Alpine & Renault

The Development of the Revolutionary *Turbo* F1 Car 1968 to 1979

Roy Smith

Other great books from Veloce –

www.veloce.co.uk

First published in September 2008 by Veloce Publishing Limited, 33 Trinity Street, Dorchester DT1 1TT, England. Fax 01305 268864/e-mail info@veloce.co.uk/web www.veloce.co.uk or www.velocebooks.com.
ISBN: 978-1-84584-177-5/UPC: 6-36847-04177-9
© Roy Smith and Veloce Publishing 2008. All rights reserved. With the exception of quoting brief passages for the purpose of review, no part of this publication may be recorded, reproduced or transmitted by any means, including photocopying, without the written permission of Veloce Publishing Ltd. Throughout this book logos, model names and designations, etc, have been used for the purposes of identification, illustration and decoration. Such names are the property of the trademark holder as this is not an official publication.
Readers with ideas for automotive books, or books on other transport or related hobby subjects, are invited to write to the editorial director of Veloce Publishing at the above address.
British Library Cataloguing in Publication Data - A catalogue record for this book is available from the British Library. Typesetting, design and page make-up all by Veloce Publishing Ltd on Apple Mac. Printed in India by Replika Press.

Alpine & Renault

The Development of the Revolutionary *Turbo* F1 Car 1968 to 1979

VELOCE PUBLISHING
THE PUBLISHER OF FINE AUTOMOTIVE BOOKS

CONTENTS

INTRODUCTION

Where to start? This was the question I was faced with. I need not have worried, however, as the help and support I have been given in the preparation of this work have been extraordinary. I hope it will be enjoyable to the reader as well as provide some details which have not been published before.

Everybody approached had a tale to tell and many are recounted here. I owe a huge debt to my partner, Helen, without whom this study would have been impossible to produce. Originally it was going to be a small book about the Alpine A350 and A500, but what was to unfold was the story of an incredible adventure; everyone involved has used these words, and so it has proved for me. Although the subject is big – Renault is big, Formula 1 is big – talking to all those involved has been like meeting a family: always friendly, generous and passionate about their subject. I hope the reader will find it equally absorbing.

I have been fascinated by Alpines since the 1980s, and it was while I was looking for information on the Alpine A500 laboratory Formula 1 car for a magazine article, that I realised there was very little on the subject in English. Further investigation led to the same conclusion concerning the early Renault turbo Grand Prix cars. There are snippets and short articles in many books, magazines and articles on websites – some accurate, some not – so I decided that now was the time to write something on the subject before this great adventure is lost in the mists of time.

We begin with a look at the history of the companies involved, so setting the scene and demonstrating where each of the famous names fits into the study. We take a close look at the first Alpine Formula 1 attempt in the 1960s: the very real but aborted Alpine A350 Renault Gordini normally aspirated car entered for the 1968 French Grand Prix. Some may think the A350 is irrelevant, but one needs to look at the 1960s, the regulations for Grand Prix cars set in 1966, and the men who were to be involved later: Castaing, Bande, Dudot, Boudy, etc. We see the difference in the environment and attitude to going motor racing in the 1960s, and how the scene changed from carefree enthusiasm to the dogged attention to detail that would be necessary for every team into the 1980s; and all before the computer was readily available. We watch the development of the

(© Renault Communications)

Alpine A500 turbo development car.

first idea for a turbocharged engine at Alpine, the Elf and Renault investments, and the acquisition by Renault of Gordini and Alpine. Eventually, we come to the first of the modern era Renault Grand Prix cars, from the mid-1970s to the year of the first victory in 1979.

But we don't stop there, as we take a brief look, race by race, at what followed. The study reaches conclusion with a glance at the legacy that led to the development of the turbo as it became available to everyone. Finally, we look at the great idea that became Renault Histoire & Collection, where a group of dedicated professionals keeps these cars of yesteryear alive for today's enthusiasts.

I have tried to present a complete picture for those unfamiliar with the early days, and so crave the indulgence of those readers who already have experience of the 1960s and 1970s because they were involved, or merely because they were around at the time or, perhaps, have studied the subject. Formula 1 development never stands still, and much has already been written about the later years of incredible turbo power outputs, but here we see how it all began.

I hope this book will have an appeal the world over for those interested in motor sport in general, Formula 1 enthusiasts in particular, Alpine and Renault enthusiasts for sure, and anyone interested in how Renault, a major company in the automotive world, became involved in a great Grand Prix gamble.

Also covered is the input of the Elf oil company and the eventual development of an engine whose power was to change the thinking of the world's engine constructors. In the 1970s, significant horsepower requirements for F1 led to 8- or even 12-cylinder designs. It is true that, when a 3-litre V8 Cosworth was putting out 450 or so bhp, few believed it possible that a small V6 1500cc engine could ever produce as much as 1200bhp (more in some cases), but, by the mid-1980s, these were the figures that were being achieved.

Turbocharging itself is not new, the first known concept being that of Dr Alfred J Buchi, a Swiss gentleman, somewhere around 1909-1912, whilst he was working for Sulzer Brothers. Louis Renault was also to patent a unit before World War 1, and exhaust-driven superchargers, now called turbochargers, were used on heavy vehicles towards the end of World War 1 and on aircraft long before World War 2. It is known that, in England in the 1920s, there existed a car called a Halford Special, featuring an exhaust-driven, turbo-style supercharger deemed revolutionary at the time.

But it was in the early 1970s that the concept was considered by Alpine and Renault. Porsche was also experimenting with

turbocharging engines, the impressive 917 Can Am car being an example. In the USA the famous oval racing and Indianapolis cars were familiar with the process; however, the units themselves were relatively large and unsophisticated, and similar to those in operation in the truck industry. No one had used a turbocharger in Formula 1, though in 1976 and since 1966, the regulations did allow both supercharging and turbocharging.

It was a young Bernard Dudot at Alpine who first fitted a turbo on a 1600cc Renault engine in an Alpine A110 for Jean-Luc Thérier to drive in the 1972 Critérium des Cévennes. He had no idea that his actions would lead to the greatest chase for power the Grand Prix world had ever seen.

This is the story of how it all began ...

ACKNOWLEDGEMENTS

My thanks to:
Authors on motor sport: Jean-Louis Moncet, Jean-Marc Cotteret, Jean-Luc Taillard, Dominique Pascal, Raymond Marescot, Ed McDonough, Jean-Jacques Mancel, Mike Jiggle; all who have helped personally and whose work has been a respected source of information, inspiration and encouragement.

Renault, Alpine, Michelin and Elf people from yesteryear and today: Richard Bouleau, Mauro Bianchi, Jacques Cheinisse, Henri Gauchet, François Castaing, Jean-Pierre Boudy, Michel Têtu, Pierre Dupasquier, Bernard Dudot, François Guiter, Jean Sage, Gérard Larrousse, Christian Schmaltz, Jean-Louis Le Tohic, Thiérry Villain, François-Xavier Delfosse, Jean-Pierre Jabouille; all of whom have been interviewed and been of immense help in ensuring that factual reality prevailed over the sometimes more attractive mythology.

Jean-Claude Fayard, Jacques Poisson, André Renut, Hervé Guilpin, Sir Jackie Stewart; each of whom checked information or communicated in writing or by phone.

Renault archives in Plessis-Robinson, Paris, and Renault Flins, home of Histoire et Collection.

Renault UK; Tim Jackson and Mandy Hopkins, who arranged early meetings and have been an ongoing source of encouragement.

Association des Anciens d'Alpine and its members who provided historical information relating to the early years.

Motor Sport magazine for the use of Mr Jenkinson's article about the launch of the turbo car (© Doug Nye/The Denis Jenkinson Estate as first published in Motor Sport).

Club Alpine Renault (in UK) archives, its magazine, Le Journal, and Tim Moores, Alpine A110 historian in the UK.

PHOTOGRAPHIC ACKNOWLEDGEMENTS

All of the photographs within this work not individually attributed as the copyright property of a particular source are the sole copyright of Renault Communications, supplied by Phototèque Renault to be treated as © Renault Communications, all rights reserved. My thanks to Stéphanie Lévêque for all her help.
© DPPI/Renault Communications is identified as © DPPI/Ren. In these cases the identity of the photographer is unknown and the copyright is held by DPPI/Renault Communications, all rights reserved.
© Bernard Asset: courtesy of Bernard Asset.
© Michel Morelli: courtesy of Michel Morelli.
Jean Sage archives: photographers unknown.
Photographs marked © AAA Dieppe are courtesy of Association des Anciens d'Alpine in Dieppe.
Photographs identified with the words © TVA are from the archives of Thiérry Villain.
© RS is the copyright of the author Roy Smith.
The statistics and results charts are the copyright of Chronosports (www.chronosports.com) and Michèle Merlino, FORIX.com.
Drawings are the copyright of ETAI unless otherwise specified.
Mille Miles photographs, © Jean-Marc Cotteret.

Special personal thanks go to:
Jean-Louis Moncet, Bernard Dudot and Jean Sage for allowing me to use various items from their book, *Renault F1: Les Années Turbo*, published in French by Albin Michel, 1991. This includes technical items relating to the engines and race and testing records. Also special thanks for the great encouragement and help given by Ed McDonough who introduced me to Veloce Publishing. Thank you to Veloce for taking up the idea and bringing it to reality.

AAA (Association des Anciens d'Alpine) for allowing me to use details from works previously published on behalf of AAA in French.
Mille Miles magazine, for authorisation to use information from work previously published therein in French.
Mauro Bianchi, Bernard Dudot, François Guiter and Jean-Pierre Jabouille, who have each done me the great honour of providing a preface for this work, reflecting their individual experience of this period.
Acknowledgements go to various additional bibliographical sources of information, unverified but which nevertheless have yielded some additional snippets of historical information: *Berlinette* magazine, *Motor Sport*, *Autosport*, *Great Encyclopaedia of Formula 1*, and works by Frederick Lhospied, Maurice Louche, Christian Huet, Ian Bamsey, and Doug Nye.
Even in a work where one has conducted many interviews and made every attempt to verify comments, statements, data and information, there may be omissions, and/or some differences of opinion. I hope the errors are few, and although everything contained within this work is published in good faith, I apologise now for any technical, photographic or acknowledgement errors or omissions.

A few special words of thanks must be set aside here to a person whose ability and accuracy in translating from French hundreds of documents, interviews, e-mails and letters, and writing letters and e-mails in French when required, have allowed this story to unfold and be told in English for the first time. Without her tenacity and great sense of humour, this work could not have been written. Thank you, Helen, for your patience, dedication, and truly excellent work.

**Roy Smith
Milton Keynes
England**

(Courtesy *Mille Miles*)

MAURO BIANCHI

The first part of this story tells how the passion of an unusual man, Jean Rédélé, brought together a group of men chosen for their talent, ability and courage, and, with the indispensable aid of Renault, was able to help return France to the forefront of the highest level of racing competition.

I had the extraordinary good fortune, together with a group of other men who shared my passion, to work with Jean Rédélé in those early days in the mid-1960s, and to play a small part in this renewal of French motor sport.

When Roy Smith asked me to contribute to this book, I was won over by his great enthusiasm, and it was a real pleasure to help him.

From Alpine's timid beginnings in single seaters in 1964 at the Pau Grand Prix in Formula 2 (where, by chance, at the first appearance of a single-seater Alpine I had the joy of being fastest in practice in front of 'Mr' Jim Clark himself), to the later Formula 1 victories, what a road those men had to travel! What superhuman efforts would be required of this army of true fanatics!

I had only a fleeting experience of what Formula 1 might be like with the Alpine A350 in 1968, but, unluckily for us, we were perceived to be ahead of our time; Renault was not yet ready for the great adventure that was to happen later in Formula 1 and our dream faded away. Other devoted men were to reach this target in due course; their combined efforts forged the 'Alpine legend' which eventually saw some of them scaling the Everest of motor sport that was to be the turbo era of Grand Prix racing.

Roy Smith has brought all these elements together in this extraordinary story which he tells here with talent and passion.

Thank you, Roy, for giving these pages of history to all those who love motor racing!

Mauro Bianchi
La Garde-Freinet
France

BERNARD DUDOT

This period of Renault's competition history, related with passion and competence by Roy Smith, shows in detail how Renault tiptoed onto the hallowed ground of F1 to become one of its major players. This adventure, in the etymological sense of the word, in which the rational runs alongside the irrational, is primarily a history of men as well as the emergence of a new technology, of which the turbocharged engine is the central element.

With the passage of time, I realise how much passion for his craft and patience, given the difficulties encountered by his team at Viry-Châtillon, were needed for Bernard Hanon – then chairman and managing director of Renault – to back such an adventure. Dr Fuhrman, chairman of Porsche at the time, declared, without mentioning his name, "I would not like to be in the shoes of the man who decided to bring this project to fruition." Bernard Hanon believed in the concept of the turbocharged engine and wanted to give Renault an international image through Formula 1.

Outside of the Renault group, François Guiter, in charge of marketing at Elf, had supported the idea, and had, for many years, encouraged Renault, up till then successfully involved in rallying at the highest level, to return to circuit racing by way of Formula 3 and then Formula 2. It was François Guiter who then acted as the catalyst of the 'turbo' concept by offering to pay Renault for the development of the first two engines to "see what happened."

At Viry-Châtillon, under the direction of Gérard Larrousse, we were a handful of young, passionate engineers, including François Castaing, then technical director of Renault Gordini, who had 'sold' this rather mad project to Bernard Hanon. The Viry-Châtillon team needed a large dose of the recklessness, heedlessness and passion which only youth can provide.

The first circuit tests at Jarama, with Jean-Pierre Jabouille at the wheel of the A500, revealed the huge problems we would have to overcome. Nothing worked as planned; the response time of our turbo engine was not suited to the sinuous track at Jarama, and we could only imagine how it would behave at Monaco! Jean-Pierre Boudy, head of the project at that time, was close to despair. Gérard Larrousse, who had tested the engine under other conditions, told us that it worked like a lift: you pushed the button but the lift didn't operate until the doors were shut.

At that time, we had no telemetry, and the only information we had came from the drivers. The operation of a turbo engine depends on the interaction between the speed and temperature of the exhaust gases, themselves a function of the fuel dosage and the ignition advance. Jean-Pierre Jabouille's ability to analyse this very complicated process was enormously helpful to our progress.

Gérard Larrousse understood the importance of geographical proximity between the engine and chassis departments if we were to develop a single-seater with this special engine. This operation, which led to moving the Dieppe chassis team to Viry-Châtillon alongside the engine team, was not achieved without some casualties, and some members of the team didn't make it. The transfer resulted in the creation of 'Renault Sport' and the birth of the RS01, the first Renault F1 with a turbo engine. This single-seater, created under the aegis of François Castaing, was a great success aesthetically, and more than met its specification. Its external appearance gave little evidence of the huge space needed for the engine. However, the base was healthy; it remained to be seen how well it would perform on the track.

We had a lot to learn, and we had to help our partners to develop their technology. I remember a letter from a supplier of rod bearings telling me that it was impossible to meet such a demanding specification! In the end, another manufacturer dived in at the deep end to help us. The gearbox and transmission had to be capable of bearing unusual amounts of torque. Without the smallest point of reference, the team discovered the importance of aerodynamics. The construction of the Michelin tyres was also new; here again, there was no point of reference to judge our performance compared with the competition. The operation of the engine, with its famous response delay, was an additional problem in our understanding of the behaviour of the tyres and the link between the two. In short, lots of unknowns and not much data.

Many men were part of this project at different times, either at Dieppe, Viry-Châtillon, Clermont-Ferrand, or Billancourt. All made a contribution to what has become the Renault F1 team of today. There is no doubt that this was a period when Renault and its partners needed to invest resources in order to reap the benefits in the 1990s with the V10 concept, and later the V8 of the 2000s. Still today, the engine team at Viry-Châtillon includes some of the men who were present at the start of this fantastic adventure, so ably related by Roy Smith in this book.

Bernard Dudot
Paris
France

JEAN-PIERRE JABOUILLE

Everyone will tell you that this was a great adventure, and, indeed it was, for me as much as anybody.

When I went to Alpine in 1969 as a professional driver to do the F3 Championship with Patrick Depailler, I was already passionate about technical things, suspension and so on, so of course soon got myself into trouble – a young driver trying to take charge! – but we began to win races with the famous Alpine F3. Of course, Alpine had run at Le Mans many times with the prototypes, but that was the old generation. Then, as Renault became more involved, Alpine was asked to build a new sports car for the Castaing-designed engine for the 2-litre class in the European Championship; that car was to be practically unbeatable. Jean Terramorsi had thought about turbocharging and put Bernard Dudot on the project. I was driving in F2 and the sports prototypes when I got to hear about it and I thought it was a great idea. It was launched by Terramorsi and François Guiter of Elf. Guiter and Elf had financed the 2-litre sports car engine in 1973 and now, again with Elf, he had the first two F1 engines built at Renault.

Before the 1500 engine was placed in a single-seater chassis, it was mounted in an A442 prototype with different bodywork. I remember that I did a lap, returned to the pit, and told Dudot that it might be better to stop right away because it didn't work at all. However, as Roy explains in this book, they eventually got the engine sorted out and I became involved in the development of the car, whilst at the same time concentrating on winning the 1976 Formula 2 Championship. It was quite difficult for me, although people didn't realise it at the time, because we had a new chassis, new engine, and new tyres. But I was passionate about technical stuff so I found it very interesting. Michelin, too, had its sights on winning in F1 and wanted to use radial tyres, whereas at the time Goodyear and Firestone were using conventional tyres. With that new radial tyre, when you pushed hard in a corner the car held on and held on, then suddenly let go – you had to be quick to catch it.

We used to go out on the tracks on Mondays and Tuesdays for testing after the Grand Prix, and gradually we began to make progress. By 8 December 1976, we had finished testing and the car had been painted yellow for a press launch – that was the day that Bernard Hanon said, "OK, we're going into F1!" That first car – the A500 laboratory car – had done its job.

The RS01 was the first real Renault F1 car. It wasn't bad but it wasn't up to the level of our competitors. I was closely involved in the creation of the RS01 with Jean-Claude Guénard. It worked okay and we did a lot of development work; it was truly an adventure. Sometimes things went well; at other times we weren't making any progress – not funny at all.

In 1979 we made the leap, and big breakthroughs came with the twin-turbo ground-effect car. It was resilient and super-efficient, and from that moment on we began to win races. Dijon – that first win was fantastic, for Michelin, for the turbo engine. I was really happy because it was all French equipment, winning in France. We had won our first Grand Prix with technology that, at the time, was very different from what others were using. Both René Arnoux and I went on to win quite a few more races.

It's a fascinating story, full of politics, egos, dreams, frustrations and great excitement. Roy Smith has covered it all in significant detail.

Jean-Pierre Jabouille
Dannemarie
France

FRANÇOIS GUITER

(Courtesy *Mille Miles*)

Roy Smith has produced a very comprehensive book on the beginnings of the turbo 1.5-litre F1 engine, the first in English. Here are some of my personal memories of this great adventure.

It all began in 1968 when Jean Terramorsi won the Grand Prix for publicity for Renault, and I won the same title for the launch of Elf. At that time, F3 Matras dominated the championship: 17 victories in 20 races in 6 months. The Alpine Renaults were hampered by their fragile engines.

Elf and Renault immediately thought: "Why don't we do business together?" An exclusive contract was signed between them and is still in force today for lubricants for production cars.

At the time, Alpine Renault shone in rallying, winning the first World Championship in 1973. In endurance circuit racing, there was success for the little prototypes in the performance index, but things were not going too well for the 3-litre Alpines, which suffered heavy failures and were abandoned.

When we finished our contract with Matra at the end of 1970, we took a joint look at what we could do with Alpine and Renault in circuit racing in 1971. It was at this time that the drivers, Jabouille and Depailler, came to see me to tell me that they had a wonderful chassis, and that the new R16 engine could probably be adapted for it.

So began an enthralling adventure: André de Cortanze for the chassis, Marcel Hubert for the aerodynamics, Bernard Dudot for the engine – together, during the season they were to create a wonderful Formula 3 car in which the drivers would win the French Championship, with Depailler first and Jabouille second.

The idea was to create a racing V6, initially intended for a 2-litre prototype, but, of course, we had other plans as well. In its second year this V6 was to win all the races, and the women's team of Marie-Claude Beaumont and Lella Lombardi could have won Le Mans if they hadn't run out of fuel ...

A clever manoeuvre at the FIA of the time made our V6 eligible for Formula 2, which it won twice in a row, Jabouille then Arnoux beating the BMWs, the almost unshiftable winners of the Formula 2 titles.

At the same time, Terramorsi had the brilliant idea of sending Dudot to California to learn about turbos and investigate the possibility of adding one to our V6. This would eventually be the 2-litre turbo which won Le Mans in 1978, driven by Pironi and Jaussaud.

But that wasn't enough for us: we wanted to go into Formula 1. Why not a 1.5-litre turbo engine, which all the great engine technicians of the time thought was impossible? We ordered one from Renault, like the V6, and after a difficult start this engine would completely revolutionise Formula 1 racing, as well as our fuels. It should have ended with a firework display, winning the Formula 1 Championship with Prost in 1983, but illegal fuel used in the Brabham BMW prevented it. Renault never filed a complaint, not wishing to win on appeal – such a pity!

The Renault F1 turbo engines were in use for some time and saw the first victories of the legendary driver Ayrton Senna, king of pole position. Eventually, they were stopped as they were too powerful – beyond the measurement capabilities of the test benches!

This marvellous joint adventure reminds us once again what can be achieved by a group of men who share a passion. For all the wonderful times we spent together, my thanks to them all!

François Guiter
Formerly Marketing and
Promotion Director, Elf
Paris
France

PART 1

In the beginning

RENAULT

Renault, Alpine, Gordini: some of the most evocative names in French motor sport, whose products were to influence the world's automotive industry, and, in the case of Renault, still do today. So just who are these three? We will start with the survivor, Renault, the power behind the team in more ways than one, which was to take over the other two during the period of our story.

It was Louis Renault who started it all. He was born in Paris on 15 February 1877, the fourth of six children; his father had developed a small drapery business in the Place des Victoires where he specialised in making buttons. His mother, Louise-Berthe Magnien, was a devout member of the Tiers-Ordre (an order of lay sisters, which could be described as bourgeois).

Louis loved engineering, creating new ideas and new techniques for applying his talents as a mechanic. In his teens this desire drove him to spend a lot of his spare time with Léon Serpollet, who was building steam cars in his workshop in the Montmartre area of Paris. The Renault family had a second home in the Billancourt area of Paris, and Louis Renault set up his own workshop in a shed in the garden, where he designed and built a small four-wheeled car powered by a de Dion-Bouton engine in 1898 and equipped it with an invention of his own, a direct drive system. At the end of 1898, he was to spend Christmas Eve with friends at a cabaret, and drove there in this, his first car. To

> **"... Louis Renault set up his own workshop in a shed in the garden, where he designed and built a small four-wheeled car powered by a de Dion-Bouton engine in 1898 and equipped it with an invention of his own, a direct drive system."**

prove its capabilities to his friends he drove it up a steep incline, the rue Lepic in Montmartre. The little car, with a colleague as passenger, went up the 13 per cent gradient without difficulty. It was the first time a horseless carriage had done this, and, by the end of the evening, Louis Renault had orders and deposits

Louis Renault's workshop.

Renault in his workshop, 1898.

Madame and Marcel Renault in the Renault 1CV 3-4 monocylinder Type A.

Louis Renault: Paris-Madrid, 1903.

for twelve cars to be built by the end of 1899. His personal adventure had begun.

He patented his direct drive system during 1899, and established the Renault Frères company with his two elder brothers. The rest of the world's motor industry soon took up Renault's patented drive idea and so he quickly acquired a reputation. Right from the beginning, the Renault brothers had fully understood that participation in car races could provide valuable promotion for their products, and they began with the Paris-Trouville race the same year. As the months and years passed, they claimed victory in most of the town-to-town challenges of the period, such as Paris-Bordeaux, Paris-Ostend, and Paris-Berlin, topping it off with Paris-Vienna, which, by 1902, made Marcel (the main racing driver among the brothers) a highly respected competitor. Of course, the cars got bigger and the publicity surrounding these victories led to numerous orders, with Paris-Toulouse alone generating many of them.

Success turned to tragedy, however, when the 1903 Paris-Madrid race finished with twelve people dead, among them Marcel Renault. Louis gave up competing and concentrated on selling his cars to other drivers, and not only in France, also continuing to create technical innovations which contributed to expansion of the firm.

"... the 1903 Paris-Madrid race finished with twelve people dead, among them Marcel Renault. Louis gave up competing and concentrated on selling his cars to other drivers ..."

Some years previously, in 1895, an organisation named the Automobile Club de France (ACF) had been formed which, on 26 June 1906, held the first French Grand Prix at Le Mans on the circuit created in the department of La Sarthe. That first Grand Prix was won by a Renault car driven by Ferenc Szisz, who covered the 12 laps of the circuit in 12 hours, 14 minutes; it would be 73 years before a Renault would again win the French Grand Prix. In 1909, Louis and his brother, Fernand, who had been ill for some time, decided to close the original company to allow Fernand to retire; sadly, he passed away a few months later.

Louis Renault then decided to create Automobiles Renault (L Renault Constructeur). He extended the lease on his factory and took complete charge of an organisation which, by then, was employing around 2500 people and manufacturing 4500 cars a year. Over the coming years he became the first car manufacturer to branch out into another field of new technology which appealed to him: aeronautics, a business he remained involved in until 1939.

It is also interesting to note at this point that one of Renault's patents before World War 1 was for a turbocharger, believed to be the first time the function of the idea had been patented.

In 1912, Renault visited Ford in the USA, where he saw the production lines that gave a decisive advantage for volume manufacture of cars, an implementation of the system known as Taylorism. An excited Louis Renault returned to France and instigated the production line process. His employees were less enthusiastic, however, and did not see things the same way, realising that jobs would certainly be cut with this new working method. For the first time, Louis was faced with strikes.

"... one of Renault's patents before World War 1 was for a turbocharger, believed to be the first time the function of the idea had been patented."

Renault survived, of course, and, by the start of World War 1, the company was employing around 5000 people. With the outbreak of war factories turned their efforts to armament manufacture, and, as Renault's men were called to serve at the front, their work in the factory was frequently taken over by their wives; a crèche and school were installed to cater for the children. The workforce had increased, too, to meet the demands of the military, and, by 1918, Renault was employing 22,000 people, many of them women.

In 1918, Louis Renault was awarded the Légion d'Honneur. It seems that he had also developed a taste for the ladies and had proposed to several women by the end of the war, having earlier in 1899 told his brother, Marcel, "I shall not marry until the factory has 5000 workers." By 1919 it had considerably exceeded that figure, so at the age of 40 he went out and found a wife, Christiane Boullaire, the 21-year-old daughter of a Parisian lawyer.

The period after World War 1 was difficult, bringing fierce competition and rivalry between Renault and André Citroën that continued until 1935, when Citroën died.

In 1926-27, Renault factories were opened in Belgium and England, but the market in Europe now had to contend with competition from the powerful US manufacturers; as a result,

ACF Grand Prix (La Sarthe Circuit): Ferenc Szisz on the starting line, June 1906.

Challenging the world's terrain and breaking records for distances travelled: Africa 1925 expedition to the Cape by land.

many of the small European companies closed down. Renault was neither small nor one to fail, and Louis maintained his publicity with Renault cars by beating record after record for endurance, fuel economy and speed.

Renault 4CV Luxe model at the Trocadero in 1948.

Billancourt plant 1958.

By 1929, Renault had thirty subsidiaries and was selling in 49 countries. However, this was the year of the stock exchange crashes which sent a shock wave around the world, putting millions out of work and, in part, fostering the political climate that allowed Hitler to come to power in Germany four years later.

By 1935, France had 500,000 unemployed, causing a drop in demand for cars. As his other markets were suffering from worldwide recession, Renault was forced to reduce his workforce and the number of hours it worked. Many strikes followed and, by the end of 1938, Renault's employees were even occupying his factories, leading to violent interventions, mass arrests, and many dismissals.

World War 2 was not a good time for the Renault company, and nearly brought about its end. For Louis personally it was a disaster also, as he was charged with collaboration, leading to incarceration in the notorious former Nazi-controlled Fresnes prison close to Paris. It was there, under suspicious circumstances, that he became ill and was taken to the St-Jean-de-Dieu Hospital in the rue Oudinot (Paris). He died on 24 October 1944.

His factory was nationalized after the war, and Pierre Lefaucheux, an engineer and member of the French Resistance, was placed in control of the new company, La Régie Nationale des Usines Renault. A born leader, Lefaucheux was ordered by the new government to make trucks, but also managed to obtain permission to manufacture a few private cars. Lefaucheux introduced the famous 4CV, which was displayed at the first post-war Salon.

By 1954, Renault employed more than 50,000 people and sold in over 1000 outlets worldwide. Unfortunately, Lefaucheux died in a car accident in 1955 and his place was taken by Pierre Dreyfus, who set about improving social cohesion within Renault, signing the first company agreement with the trade unions, and introducing more paid leave and a pension scheme.

"In 1956, Jean Hébert was to break the world land speed record for turbine-powered cars at 192mph (307kph) with the Renault prototype 'Etoile Filante' and a Turbomeca turbine."

Motor sport, too, had begun to lift its head after the class victories in the Mille Miglia with the 4CV in the early fifties. In 1956, Jean Hébert was to break the world land speed record for turbine-powered cars at 192mph (307kph) with the Renault prototype 'Etoile Filante' and a Turbomeca turbine.

That same year the Renault Dauphine was created; just 4 years later, 1,000,000 had been produced. Amédée Gordini now appeared in the frame with the Dauphine Gordini, and then again in 1964 after the introduction of the legendary Renault R8 Gordini.

Renault eventually took control of Automobiles Gordini in 1969, while, at the same time, Jean Rédélé and Alpine were also strengthening their links with Renault.

In 1966, Pierre Dreyfus had concluded an agreement for technical collaboration with Peugeot, which would eventually extend to Volvo to form what became the PRV framework agreement. Dreyfus took them into the 1970s with a positive sales programme and a new car, the R5, which, by 1973, represented 60 per cent of the firm's production. This was the

> ## "Renault eventually took control of Automobiles Gordini in 1969, while, at the same time, Jean Rédélé and Alpine were also strengthening their links with Renault."

time of the Yom Kippur War and the Middle East crisis, which led to a huge increase in the price of oil. Dreyfus – conservative in his decisions – was an astute man who allowed his management to investigate various motor sport options, having refused for several years to be involved in anything other than rallying through Alpine. However, the company employed some creative thinkers and their ideas led to the Renault V6-powered Alpines dominating the 1974 European Sports Car Championship.

When Dreyfus retired in 1975 he was replaced by Bernard Vernier-Palliez. A key appointment made at the same time saw Bernard Hanon become a board director. Hanon was to prove highly influential in the story of the Grand Prix cars, and, like Louis Renault himself way back in 1900, was an enthusiast for motor sport and the publicity it could bring. It was he who announced in December 1976 that Renault was going into Formula I, eventually taking six world manufacturer titles between 1992 and 1997, followed by two more in 2005 and 2006.

'Etoile Filante' at Bonneville.

Dauphine Gordini, 1958.

ALPINE

Jean Rédélé, founder of Alpine, was born in Dieppe on 17 May 1922; perhaps his destiny was already determined, as he was to be one of the major achievers in the field of French motor sport. Creating a series of cars that carried the Alpine name, his company was to become the darling of France, his cars to this day revered for their performance and beauty.

Born into a motoring family, Rédélé took charge of his father's Renault agency in Dieppe in 1946, where he was to have the chance to develop his love of the sporting side of motor vehicles. In 1952, Jean Rédélé and Louis Pons took a class win in the Mille Miglia with a Renault 4CV 'Normale;' Rédélé went on to win his class in the Tour de France and Liège-Rome-Liège.

The same year he met Giovanni Michelotti, whom he asked to design a sports coupé based on the 4CV chassis; the car, called a Rédélé Special, had an aluminium alloy body manufactured by Allemano and weighed just 550kg (1210lb). With this car he won the 1953 Rally Dieppe and went on to win the up-to-1300cc class in a prestigious race at Rouen-Les-Essarts, as well as the up-to-1300cc category on the first stage of the Lisbon Grand Prix.

In 1954, a second car known as the 'Marquis,' was built and exhibited at the New York Motor Show in January. A production licence for the 'Marquis' was arranged but did not result in the manufacture of any vehicles. Back in France, Rédélé met the Chappe brothers, coachbuilders based in Saint-Maur who carried out an initial study for the Coach Alpine in preparation for production. Alpine was the name chosen for the marque as a celebration of two consecutive class wins, in 1953 and 1954, by Rédélé and Pons in the Coupe des Alpes.

Production of the Alpine type A106 began, and a Certificat de Dépôt d'Acte was issued by the Tribunal de Commerce de la Seine on 6 July 1955, recognising the official foundation of Société des Automobiles Alpine on 22 June that year.

Three cars – one blue, one white and one red – were shown to Pierre Dreyfus, new managing director of Renault, at Renault's Boulogne-Billancourt HQ in July 1955, but did not elicit any support from Renault; it may be that it was too early in Dreyfus' reign for a decision to invest. The cars, now made with glass fibre bodywork, had their first public showing at the Paris Salon in September 1955. Full production began at the Dieppe plant,

Jean Rédélé at the 1951 Monte Carlo Rally.

The red, white and blue cars presented to Pierre Dreyfus.

and, following a class win in the 1956 Mille Miglia by an A106, it was decided that the name Mille Miles should be used as a designation for the high-performance variants of the cars.

A Michelotti-designed A106 cabriolet, incorporating for the first time the centre tube chassis in place of a Renault floor pan, was completed in Turin on 3 May 1957; then, in 1959, the A106 coupé version appeared at the Paris Salon, and preparations began for the A108 berlinette.

The A108 made its competition début on the 1960 Tour de France in September, just prior to the Paris Salon of that year. It incorporated the mechanical components of the Dauphine Gordini, in place of those of the 4CV, with the engine enlarged by Mignotet to 998cc and producing 70bhp.

> ## "A Michelotti-designed A106 cabriolet, incorporating for the first time the centre tube chassis in place of a Renault floor pan, was completed in Turin on 3 May 1957 ... "

In 1961, Jean Rédélé began discussions with Willys Overland to produce A108 berlinettes at São Bernardo do Campo in Brazil, and a French-built berlinette with 'Interlagos' badging was shown at the São Paulo motor show in December.

The iconic A110 berlinette was launched at the Paris Salon in October 1963 – a development of the A108 but with mechanical components now taken from the R8, the rear body shape modified by Alpine designers to take account of the new engines and rear-mounted radiator. Although the shape was thought to be near-perfect, its mechanical side, as Mauro Bianchi says, "... needed quite a bit of sorting out." However, after much work, the 1000cc A110 berlinette was homologated as a Group B GT car, and the same year Alpine introduced the M63 sports racing car with a 996 engine for the prototype class.

After Brazil and the Willys connection, Mexico was next, and in 1964 production of the 956cc-powered A110 berlinette began there, badged as 'Dinalpin.' In France the sports cars were further developed with the introduction of the M64 1149cc, which achieved the top spot in the index of thermal efficiency at the Le Mans 24 Hours. This was also the year that the Alpine P64 single-seater cars appeared in Formula 2 and Formula 3 classes. In 1965, a 1296cc-powered M65 achieved class wins at Reims and the Nürburgring, and the single-seaters continued to feature regularly in the top five places in Formula 3.

Fabulous A106 Mille Miles. (© J M Cotteret *Mille Miles*)

Le Mans 1966. Note the huge Alpine entry. (Archives AAA Dieppe)

Patrick Depailler in a Formula 3 Alpine. (Archives AAA Dieppe)

Monte Carlo, 1973: 1600S Andersson/Todt.

By 1966, 1296cc variants of the A110 – intended principally for competition use and called simply '1300' – were introduced and a new racing Alpine, the A210 sports prototype car, appeared in the May 1000km at Spa (Belgium).

In 1967, a new A110 variant was introduced at the Paris Salon: the 1300S with 120bhp available for works competition cars. The A280 F2/F3 car, a development of the 270, was completed, followed by the A330 in 1967. Licensed production by FASA of A110 berlinettes was begun at Valladolid in Spain in March, and an agreement was signed on 27 September to allow berlinettes to be built at the Renault factory in Plovdiv, Bulgaria, to be known as 'Bulgaralpine.' The 210 sports cars appeared at many of the European sports car races. Patrick Depailler shone in the F3 Alpines.

By 1968, Jean Rédélé had at last been able to persuade Renault management to allow Alpines to be sold in Renault agencies. An initial design sketch for the first A310 was also completed by the design department, and this was the year that the A350 single-seater, originally a research project, was secretly designed and built by Richard Bouleau's team in-house in Dieppe as an experimental car for a new type of suspension, but quickly turned into the first attempt at a Formula 1 car intended to be driven by Mauro Bianchi. The full story appears in Chapter 3.

"Jean-Claude Andruet won the European Rally Drivers' Championship in 1971, and Alpine finished second in the European Rally Championship for Makes."

It was in 1969 that a new purpose-built factory was opened on a Dieppe industrial estate. The 1565cc A110 model was upped to 138bhp and became the 1600S. Unfortunately, a bad weekend at the Le Mans 24 Hours in June was to spoil things, as the V8-engine cars failed to finish, with only the 1150cc A210 of Serpaggi/Ethuin redeeming honour by winning the index of performance. Renault's influence was already considerable; it ordered a halt to the A350 Grand Prix car and now ordered Alpine to cease sports car racing.

Jean-Claude Andruet won the European Rally Drivers' Championship in 1971, and Alpine finished second in the European Rally Championship for Makes. In single-seaters the André de Cortanze-designed A361 appeared. Elf became involved and Alpines dominated Formula 3 with Patrick

Depailler and Jean-Pierre Jabouille driving. The following year, Alpine won the European Rally Championship for Makes. Jean-Pierre Nicolas was French Rally Champion and Christine Dacremont was French Women's Rally Champion.

Although sports car racing had been shelved since 1969, single-seater cars were still designed and built, and a new F3 was unveiled, the A364, nicknamed the 'Dinosaur' because the slotted engine cover looked a bit like the notches on a dinosaur's back: a beautiful-looking car. This was the early days of the aerodynamics period during which wild wing formations started to appear.

It was also in 1972 that Bernard Dudot tried fitting a turbocharger to a 1600cc engine, giving it 200bhp. With this car Jean-Luc Thérier wrestled the A110 berlinette to victory in the Critérium des Cévennes; the first win for a post-war, modern-era, turbocharged car. Alpine also unveiled the Marc Mignotet-prepared 180+bhp 1800cc A110.

The following year Alpine went even further, and, in a giant-killing performance, won the inaugural World Rally Championship, whilst Jean-Luc Thérier was crowned French Rally Champion.

Renault was to take a majority holding in the Alpine company, changes were instigated with a view to developing a new sports car. The single-seaters proved impressive in the hands of Patrick Tambay, Michel Leclère, and Alain Serpaggi. The A367 Elf-Hart was driven by Patrick Depailler and Jean-Pierre Jabouille.

In 1974, the new A310 made its rally début, achieving its first win in July/August on the Boucle du Vercors-Vivarais, driven by Bernard Darniche. The Alpine 440 and 441 sports cars dominated the European 2-litre championship, with Alain Serpaggi crowned champion ahead of Gérard Larrousse and Jean-Pierre Jabouille. Bernard Dudot was moved from Alpine in Dieppe to Renault-Gordini in Viry-Châtillon to join Jean-Pierre Boudy to design and develop a turbocharged version of the François Castaing-designed V6 2-litre engine for the sports cars, which, although it won first time out, subsequently failed to deliver at many of the other races. Undaunted, in 1975, the idea of building a Formula 1 car was first secretly discussed in-house, and Jean Terramorsi, then head of Renault Gordini, asked Alpine to design and build a chassis to take the V6 engine. André de Cortanze and André Renut began work on a project that was at first thought by the outside world to be an F2 car, theoretically for the new 1976 season rules. However, it was but a small step to the creation of the Alpine A500 laboratory F1 car. At the same time, the new A442 sports car saw the light of day as the dream to win the prestigious Le Mans 24 Hours was openly discussed.

The A441T (turbo) winning at Mugello, 23 March 1975.

Gérard Larrousse was to become Director of the new Renault Sport organisation in 1976, charged with the complete reorganisation of both Alpine and Gordini. It was in December of that year that the Grand Prix project was unveiled by Renault Director, Bernard Hanon, after the Alpine A500 had completed secret testing during the summer. A new all-Renault Formula 1 car, the RS01, was already being created by Renault Sport in Viry-Châtillon, where many of the design team had been relocated from Dieppe.

"In 1974, the new A310 made its rally début, achieving its first win in July/August on the Boucle du Vercors-Vivarais, driven by Bernard Darniche."

The 150bhp A310 V6 was presented in September, making its rally début on the Tour de France, driven by Jean Ragnotti. That same year work began on a new Renault Sport workshop in Dieppe, in order to concentrate effort on winning the Le Mans 24 Hours.

Bernard Hanon oversaw complete control of Alpine in 1977,

The winning car, Le Mans, 1978.

and in July the last French A110 left the Alpine production line in Dieppe. Guy Fréquelin was crowned French Rally Champion in the A310 V6, and Jean Ragnotti won the European Rallycross Championship, also driving what was now a Renault Alpine as opposed to an Alpine Renault following the takeover. No fewer than 3 Alpine-badged A442s were entered by Renault at Le Mans, and, although this attempt came to nothing, glory was just a short step away when, in 1978, after 3 years of trying at Le Mans, Renault won the 24 Hours with the turbocharged Alpine A442B driven by Didier Pironi and Jean-Pierre Jaussaud.

1979 and 1980 saw the first appearances of a new mid-engined car built in Dieppe – the Renault R5 Turbo (1st series). Based on an R5 shell with aluminium roof and doors, it had been under development since 1976 and was now shown completed at the Brussels Salon. Built at the BEREX (Alpine) factory in

Dieppe, it was the most powerful French production car of the period and also the first road car to have a turbocharger fitted to its 1397cc engine, producing 160bhp. At the end of May it was homologated in Group 4 and a competition-client version called Cévennes was presented at the Paris Salon. In 1981, Jean Ragnotti and Jean-Marc Andrié won the Monte Carlo Rally in an R5 Turbo.

Meanwhile, the designers at the Centre de Style Renault at Rueil-Malmaison and BEREX, together with the stylists at Heuliez, were charged with developing a replacement for the A310. (BEREX was a Renault company set up in Dieppe after the changes at Alpine following the takeover, and the decision to quit sports car racing after the Le Mans 24 Hours victory.) 1982 saw the appearance of a competition variant of the R5 Turbo which was considerably modified to produce the Maxi Group 4

Jean Rédélé in 1951.

R5 Turbo, Giro d'Italia, 1979.

with 250bhp; Jean Ragnotti and Jean-Marc Andrié won the Tour de Corse in it. Moving to 1985, we see the final examples of the A310, and, for Group B rallying, the R5 Turbo Maxi 2 appearing on the scene with 1527cc producing 350bhp.

In 1986 the A310 replacement, the GTA, first appeared in the catalogues and was displayed at the Birmingham Motor Show. Its production in various forms continued up to 1991 when the A610 was introduced at the Geneva Motor Show in March for sale during 1992. Special editions followed – the Le Mans and Magny-Cours – until 1995, when the final A610 rolled out of the Dieppe factory and the production of Alpine-badged cars ceased after 40 years.

Jean Rédélé, its founder, was to enjoy his retirement, spending many anniversaries with his now older team of passionate employees until his passing on 10 August 2007.

With its motor sporting pedigree, the Alpine marque grew out of the desire for competition, so it is with this background that we now move on to take a look at the short and troubled life of the first attempt at Formula 1, though it was to be several years before the Régie had sufficient confidence in a reorganised Renault, Gordini and Alpine company to take the great gamble and try again in Formula 1.

Grand Anniversary, 2003. L to r: François Lhermoyé, Alain Prié, Philippe Charles, Jean Rédélé, Claude Foulon, Jean-Pierre Limondin, Jean-Luc Brodin, André Desaubry, Alain Serpaggi, Jean-Pierre Buirette, Gilbert Harivel, Henri Gauchet. (© J M Cotteret, *Mille Miles*)

THE ALPINE A350 EXPERIMENTAL GRAND PRIX CAR

A350 At Garage Rédélé. (Archives AAA Dieppe)

Chassis:	Tubular, polyester body
Engine:	Renault-Gordini V8
Capacity:	2996cc
Cylinder heads:	Hemispherical, aluminium
Valves:	16 (4 per cylinder)
Carburation:	Weber 4 twin-choke 45s
Ignition:	Marelli with coils
Power:	Claimed 310bhp at 7500rpm
Transmission:	BV Hewland DL200 5-speed
Brakes:	4 ventilated discs by ATE
Suspension:	Flat suspension (Richard Bouleau)
Shock absorbers:	Le Carbon
Weight:	540kg (1188lb)

To quote from an interview in 2007 with Mauro Bianchi: "In 1968, many of us at Alpine had great dreams. Of course, our hopes were encouraged by the good results of our little prototypes and some good performances of our single-seaters in F2 and F3. In fact, both showed themselves to be astonishingly competitive in spite of power ratings that, in all decency, I can only describe as 'reasonable.' We therefore started to dream of a Formula 1 programme."

THE DESIGNER – RICHARD BOULEAU

Richard Bouleau, born on 12 September 1935 in Sens, was firmly linked with the first steps of the great adventure that was Alpine. Although playing no part in the later turbo F1 car, he was to bring André de Cortanze onto his design team, where Bouleau's work had included the chassis and suspension systems on the successful early prototype sports cars and single-seaters, then the road cars. (André de Cortanze eventually became leader of the design team for the A500 and RS01 turbo cars.)

With a career that ran from 1962 to 1995, Richard first worked pre-Alpine on the design of a chassis for a racing car for his friend Bernard Boyer. Although his background was in cars,

André de Cortanze and Richard Bouleau (late 1960s).

he had not been involved in competition until he attended a few events and began to form his own ideas. Working for SAVIEM (Renault truck division) in Paris after finishing his studies in Saumur, he joined a group of enthusiasts who used to meet for dinner at the Bar de l'Action, close to the Etoile. This little group included not only Richard and Bernard but also Jo Schlesser, Amédée Gordini, Jean Lucas, José Rosinski, and Gérard Crombac. Richard says, "I remember the very first draft of *Sport Auto*, with its Ferrari single-seater on the cover, being discussed excitedly by everyone round the restaurant table on one of those evenings … At the time, Renault was supplying engines to René Bonnet to run at Le Mans. Jean Rédélé, not wanting Bonnet to have an advantage, asked the Renault Board to do the same for him. An agreement was made subject to the presentation of an Alpine project for Le Mans. It was Bernard Boyer who introduced me to Jean [Rédélé]." Rédélé didn't really want a new designer but he was impressed by Bouleau's experience in Mexico, where he had been for SAVIEM, and so he was taken on as assistant in the department that dealt with Alpine licensees abroad. It was November 1962 and, in addition to helping the licensees department, Richard was asked to review some drawings for a possible Le Mans car.

Richard: "At that time Alpine only had a little shack at the end of the Renault building: no office, just a little glass cage for the secretary in the middle of the workshop! We had to set ourselves up, so we bought two drawing boards and began to design a car in Jean Rédélé's apartment. In fact, I never did get round to working for the licensees abroad!"

His first chassis design was the M63 sports car prototype for the 1963 Le Mans 24 Hours. Richard: "The same team that assembled berlinettes during the week used to work with the competition cars at the weekend, returning to the production line when they got back from the circuits." Richard laughs. "It has to be said that they didn't bring out many berlinettes, as the total staff of about 45 were always tired!"

After the M63 he developed its successor, the M64, and, during the 1965 season, the M65, which was eventually called the A210.

Richard Bouleau: "When we first saw the V8 Gordini engine which was placed at our disposal, we realised right away that it needed an entirely new chassis. This was to be the A220."

On the single-seater front, after early attempts to utilise Brabham technology in F3 and F2 in 1963, Jean Rédélé decided that Alpine should design its own cars, and here Bouleau's skills were to come into their own. It was during this period that the idea for the 'flat suspension' originated.

Richard, in the middle, in coat. (Archives AAA Dieppe)

Richard: "I had this idea in 1965. I did a lot of trips between Paris and Dieppe. Driving for a long time you have time to think and when I reached my destination I would put my ideas down on paper. Then in 1967, I believe it was, we started to think about a car to test the theory on." That car was to be the A350, designed and built to F1 regulations of the time for 3-litre cars (or 1500cc supercharged). Richard again: "I saw it purely as an

"After the M63 he developed its successor, the M64, and, during the 1965 season, the M65, which was eventually called the A210."

experiment. It was built in secret – well nearly, anyway – but Mauro (Bianchi) and others persuaded Jean Rédélé that we should try to enter it in F1." … "With the A350 we worked a lot with Mauro; he was an excellent driver and had also helped to develop the A110 by testing nearly all the cars we made during that period. After his horrific accident at the 1968 Le Mans 24 Hours, he decided to stop racing and devote all his time to

Bianchi in 1965 with team-mate Roby Weber. (Archives AAA Dieppe)

testing and development. After the A350 project was halted in 1968, I started working on the new A310 GT-style sports car, a complete secret at the time. A young man joined me in the design office – his name, André de Cortanze. Already with the team as a project engineer and driver, he had been involved with several of the Le Mans cars, and it was he who was involved with the design of the Alpine A500 for the turbo engine that was later developed by Bernard Dudot, who had joined Alpine in 1968."

Richard was eventually to move into BEREX, the company newly created by Renault in Dieppe which became the Design and Exploratory Research Office. BEREX was to specialise in projects for sports or marginal vehicles such as the R5 Alpine, the R5 Turbo, and many more vehicles which never saw the light of day. "We even nearly brought out a new berlinette!" Richard says. BEREX closed at the beginning of 1995 and Richard decided to retire.

THE DRIVER – MAURO BIANCHI

Mauro Bianchi was born on 31 July 1937 in Milan. He joined Alpine in 1964 and became not only a prolific race winner, but also a fine test driver and development technician of many Alpine cars for a number of years.

In the early 1960s he was three times World Champion in the GT sports car class, as a result of which he received a phone call from the director of Shell's competition department (which

was sponsoring Alpine at the time), suggesting a meeting with Jean Rédélé. Mauro, who was aware of Alpine, but who found himself unemployed in spite of his successes, with a wife and family to feed, went to Paris. This young, ambitious and ebullient character had already demonstrated his talents and Jean Rédélé decided he had found the man he was looking for. "We're going to France, to Dieppe, to live beside the sea in a beautiful villa – it's going to be wonderful!" he told his somewhat alarmed wife.

His first task was to evaluate the first A110 prototype with the 1100cc engine. Apparently, so Mauro says, it was nicknamed the 'Monster' because of its peculiar handling. Mauro: "I got out of the car and asked them 'What are you planning to do with that?' An engineer replied with the understatement of the century: 'We haven't a clue!'" The car held the road well and was very fast, but had no stability when driven in a straight line. But, Mauro says, "I remember the team was highly motivated and little by little we got the car sorted."

Interestingly, a (then young) man, Michel Petitpas, who lived nearby at the time, recalls, "I remember the little Alpine cars tearing up and down the road – it was an unforgettable sight and sound, though there were often loud bangs when something broke! I lived on the avenue Alexander Dumas, the last straight part leading to the village of Puys, a small village to the east of Dieppe, where the Canadians landed in the World War 2 raid of 1942. At the time I had a VAP motor scooter and would ride

> **"His first task was to evaluate the first A110 prototype with the 1100cc engine. Apparently, so Mauro says, it was nicknamed the 'Monster' because of its peculiar handling."**

home from the Lycée Jehan Ango where I was studying. It was hard, because come wind or come rain I had to go to school! Often when I was approaching our house, coming from Dieppe, I would see a little blue car crackling along at a good speed – an Alpine berlinette! Whose was it? I had no idea, but I was curious, and one day found out that it was Mauro Bianchi coming home for lunch – he lived in Puys. At that time, any sports car which drove past would be noticed and admired. I was fortunate to go sailing with the father of Alpine, as I was a member of the Dieppe sailing club and Jean Rédélé kindly invited me one day to join him, as he was looking for a crew member. He had a wonderful, thoroughbred boat. In 1964 at Haras de Janval,

Dieppe, the French Equestrian Federation was training horses for the Tokyo Olympic Games. I was employed to help train them in the fields around the little aerodrome above Dieppe, alongside a completely straight road, some 6.8km (4.2 miles) long near to the fields. I often heard the sound of an engine being driven full speed at the end of this long straight. It was, of course, the Alpines being tested! One day I heard the sound of an engine coming to its end; sort of 'Cling! Ratatabreeng! Clang, clang, clang!' ... followed by a penetrating silence. The car was immobile, the engine blown up! I felt sorry for the poor drivers, as at that time there were no mobile telephones to call the factory – they had to go to the nearest farm to use the telephone."

"In March 1969, Mauro made a return to driving after an horrendous crash in the 1968 Le Mans 24 Hours which nearly claimed his life."

Mauro's place in the team was assured, and he was to drive the Richard Bouleau-designed A270 and 280 single-seaters. He also turned his hand to rallying in the 1964 Critérium des Cévennes in a berlinette, and in the 1965 Tour de Corse; he finished second overall, co-driven by Gauvain. In Formula 2, for the Pau Grand Prix, he finished fifth after putting his car on the grid in front of the Lotus of Jim Clark and Peter Arundel. At the Le Mans 24 Hours, he teamed up with Jean Vinatier in an M64. Then, in 1965, he won the Nürburgring 500 kilometres with his brother, Lucien, in an Alpine M65. He won again in F3 at Wunstorf in Germany, and at the 1966 Le Mans drove an A210 1300 with Jean Vinatier, finishing thirteenth. During 1967-68, Mauro worked on the two secretly-prepared new cars: the A220 (a V8 Gordini-powered sports car), and the single-seater A350. Mauro: "We started to dream of a Formula 1 programme. We did secret private testing on the circuits at Zolder and Zandvoort."

But, as you will read later, the project was not favourably received by Renault management in Boulogne-Billancourt and their dreams were dashed. In March 1969, Mauro made a return to driving after an horrendous crash in the 1968 Le Mans 24 Hours which nearly claimed his life. Mauro: "We had had brake problems. I left the pits but, in the turmoil, I forgot to pump the brake pedal to check it, and when I arrived at the Forest bends the pedal went right down to the floor!"

It was a bad time, but he decided to try again and took part in testing at Le Mans the following year. But personal tragedy

The accident. (Archives AAA Dieppe)

struck again: this time it was his brother, Lucien, driving an Alfa Romeo 3-litre 33/3, who was killed in a crash at the end of the Hunaudières straight. Devastated, Mauro decided to quit racing, but remained with Alpine, directing the test department until 1976. He had participated in 300 races, secured 35 victories, three times World Champion with Abarth; with Alpine he was there at the beginning of the racing legend.

THE A350 – JUST AN EXPERIMENT?

The mid-1960s was a period of great activity and massive change in Formula 1 when Grand Prix racing moved into a new era. New regulations drawn up in 1963 stipulated that, as from 1966, engines should be 3-litres or 1.5-litres supercharged. Honda, Maserati, Repco, Weslake, Ferrari, Cosworth – all were on the scene by 1968 with 3-litre engines powering a wide range of cars, including Lotus and Brabham. Matra even had its own ideas and its own engine, a fabulous V12.

Jean Rédélé was also secretly interested in Formula 1: in 1963, he had approached Renault with a project that would see an Alpine Renault F1 car on the grid. Unfortunately, Renault's conservative management decided to say "no." But Rédélé was keen to do something, as were his engineers, and it was well known that Amédée Gordini had built a 3-litre V8 engine. Alpine was aware though that there was something not quite right, in

Matra V12. (Courtesy Ed McDonough)

Gordini V8 3-litre engine – Jean Rédélé with Amédéé Gordini, 1968.

fact it was not delivering the performance promised on the test bed; in addition, it had a vibration problem that caused many component failures.

The French government had become interested in Formula 1 as a way of demonstrating the excellence of French engineering, and raising the country's industrial profile. It decided to offer a grant to the constructor who presented the most attractive project for the concept and construction of a 100 per cent French Formula 1 car. Matra was known to be ready to present its new V12, which promised to be technically very impressive, and, because it was an all-French car, would meet the engineering criteria for the government grant.

Of course, Amédée Gordini would have been very happy to receive this grant, but, in his mind, only in order to perfect his V8, primarily designed for endurance racing. His engine was not yet injected like the Matra but was fed by an array of four twin-choke carburettors. In reality, from what we know now, it stood no chance. Amédée had also been thinking about Formula 1, but in terms of two or three years hence.

The young technicians at Alpine had witnessed that, over the two years since 1966, when the new rules had specified a 3-litre formula, Formula 1 had been won by the Brabham team two years running, a team which, at that time, possessed only the modest Repco engine that developed just 300bhp. Alpine was thinking that, if it was possible for Jack Brabham to become World Champion in 1966 with so little power, followed by his team-mate, Denis Hulme, the following season, maybe it had a chance ...

Elf, the state-owned company, had the resources to support a similar programme with another French concern as well as Matra, but not much more was done except to talk and supply lubricants.

Jean Rédélé was in a bit of a quandary, too, remembering that at the 1965 Salon de l'Automobile the directors of Renault had forbidden him to carry the Renault name on the bodywork of his cars or in his catalogues, with the same scenario for the single-seaters. Amédée Gordini's V8 was, of course, carrying the name Renault-Gordini as Renault was investing heavily. Rédélé's team was excited by the prospect and pushing him to do it. He was persuaded and went on to adopt what has become known as his 'tightrope strategy.'

Mauro Bianchi again: "Carried along by the enthusiasm of youth, we had at least been able to persuade 'le patron' to get on and build a '3-litre single-seater'. We called it a laboratory car, but, secretly, we were already hoping for a place in a Grand Prix ... provided it turned out to be powerful enough, of course!"

The so-called experimental laboratory Formula 1 car was referenced in the Alpine records as the A350. It was to be built in the utmost secrecy in a corner of the Alpine workshops in Dieppe, officially with the aim of testing new suspensions for Formula 2. Richard Bouleau emphasised, "For me, it was a car to test my suspension theories, but my colleagues encouraged me that we could go for Formula 1." Whilst pretending to the outside world to know nothing about what was going on in the depths of his workshop, Rédélé would dash down there each morning to check on the progress of the work. The risks were high, of course, and he knew it might only be a matter of time before news reached Renault. In order to avoid any misunderstanding, Jean Rédélé eventually decided to go to the directors of Renault to tell them that he was building an experimental car to test components, emphasising the fact that he was paying for all the parts. In his private capacity as a paying client, he could build any car. The results of the studies, he told them, would be directly applicable to the berlinettes and thus to the benefit of Renault if they were victorious.

This was good news for Richard Bouleau, who could, at last, freely test his theory for pendular suspension; as for Mauro Bianchi, he had a contract as test driver with the promise of an early début in Formula 1.

All were very aware that the level of power demanded would rise considerably: there was talk of 400bhp for the V8 Cosworth and 420bhp for the V12 Ferrari and Matra! To remedy this, Richard was convinced that he had no choice other than to be really inventive and design a single-seater that would have better handling than the competition. They also had what they believed would prove to be the considerable advantage of a new design of Michelin 'radial' tyre, which none of the competition had.

"Bouleau came up with ... the 'flat suspension' which was to be a feature of the A350 and also eventually fitted to the rear of the A220 and A221 sports prototypes."

Chassis and suspension working in unison – along with the tyres – are, of course, the vital organs that give a car its handling capabilities.

Richard: "Each constructor had his own philosophy on suspension design which could only be a compromise.

The car first sees the light of day, Garage Rédélé. (Archives AAA Dieppe)

There was no miracle geometry to maintain the wheels under satisfactory camber, whatever the roll of the body in cornering. In this respect, some wild dreams existed on paper, but they only produced theories which were as mythical as they were complicated."

Bouleau came up with an idea which seemed more realistic, although it wasn't particularly simple. He called it the 'flat suspension' and it was to be a feature of the A350 and also eventually fitted to the rear of the A220 and A221 sports prototypes.

Here, briefly, is an explanation of the working principles of this design. Richard Bouleau again:

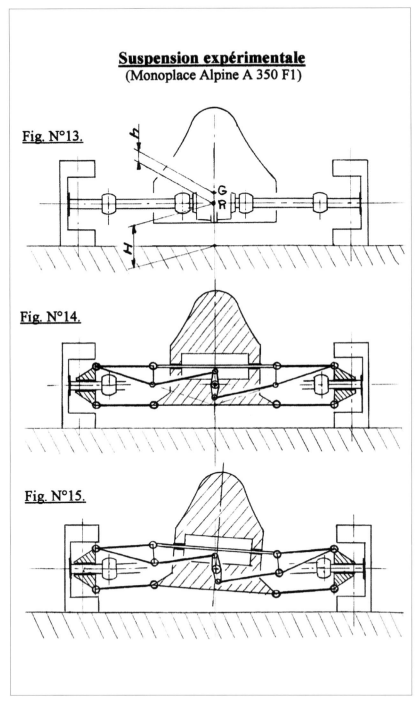

Suspension expérimentale
(Monoplace Alpine A 350 F1)

Fig. N°13.

Fig. N°14.

Fig. N°15.

Experimental suspension. (Drawing courtesy Richard Bouleau)

"It is vital to keep the wheels theoretically perpendicular to the road, whatever the inclination of the chassis. So the wheels must remain parallel to each other. This parallelism can only be maintained by superimposed suspension arms forming a frontal parallelogram; in other words, the arms must be equal and parallel. Now, if the arms were anchored to the chassis, the wheels could not be kept parallel to the frame. So the upper arms must be disconnected from the chassis and hung from a moving frame which moves in the chassis during inclination.

"The upper arms have a reaction point placed below their axis of rotation with the frame. These reaction points are then connected by two rods at the ends of a rocker whose axis is located in the centre of the chassis, which makes the movements of the two reaction points symmetrical. By positioning the reaction points correctly, the displacement of the moving suspension frame allows the wheels to remain perpendicular to the ground in any circumstances. The rear part of the chassis is made removable by a threaded joint on each tube at the front of the rear panel between cockpit and engine."

Bouleau continues: "When we tested at Zolder we found that the behaviour of the car was as surprising as it was interesting. In the chicane which comes before the stands at the Zolder circuit, it could be seen from the front that there was absolutely no sign of roll. It was so unusual that it caught the attention of a waiter in the restaurant above the stands, who came down to tell us how mystified he was. On this chassis, with the centre of gravity of the rear axle being close to the roll centre, no significant torque could be detected that was able to produce roll. With the virtual absence of roll, as the body doesn't drop, the front wheels don't drop either."

"The main idea was to develop a suspension which was not sensitive to variations in expansion, compression, stability and rolling."

In close collaboration with the Michelin Clermont-Ferrand engineers, including a young Pierre Dupasquier (of whom more later), Richard Bouleau was to find that the temperature of the tread was directly linked to variations in the wheel camber. The main idea was to develop a suspension which was not sensitive to variations in expansion, compression, stability, and rolling. Technically, the left and right wheels were not independent but interconnected by the upper triangulation, which was itself linked to a false chassis by a reverse thrust. Result: the camber of the four wheels was invariable and it was the chassis which leant into a corner. Richard Bouleau continues: "The A350 front suspension worked according to the same principle as the rear."

The completed car first saw the light of day in April 1968, seen here on the pavement of the rue Pasteur in Dieppe.

Mauro Bianchi, the test driver, takes up the story: "Richard surprised us all by designing a totally original system. The first shakedown tests took place on the Michelin test circuit at Ladoux in late April 1968. We learnt a lot from this first outing and, whilst we found many small adjustments were necessary, as per usual in an initial test, the first running was encouraging, so we decided to continue its development on the Zolder circuit. The car still had some faults, some of which were fairly severe but could easily be put right at this stage of its development. Through all this, though, I could see straightaway that it had great potential. Its strong point was the braking: with three times the power that I had been used to and 100kg (220lb) extra weight, I could still brake using the same markers as for an F3 car! The explanation lay in that flat suspension design which allowed us always to use 100 per cent of the width of the tyre tread." Because the centre of gravity and the roll centre were practically at the same height, the car could do without anti-roll bars, which gave the system maximal movement.

This rear view of the A350 shows details of the suspension, in particular, the two tubular tetrahedrons which serve as upper arms, right and left.
(Archives AAA Dieppe)

Chassis construction. (Archives AAA Dieppe)

Chassis construction. (Archives AAA Dieppe)

Dieppe, March 1968. (Archives AAA Dieppe)

First test, spring 1968. (Archives AAA Dieppe)

Mauro: "In terms of performance we were very satisfied and our lap times were fair. We then went on to continue our tests on the Zandvoort circuit, site of the Dutch Grand Prix, on 23 June; the performance achieved confirmed the competitiveness of the A350. There, too, my lap times would have assured me a place in the middle of the grid in the previous year. Without doubt, we had a very good chassis base. The handicap was going to be the engine.

"Its strong point was the braking: with three times the power that I had been used to and 100kg (220lb) extra weight, I could still brake using the same markers as for an F3 car! The explanation lay in that flat suspension design which allowed us always to use 100 per cent of the width of the tyre tread."

"We immediately made plans to enter the A350 in the French Grand Prix which, that year, was to take place on 7 July at the Circuit des Essarts in Rouen. Our strategy was clear: once the car was lined up for competition, we thought it would become evident to Renault that, on the one hand, the Alpine team with me as driver was capable of competing at this level; on the other hand, the V8 Gordini, with its 300bhp at 7200rpm, was truly too slow. In our minds, the Renault management would have no choice but to begin designing a true racing engine conforming to the requirements of Formula 1, and we had no doubt at all that a new engine would be absolutely competitive. We applied to enter the French Grand Prix."

Mauro continues: "All was set ready to go when we were hit with a huge shock; a firm message was sent to Jean Rédélé from Renault. They had issued a categorical injunction: 'We forbid the use of our V8 3000cc engines in a single-seater in competition.'"

This part of the story may appear irrelevant, but it is useful to look at the history to understand what came next. Here we have a team dedicated to competition but stifled in its efforts. It did not stand alone in this, as evidenced by a trail of attempts, successes and failures by private teams and major players over the years. Formula 1 in the 1960s was full of almost amateur enthusiasm, and was still virtually the same into the early 1970s.

Alpine had attempted to enter at a time when the Cosworth-powered Lotus 49 was about to take the Grand Prix world by storm. Whether the Alpine A350 could have risen to the challenge we shall never know ...

Alpine, Mauro and Richard believe they were right to try, but perhaps it was a bit too soon. Carried along by their enthusiasm and technical capability, they had not foreseen the political reasoning and reactions of the Renault management, which was clearly concerned about the performance of the Gordini V8 and the company's image. Renault's decision was proved correct, however, as the V8 Renault-Gordini did not achieve even 300bhp, which was 120bhp less than a good Ford-Cosworth at the time. A year later in 1969, Renault abandoned the development projects for 3-litre V8 engines, and also any thoughts of Formula 1.

"... the V8 Renault-Gordini did not achieve even 300bhp, which was 120bhp less than a good Ford-Cosworth at the time ... This unique, experimental single-seater was destroyed a few months after the French Grand Prix débâcle. Nothing remains, except the body moulds and the wheels ..."

This unique, experimental single-seater was destroyed a few months after the French Grand Prix débâcle. Nothing remains, except the body moulds and the wheels, photographed in 2007!

Renault was not in the mood for any more Grand Prix ideas for a very long time. As for Elf, the petrol company henceforth gave its financial and material help to the team directed by Ken Tyrrell, by then running the Matra. Elf would be back, but for the passionate professional enthusiasts at Alpine, F1 had not materialised.

A350 mould master. (© RS)

The wheels. (© RS)

GORDINI – THE NAME ON THE ENGINE

Amédée Gordini, 1899-1979.

Mention Alpine or Renault to anyone interested in competition cars of the 1950s, 1960s or 1970s, and the name of one man immediately springs to mind: Gordini, 'le Sorcier' (the Wizard), in his time one of the greatest automotive engineers, who specialised in making little cars go fast.

Born in Bazzano in Italy on 23 June 1899, Amédée Gordini eventually moved to Paris to establish his first garage, and was to race and tune cars during the 1930s, enjoying some success with his Fiat-engined sports cars. After World War 2 he restored

French pride through the little blue cars that resurrected the nation's motor racing heritage after the catastrophic wartime occupation, despite a continual lack of funding. The first Gordini single-seaters came in 1946 when 'le Sorcier' ran Fiat-engined cars for himself and José Scaron.

Gordini won races in Marseilles, Dijon, Forez, and Nantes, and Scaron won in Nice and St-Cloud. In the late 1940s the company expanded into workshops in the boulevard Victor in Paris, and, whilst Scaron and former Le Mans 24 Hours winner, Pierre Veyron, concentrated on sports car events, Gordini persuaded the new names in French racing, Robert Manzon and Maurice Trintignant, to drive with the top men of the time, Jean-Pierre Wimille and Raymond Sommer. Victories came in abundance, though, sadly, on 28 January 1949, in practice for a race in Buenos Aires, Argentina, Jean-Pierre Wimille was killed whilst driving a Gordini.

In 1950, Gordini supercharged a Simca engine for the newly-established Grand Prix World Championship. There were no major victories in what was to be called Formula 1, but Gordinis did prove successful in Formula 2. 1951, though, saw the first appearances of Jean Behra in the little Gordini Formula 1 car, and a year later he was on winning form, beating even the Ferraris at Reims. Gordini continued to enter cars and race tuned engines for others up to 1957, when he became a consulting engineer to Renault. This led to the first official appearance of a Gordini engine in a production Renault at the Salon de l'Auto in 1958, when the Gordini-powered Renault Dauphine was presented to an eagerly-awaiting press.

Gordini was by then well known, but, with a small company of some 20 employees, was a minnow in comparison to the likes of Renault. Plus, all the years of racing on tight budgets had taken their toll on him and the financial status of his company and he wanted to expand sales of his technology. The problem was, how to do it and who to do it with? A clever man – and not just as an engineer – Gordini had set his sights on Renault, but his early approaches fell on deaf ears.

How could he progress his plans? Perhaps through an intermediary? At the time, a good friend of his was the French Consul in America who, as luck would have it, knew well engineer Fernand Picard, head of the design department at Renault. Through this introduction Amédée Gordini was able to show Renault management the creative design of his modifications to the Dauphine power unit, and his unique 4-speed gearbox design that he had fitted into the casing of the existing Dauphine gearbox designed for 3 speeds. Renault and its engineers were enthusiastic and the Renault Dauphine Gordini, and along with it a long association, was born.

Initially, a hundred cars were built at Gordini's workshop in the boulevard Victor, eventually resulting in many thousands being built at Boulogne-Billancourt. Other projects were to follow, including a Dauphine Gordini-powered speedboat with a modified Z-type gearbox.

The Dauphine Gordini was a complete success and Amédée had begun looking for his next project when Renault produced the R8. Paul Frère, a famous motoring journalist of the period, commented, "The R8 is the car we have all been waiting for." It produced a top speed of 82mph (132kph) from its 1108cc, 50bhp Major engine. Amédée Gordini saw the potential and developed the engine to give 95bhp. The R8 Gordini was to become famous around the world; with a top speed of 105mph (169kph), and an 18 second quarter mile, this car was one for the racers. So it proved to be; even today many classic and historic rallies feature one or more R8 Gordinis on their entry lists.

Gordini and his Dauphine.

> **"The R8 Gordini was to become famous around the world; with a top speed of 105mph (169kph), and an 18 second quarter mile, this car was one for the racers. So it proved to be; even today many classic and historic rallies feature one or more R8 Gordinis on their entry lists."**

With the new orders for the R8 Gordini the workload was burgeoning, and Amédée was thinking of a move to expand his now cramped workshops. At the time, he may also have been thinking of something other than continuation of his alliance with Renault, or maybe he just wanted the Régie Renault to take a more serious view of this. Whatever his ideas were, he certainly looked at buying land to the west of Paris in Noisy-le-Roi, although the true reason for this was never divulged.

Renault was already heavily involved with Gordini and it was at the end of 1967 at the Gordini works annual dinner that Amédée announced that Gordini would move to a new home; not Noisy-le-Roi but Viry-Châtillon, close to the Autoroute du Sud where his good friend Henri Longuet was mayor. Of course, the directorate of Renault had brought its influence to bear. Construction started early in 1968, and, on 3 February 1969, the Gordini company officially began the move to the new buildings in Viry. The change was dramatic, quoted at the time as "... different as chalk from cheese;" the plant was immediately to become more Renault than Gordini.

One of Gordini's own projects in the mid-1960s was the design and build of the V8 engine. Renault was not too keen about it as, by 1968, it was heavily involved with subcontracting several other development projects to Gordini and although giving approval for it to be built for Sports Prototype use and a future road car Renault was not overly willing to progress this engine over other projects; the company was horrified upon discovering that Alpine had fitted the V8 into a proposed Formula 1 Alpine A350!

Renault 8 Gordini cup race Le Mans, 27 September 1970.

Renault immediately enforced an embargo on its use in anything other than the Alpine sports cars, as it was also becoming more involved with Jean Rédélé's Alpine company in Dieppe.

Renault also decided it did not want to get involved in the R8 1300 Gordini that Amédée had created, as it had done with support for the R8 1100 and the Dauphine prior to that. However, in spite of their differences of opinion, Gordini needed Renault, and his team continued its work for Renault, though, given the pleasurable experience of the early years, he was, perhaps, a little less enthusiastic than before.

Gordini's staff had continued to grow, and by 1969 some

forty people were employed in various capacities. 'Pépère' ('Grandpa,' the employees' affectionate nickname for Amédée) and Marc Bande, one of his technicians, had astutely employed a number of young engineers who went on to great careers. François Castaing, who was to come to the fore a few years later, first appeared to work in boulevard Victor, prior to his military service. The young Jean-Pierre Boudy also started at Gordini after meeting Marc Bande, and, in the design office, the two enriched the group of engineers working alongside Giuseppe Albarea.

It is interesting to hear from future director, François Castaing, at this point: "In my last year at the Paris Industrial University, after having begun in Aix-en-Provence, I was asked to work on a very special subject for the end-of-year dissertation. My professor knew that I was interested in cars and gave me a study commissioned by Amédée Gordini! That year [1968], Amédée was still chairman of his own company, Automobiles Gordini. It seemed he was not entirely happy with his collaboration with Alpine and wanted to build his own car for his V8 3-litre engine. He commissioned studies from various universities. On his behalf we had designed a chassis with Elva suspension, to which he was very partial; then we made a wind tunnel model and in July I knocked at his door in the boulevard Victor and he hired me."

Castaing continues: "At the time we were pioneers, and my first mission was the 1968 Le Mans 24 Hours, which was to be held in September because of the strikes and unrest during the summer. You can imagine I was somewhat concerned when, during the race, the guys in the Gordini part of the team left for their hotel at 11pm, while the cars were on the circuit! Alain Marguet and I were the only ones who stayed in the pits; we were by then worried about the relaxed attitude to racing."

Before leaving to do my military service, I had adapted the Kugelfischer injection to suit the little Gordini twin-cam 4-cylinder – this was the engine fitted to the Killy-Wollek Alpine that ran at Le Mans in 1969."

> ## "That year [1968], Amédée was still chairman of his own company, Automobiles Gordini. It seemed he was not entirely happy with his collaboration with Alpine and wanted to build his own car for his V8 3-litre engine."

Alain Marguet, who joined as an engine technician, was to be one of the few technicians still at Renault Sport in 1975, along with François Castaing and Marc Bande, to have worked first of all for Amédée Gordini in his workshop in the boulevard Victor in Paris, then at Renault Gordini, later Renault Sport, at Viry-Châtillon. Marguet left his studies at 20 years of age to go from Arras to Paris and begin working at Gordini. Marguet says in the 1991 book, *Les Années Turbo*: "From what I had learned at school and what I had learned about Gordini's sporting prowess, I expected something more modern when I arrived in the boulevard Victor. I was very surprised." When the time came for the move, he says, "Unlike the older employees at Gordini, the move to Viry didn't concern me very much. On the contrary, I

The Gordini V8 engine. (Archives AAA Dieppe)

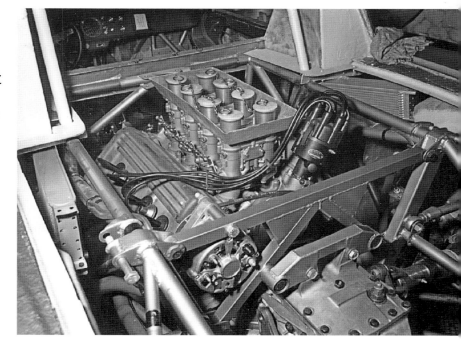

V8 in the A220 prototype sports car. (Archives AAA Dieppe)

Gordini with Terramorsi at Le Mans.

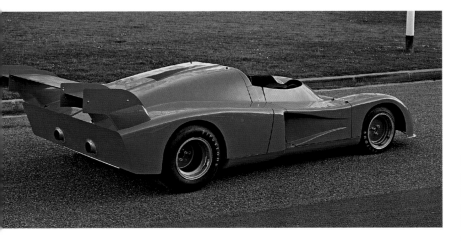

The new A440 outside the workshop in Dieppe in 1973.

thought it essential. The test bench on which I had been working at boulevard Victor was installed under a fragile roof, and I remember that when we were running the engines late into the evening, people living nearby would throw things at our roof."

The start of the move, which took place in February 1969, was to cause quite a few problems with the engineers, who couldn't stop working because they were preparing for that year's Le Mans 24 Hours. The V8 engines were to be assembled in Viry,

but the test bench had, at that point, not yet been resited, and the V8 had to be sent back to the boulevard Victor for testing. The 1969 Le Mans race was to be a disaster for the V8 engine; in fact, as one ex-employee says, "Le Mans had been a total fiasco. It had not been helped by the upheaval of the move but, unfortunately, it was the death knell for this engine, and the management at Alpine and Gordini were instructed by the Renault directorate to stop all V8 development and sports car competition racing."

1969 was to herald more changes than just a factory move when, in June, a meeting of the administrative committee of the Régie-Renault and Gordini confirmed the acquisition of 70 per cent of the capital of Gordini. Renault appointed a new director to work with the Renault-Gordini company alongside Claude Haardt: Georges Sauvan, previously with Peugeot and recently with Gordini. Also at about the same time Jean Terramorsi was appointed to join the senior management of the new organisation; a man who was to play such a prominent role in the turbo story.

"Le Mans had been a total fiasco ... it was the death knell for this engine and the management at Alpine and Gordini were instructed by the Renault directorate to stop all V8 development and sports car competition racing."

At that stage, Gordini was still PDG (President Director General). However, it was becoming obvious to him that he was gradually being sidelined by the new structure. Gordini was an extraordinary engineer though, perhaps, by this time, a little disillusioned and weary of the politics involved. As a director he had an office in Viry, although was becoming less involved in the day-to-day running of the company as the months passed. His visionary mind began to wander; he had an idea, and suggested that he go back and set himself up in the old premises to design an engine without a cylinder head, ie with block and cylinder head in one piece. Gordini got his wish and Marc Bande went with him and Giuseppe Albarea to the boulevard Victor in mid-September 1970.

Amédée Gordini's thinking was to use modern metallurgy to save time in the fabrication of engines. However, it comes as no surprise that, now he was away from Viry, he was to play no further part there. Bande, however, was called back to Viry in

1971 to work on a number of projects relating to the V6 PRV, a concept of the Peugeot-Renault-Volvo collaboration. Then Giuseppe Albarea was also recalled from the boulevard Victor by Georges Sauvan.

François Castaing, on returning from military service, went direct to Viry and several new projects, which included an updated version of the Renault 16 engine and preparation of engines for customer competition use. Then, in 1972, Castaing got the green light for a new engine: a V6 2-litre, which was to carry the Gordini name. With Elf money, Renault put out a commission to the Viry-Châtillon team to design a new V6 1997cc atmospheric engine to compete in the 2-litre European Sports Car Championships. Renault was returning to high-profile racing competition with Elf, led by François Guiter, who had managed to persuade his boss, Jean Prada, that such an investment would be good for Elf's image and publicity. Negotiations with Renault, Alpine, and the Viry-Châtillon Renault-Gordini team resulted in Alpine being given the contract to design the new sports car, which was eventually to appear in 1973 to compete in the 2-litre European Sports Prototype Championships in 1974.

It is definite that Formula 1 and the Gordini V8 were distant memories by 1973, and F1, especially, was far from the minds of either Alpine or Renault or, in fact, any of the design team. However, that same year Renault took a major share in the Alpine company, until then owned by Jean Rédélé, thereby strengthening ties between Renault, Alpine, and Gordini. Rédélé stayed on as a director but inevitable changes occurred: the competition service department was completely reorganised, and the man who was key to many Alpine victories, Jacques Cheinisse, became its head.

Tragedy had struck the Viry operation in November 1972 when Claude Haardt was killed in an accident in the Bay of Arcachon in a boat owned by Renault Marine. Jean Terramorsi replaced him as principal of the Renault-Gordini company.

Back in boulevard Victor during 1972, Amédée Gordini had continued to work on, but Renault had by then taken stock of the potential market for this all-in-one cylinder block and head. Alas, although studies showed that the idea wasn't bad, it was not going to suit the way the business of producing volume automotive engines was going, and so it was against proceeding further. The project to develop a 4-cylinder engine with no cylinder head was cut short in 1973. Soon afterward the workshops in boulevard Victor were sold and Amédée decided to call it a day and retire.

A new era was set to begin when Gérard Larrousse – who

Usine A Gordini.

had featured in Alpines since his early forays into rallying in the 1960s, and had had a legendary career; a prolific winner not only in Alpines but notably in Porsches and many others – returned to the Alpine fold to use the A440 and 441 in his own team, Elf Switzerland, in 1974.

Renault was watching his progress and, just before what was to be his last competitive drive on the Tour de Corse in 1975, where he drove a 1774cc Gordini-powered Alpine A110, he was made an offer he could hardly refuse. That rally entry was also the last time Alpine would enter a factory car under its own name. From the beginning of 1976, Larrousse was made head of the sporting ambitions of Renault, and created the organisation known today as Renault Sport, with responsibility for Le Mans and Formula 1 projects.

The ageing Amédée Gordini, who had already decided on a quieter life, eventually sold all his remaining shares to Renault in 1977, giving total control to the Régie. Fortunately, Gordini lived to see his name on the engine that was to change Formula 1 for ever, and was able to visit the races as well as witness the 1978 Le Mans victory. The name Gordini lives on today, and, whilst he may have faded a little in later years, his presence was felt long into the turbo era. After his death on 25 May 1979, the factory in Viry-Châtillon was formally named the 'Usine A Gordini.'

No one would ever forget 'le Sorcier,' in his heyday one of the great engine magicians.

Part 2

THE DEVELOPMENT OF AN IDEA

In 1970, Pierre Dreyfus, PDG (President Director General) of the Régie Renault, and Marc Ouin, his secretary general, were pretty unimpressed about the benefits of racing after the high-profile failures of the Renault-Gordini-engined 3-litre V8 Alpines at the 1969 Le Mans, except, that is, for Alain Serpaggi and Christian Ethuin, who won the index of performance in the 1150cc class. Theirs was the only car to cross the line at the finish and the other six cars had nothing to show for their efforts. Alpine had tried hard, but, even with the sleek design of its cars, it had not been as successful with the big V8 Renault-Gordini engine as it had previously with the smaller capacity units, as the V8 was not developing the power or reliability of its competitors. Moreover, a study of the circumstances seemed to indicate a lack of communication and coordination of the task in hand from the three parties involved: Renault itself, the new Renault-Gordini plant in Viry, and Alpine in Dieppe. It is possible that the disruption of the move to Viry, the differences of opinion between Amédée Gordini and Jean Rédélé, and the casual approach of some team members involved all who contributed.

Something had to happen if Renault-Gordini was to go racing again. Mauro Bianchi says: "The small-engined cars were always good; Marcel Hubert was brilliant with the aerodynamics. The A220 was good eventually, after some early problems, but, sadly, that engine was our downfall, and we had 100bhp less than the Matras." Renault was investing heavily in Gordini and was losing patience. From that time on, Renault decided to agree only to the Dieppe Alpine's participation in rallies.

For Elf this was a setback. Founded in 1967, the new state-owned petrol brand was looking from the start to create an image of technical quality with a creative and dynamic outlook for its company, openly expressed to the public through competition. Market research had shown that, in the new vibrant economy, the man in the street took notice of winners, especially in the high-profile world of motor sport. In this objective, Elf had started and succeeded with an association with Matra, which had the same ambitions, and had won the French Formula 3 Championship (1967), the European Formula 2 Championship (1968), and the Formula 1 World Championship (1969). The next target was to be victory in the Le Mans 24 Hours in 1970.

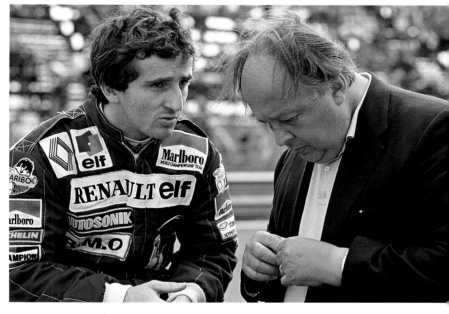

Alain Prost with François Guiter at Zeltweg, 1983.

However, the rules of the ACO (Automobile Club de l'Ouest) placed the 3-litre cars in the prototype class alongside the domineering Porsche and Ferrari teams. Victory eluded Elf and Matra was by then in partnership with Simca, which was owned by Chrysler. The contract with Elf was up for renewal and Elf had to make a choice to go on with an agreement whereby it might be competing with Chrysler's partner, Shell, or go it alone with Renault. It was François Guiter who was to persuade his boss Jean Prada to go with Renault.

In fact, since 1968, Elf had had a contract with the management of Renault to use its lubricants for every road car that left the production line, with the spin-off that Elf would be recommended to customers of Renault in aftersales and advertised as "Used by the Alpine Renault Rally team." This contract, too, was up for renewal at the end of 1970, and Elf wanted to put money into a competition programme, because, without Matra, it would no longer have a circuit racing presence.

Jean Terramorsi.

Claude Haardt was a formidable leader of men and an unrivalled salesman. On joining Renault he was put in charge of marketing in the engine division. In this capacity, he sold engines to DAF, was responsible for Renault-Marine-Couach (specialists in marine engines in Arcachon), and undertook the sale of engines to the Americans. In June 1972, he was appointed chairman and managing director of Renault-Gordini in Viry-Châtillon.

It was earlier, under his direction, that Amédée Gordini had abandoned his plans to move his company to Noisy-le-Roi from the boulevard Victor, and instead relocated to a new factory in Viry-Châtillon in 1969. As we have read in a preceding section of our study, 'le Sorcier,' at first happy with the move, did not agree with all the changes Renault was making, and returned to the boulevard Victor to continue his research into a new, small engine. Jean Terramorsi was working for a publicity and marketing company, one of whose clients was Renault, where he was to take over the job of managing the Renault publicity department from Marc-Antoine Pampuzac. François Guiter had been in contact with Terramorsi since early in 1970. Enthusiastic, passionate about cars and competition, Terramorsi was a man full of ideas – original, imaginative, and visionary. He possessed charisma, was receptive to the ideas of others, and had a good, respectful, yet open, relationship with top management. Because of this he was given special marketing responsibilities which included overall management of Renault's competition interests.

> **"Enthusiastic, passionate about cars and competition, Terramorsi was a man full of ideas – original, imaginative, and visionary. He possessed charisma, was receptive to the ideas of others, and had a good, respectful, yet open, relationship with top management."**

Though it was bright, promising and successful, Alpine-Renault's rally programme – favoured by Renault – was not sufficient to satisfy the dynamic management in the Elf boardroom.

Renault and its management, unfortunately, could not be persuaded to go further. François Guiter, project manager for Elf's sport strategy, set about securing agreement from Jean Prada to organise and finance a programme with Alpine, utilising its successful Formula 2 or 3 cars. Guiter could not go too far, however, and had to make do with the finance available, at the same time avoiding offending any sensitivity within Renault management. How could it be done? As luck would have it, an opportunity arose with the new Formula 3 regulations, which were now open to engines that had to come from a series production unit with a capacity of 1600cc, and fitted with an inlet restrictor. Bernard Dudot in Dieppe was already working with Marc Mignotet to provide a suitably tuned unit for the new Alpine single-seaters.

The Renault R16 engine was perfect for the task. But before suggesting any plan Elf management had to decide where it could get the support within Renault, and maybe Alpine if that route was taken. Elf found three men at Renault: Claude Haardt, Jean Terramorsi, and Christian Martin, and a man at Alpine who would provide essential support: Jacques Cheinisse.

Christian Martin was in the commercial management department, an acquaintance, though not a close friend, of Jean Rédélé, and had a soft spot for Alpine and its efforts. He discovered a personal liking for racing while on business for Renault in Brazil, where Alpine was having the Interlagos berlinettes built under licence by commercial vehicle builder, Willys Overland. Willys regularly raced the Interlagos cars in South America.

Others within Renault management were not so keen on

the members of the small company from Dieppe, whom they regarded as 'mercenaries.' But, like Terramorsi, Martin had a greater vision and could see a time when they might achieve what the sceptics wanted through success in competition.

The last man in the link was Jacques Cheinisse, a superb rally strategist. Cheinisse was open-minded and perceptive enough to see a potential in a joint initiative with Elf that involved Alpine. Well known in motor sport circles and in rallying, he would lead Alpine to the first World Rally Championship title in 1973. His interest and enthusiasm may, in fact, have been the first building block of the team that led Renault into Formula 1.

"Christian Martin ... discovered a personal liking for racing while on business for Renault in Brazil, where Alpine was having the Interlagos berlinettes built under licence by commercial vehicle builder, Willys Overland."

So François Guiter had his men, and, with the enthusiastic Haardt and Cheinisse, they decided to take the risk and hope that, with the persuasion of Terramorsi and Martin, Renault senior management would get involved in this joint competition venture. Elf had agreed to put up the finance and, with the tacit support of his accomplices in Renault management, Cheinisse began to put together a small group that included three of their talented, forward-thinking design engineers: André de Cortanze (chassis), Bernard Dudot (engine), and Marcel Hubert (aerodynamics). Their objective was the French Formula 3 Championship for the 1971 season.

André de Cortanze was a graduate of INSA Lyons (National Institute of Applied Sciences) who had an interest in design. Then working with Richard Bouleau, he had earlier been made project manager for the 3-litre prototypes. Bernard Dudot had joined Alpine in 1968 after persistently offering his services to Jean Rédélé following graduation from CESTI (engineering college). He was to revamp and co-ordinate the activities of the engine department at Alpine.

Alpine had previously utilised the resources of several outside partners, dependent on the area in which they specialised. For engines these had been Renault, Renault-Gordini, Mignotet, and Moteur Moderne. Dudot and his team were given the responsibility of developing the R16 engine on the one test bench they had at their disposal, their task being

Christian Martin.

Jacques Cheinisse (centre) with Jean-Luc Thérier and Marcel Callewaert, 1970.

The team in 1969 with the 220B 3-litre prototype of Andruet and Grandsire; de Cortanze fifth from left. (Archive AAA Dieppe)

Marc Mignotet in 1997. (Courtesy *Mille Miles*)

to turn it into a Formula 3 competitive unit. Dudot was to work closely with Mignotet during this period.

Bernard Dudot: "Marc Mignotet was a clever man. He taught me a lot. He could see things in his mind and create cam profiles just by analysing the situation and directly machining the component. If I had a problem, perhaps, say, with piston design, he would not tell me the solution but would put things in front of me to see for myself the way forward. He didn't get on with everybody but, for me, he was inspirational."

Marcel Hubert was the very experienced Alpine aerodynamicist. He had studied at the Romani School and joined Alpine in 1962, first as a freelance then as a company employee. He had worked on all the prototypes and berlinettes and had been involved in the A350 in 1968. His aerodynamic work played a major part in the amazing performances achieved at Le Mans over the previous years of the mid-1960s by the small-engined Alpines.

A master of the situation, Hubert knew how to work in a team, taking into account the comments of the drivers and the requirements of the engine people or chassis designers. François Castaing: "Marcel Hubert was Alpine's secret weapon; he was simply a genius. Where computers were not even thought of for designing, his mind worked like one, able to turn two-dimensional concepts into three by literally cutting some wood or foam to shape to demonstrate what was in his mind."

"Marc Mignotet was a clever man ... He could see things in his mind and create cam profiles just by analysing the situation and directly machining the component ... He didn't get on with everybody but, for me, he was inspirational." – Bernard Dudot

For the drivers, François Guiter was to enlist the proven expertise of Patrick Depailler and Jean-Pierre Jabouille. Jean-Pierre Jabouille says, "I went to talk to François Guiter. I thought Alpine had something interesting for us, so we went to see them. But, in fact, I think the first car needed some fine tuning – the chassis, that is. As you know, I was already passionate about technical things, suspension, etc, and so quickly made friends with the Alpine engineers and tried to make them understand. Of course, I got into trouble – a young driver trying to throw his weight around. But there was a chief mechanic who understood things; he told me to let them say what they liked and he would see they did what I wanted. So we made various adjustments and the car ran much better. Gradually, the engineers came round; of course, it wasn't only me testing the car: there was Patrick too."

"Marcel Hubert was Alpine's secret weapon; he was simply a genius. Where computers were not even thought of for designing, his mind worked like one, able to turn two-dimensional concepts into three by literally cutting some wood or foam to shape to demonstrate what was in his mind." – Castaing

Would this set-up – Elf financing, Alpine's specialist chassis knowledge, and Renault engines – be sufficient to impress Pierre Dreyfus? Unfortunately, his ultra-conservative thinking saw it as a risk: suppose they should fail? It was Renault's name on the engine! So it was, on reflection, no surprise at all that, during the official launch of the 1971 competition programme, at the very last moment the promotional information documents relating to Formula 3 were withdrawn from the press pack. It was a shock to the team at the time, but a few insiders had convinced some of the senior management. Dreyfus knew this and some of his team were keen, others would tolerate it, but … he didn't approve.

Elf personnel, the men at Alpine, and the committed believers in Renault wore broad smiles when, come the end of the season, Depailler and Jabouille had dominated the French championship. At last! Now would Renault come in from the cold? The problem was that Renault had no engine in its programme capable of taking the next progressive step.

Elf did not want to stand still: much effort had been expended to get the F3 cars to the top of the podium; now that it wanted to go the next logical step, Renault was not going to prevent that. With or without Renault, that was the plan.

André Renut: "The Elf F2 single-seaters were designed in our design department at Alpine. As for the build, we did some things and other parts were entrusted to an external team." So, as we see, Alpine was asked by Elf, with tacit agreement from Renault, to build a Formula 2 single-seater. Whose engine would be used? Renault did not have one, and nor was it interested in building one. The decision: a Ford-Hart engine! Cheinisse gave it the thumbs-up. Terramorsi and Martin gasped and put their hands over their eyes, but still parted their fingers to watch!

Marcel Hubert, Viry-Châtillon, 1975.

De Cortanze was put to work to design the car, an Alpine A367 named the Elf 2 and, in May 1972, Depailler, Jabouille, and François Cevert tested it at Magny-Cours. The team was run by an Englishman, John Coombs, and named Elf Coombs. Jabouille finished in 14th place that first year in F2. The team continued through into 1973 with this car, though with limited success.

As one might imagine, there were gasps of anguish at Renault, and the pressure was further increased when François Guiter persuaded Jean Prada to ask Renault to make a real competition engine for Elf to use. Renault had gained some considerable advantage, publicity-wise, on the back of Elf's successful efforts, plus it was a state-owned company, and it was unthinkable that Elf could, if pushed, withdraw from Renault.

François Guiter had also quietly made direct contact with Claude Haardt to try and convince Renault to build a true competition engine. It was all that Haardt wanted. François Guiter: "I arranged a visit to Cosworth in the UK through my good relations with Ken [Tyrrell]. Ken set up the visit and François Castaing, Bernard Dudot, Claude Haardt, Terramorsi, Ken and I went to Cosworth. You should have seen Keith Duckworth's face when a delegation from Renault turned up! In fact, it was a very interesting visit and Castaing and Dudot saw that the metrology and quality control department was very specialised, to the point that they rejected any component that did not exactly meet the

45

tolerances required – and boy, those tolerances, they told us, were pretty tight! We learnt a lesson that day. Claude Haardt had already said to me, 'My dream is to create a French Cosworth.'"

But, once again, after presentations to top management, to Haardt's amazement its members stood firm behind a curtain of caution. Even the perceived taunt with the Hart engine in the F2 car had not worked. Although, Dreyfus and his team could see that, maybe, there could be some mileage in the idea this time, they were not prepared to put in their own money; their stance was: "If Elf wants an engine, OK – let them order it and pay for it!" Elf's simple reply was "How much?" A figure of 300,000 francs was suggested. Elf immediately sent a cheque. However, in the letter written by Christian Beullac, then number two within Renault management, to Jean Prada at Elf acknowledging receipt of the order and the cheque, he wrote, "Have we got the men capable of doing this? And what can we do about it?" Still Renault lacked enthusiasm.

The order was passed to Claude Haardt and Georges Sauvan at Renault-Gordini in Viry-Châtillon. Sauvan put François Castaing in charge of it. Castaing: "When I returned from military service in spring 1970, Renault had completely taken over Gordini and I found myself in Viry. We had a great deal of difficulty in 'placing' our engines at Alpine, who, at that time, preferred to develop their own association with their own man, Bernard Dudot, and the links with Mignotet, and we had to prove that we were just as good at developing the small 1600cc engine by doing some customer projects. We also worked on the PRV multi-valves and on the R12 Gordini engine, until Sauvan came to me in 1972 and asked me to make the new competition engine ordered by Elf."

Renault had an image; the design was to be specific and not exceed 2 litres, a capacity which, coincidentally, suited participation in the European championship for 2-litre prototypes, against BMW, Ford, and Abarth. Elf agreed that sports car racing would be fine for its purposes, and perhaps Alpine could design and build a car?

When at Peugeot, Georges Sauvan had worked on the design of a top-of-the-range engine which would be used by the Peugeot, Renault, and eventually Volvo, partnership. Peugeot, the project manager, originally planned a V8/V6 declination which could be built on the same production lines (like Buick in the USA) but, because of space and financing concerns, it was reduced to V6, even if it did mean dealing with certain difficulties. The Peugeot 604 finally appeared after the Renault R30 (unveiled in the spring of 1975), but to ensure that the public knew it had designed this 'prestige' engine alone, Peugeot had taken the wind out of Renault's sails by releasing details during

1972, before Renault had thought about saying anything. The management decided that if it was going to build this engine for Elf, the specification of the Castaing-designed competition engine should be 6 cylinders, the same declination as the Peugeot unit, to create a perceived marketing opportunity from it. Secretly, Renault was not best pleased that Peugeot had gained capital from the partnership, and wanted to have the public believe that its competition 6-cylinder was by association the same engine as that for the partnership. The illusion was intentional and made completely feasible by suggesting to Castaing that he build a 90° V6.

Although the specification was determined to ensure a marketing success for Renault, in reality, the two engines had nothing in common. However, the choice of a 90° V6 gave Castaing a lower centre of gravity than a classic 60° V6, and allowed the fuelling system and other items to be placed in the middle of the V, making the unit compact.

Castaing's work was completed in record time due to the close cooperation of Moteur Moderne, which had previously worked with Alfa Romeo and Matra, the engine layout being nearly identical to that of half a V12 Matra. The green light was given in April 1972 and the engine was running on the dyno in the first few days of November.

Alain Marguet (*Les Années Turbo*, 1991) says: "It was designed and built extremely quickly. I remember the first day it ran: most of the factory staff were assembled in the corridor behind the dyno. It started with no problem, and the first apparent fault was very minor: a leak in the crankshaft oil seal at the level of the distribution pulleys a few minutes after it was started up. It was nothing. It seems laughable now, but it was one of my proudest moments, as I was the one working the dyno. The atmosphere at that time was incredible: François Castaing led the team, giving it huge dynamism. It was an intoxicating period."

Sadly, on 11 November, just before Claude Haardt was due to go to the USA, he and his son were killed in an accident in one of the Renault Marine powerboats during a trip on the Bay of Arcachon. In memory of Claude Haardt, the engine was officially christened the CH1 when it was revealed on 15 January 1973 at the Armenonville Pavilion in Paris.

Jean Terramorsi was appointed to take over from Haardt as chairman and managing director of Renault-Gordini. It is believed that around twenty of these successful engines were constructed between the first running in November 1972 and October 1974.

Although Pierre Dreyfus had not readily approved of Renault in competition, he believed in outside company partnerships where an advantage could be gained for Renault. Alpine had some difficulties at the time of the fuel crisis, and, in 1973, Renault had undertaken a preliminary acquisition of holdings in Alpine to look after its investment. The competition department was placed directly under the full responsibility of Jean Terramorsi and attached to the planning department of the Régie, by now headed by Bernard Hanon. Hanon held world ambitions for Renault and was convinced of the media impact of competition. He felt that rallying, whilst popular, only reached a restricted market, plus, it could be seen that the regulations were going the way of increasingly restrictive rules. Circuit racing, on the other hand, allowed the boundaries to be pushed. Hanon had the ear of Dreyfus who, though cautious, trusted him as he did Marc Ouin, who was already convinced. Terramorsi was in charge of competition and Hanon had the confidence and influence at the top of the organisation.

Jean Terramorsi had watched Dudot's efforts with the F3 engines and the turbo, and had noted Thérier's win with interest. Terramorsi wasn't a great technician, but was both open-minded and intuitive, and respected the views of Jacques Cheinisse. The two agreed that Dudot should go down to Viry, and it was from there that Terramorsi was to agree with Dudot on a mission to study turbos in the USA. Dudot went off to California to see what was being done there in the field of turbocharging engines. Whilst there he formed a very positive relationship with Garrett and became convinced that here lay the future.

Engine CH1.

"It is believed that around twenty of these successful engines were constructed between the first running in November 1972 and October 1974."

Back in Dieppe, André de Cortanze, André Renut, and Marcel Hubert had started to work on the new Alpine A440 sports car, to take the new Castaing-designed V6 2-litre engine. It was first shown in January 1973, then tested at Dijon before taking part in its first race on 1 May 1973 at Magny-Cours, with Jean-Pierre Jabouille at the wheel. Its first victory came just a few weeks later at Croix-en-Ternois.

While Dudot was in the USA at the end of 1973 a decision had been taken to try to fit a turbo to the V6 2-litre with a unit from Garrett. Unfortunately, the Yom Kippur War, and the petrol embargo which followed it, alarmed everyone; early in 1974, Dudot received a telegram in the USA informing him of the

end of the project. The team now had to review its position. However, Bernard Hanon felt convinced that, on paper, a turbocharged route for the future was justified, though still had to demonstrate this in practice. They had to acquire the know-how which could be applied in order to move on further.

By May 1974, the fuel situation had improved, the depression earlier in the year replaced by new-found optimism. Also, the normally aspirated 2-litre A440 and 441 cars were beginning to dominate the 2-litre European Sports Car Championship. Enthusiasm was high and thoughts of a possible victory at Le Mans – that magical dream – were coming to the fore. But more power was needed to win that outright, and this was the originally intended destiny of the Turbo.

At about the same time, an interesting development occurred at a meeting between François Guiter and the rule makers of Formula 2. Currently, F2 engines had to be based on production units used in a manufacturer's road cars. François Guiter: "Well, we were talking and I suggested quietly it would be good for the sport if the engine regulation were relaxed. My colleague at the meeting thought for a few moments, then, just

Testing at Paul Ricard, 19 March 1973.

Winter 1974: testing the A441T at Paul Ricard. (François-Xavier Delfosse Archive)

sports cars would also now be eligible for use in Formula 2 two years later.

From the start of 1974, Gérard Larrousse had formed his own team, Elf Switzerland, using the Alpine A440 and 441 2-litre, normally aspirated engine sports cars. Larrousse had taken over the Ecurie Archambaud team with the blessing of Jean Terramorsi, who saw it as a spur to help push the Alpine factory team. The result was eventually total dominance in the 1974 European championship – seven victories in seven races, the constructors' title for Alpine-Renault, and the drivers' title for Alain Serpaggi.

With the engine proven a winner, it was decided to try a turbo-boosted version. This was tested, and one car, now called the A441T, was to start the 1975 season entrusted to the Gérard Larrousse/Jean-Pierre Jabouille team, to contest the World Sports Car Championship. The car won on its first outing at the Mugello 6 Hours, then, unfortunately, failed to fulfil its early promise. The season was almost a complete failure, made worse when a near dream victory at Le Mans saw an outright win slip from the grasp of the factory team when the car ran out of fuel! However, even before that first turbocharged car had appeared in public, the engineers involved with the engines in Viry-Châtillon – Castaing, Dudot, Boudy – were secretly beginning to dream about F1: it would be good for Renault's image, wouldn't it? Jean Terramorsi was told what they were thinking and François Guiter became involved; they had started to look ahead. Guiter was convinced, though those around him thought he was mad to try. However, at that time, it was still a secret known only to a few insiders.

Formula 1 was then open to normally-aspirated, 3-litre or boosted 1.5-litre engines. The engine designers knew there was absolutely no technical correlation between these two formulae, but this could, they thought, give the team an opportunity, though the closely knit little group at Renault felt that Formula 1 was surely just a dream as long as Pierre Dreyfus was in command. To avoid the certain veto of the chairman and managing director, they knew the capacity of the engine could not really be increased, though Castaing had thought of a W-format 3-litre. Guiter spoke secretly to Ken Tyrrell, who pointed out that Renault was not Ferrari or Cosworth, so to try and build a 3-litre engine would be a waste of time. Why not try the turbo route, which, if it worked, would be put in a new car that his team was thinking about?

That decided it. Guiter met with Terramorsi, Castaing, and Dudot. The only chance to employ a Renault-approved engine lay with the possibility of using the regulations to build an engine with an exhaust-driven supercharger, otherwise known

as everyone was going out of the room for lunch, he looked at me and said, 'Yes, OK!' and as he was in charge of the governing body he was able to make this decision. So he did it and changed the rules. From 1976 the new regulations for F2 would be 2 litres, and engines would no longer have to be based on series production units." After lunch the the new rule was ratified; thus, the Elf-financed V6 used in the Renault-powered as a turbocharger, and hadn't Louis Renault patented an idea before World War 1? What a story this would be! Jean Terramorsi took the decision and secretly asked Alpine to design and build a single-seater destined to receive a V6 engine.

André Renut: "My role was as a chassis designer in the competition department. From 1964 to the end of 1978 I worked on the design and build of all the racing cars, apart from the engines and aerodynamic design of the bodywork. We had a request to build a new single-seater. Remember, we had no computers! We created a new chassis known as the A500."

Jacques Cheinisse: "Actually, de Cortanze didn't wait for orders before beginning a design!"

To gain the agreement of general management for a chassis it was also essential that this single-seater didn't look like a future Formula 1 car. It must not give the impression that Renault was involved in a Formula 1 car or that it was considering taking part in the Grand Prix World Championships. Formula 2 was going to be for V6 2-litre engines in 1976; this was the cover story. The plan to change the regulations had enabled an F2 V6 to become a reality.

Sadly, two years before this momentous decision, Jean Terramorsi had been diagnosed with serious heart problems which he chose to ignore, carrying on his expansive, larger-than-life existence as before. However, his health was affecting his concentration at work and, as his authority relaxed, some results were affected and rumours began to fly. A prominent member of the racing team says, "The 2-litre turbo sports car was an excellent car, but, unfortunately, the lack of discipline and organisation at the factory had become a handicap with the turbo version. Often the cars would fail through some small part. It was very difficult: parts of the organisation were each doing their own thing and nothing seemed to be coordinated."

François Castaing: "By the beginning of 1975 I was no longer personally concerned with the sports car engines but had become involved in other areas. Bernard Dudot was working on the turbo; Jean-Pierre Boudy was in the design office. They were working on the secret 1500 F1 unit. During the summer we had noticed tension between some of the people up in Alpine and Georges Sauvan. It looked as if something was going to happen. One day Sauvan got us all together and announced that he was going to reorganise the design programme, and I was moved up to be part of the overall technical management of Renault-Gordini." Terramorsi's health was failing him at the same time as changes were scheduled to take the team into a new era.

In early autumn 1975, Bernard Hanon approached Christian Martin to ask Gérard Larrousse to take charge of coordinating

and organising a separate department with the blessing of the Renault management, which had decided to set its sights on the biggest prize of all, the publicity that could be gained from victory in the Le Mans 24 Hours. Gérard Larrousse was coming to the end of a brilliant and eclectic career as a driver. He had made his name in rallying, luckily seizing the occasion of his transfer from Alpine, at the end of the 60s, to try his hand on the circuit. He had driven for Porsche and also teamed up with Henri Pescarolo in the conquest of two consecutive world titles for Matra in endurance, and had won two victories at Le Mans. Apart from his commitments as a factory driver, he had also undertaken personal projects which demonstrated his organisational talents. Bernard Hanon said, "Gérard Larrousse brought together all the qualities necessary in my view to assure his role. He had a deep knowledge of racing lived from the inside; he was a good manager, and he would fit in well with the structures we had at our disposal. He seemed to me to be well qualified to train, communicate, explain, define, organise. He was balanced and thoughtful."

Gérard Larrousse: "It was at Vallelunga on 12 October 1975 that they spoke to me and a contract for the new plan was agreed. I had to sign a contract that forbade me to race again!"

In January 1976, Larrousse took charge of the competition interests of Renault under the direction of Christian Martin, and created the name Renault Sport. At the same time, following changes at the very top and the retirement of Pierre Dreyfus, who had been replaced the year before by Bernard Vernier-Palliez, Bernard Hanon was promoted to the position of director on the management top rung. From that time on, Hanon wanted an open door policy between racing and general management.

It was clear that order and discipline had to be imposed. Larrousse agreed on a top priority: he had been given his target – the Le Mans 24 Hours – but he also regrouped all top level sport activity into Renault Sport, and had the new building built in Dieppe, no longer for Alpine alone but for Renault Sport: it was here that the sport prototype department would be based until the eventual victory at Le Mans in 1978, which was to mark the end of Renault and Alpine sports prototypes. The offices were later inhabited by BEREX, the new prototype design arm of Renault where many of the Alpine people were eventually to work on various concept projects. The arrival of Larrousse was met with a guarded response from the workforce. The task looked thankless and difficult. For Terramorsi and Cheinisse, and his faithful team at Alpine, it was quite a surprise.

Renault and its sporting ambitions was under new management ...

François Guiter: "At the time [1974] we were still under contract and had a sponsorship deal with Ken Tyrrell. After secret discussions with Tyrrell and consultations with Matra, Castaing and Dudot faced the fact that the atmospheric solution would lead them up a cul-de-sac. The Renault engine team could not imagine that they could do better than Ferrari or Cosworth. So it was very tempting to take an original step by pursuing the turbo route." An insane gamble? Porsche, master of the subject at the time, said it was doomed to failure; the handicap imposed in F1 (capacity reduced by half) seemed insurmountable.

Castaing: "It was a much more difficult challenge than in sports cars, where the rules allowed us to go up to 2.2 litres. I had the alternative of a W9 3-litre in my mind."

In the end, Renault had wanted a V6 for the sports cars, so there was only one course to take; it would try to create a small V6 from the big V6. Could this be done? Would it be within the rules of F1 at the time? The Grand Prix regulations had been set up some twelve years previously, so, to find the answer, we need to go back to 1963.

The Formula 1 rules in 1963 called for engines to be of 1.5 litres, and that regulation was set to stand until the end of 1965. In January 1963, at the meeting of the CSI (Commission Sportive Internationale), a new set of rules for 1966 onward was planned and discussed, supposedly designed to allow more reliability and better economics, and provide a new challenge to the designers. 3-litre engines were to be used, however, in 1963, no one knew the cost or who would build the engines; several companies had the capability, but would there be enough engines in production to supply a full grid of cars? The CSI, therefore, decided that to give time for the new formula to bed itself in, an interim solution would be proposed to allow 1.5-litre engines to be used alongside the 3-litre units.

Of course, a normally aspirated 1500cc against a 3000cc unit would be no contest, and would render the 1.5-litre useless unless it was a forced-induction, supercharged engine, a technology which had found success before World War 2, not only with the Mercedes and Auto Union teams, but also Bentley, and even on small, under-1-litre specials. It was, therefore, proven technology, which worked well, produced a

large boost in power, and involved a relatively simple process. Thus it was that, at its 1963 meeting, the CSI decided to apply an equivalency formula which would theoretically equate a supercharged 1.5-litre to the 3-litre engine.

As time passed, the mathematicians, physics specialists and major engine builders continued to argue that an equivalency formula such as that proposed was not realistic: the calculations and assumptions were wrong; it was useless. But the technical regulations set in 1963 were fixed, and so that was that. The interim equivalency formula was ignored but not removed from the statutes.

"... Renault had wanted a V6 for the sports cars, so there was only one course to take; it would try to create a small V6 from the big V6. Could this be done? Would it be within the rules of F1 at the time?"

History has shown that plenty of 3-litre engines became available in a short space of time. Honda, Maserati, Repco, Weslake, Ferrari, and Matra all built engines, but the king of them all was eventually to be the Keith Duckworth-designed Cosworth, a customer engine for the car manufacturers. As the years passed, all of the car manufacturers, Ferrari and Matra excepted, were to use Cosworths, even the Ken Tyrrell team Matras. By the start of the 1966 season, the equivalency formula and the forced induction engine had been pretty much forgotten.

It was in the early 1970s that several engineers began to think about extracting extra power from existing, normally-aspirated petrol engines. In the USA, forced induction engines – first supercharged then turbocharged – were being used on the oval tracks and for Indy Car Racing.

Back in 1963 the original rule makers of Formula 1 had only envisaged forced induction by supercharger, where the air is forced into the combustion chamber by a mechanical means driven by a belt or a crankshaft, etc., thus requiring some of its extra power provided to the engine to drive the system. With a turbocharger the forced induction of air is introduced by a turbine being driven by the flow of the exhaust gas exiting the combustion chamber; the turbine on its shaft in one housing drives a second turbine, a compressor, in an adjoining housing that is sucking air in and forcing it into the combustion chamber in the cylinder head, along with the required amount of fuel. It is a lighter weight installation and absorbs no mechanical power from the engine's moving parts to turn the turbine; it is also more efficient. Turbocharging was definitely a forced induction system, so although the rule makers in 1963 had been thinking about superchargers, it seems that they had forgotten about the existence of turbocharging. In fact, it had been used for some time in the aircraft industry to ensure the maintenance of the intake manifold pressure when flying a piston-engined aircraft at high altitude, the power output being related to the rate at which air can be introduced into the combustion chamber with the relevant combustible medium – inflammable fuel. And, of course, for many years turbocharging had been used to give more power to diesel engines.

Because barometric pressure falls as height is gained (it is 1 bar at sea level), one can see that at, say, the South African circuit of Kyalami, situated at around 1800m (5905ft) above sea level, or Mexico at around 2200m (7218ft), a normally aspirated engine designed to run at sea level will lose power. In a normal car one might not notice the slight drop-off, but in a racing engine designed for absolute peak performance the slightest variance in pressure can result in a loss of vital fractions of a second per lap.

Ken Tyrrell, boss of Tyrrell F1 and a very experienced Grand Prix team owner who had used several types of engine in his time, favoured the idea, and suggested to François Guiter that he would have one of these engines if the project went ahead. The team at Viry-Châtillon knew that Renault was not going to sanction the building of anything for racing on its own initiative, as we have read in preceding pages, but, if Elf wanted to pay for it again, the team thought perhaps it could do it, if it could find a reason to! Guiter made out the order. Terramorsi's engine team gave the design a budget of 500,000 francs. François Guiter did not have this sum in his budget but went and knocked on the door of his friend, Roger Clairet, the commercial financial specialist within Elf who had negotiated all of the contracts with Renault, including the sole supply of lubricants some years before, and who had also administered the recommendation budget on the previous V6 2-litre engine.

François Guiter: "He said to me, '500,000 francs – what for?' 'To build an F1 engine.' 'But the president of Renault has forbidden it!' … So we called the budget 'Testing of a performance engine'."

However, getting it built secretly in the Renault-Gordini works without telling the Régie directorate looked as if it would be a problem. But Guiter had an idea that they could order it as a research project. All was agreed and officially in the Viry-Châtillon records appeared an entry for the "design of a performance engine." The date: February 1975.

In fact, it was two engines: 1.5-litre turbocharged prototypes to be built in parallel: the 32T had a bore reduced to 80mm and was first run on the test bench dyno on 23 July; the 33T had the same bore as the 2-litre – 86mm – and was running a fortnight later on 8 August.

There was a lot of learning to do, but with perseverance the engine team continued to increase its knowledge and to understand how the turbocharger could be applied, in particular the dimensions of the turbine and compressor housings. In the beginning, the team used a single Garrett turbocharger, a standard production item mainly used on diesel engines for trucks; it knew that it was best to run lower compression ratios, and, with standard production pistons, improved the cooling and began to employ sodium-filled exhaust valves. A Kugelfischer metering system controlled the fuel injection; this had a pneumatically-controlled 3D cam to adjust flow according to boost pressure, as well as monitor and react to throttle action.

A miracle: the 32T straightaway registered 500bhp, the target the team was after, but this power level was not achieved again for some time. It was, however, a very encouraging sign.

"A miracle: the 32T straightaway registered 500bhp, the target the team was after, but this power level was not achieved again for some time. It was, however, a very encouraging sign."

These engines were discreetly baptised on the circuit on 21 November (33T) and 19 December (32T) 1975, hidden under the bonnet of an A442 prototype which had no distinguishing features except for the drivers summoned to do the testing – Jabouille, Larrousse, and Depailler. Unfortunately, we have no photos of this test but Gérard Larrousse tried the car and says, "It was quite a surprise after the sports car. Although I knew the chassis well enough, the engine was a violent, powerful monster when it was working properly. Unfortunately, you didn't know

Engine 32T.

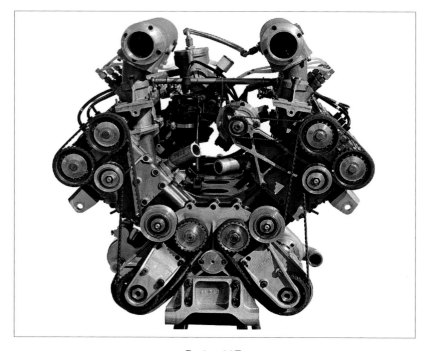

Engine 33T.

when it was going to work properly and it happened suddenly. The throttle/turbo lag was very tricky to master. I was full of admiration for any driver who was going to handle this thing."

Jean-Pierre Jabouille: "I was told we were going to test this new engine secretly in a prototype with different bodywork. I went down to Paul Ricard and saw it in a car for the first time. It was the A442, I think – a sports car with this 1500 in it. I remember that I did a lap or two and returned to the pit and explained to Dudot that it might be better to stop right away because it didn't work at all. You would come out of a corner onto the 200- or 300-metre straight before the Signes corner and ... there was nothing, it didn't work and I had an engine of 100bhp! Dudot suggested, 'We'll change the turbo and you can tell us what it's like.' So they changed the dimension of the turbo – at the time, the greater the diameter the higher the power but the longer the response time. He put a little turbo on – I don't know how much power I lost but it didn't matter much because the target wasn't power, the target was to be able to use it – and the response time was cut in half, so I said that if it produced that effect, certainly with some work it might be OK ... But it was a lot more difficult than we had foreseen."

Patrick Depailler, who also tested it, had just finished his second Formula 1 season with Ken Tyrrell, and it was logical for Elf to combine Renault and Tyrrell. In fact, a model of the 1500 turbo had been delivered to the English team to be fitted to its car, as well as one delivered to André de Cortanze up in Dieppe for what was being called the A500.

In these later months of 1975, there was still a long way to go: as the saying goes: "Many a slip between cup and lip." Plus, the prototype 2-litre turbo unit's failure in the Sports Car World Championships – apart from the Mugello victory – didn't auger well for greater ambitions and wider use.

There was, however, a belief within Elf and among the Renault Sport engineers that they had got something special. As the months went by, management in the Régie got to know about the 'design of a performance engine' and the Alpine chassis. The two had been brought together and tests were taking place. In July 1976, the Renault management decided internally to commit to both the existing target of Le Mans and now a Formula 1 programme. Renault had already brought together the sporting activities of its own department and that of Alpine and Gordini directed by Gérard Larrousse under the Renault Sport title. Studies were showing promising results and a report on the whole programme had been presented to Bernard Hanon at board level.

There was an interesting aside early in 1976; here is

what François Castaing says about it: "We had a call from management: apparently, François Guiter had presented a case which suggested that it might be better to have two teams running the turbo engine to allow comparisons, and, as they were sponsoring the Tyrrell at the time and Ken had visited us earlier, he wanted us to send a set of parts and an engine to Tyrrell. When Ken Tyrrell had presented his spectacular six-wheel, single-seater [four wheels being steered] with a symbolic yellow stripe on its blue paintwork, it was thought that it would eventually be powered by Renault." At the presentation it had a Cosworth in it. Castaing continues: "A little while later we went to the UK in the spring and saw a section of the back end of a car – I don't remember if it was the six-wheeler; it might have been." [François Guiter: "It was definitely the rear of the six-wheeler."] "The shock was what they had done with our engine: it had been turned through 180°, the turbo moved, and there was a shaft going to a compact gearbox. We were, of course, all very polite, but it was clear to us that this was not a serious proposition and had probably been done to keep the sponsor happy." (François Guiter: "He could be right!") "Well, as it turned out, Ken decided against using our engines. In spite of a contract signed by the two sides, the association never saw the light of day in the form in which it was originally envisaged." Some five years later, in the early 1980s, Ken Tyrrell turned out to be one of the fiercest to argue for the rules to ban turbos – then, later in the 1980s, he started to use them!

By early spring 1976, the chassis had arrived in Viry, and the revised engine first ran on a track in the single-seater A500 Alpine on 23 March at Michelin's Ladoux test facility, near Clermont-Ferrand. The story of the car and the tests follows shortly.

On 12/13 June 1976, the first Alpine A442, 2-litre turbocharged car, a single entry, ran at Le Mans. It took pole position in qualifying and fastest lap in the race, but, after this early promise, failed to finish. Undaunted, Dudot and the team were now sure that the turbo engine was the way to go. This time Renault management was listening and decided to take the huge but calculated risk. In December, Bernard Hanon announced to an eager international press that Renault was going to enter into a feasibility study for a new Grand Prix team, whilst also continuing to put maximum effort into winning the Le Mans 24 Hours.

Alas, Jean Terramorsi, the great enthusiast for the project and instigator of the development of the turbo, had passed away in August 1976, but his vision of the turbo and his enthusiastic commitment were beginning to bear fruit, to be proven in the years to come. Likewise, his dream of seeing the turbocharger developed for use in normal road cars was to come to fruition

The engine comes to Dieppe.

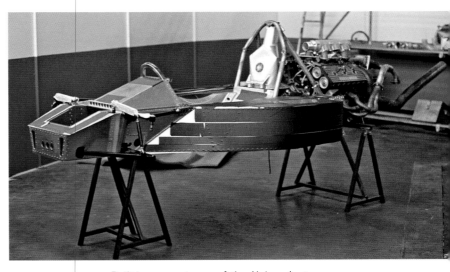

Built in a secret area of the Alpine plant.

with the introduction of the rear-engined Renault 5 Turbo a few years later.

Elf had seen that Renault had the capability to build a new racing engine; having put up the initial money, the engines worked and, though faster progress had been hoped for, it wasn't to be. However, François Guiter was convinced; it took a long time, but his faith in the idea was vindicated when eventually the turbo became a realistic proposition.

THE BIRTH OF THE ENGINE, FROM THE KITCHEN AT ALPINE TO FORMULA 1

Bernard Dudot testing at Nogaro, 1981.

Jean-Luc Thérier, Critérium des Cévennes, 1972. (Courtesy Michel Morelli)

François-Xavier Delfosse: "The first 1500cc engine was secretly installed in a sport prototype, with Jean-Pierre Jabouille taking the wheel at the Paul Ricard circuit. And at the end of one lap, he stopped to tell us in desperation, 'We'll never make it!'"

Jean-Pierre Jabouille: "It was awful! Can you imagine, there was so much turbo lag it was impossible to drive!" We have already read Gérard Larrousse's comments. Desperate times, maybe, but nothing is ever easy when new technology is being developed.

Bernard Dudot: "When I joined Alpine in 1968 after chasing Mr Rédélé for many months, he said he wanted me to develop an engine department. They were working with Mignotet, Gordini and Moteur Moderne, but Jean Rédélé wanted his own development department. It seemed that relations between Rédélé and Gordini were not too good. Anyway, after a while spent getting the engine side of things more coordinated I was allowed to set up my first test bench (the first dynamometer in Alpine Dieppe – I think it was 1970) in the kitchen, because I needed a good supply of water! And it was there in that kitchen that, after working on several other engines, I had the idea – or maybe it was Terramorsi or Jacques Cheinisse, I don't remember clearly – but anyway I started to look into the idea of using a turbocharger, and contacted the British company, Holset. I remember they were very helpful and I fitted and tested a turbocharger for the first time on the 1600cc unit! Yes, we started it all in the kitchen amongst the cups and pans – that was the first Renault turbocharged engine!"

That engine in that car won on its first outing. The turbo lag was terrible, but Jean-Luc Thérier was so good that he was able to overcome this failing, and used the enormous power in the 200bhp Alpine A110 to the full. The engine was also put in a single-seater for Formula Libre.

Moving ahead three years, Bernard Dudot explains: "From the beginning in the kitchen we had come a long way, and, as we have seen, following our enthusiasm and hopes of entering Formula 1, François Guiter and the general management had decided early in 1975 that we could build a prototype Formula 1 engine based on the 2-litre turbo, though it was not a straightforward matter at the time for the management of a company like Renault to evaluate our chances of success, and, more still, the consequences of failure.

"Everything began at Viry-Châtillon on tiptoes and in the greatest secrecy. It was Jean-Pierre Boudy who took on the project. Almost the whole of the Renault Gordini factory was occupied with the 2-litre turbo programme, with victory at Le Mans as its main objective. As a result, Jean-Pierre's team was cut to the limit: two mechanics and a designer under the direction of Giuseppe Albarea, the head of our design office, took on this Formula 1 project. Two secret prototype engines based on the 2-litre turbo V6 were built. The new capacity of 1500cc had been obtained by reducing the stroke from 57.4mm to 42.8mm while maintaining the 86mm bore of the 2-litre, and, on the other engine, by reducing the stroke to 49.4mm and the bore to 80mm. The first solution, considered at the time to be extreme because of its bore/stroke ratio of 2, allowed us to reuse the 2-litre cylinder heads without modification. We had set our sights, to begin with, on attaining the crucial 500bhp claimed by the competitors' atmospheric engines at the time, like the Cosworth.

> ## "Almost the whole of the Renault Gordini factory was occupied with the 2-litre turbo programme, with victory at Le Mans as its main objective. As a result, Jean-Pierre's team was cut to the limit: two mechanics and a designer under the direction of Giuseppe Albarea, the head of our design office, took on this Formula 1 project."

We estimated that this level would be the minimum requirement, as we had to compensate for the response time associated with turbo engines.

"Knowing that our 2-litre atmospheric unit had developed 300bhp, a rapid calculation decided the necessary overboost pressure at around 2.5 bar absolute. On that basis, we could determine the volumetric ratio, and the dimensions of the turbocompressor and heat exchanger to reduce the induction temperature at the entry to the engine."

Volumetric ratio? Dudot: "To achieve the best possible combustion efficiency the engine technician had to choose a high volumetric ratio. All other things being equal, the volumetric ratio determines the maximal pressure obtained in the chamber during combustion. At that time, we didn't know enough about

the combustion process because we lacked the means to define it, and in particular all the parameters linked to it, to determine straightaway the optimum volumetric ratio for any given fuel. Notably, the shape of the combustion chamber, the nature of the thermal exchanges between gas and surface, the sweep of the chamber by the fresh gases, are vitally important elements in the choice of volumetric ratio. As you have to begin somewhere, more often than not you based it on an analogy with known engines. If you did not have these references at your disposal, calculation provided a theoretical approach, but it does not take into account the particular characteristics of the engine.

"So: if VA is the volume swept during compression by the piston between the bottom dead centre and the closing of the induction valve;

if V is the unit capacity

$$X = \frac{VA}{V}$$

$\dfrac{P_2}{P_0}$ = the overboost ratio of the engine

$\gamma = \dfrac{C_p}{C_v}$ the polytropic coefficient of the fresh gases

εa = the volumetric ratio of the engine in its atmospheric version

$\varepsilon_{T'}$ the volumetric ratio of the same engine when overboosted, will be

$$\varepsilon_T = \frac{X-1}{X} + \frac{X(\varepsilon a - 1) + 1}{X \left(\frac{P_2}{P_0}\right)^{\frac{1}{\gamma}}}$$

However, the values thus obtained are generally lower than it is possible to reach, and only methodical experimentation will allow optimum values to be achieved.

"Then we come to the turbocompressor – the means by which the engine is overboosted. As we have seen, the idea had been thought of before – and even by Louis Renault – but it was the French engineer, Rateaux, who was the first to actually

use it in 1917. Since that time, the use of engines overboosted by turbocompressors has been widespread, but mainly in aeronautics where they were used to re-establish at altitude the induction conditions of piston engines at ground level. A turbocompressor is a kind of mechanical device composed as follows:
- a hot section receiving the exhaust gases: the turbine (rotor wheel and housing)
- a cold section which compresses the air destined for the induction: the compressor (rotor wheel and housing)
- a shaft which links the turbine and compressor rotor
- a central housing supporting the shaft and the rotors and linking the turbine and compressor rotor

"The shaft supporting the wheels (rotors) is mounted in the housing on floating bearings which turn at about half the speed of the shaft, and the whole assembly is lubricated under pressure by a diversion of the engine's lubrication circuit. The lubrication also eliminates part of the heat flux produced by the turbine.

"An internal combustion engine delivers exhaust gases at a high temperature and, at a sufficiently high speed, traps part of them while they are in the gas turbine. It is this energy which is recuperated in the turbine and causes the compressor wheel to speed up. Air is taken at the inlet of the compressor at atmospheric pressure and put under pressure in the compressor chamber by centrifugation. The moving assembly of shaft and wheel can reach 180,000rpm in the case of small turbocompressors such as those used in Formula 1 V6 engines.

"The available power in a turbine is expressed by the following formula:

$$W_T = \eta_T \; Q_T \; C_p \; T_3 \left(1 - \frac{1}{\pi_T^{\frac{\gamma - 1}{\gamma}}} \right)$$

where η_T is the efficiency of the turbine at the speed and pressure under consideration
Q_T is the throughput of exhaust gases
C_p is the specific heat of the exhaust gases
T_3 is the temperature of the exhaust gases
"There is also a certain ambiguity in the value of γ of the exhaust gases because their measurement needs to be very precise.

"It is worth noting in passing that the turbine power is a direct function of the following:
- the efficiency of the turbine ηT depends on the correct adjustment of the turbine to the output characteristics of the engine (this is the engine technician's job), and also the quality of the design of the turbine wheel/housing assembly (which is the responsibility of the turbine technician)
- the mass throughput of exhaust gases Q_T linked to the engine capacity and at the level of the pressure of the gases
- the exhaust temperature T_3, which should be as high as possible, is limited only by the characteristics of the turbine rotor. This temperature aspect is particularly crucial under re-acceleration, affecting the length of the response time

"The expansion rate π_T in the turbine should be as high as possible.

"The engine technician has responsibility for the design of the exhausts and especially the turbine discharge.

"Once the calculations have been done, taking into account the temperature levels attained in Formula 1 engine exhausts and their gas throughputs, one can achieve available power in the turbine of around 80kW at high revs, or nearly 110bhp. This is considerable, and generally far higher than the needs of the compressor. This is why at the turbine inlet one uses only part of this power – the amount strictly necessary for the compressor to reach the required inlet pressure level. The excess energy is evacuated direct to the atmosphere prior to the turbine inlet

> **"Once the calculations have been done, taking into account the temperature levels attained in Formula 1 engine exhausts and their gas throughputs, one can achieve available power in the turbine of around 80kW at high revs, or nearly 110bhp."**

through a by-pass usually known by turbine designers as a 'waste-gate,' referring to the wastage of available power in the exhaust and its direct return to the atmosphere. Initially, the waste-gate was used in the simplest possible way, and just as it was delivered to us by the turbo-compressor manufacturer. A spring held a supporting valve in its seat and, when the induction pressure was reached, the pneumatic effort exerted on a membrane counterbalanced that of the spring, the valve opened and the excess exhaust gases escaped into the atmosphere.

"Little by little, these parts associated with the turbocompressor became more sophisticated in order to reduce their weight, and especially to control them both in accordance with the driver's needs and as a function of the feed pressure characteristics, which were predetermined and loaded in the memory of a simple onboard computer. This sophistication could only be attained thanks to simultaneous progress being made in electronics, which eventually, by 1985, allowed us to adjust the overboost pressure graphs as a function of the engine speed and circuit by circuit, by integrating the special characteristics of each one – a luxury we did not have in the beginning in 1975-6."

The continuous growth in power of Formula 1 engines, both in racing and especially in qualification, resulted in a diminishing of the by-pass waste-gate's role as the seasons and races progressed. By the beginning of the 1985 season, at Renault Sport waste-gates were purely and simply taken off for qualification. Dudot: "We therefore had at our disposal at the compressor the total power available to the turbine at all levels. On the 1986 engines we easily exceeded an overboosting rate of 5 bar without any particular negative effect on the engines. Over 1200bhp could be seen in qualifying."

"The continuous growth in power of Formula 1 engines, both in racing and especially in qualification, resulted in a diminishing of the by-pass waste-gate's role as the seasons and races progressed."

Dudot continues: "Jean-Pierre Boudy, using as his model the work being done on the Le Mans engine, had chosen a single turbocompressor. We were very familiar with this type of installation and Garrett had the materials we needed in its range.

"450bhp was achieved fairly easily during the summer of 1975 with a short run giving 500bhp at 9000rpm. Meantime, the problems that faced us were shown to be:
- an insufficient usable rev range, as the engine overboost began at too high a speed
- poor behaviour of our pistons; pinking causing failure all the time

In summary, these problems are quite normal for this type of engine, but they are tricky to resolve and would not at that time be remedied in the short term.

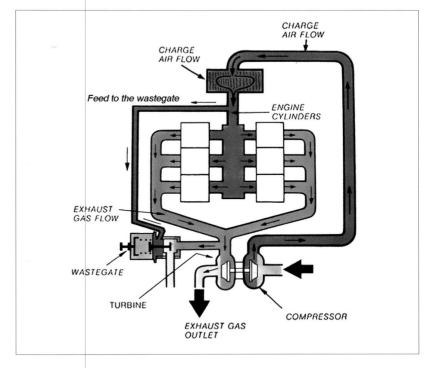

Gas flow.

"To improve the running range of the engine, Jean-Pierre Boudy suggested a composite turbo with a large compressor in relation to the turbine. Within the Garrett range, his choice was a T04 turbine and a T05 or TV61 compressor, two assemblies that were not directly compatible. We therefore had to design special linking parts and in particular a central housing, a welded steel fabrication. The problem was that things took a turn for the worse in terms of reliability. Breakages of turbo shafts, bearings and turbine rotors were frequent occurrences."

Jean-Pierre Boudy: "Garrett had warned us about the difficulties we would face but, at this time, we had very little contact with the design offices in Los Angeles. Though they were nice people, these manufacturers kept their secrets very close to their chests. Garrett was a big company and not interested in being involved in building a specific 'Formula 1' turbo. Little by little we overcame the problems, but at the price of costly technological studies and manufacturing delays."

Bernard Dudot: "Another problem, relating to the behaviour of the pistons, was much more complex. While we maintained the power around 500bhp, all went well; beyond that, problems arose as bhp increased. During 1976 it took all our faith, and that

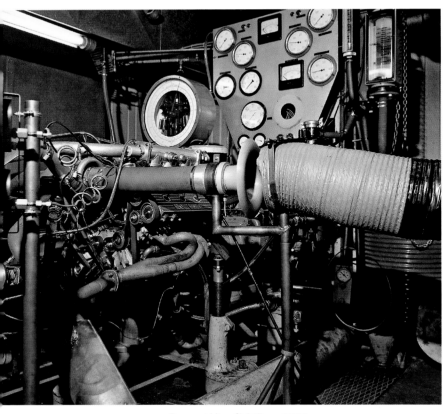

Dyno at Viry-Châtillon, 1975.

valves with stems measuring 100mm in length and 7mm in diameter."

Bernard Dudot: "In the end everything was done, but not quickly, and while our role as pioneers in the field was fantastic in the sense of technical progress, it had to be paid for by many long nights and the wiping of tiredness from everyone's eyes. With the benefit of hindsight, we would later understand all our earlier difficulties."

Dudot continues: "At the time, though, it was not a simple

"Another problem, relating to the behaviour of the pistons, was much more complex. While we maintained the power around 500bhp, all went well; beyond that, problems arose as bhp increased."

feat to convince the management, even if they were enthusiastic, that our setbacks were an essential part of the process, and I well remember to what extent François Castaing and Gérard Larrousse needed persuasion and faith in our future to get it accepted.

"An anecdote, to illustrate the technical context in which we were working. I remember the reply of one bearing manufacturer, who shall remain nameless, but we can say they were English and located just off the M4 motorway west of London, whom we consulted for bearings for our Formula 1 engine. The correspondence I sent them included the specification of the engine. A few weeks later I received a letter written with great English courtesy, explaining that they did not wish to participate in our project, which they considered unrealistic, and saying that they didn't believe a 1500cc engine could ever achieve 500bhp; what's more even if it could, we [Renault] would not be the people to do it! Luckily, a German sub-contractor had a little more confidence and supplied us for the complete project."

But let's go back to the theory again to explain what happened next.

Bernard Dudot: "It is interesting to look at the process which rules the engine-turbocompressor assembly and to see how it can work without harming the breathing of the engine.

"In the case of an engine with controlled ignition, we accept that 35 per cent of the energy released by combustion is evacuated in the exhaust gases. Only a part is recoverable:
–   half of this energy goes out into the environment
–   a quarter is lost, because the gases cannot be evacuated at the ambient temperature and pressure

of Jean-Pierre Boudy, to explain to the little group of technicians working on the project that it was normal to set up three engines on the test bench in order to produce one in good condition, which itself would break after only a few runs on the dyno."

Why were there so many problems? "It was partly due to the level of knowledge of our sub-contractors, which was rather limited at the time, relating to thermal and mechanical loads on such small parts. For example, Mahle, our piston supplier, had good experience with large pistons for high-load diesel engines, but with bores larger than 200mm. Cooling of pistons by oil circulation was considered but it was impossible on bores of 80 or 86mm. We had to do it though, and we did it together. We repeated the same cooperation with our various other suppliers."

Jean-Pierre Boudy: "Our piston technicians learned to make pistons with a bore of 80mm and an oil circulation gallery; our piston ring suppliers learned to add ceramic [yes, already in 1976] to piston rings of 1.5mm thickness; and our valve manufacturer gradually mastered the construction of hollow

– the excess energy represents 8 to 10 per cent of the energy of the fuel and is sufficient to compress the inlet air from 1 to 5 per cent of this energy

It is this part that is recovered in the turbine.

"So, how do we adapt the compressor to match the engine? Once the desired level of performance is known, the engine technician can calculate the overboost pressure level required and estimate the air throughput consumed by the engine. It should be noted, however, that, with the same overboost pressure, there can be considerable differences between F1 engines of similar power, which derive from the ratio of the fuel air fill and swept volume of the combustion chamber. Some of the fresh fuel/air mix that travels through the combustion chamber at the beginning of the induction phase goes directly to the exhaust while the exhaust valves are still open. In fact, part of the fresh mix, under the effect of the inertia and the difference in pressure which exists between the induction and the exhaust, goes directly to the turbine inlet. This portion of fresh mix plays a considerable role in the cooling of the exhaust valves and top of the piston, but with negative effects on fuel consumption. This effect can be expressed as the 'sweeping efficiency:'

$$Rb = \frac{Mm}{M}$$

Mm being the mass of gas retained by the engine and M the mass of air going through the compressor.

"The sweeping efficiency is generally between 90 and 98%. When these data are evaluated, the turbine technician will suggest the compressor whose overall characteristics are expressed by its range. The range of a compressor brings together in one place:

– the rotor speeds and their lower limit as well as their upper limit
– the efficiencies as a function of the throughputs and pressure ratios

For the engine technician the trick lies in placing the representative points of the engine's air requirements in the best possible efficiency zone whilst remaining short of the maximal speed of the compressor. To achieve this, the turbine technician makes use of the 'mechanical' construction of the turbocompressor, for which he needs to choose, within its range, the dimensions of the compressor housing and wheel.

"The first variable is what is known as the A/R of the compressor housing:

A being the area of the section of the volute (scroll) at the inlet mouth

R being the radius of the centre of the section

"In general, an increase in the A/R favours high throughput points and medium compression ratios within an unchanged throughput range.

"The second variable is the rotor trim:

$$Trim = \left(\frac{d}{D}\right)^2 100$$

"The increase in the trim $(d/D)^2 100$ displaces the usage zone globally towards the largest throughputs and the highest compression ratios. Generally, the choice of elements which make up the compressor is done on the dyno.

"The turbine is adjusted differently. The necessary 'turbine ranges,' documents which bring together as graphs all of the thermodynamic characteristics, are much more confidential than those for the compressor. We had to lobby both Garrett and KKK for a long time before they would send us these documents. It was only when an atmosphere of trust was established and the adjustment of the turbine was almost complete that we were sent them.

"The 'turbine ranges' supply two important items of information: the value of the exhaust gas throughput as a function of the expansion ratio, and the turbine efficiency at the same speed as a function of the expansion rates. The first of these allows one to choose the dimensions of the turbine, and especially the A/R. The second piece of information should confirm that the chosen turbine adjustment (A/R and rotor trim) will supply the correct efficiencies. During the first tests

"The 'turbine ranges' supply two important items of information: the value of the exhaust gas throughput as a function of the expansion ratio, and the turbine efficiency at the same speed as a function of the expansion rates."

on the dyno, one chose a fairly large turbine A/R. Sweeping is a function of the camshaft profile and is also in direct relation to the value of the exhaust pressure, the cylinder emptying more efficiently as the exhaust pressure at the turbine inlet is lower. The smaller the A/R chosen, the higher the pressure at

The all-new A500 chassis.

the turbine inlet for the same induction pressure. In general, after a first test on the dyno, all the rest is done on the car. The work revolves around the choice of A/R in order to widen the usable range of an engine, particularly at lower speeds. Finally, it is worth choosing the smallest possible A/R compatible with the determined level of power and the sweeping value below which you don't want to fall. This sweeping value is quantified approximately by the difference between the induction pressure (P2) and the exhaust pressure (P3). It can happen that where the

adjustment is extreme and at high speed, the difference between P2 and P3 becomes negative. In this case, it is worth checking the behaviour of the exhaust valves and pistons as this situation generally produces pinking due to an increase in temperature.

"The first test of our new engine in a car was a great moment. It took place at the Paul Ricard circuit at Le Castellet in November 1975. In the greatest secrecy, we had fitted one of our Alpine A442 sports prototypes with the first 1500cc turbo destined for the test circuit. Another A442, fitted with the 2-litre turbo engine, acted as a control. Jean-Pierre Jabouille moved from one to the other to compare engine behaviour. On this first occasion it was a matter of clearing the ground to make way for more significant tests.

"Obviously, our target was to do as well with the 1500 as with the 2-litre. The most obvious fault, as was to be expected, was the response time, which was considerably higher than with the 2-litre turbo. The richness settings fixed on the test bench didn't seem to suit the needs of the engine in the car. Jean-Pierre Jabouille, who had wide experience in evaluating the behaviour of engines in general, proved a valuable asset in the tuning process. At first the turbo lag was a disaster. Jean-Pierre was not happy, but as we improved we managed to get this first engine to run for 600km (372.8 miles) of tests. It was our first result, and we were sure that if we had the reliability the tuning would progress. After this first contact with our future engine, Jean-Pierre Jabouille was guarded in his enthusiasm. However, although only a few people from the factory were directly concerned in this first trial run, enthusiasm within the Viry-Châtillon team was high."

Dudot continues: "The second test, still in an A442 prototype, took place a few weeks later in mid-December, this time with a new fuel injection cam and a Garrett T04/T05 composite turbocompressor whose turbine and compressor did not belong to the same family in the constructor's range. This time, Jean-Pierre Jabouille lapped within the times of the 2-litre turbo, despite a response [turbo lag] time which was still lower but, it seems, compensated by higher power. Jean Terramorsi had wanted to define the car's field of use by experimentation in the A442 sports car without prying eyes seeing the engine or people raising questions, either inside or outside the team. His way of working was to allow the tests to develop, which had the advantage of revealing a number of problems that cropped up relating to the likely mounting of a turbo engine in a single-seater. Serious efforts had been made to make the turbocharger unit more compact, to ensure the ventilation of the hot spots, and to supply the cold air to the compressed air circuit heat exchanger. This car also was to allow us to make an appraisal of the transmission and to polish the rough edges off a number of chassis questions.

"At the speed at which we were progressing, and to Jean-Pierre Boudy's great joy, it was becoming urgent to move to the

final stage. The A500 laboratory car project was taking shape up at Alpine in Dieppe under the direction of the chassis engineer, André de Cortanze. It was a single-seater directly inspired by the Formula 2s of the time. However, it was an all-new chassis designed to carry the Formula 1 engine."

RENAULT-GORDINI-ELF F1 ENGINES – BENCH DYNO TESTS

	32T	**33T**	**41T**	**53T**
Date of first test	23.07.1975 Size 80 x 49.4	08.08.1975 1st boost test. Size 86 x 42.8. 950g pressure: 360bhp at 11,100rpm	26.2.1976 Size 80 x 49.4, 1500g pressure: 502bhp at 10,500rpm. Torque: 37mkg at 9000rpm	27.9.1976 Size 86 x 42.8
2nd session	22.8.1975 1200g pressure	11.8.1975 Camshaft setting tests	7.7.1976 Turbo modification (response time). New inlet collector (inertia of new turbo reduced by 20 per cent)	3.1.1977 507bhp at 10,500rpm. 40mkg at 8200rpm
3rd session	4.9.1975 1500g pressure: 478bhp at 10,500rpm	1.9.1975 1250g pressure: 422bhp at 10,500rpm	6.9.1976 Testing of turbo collectors & camshafts	–
4th session	3.10.1975 1500g pressure: 502bhp at 10,800rpm	23.9.1975 1500g pressure: 491bhp at 10,800rpm	5.1.1977 Bench dyno tests pre-delivery to Renault Sport (test emergency engine) for Ricard January 1977. Power well above 500bhp	–
5th session	10.11.1975 Delivery to Alpine-Renault (488bhp at 10,500rpm)	30.10.1975 Delivery to Alpine-Renault	–	–

	32T	**33T**	**41T**	**53T**
6th session	9.12.1975 Last bench dyno test before delivery to Alpine	3.3.1976 Tests on new guillotine cylinder heads	–	–
7th session	28.4.1976 General bench dyno tests (520bhp at 11,000rpm)	8.3.1976 Bench dyno test pre-delivery to Alpine (with old cylinder head)	–	–
8th session	1.11.1976 Bench dyno test pre-delivery to Renault Sport and with low boost	5.5.1976 Delivery to Alpine (513bhp)	–	–
9th session	24.11.1976 Tests on richness cams	27.10.1976 Turbo tests	–	–
10th session	–	9-11.3.1977 Testing of new camshafts and new central collectors	–	–

THE ALPINE A500, NICKNAMED THE 'PHANTOM,' BECOMES REALITY

André de Cortanze, with André Renut and Marcel Hubert, had set to work on the creation of a car in 1975 that was to be the Alpine A500, a steel tube and semi-monocoque single-seater. Although shrouded in secrecy, inevitably news of the project leaked out and things nearly went seriously wrong, both politically within Renault and for the project itself. Work began behind screens in what was thought to be a secure area in the Alpine plant in Dieppe, but a visiting journalist got a picture taken over the top of the screens, and, before long, people were asking questions and news was filtering out about a new car. As it was difficult to deny the activity, the team let people believe that it was working on a new Formula 2 Alpine: after all, it was known, as previously stated, that the 2-litre engine would be eligible for this discipline in 1976. Alpine could, then, quite logically be involved. However, the nosy journalist was surprised by the dimensions of this car, though de Cortanze's reply to leading questions on this matter was that the tank was much too small to cover a Grand Prix distance. In fact, it was just about the only thing he had done to make his car ineligible for Formula 1!

As is the way with secrets, the cat was very nearly let out of the bag when *L'Equipe* (the French daily sports newspaper) revealed what it called an Alpine Formula 1 scoop. "It was a terrible shock," de Cortanze says [*Les Années Turbo, 1991*] "If I hadn't been able to defend myself, if I hadn't been able to prove that the single-seater photographed in Dieppe was not an F1 but an F2 car, I would have been fired on the spot and Jean Terramorsi, who had taken great risks, would have found himself in a very difficult position." It was a close-run thing, Terramorsi had to quickly bring Bernard Hanon in on the idea.

Jean-Pierre Jabouille takes up the story: "The car with that big nose? I don't remember, perhaps I did a couple of laps in it, but the one with the wing in the nose cone and the one with the wing on top were the most interesting. The important thing in aerodynamics is to avoid aerodynamic movement, and when

Top right: The early chassis.

Right: The first design, thought never to have been tested on a track. It *was*, however, tested in the wind tunnel. (© Dominique Pascal)

First wind tunnel tests. (© Dominique Pascal)

With curved nose. (© Dominique Pascal)

there is a mass like that one with the flat, full-width nose near to the ground you create movements of the trim, and when you brake the rear lifts and – oops! So that one didn't work. But in the wind tunnel, in a straight line, it's fine, it's interesting, but no good to use. Afterwards a decision was taken to start with the one with the wing on top."

Various body design changes were to take place after testing in the wind tunnel before the car was tried at the Ladoux test track. These photos show some of the tests that were carried out in the wind tunnel on different nose cones and front wings in late spring 1976.

The car in this format was tested on the track at Paul Ricard but discarded in favour of the one-piece front wing seen here.

The car, with its high, nose-located front wing, then went on to Dijon, Jarama, and Paul Ricard; eventually, after a repaint it went to Nogaro for more track testing.

The first outings of the secret (or by now, not-so-secret) A500 car in early 1976 sadly, were disappointing for the engine technicians. The car would not perform properly, some of the problems being associated with the mechanical grip of the tyres. The first test took place on the Michelin circuit, which was used because it was possible to run there 'behind closed doors' and because, at that time, Michelin already had fairly sophisticated measuring equipment which it could use.

> ### "Various body design changes were to take place after testing in the wind tunnel before the car was tried at the Ladoux test track. These photos show some of the tests that were carried out in the wind tunnel on different nose cones and front wings in late spring 1976."

Because of the grip problem different tyre set-ups were tried. François-Xavier Delfosse explains: "We were having great difficulty getting the car to work properly on the Michelin tyres. Pierre Dupasquier had done a good job getting us the type of tyres we thought we needed, but somehow the grip wasn't there, so, much to the horror of the Michelin people, we fitted some ready-prepared Goodyears to continue the test. Happily, Michelin responded shortly after with a better tyre and we went off to Dijon for more tests."

Jean-Pierre Jabouille: "It was very difficult for me, although people didn't realise it at the time, because we had a new chassis, new engine, new tyres, and each time I stopped the engine after about five laps something was broken. And each time there were the Michelin people climbing all over the car, the engine technicians at the same time and the chassis man – it was tricky to concentrate on what I needed to do: to test the car. So it took a long time to make the necessary progress. Thankfully, gradually we did. I was passionate about the technical stuff so it was really very interesting for me."

"This first trial run, and the following one carried out at Dijon on a short circuit, were dogged by mysterious fuel supply problems in the engine. Nevertheless, Jean-Pierre Jabouille eventually managed to achieve 1min 03.3sec ..."

This first trial run, and the following one carried out at Dijon on a short circuit, were dogged by mysterious fuel supply problems in the engine. Nevertheless, Jean-Pierre Jabouille eventually managed to achieve 1min 03.3sec, which, at the time, was considered excellent.

Jean-Pierre again: "Michelin had a problem, too. They wanted to win in F1 but they wanted to use radial tyres, whereas at the time there were Goodyear and Firestone who had conventional tyres. The conventional tyres were of a totally different construction: the tread of a Michelin was very rigid, which meant that they didn't distort much in running, while the Goodyears and Firestones did. The conventional tyre was much easier to drive; it began to slide at the rear under power but progressively. With the radial tyres they held on and held on and suddenly they went and there was no control. I tried to explain to everyone, but it was difficult for them to understand until they could see that, in the little corners, the drift was much easier and more constant with a conventional tyre but with the radial there was no drift, just grip and then – bang. It took time to learn the way they worked and we also worked on the steering and suspension to help improve the tyres. Eventually, it was as easy to drive as a conventional tyre – not only Goodyear, but conventional tyres in general."

François-Xavier Delfosse again: "Our first really significant test with this car took place in Jarama on 11-14 May 1976, on a circuit on which comparative lap times were available as it was the traditional location of the Spanish Grand Prix. It was during these first tests that we were able to measure how far we had to

With high front wing – the one eventually chosen. (© Dominique Pascal)

Rear view. (© Dominique Pascal)

Note the tyres. This was at Ladoux, Michelin's private test track!
(Archives AAA Dieppe)

At Jarama.

go to be really on the ball. The Jarama circuit has a slow section in which there are two right-angle turns, first a left and then a right, separated only by a 30m (32.8yd) straight, before a rapid section uphill. It was in this sequence that we were able to assess the problems."

Delfosse continues: "In fact, the engine in its atmospheric phase developed 130bhp compared with some 520bhp when the turbo pressure was established. We could see how difficult it was to drive: imagine an engine which went from 130 to 520bhp almost instantly but within a very variable period. However, three days of tests allowed Jean-Pierre Boudy, the engineer in charge of the development of this engine, to make considerable progress on the fuel injection settings, especially when the turbo pressure began to increase. The settings finally chosen proved to be some way from those set on the test bench, and we learned essential lessons for the future."

Bernard Dudot: "Once this work was done, we found we were still behind the expected performance, and we decided to make a comparison with some tests between the F1 engine and a 2-litre turbo derived from the A442 by putting the A442 engine into the A500 chassis.

"This allowed us to evaluate with a proven unit some of the difficulties that were facing us. I remember Jean-Pierre Boudy brooding in despair in the shadow of the pits and Jean-Pierre Jabouille fuming with rage in the face of our inability to solve the problems. This session put the engine technicians' nerves, as well as Jean-Pierre Jabouille's, to the severest test, but it gave us the chance to assess what we still had to learn and the things we had to do to be competitive, even if the fine enthusiasm of our too-easy earlier days was taking a knock."

Jean-Pierre Jabouille: "It was decided as part of the philosophy of Castaing, Boudy and Dudot development programme to take this car to the tracks on Mondays and Tuesdays after the Grand Prix. In Madrid [Jarama] there is a straight and then you turn and there is a very tight bit. I learned something that was very useful for what followed. We started testing and it didn't work too well because there was a whole range where the turbo didn't come in quickly enough, or it came in just at the moment when I had to brake and I, who had driven the whole time, said, 'It's not the power that bothers me, it's the use of the engine. Please do me a favour, so that you can understand: bring me down a 2-litre turbo prototype engine (which had the same power at that time).' I wanted to show them that it wasn't a question of power, but of flexibility in use. Jean-Pierre Boudy telephoned Viry-Châtillon and they sent an engine down overnight. When it was fitted I went out and straight away gained 2 seconds per lap, just from the better utilisation and flexibility in use of the engine. It proved my point that it was use, not power, that was at fault. So they were convinced and for a long time we kept the same 500bhp 2-litre turbo in it but worked on the utilisation of the power. From that moment we started to develop in the right direction. For me it was very important."

The specification of the experimental car at this stage at Jarama was described thus:

Chassis: part tubular steel, part monocoque reinforced with duralumin
Body: polyester
Engine: 1500cc V6 90°, cast-iron block with aluminium heads
Valves: 4 per cylinder
Fuel feed: Kugelfischer with a Renault-Gordini Garrett turbocharger
Power: 500bhp at 11,000rpm
Compression: 7 to 1
Transmission: BV Hewland FG 400 manual 6-speed

The following series of photographs are from the tests at Jarama in May 1976. The driver doing all the testing was Jean-Pierre Jabouille. Unfortunately, the records of these tests did not

Preparation: Jabouille waits seated behind the car.

A spot of understeer!

The first run.

Note the huge airbox; it was directly in front of the rear wing!

Fine adjustments.

A change of engine for comparative tests (the 2-litre).

The 1500.

survive, but we have the pictures of the A500 Alpine and the words of Jean-Pierre.

Asked about the chassis, Jean-Pierre continues: "What one has to understand is that we were so far off solving the problem of the tyres, the aerodynamics and the use of the engine that we weren't worrying too much about the chassis. The chassis was good enough to sort the engine out. A chassis is only good if it is good aerodynamically. It is vital that the chassis is rigid and the suspension's as rigid as possible, and then everything that has to do with the balance and the comfort of the driver comes from the aerodynamics in relation to the weight and the centre of depression, which must displace as little as possible with changes in the trim. The more stable you are in that area, the easier it is for the driver to drive well. When you manage to do that, you have a good car. There's always the question of whether there's the right amount of negative camber and how quickly the tyres wear out, and all that stuff, but it doesn't change things very much. So let's say that the chassis of the 500 was good enough to do the job, which was testing the engines."

Compact cockpit.

"... so it was that the test team arrived at the Paul Ricard Circuit, Plateau du Camp, on Wednesday 16 June 1976, where the 'Phantom' appeared for its first official public viewing. The secret tests carried out at Michelin's Clermont-Ferrand test track on 23 March 1976 – under the eyes of ... Michelin representatives, and the man from Elf, François Guiter – were over."

After the tests were completed everyone felt ready to move on to Paul Ricard. There was still work to be done, but pressure from management and press intrusion meant it was time to come clean and invite a few people to see what they were doing: it had become impossible to keep it a secret any longer. So it was that the test team arrived at the Paul Ricard Circuit, Plateau du Camp, on Wednesday 16 June 1976, where the 'Phantom' appeared for its first official public viewing. The secret tests carried out at Michelin's Clermont-Ferrand test track on 23 March 1976 – under the eyes of just the few members of the new team, Michelin representatives, and the man from Elf, François Guiter – were over. The second test at Dijon-Prenois was completed, as were those at Jarama in May. Now, word

was out: something sleek, black and coming from Alpine and Renault was at Paul Ricard ... The motoring press, by now well informed, was more than just interested; rumour had it, it really *was* a new Formula 1 car! Were the whispers true? The sceptics were out in force. It was powered by – what? A 1500cc engine? Turbocharged? Few could believe it.

It's an Alpine! It's a Renault! Powered by a Gordini! The combination was not new but the car certainly was. Conjecture was rife.

Formula 1 cars were all 3-litre – everyone knew that – but they had forgotten those 1966 regulations. The pundits went scuttling for their rule books. Of course! There it was, written quite clearly – the formula which allowed a 1500cc forcibly inducted engine.

The furore had to be seen to be believed; excited conversations down the phone lines, on the telexes, and heard in bars. At last it was revealed: the first public showing of a car powered by an engine whose format and design would eventually change the world of motor racing and rallying, and bring the power of turbocharging to the notice of the huge conglomerates that were and are the private car manufacturers.

It was not known what lay in store when Jean-Pierre Jabouille slowly drove the car out of the pit garage on Thursday, 16 June 1976. It was a misty morning; not a breath of wind could be felt on the Plateau du Camp, adding to the drama. The

69

The A500 today.

A lot of pipework!

journalists called it the 'Phantom' and it looked like one; for the invited press it sounded like nothing heard before. Christian Martin, Gérard Larrousse, Bernard Dudot, François Castaing, Jean-Pierre Boudy, André de Cortanze, François-Xavier Delfosse, Georges Bresson, and Pierre Dupasquier, along with François Guiter of Elf, all stood silently watching as the tension mounted and Jabouille nonchalantly cruised away, gathering pace whilst the whistle of the engine cut the morning air, gaining in audibility as the engine revs rose. It was the beginning of a new era as the first turbocharged Grand Prix car made its public début.

After a brief warm-up, the so-called A500 returned to its pit. The renowned French motor racing journalist, Johnny Rives, took notes and recorded what happened next at that first public test. So, from *Les Annees Turbo* in 1991:

"The Michelin technicians stop Jabouille to measure the wheel temperature before the car goes through a puddle left by an overnight shower. In charge of operations is François-Xavier Delfosse:

'How are you for temperature?' he asks Jabouille.

'The water's a little hot,' replies the driver.

Delfosse removes a cover from the right-hand side of the radiator.

'What's the pressure?' asks Boudy [one of the Renault-Gordini engine men from Viry-Châtillon].

'1.4. The engine seems much better than at Jarama.'

'Much better?'

'Much better than everything we've tried up to now.'

'Is it too rich?'

'Nothing worth mentioning.'

Jabouille turns his head. 'Take the wing off a notch.'

'So it's not worth trying a second test with the original turbo?' asks Boudy.

'Not in my opinion,' replies the driver. 'This one works much better.'

'Do you think it runs better than the one yesterday?'

'Much better.'

Once the wing has been adjusted, Delfosse, who has overseen the mechanics' work, comes up to Jabouille. 'OK.'

"The black A500 goes off again. On each lap, Jabouille seems to be progressively re-accelerating, taking two stabs at the throttle coming out of the Pont corner, maybe to avoid pushing the engine to its limits except when the car is totally stabilised on the straight. His time is 1min 16sec on the 3.3km (2.03 mile) circuit. Boudy has gone to the corner to listen to the sounds of the little 1500cc turbo engine; that will tell him how much effort is going into its operation.

"At the next stop, they decide to change the injection pump. Alain Marguet is in charge of the procedure. Boudy, watching him, asks, 'You prefer to remove the collector rather than the turbo pipe? That's how we usually do it …'

"The black A500 goes off again. On each lap, Jabouille seems to be progressively re-accelerating, taking two stabs at the throttle coming out of the Pont corner, maybe to avoid pushing the engine to its limits except when the car is totally stabilised on the straight."

'Without removing the collector?' asks Marguet. Unruffled, he continues to do it his own way. Standing up, he suddenly says, 'It's a bit hot in there,' and pulls on his asbestos gloves. Diving back down to the engine, he says, 'François! Could you put it in fifth and push the car a bit?'

Without a word, Delfosse does what he is asked. As he pushes, the engine sighs quietly. After a short silence, Marguet agrees: 'Right! We took that off …'

"Boudy is persuasive. 'Yes, we completely removed the pipe and the turbo housing.'

"A few minutes later there is deep discussion about the axial and radial play of the turbine. Marguet says, 'It's normal.'

'As it usually is,' confirms Jabouille. But Boudy has a completely different opinion: 'It's very important.' He points to the turbine blades, which are worn from rubbing against the turbo housing. Jabouille whistles. 'That can't be helping …'

"The discussion becomes heated. Delfosse is getting impatient and tries to intervene. 'Are you going to change it or not? If so, let's get on with it …'

"Castaing and Dudot had left the area, but came back just at the right moment. Castaing leant over and took hold of the axle to estimate its play. Jabouille is standing a little to one side, so I take the opportunity to ask him if the car is so delicate to drive that he must wait until he is totally straight before re-accelerating. This makes him smile. 'I don't wait at all to re-accelerate. It's the turbo that's late coming into action. That's where the whole problem lies. Nowhere else.'

"The mechanics work for an hour, and Jabouille goes back out on the circuit towards 12.30pm. Knowing that he re-accelerates from the apex in the last corner, the one before the pits, I time it from this point until the engine picks up. Between

Clearly, it's badged as a Renault.

Little comfort in the seat!

4 and 5 seconds – a huge delay … Jean-Pierre comes back to the pit.

'So?'

'At some points it's better, some less so. Either too rich or too lean. I think too lean. We'll have to test it.'

'Make it richer?' suggests Boudy.

'No, leaner. Then, if it makes it worse we'll know that that's the problem.'

'Right. Can you check your pressure at the end of the straight?'

'I did. It's a constant 1.4. Is Bresson around?'

'Yes, I'm here,' says the Michelin engineer.

'Is the rear tyre the same as before?'

'Yes, it's working on a good third.'

'Coming out of the corner, could you see your pressure?' asks Boudy.

'Which one?' asks Jabouille.

'This one.' [Boudy indicates the Pont corner before the pits.]

'Zero!'

Behind his blonde beard, Boudy is taken aback. 'Zero zero?'

'Yes,' says Jabouille.

Silence.

"Marguet adjusts the richness and when the Alpine-Renault A500 goes back out you can hear the engine backfiring all round the circuit; it really only sounds smooth at the end of the straight. Coming out of the Pont corner, the response time is up again – it seems even slower! However, Jabouille continues. 3 laps; 4 laps … 'Can't he feel that it's worse than before?' shouts Marguet. Nobody answers. On the sixth lap, the A500 does 1min 16sec and then Jabouille decides to stop. He doesn't wait to be questioned: 'Right, then. The pressure comes in earlier than with the other cam. But the engine only picks up at 8000 revs. And then there's a little flat spot.'

'At 8000 revs – you mean that you can feel the pressure coming in?' asks Boudy.

'Yes. Before, there's nothing. We have a lot of pressure, much sooner. But there's a flat spot at 8000. We're moving in the right direction. We can go leaner.'

'Is there a point that you can't go beyond?' puts in Bernard Dudot.

'It's misfiring at 8000 (at the flat spot). It looks as if that's where it's too lean.'

"They get busy with the engine; the overheated parts crackle as they cool down. While a mechanic pours fuel into the tank, the tyre man comes up to Jabouille.

'How's it behaving?'

'Not fantastic. Understeers a bit.'

'At the entry?'

'No.'

'You're accurate at the entry?'

'Yes,' says Jabouille. 'But if I press on hard, I drift at the front as if there isn't enough downforce. I don't feel the steering stiffen…'

Boudy chips in: 'Don't insist too much on the leaner engine like that, because …' and he grimaces.

"Jabouille's mind is clear at last. He says, 'The pressure is there. But the engine doesn't get going. There's a limit where it pops between 7600 and 8200.'

"When everything is ready, the driver puts his brightly coloured integral helmet on again. Narrower wheels have been mounted on the single-seater. He goes back onto the circuit at 1pm, and the engine seems to backfire more than ever.

"The Alpine goes out for another four laps, and the response time of the engine under acceleration has gone down to 5 seconds. On the straight, the sound it makes is continuous, like a triumphant bugle after an assault."

'This time he won't do more than two laps,' predicts Marguet.

Under acceleration, it's a disaster – on one occasion, 12 seconds between the car passing the apex of the corner and the clear uptake of the engine! After just one lap (in 1min 31sec) Jabouille stops. There's some grass caught in the front suspension.

'Have you brought us some flowers?' says one of the mechanics, sarcastically. Jabouille takes no notice of the joke. Concentrating on the job, he says to Boudy, 'Go back and make it a bit richer than at the beginning. Tyres seem OK but I can't see them too well because of the engine. At 8000 it picks up as if I'd pressed a button.'

Boudy, in professorial tone, replies, 'It's a function of the pressure and the inlet.'

Someone smiles, while the technicians say nothing but look on approvingly. The Alpine goes out for another four laps, and the response time of the engine under acceleration has gone down to 5 seconds. On the straight, the sound it makes is continuous, like a triumphant bugle after an assault. Jabouille stops and says, 'It works perfectly if I accelerate to three-quarters. When I give it full acceleration, the pressure falls from 1.5 to 1.4.'

'The turbo's making a strange noise,' says Delfosse. 'I've never heard that before.'

'The front tyres are faster on turn-in into the corner,' says Jabouille.

'And elsewhere?' asks Bresson.

'It's too pointy. Perhaps we should reduce the front downforce with these tyres.'

To the engine people, he says, 'If you could make it work as it does when I partially open the throttle, it would be perfect. If I put my foot down to the floor, it misfires. If I don't fully accelerate, it rises to 11,000.'

"Again the technicians lean over the engine. Jabouille has taken off his helmet and is gulping water from a bottle. He's still strapped into his narrow cockpit.

'What are they doing? Are they taking the turbo off?'

'Yes,' replies Delfosse.

'They should have told me. I'm getting out.' He unbuckles his harness and stands up. Dudot tells him, 'We're going to put on the 68.'

Jabouille's eyes sparkle. He's already in a hurry to try the little 1500 engine boosted by the new turbo.

'Let's have something to eat,' suggests Delfosse to help him relax.

"The tall man doesn't need asking twice – he's starving. Between mouthfuls, he makes a point: 'My first impression of the morning was surprise at the gentle and progressive operation of the engine. The second was that we found (with a few tricks, but at least we found it) an operating range equivalent to the 2-litre. It's encouraging because the solution came very quickly.'

"At 2.30pm he went out again on the circuit, did only three

"When Jabouille goes out again, the response time falls to 3.5sec. Lap times reflect the difference: 1min 14sec. However, Jabouille's reaction is not what they expect ..."

laps and came back in to say, 'We'll have to make it leaner again, because that changes the problem a bit ...'

'Is it worse with this turbo?' asks Boudy, worriedly.

'I don't know yet whether it's not as good, but it's certainly different. I get the impression that we need to make it leaner.'

'A lot?'

'Yes.'

So Boudy turns to Marguet and says, 'Alain, put it back two turns.'

"Delfosse says to Jean-Pierre, 'That will balance it ...'

'You can take a bit off the front, though,' the driver tells him. "Afterwards, they change a rear rod.

"De Cortanze: 'Léo, perhaps we should check the rocker gaps to see if it's changing.'

"Everyone gets on with his own area of work. Bresson, the tyre technician, ventures: 'What I find strange is that with smaller tyres it reduces the downforce.'

"Jabouille goes out for just one lap. When he stops, he speaks to Marguet. 'Put it back by one turn.' Then to Boudy: 'I gained 150g with that.'

'You got 1.6?'

'Exactly.'

'Take off 1½ turns of the valve, then,' Boudy says to Marguet.

"When Jabouille goes out again, the response time falls to 3.5sec. Lap times reflect the difference: 1min 14sec. However, Jabouille's reaction is not what they expect: 'I don't get the same result as with the other, especially under acceleration,' he says when he stops.

'Your engine runs better with this turbo, in my opinion,' replies Boudy.

"Silence for a minute. Then, 'Perhaps, perhaps,' Jabouille replies in a subdued tone. 'I've still got the flat spot at 8000.'

'And what about when you had it fully open, this morning?'

'The same ...'

"When he goes out on the circuit again, he comes in several times to change the wing settings to find the best balance. His time has dropped to 1min 13.2sec.

'We can run with the flap at 20°,' he says. 'That is, with practically no more downforce. Now we can adjust the car. Before, it wasn't adjustable; whatever we did, it didn't give any downforce. I could feel it in the lightness of the steering. Now that the rear axle is nailed to the ground, we can put the big cover on the front. I'm going to soften the front rod and stiffen the rear. Physically, you can easily tell whether there's downforce or not when you drive it.'

"Towards 5pm, the Alpine-Renault A500 is lapping at 1min 12.7sec. 'The engine's getting better,' says Jabouille. 'We could make it even leaner.' 'This cam enriches it between 500g and 1 kilo,' Boudy tells him. 'Have you still got the flat spot at 8000?'

'No, but coming out of the hairpin it isn't so good.'

"Three more laps and Jabouille says, 'It's going well at the top end, but I've got problems at the lower end.'

'Too lean?' asks Marguet.

'Perhaps. We'll have to enrich it by three turns.'

"Christian Martin, Renault management, comes back from a point on the circuit where he has been watching the black single seater going round. He says to Jabouille, 'It looks as if it's beginning to go quite well!'

'Yes.'

'With a whisker more downforce at the front it should be better,' suggests Bresson. [The front tyres of the Alpine have been changed for a wider model.] 'That will show how the problem is changing.'

"Jabouille goes out again for a series of four straight laps. The response time going out of the Pont corner is around 3.2-3.5sec. The Alpine is lapping at 1min 12.3sec. When it stops, Delfosse asks Jabouille, 'Is it still understeering?'

'Just a little,' replies Jean-Pierre. 'The engine's not going badly, but there's not enough turbo pressure. I've got problems when accelerating.'

'We'll go back to the turbo we were using this morning which worked better with this injection cam. Then we'll have another cam to test,' explains Boudy.

"The work is done and the Alpine goes back out at 6.15pm. Jabouille only does three laps and says, 'It's the same as this morning. The engine turns over, but not as strongly.'

'What's the pressure?' asks Boudy.

'1450, like this morning. 100g less.'

"The three engineers – Castaing, Dudot and Boudy – scratch their chins, perplexed.

'And what happens in the first part of the acceleration?' asks Castaing.

'It's better,' replies the driver. 'It pulls away earlier but the speed doesn't rise so quickly.'

'Yes, it gives less power,' comments Boudy. 'Show us the critical position of the throttle. We'll put a block under it and that'll give us an indication of what's happening.'

"Sitting in the cockpit, trying the throttle with his right foot, Jabouille tries to find the level that produces the hiccup. 'About there,' he says at last.

Marguet measures the displacement of the throttle on the engine to establish a test point. Then a block is placed under the throttle pedal.

'Good, let's try it like that,' says Jabouille before going out again. After two laps run at 1min 16sec, he stops and says, 'The engine doesn't pick up speed.'

'We can hear it,' confirms Boudy.

'It's a dog,' comments Delfosse.

'Shall we put the other turbo back for you?' suggests Boudy.

'Yes. And change the front anti-roll bar.' Jabouille gets out of the single seater and takes his helmet off again.

"He goes back on the circuit at 7.17pm. The security men on the Paul Ricard circuit wait patiently to be told that the tests have finished and they can go home. Three laps and Jabouille comes in to adjust the aerodynamics. Then he goes out for six laps which end the day's tests. The fifth lap was 1min 11.9sec, with a response time varying between 2.9sec and 3.3sec. His comment is: 'For me, it's too rich at all speeds, but when we make it leaner we lose at the lower end but gain at the top. When I change gear, the pressure doesn't fall to 0, only to 400g. Between 6000 and 8000rpm, the pressure needle rises gently, and then the power comes in suddenly. When we make it leaner, it is progressive but not as powerful.'

"Dudot and Boudy have listened religiously to his report. Gérard Larrousse has taken no part in the discussions between driver and technicians. Now he comes over and says, 'We'll have to stop. Jean-Pierre is shattered. It's half past seven.' A bit later, taking his overalls off, Jabouille's face is tired but his eyes are shining and happy. He gives us his personal impressions:

'I have to go fast on the big Signes corner. I arrive at

> **"For me, it's too rich at all speeds, but when we make it leaner we lose at the lower end but gain at the top. When I change gear, the pressure doesn't fall to 0, only to 400g. Between 6000 and 8000rpm, the pressure needle rises gently, and then the power comes in suddenly. When we make it leaner, it is progressive but not as powerful." – Jabouille**

11,000rpm. I cut the throttle to go round and it goes well, and I leave at 10,300rpm. That must be around 240kmh. By the looks of it, it seems to be quick.'

"The next day, Friday 18 June 1976, Jabouille's best lap in the A500 is 1min 11sec, in spite of an accident early in the morning after a wheel breaks. Two hours are lost while it is repaired and checked. Later, Dudot suggests that the test is carried out at 11,500 instead of 11,000rpm. They consider shortening the gearbox ratios, but the fitting of lower-profile rear tyres makes this unnecessary. The response time has fallen to 2.5sec. Boudy asks Jabouille, 'Do you think the engine still pulls above 11,000?'

Nogaro – the car was now painted yellow. (Archives AAA Dieppe)

'That's all it asks for,' replies the driver.

"The test finishes at 2pm. They've learnt a great deal in these three days. Jabouille, ever the optimist, carefully controls his enthusiasm when giving his report. 'The basis is serious,' he says. 'We made rapid progress. But there's a lot of work to be done to get us from doing a short series of laps like that to entering a Grand Prix. In my opinion, we should be ready to take part in the Grands Prix in 1978. But for 1977, we shouldn't expect any miracles.' However, they are in good spirits. Larrousse jokes, 'We mustn't panic the English, or they'll be spying on us everywhere …'

"And Jabouille adds, 'And I don't want to see a swarm of drivers in the Renault offices, all putting their hands up and shouting "Monsieur, what about me?" when the hard work is all over …'"

The test proved the car had potential. At the secret trials at Michelin's Clermont-Ferrand track the team had been able to get first impressions only. At Jarama and Dijon-Prenois it

was realised that those first impressions were going to lead somewhere. Then, at Paul Ricard, with its long straights and demanding corners, they could see it was going to work – but only time would tell.

Later in the 1976 season more test sessions were run at Nogaro to try new ideas aimed at improving the response time. Although still far from perfect, the engine became more docile and the car's performance improved. For the test at Nogaro the car had been repainted in Renault yellow and clearly displayed its laboratory status. With a rear wing logo depicting its purpose, it was ready for an official press launch a few weeks later.

Also in November, permission was obtained to proceed with a series of straight-line speed tests at the flight test centre at Brétigny, not far from the factory in Viry-Châtillon. These sustained full-load tests would bring some concerns about the pistons, though, above all, there were serious complaints from the neighbours about the noise! It was to be the first and last test at Brétigny, much to the team's regret, both for the practical

Unveiling to the press and Renault employees in Paris, 8 December 1976.

Black becomes yellow.

advantages and the friendly welcome it had received at the air base.

At the end of November the car was returned to Viry to be prepared for a grand presentation that was to take place on 8 December in Paris.

And so the car was launched; the purpose of the A500 was almost over and 1977 was to mark a turning point in the history of competition at Renault. The RS01, the first official Renault F1 car, made its début at the British Grand Prix at Silverstone that year.

Gérard Larrousse: "Bernard Hanon had called me to his office in July [1976]. It was just the two of us. We began talking, and he asked me if we could win a Grand Prix. I replied, 'Yes, maybe at altitude – South Africa, Zeltweg, for example.' Hanon thought for a moment and said, 'OK, go and build an F1 car for Jabouille and we'll see if we can win a Grand Prix.'"

The RS01, its construction approved by Bernard Hanon, was the first modern F1 car to take advantage of the F1 ruling which permitted 1500cc turbos to run with the 3000cc atmospherics. François Castaing, then team director of the F1 project, would succeed in producing a single-seater which perfectly integrated the characteristics of the new turbo engine. With the RS01 Renault was to establish an important landmark by moving from the experimental stage of the A500 to its use in a competition single-seater.

The laboratory test car.

Renault's adventure in Formula 1 had begun, but, as we shall learn, there would be a mountain to climb ...

Part 3

CLIMBING THE MOUNTAIN

Jabouille in the championship-winning Elf 2 at Hockenheim, 1976.

During 1976 Gérard Larrousse moved the design team that had worked on the A500 down to Viry-Châtillon in order to locate the Renault Sport F1 car department under the same roof as the engine development shop. This wasn't to everyone's liking, but the principal players either spent all their time at Viry or travelled regularly from Dieppe to Viry, or vice versa as the sports cars were being developed in Dieppe.

As we have already learnt, tests on the A500 proved interesting: the team could see that, with more work and a new car, Renault might just make it in Formula 1. Gérard Larrousse: "It has to be said that no one was talking about the World Championship!"

On 8 December 1976, a formal announcement had been made in Paris that a new car, the RS01, was already being created in mock-up format. Jean-Pierre Jabouille was to play a major part in this, and was on the scene most days to assist after his championship-winning year in F2.

The design group, led by André de Cortanze, was well on the way with the RS01 in Viry-Châtillon by 9 December 1976 when these photos were taken.

The A500 had completed its tests, and had been shown to the world's press the day before as the A500 prototype laboratory car; its job was done and it had been returned to Viry-Châtillon, not to be cut up, fortunately, but to provide test experience to help create the RS01, the first official Renault Formula 1 car.

Back in the 1970s all car makers made mock-ups; computers and electronically aided design were, as yet, unheard of. The designers were skilled craftsmen able to create ideas in 3-dimensional format and mock up the actual car, creating the final design as they went along. As can be seen in the case of the RS01, Jean-Pierre Jabouille, a superb driver, was to apply his analytical mind to the task of creating the right environment in the cockpit for the driver, whilst Marcel Hubert, the wizard of Alpine's great aerodynamic cars of the 1960s, studied the chassis design with interest, planning all the time how he could create an aerodynamic shape, whilst accommodating all of the requirements of the chassis people and engine designers. Here,

Jean-Claude Guénard. (Jean Sage Archives)

Right: Of course, the engine is of particular importance, and is one of the first elements to be presented to the wooden mock-up.

Bottom right: Jean-Pierre Jabouille is present most of the time; after all, as the driver, he has to fit in the car easily and with every control to hand. The car is virtually designed around him. Here he is seen in the mock-up.

in pictures, is the story as it unfolded in December 1976. Jean-Claude Guénard worked closely with Jabouille, having been with him as engineer on his previous cars; along with him Hervé Guilpin and Marc Bande worked on designing and drawing the parts to be produced.

The photographer of these pictures is not known (© Renault Communication), though it is known that he left the team for a few days and returned again on 16 December 1976; this is what he saw.

"On 8 December 1976, a formal announcement had been made in Paris that a new car, the RS01, was already being created in mock-up format."

Jean-Pierre Jabouille: "I can't remember the exact date that we started on the RS01, but everyone was in a hurry. I was still busy winning the European F2 championship, but saw the design team as often as possible. Some things on the RS01 were based on the lab car. In the end the RS01, being the first Renault car for F1, wasn't bad, though it wasn't up to the level of some of the other cars in F1."

The A500 lab car was a tubular chassis with panels of riveted aluminium, but the RS01 was eventually constructed with a chassis in aluminium, the first Renault Sport monocoque. Jean-Pierre Jabouille: "Castaing and the engineers were very committed – me too – and this was a car where I worked very closely with Jean-Claude Guénard and the team all the time. Marcel Hubert did an excellent design for the rear wing. He was really my teacher of things aerodynamic – fantastic."

The car was made in two ways: working in the design office at the same time as creating the mock-up, and it was made as a model to see if everything worked.

Jean-Pierre: "Jouvenot made the models – first in glass fibre then in plastic. The best wind tunnel we used was at St-Cyr, called the S4 – most of the testing was done there. To create

A quiet moment of concentration.

The A500 in the foreground and the RS01 mock-up in the background.

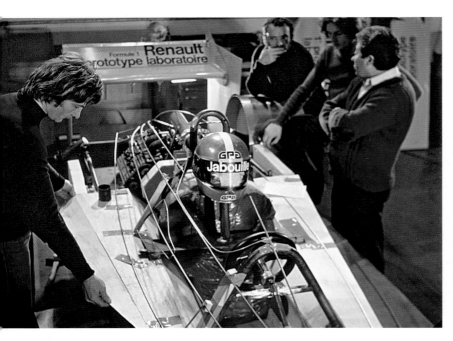

Hubert, de Cortanze, Guénard. By now they were beginning to put templates on the wooden mock-up to create the shape of the body. Parts of the A500 were used to create the design, as can be seen from the yellow-painted rear wing unit.

Getting out without becoming stuck or fouling anything is as important as getting in and sitting comfortably. Clearances are measured.

Castaing, Jabouille, de Cortanze and Hubert (+ unnamed engineer).

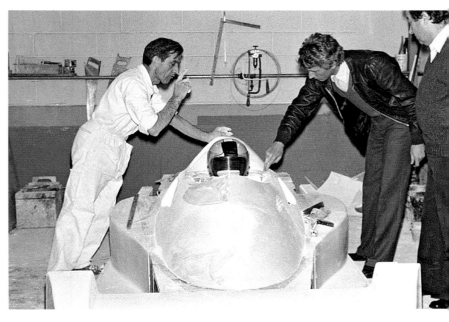

RS01: moulding the master, February 1977, Messieurs Jouvenot, Jabouille, Hubert.

A ghostly image.

the wide nose we copied the design of the nose of my Elf 2 car. It worked quite well in general, but the nose with the wings was better. In general, the RS01 is much more open at the rear compared with the lab car, and it represents typical F1 thinking in Renault at the time."

Work continued all through the spring of 1977, whilst the engine team was, of course, working flat out to build sufficient engines ready for testing and racing. Wind-tunnel testing was done with full size models.

Jean-Pierre Jabouille: "Marcel Hubert was a clever aero man – from the old school but very competent. I worked with him all the time in the wind-tunnel because for me it was one of the most exciting things in motor sport. At the time the regular fans – the public – knew little about it; even we drivers had little experience of it. It was fantastic because, if we made big modifications to the suspension, etc, it could be seen, and maybe it worked or maybe it didn't – it was a physical thing. But in the wind-tunnel we could move some small thing and it transformed the balance of the whole car. It is the only place where one and one do not always make two. In mechanical work a technician can change a few points and know in advance what will happen. In the wind-tunnel you can change something at the front and you can't see much difference, but if you look carefully you'll find that it

The S4 tunnel at St-Cyr.

Discussions with Marcel Hubert (right) during proceedings.

has changed something at the rear, and vice versa – you change something at the rear and the effect is at the front. So, all that was serious analysis and at the time there was [unlike now] little automated mathematical calculation. Yes, I liked working in the wind-tunnel."

The chassis team developed the car throughout the spring to the point where it was ready for its unveiling to the press and the public on 10 May 1977 at a gathering in the Renault showrooms in the Champs-Elysées in Paris, where Gérard Larrousse introduced all the members of the team who would be involved in running the car when it appeared on the Grand Prix circuits.

Some considerable excitement had been generated. There had been doubters, and there still would be, but, for the moment, the hour had come to present Renault Sport's first Formula 1 car to the world. The world's journalists were invited to attend. Here is part of the description from an issue of *Motor Sport* in 1976, written by the late Denis Jenkinson, one of the most famous motoring journalists of the day:

"After private (and very secret) testing had been carried out at the Michelin Tyre Company's test-track at Clermont-Ferrand in March last year, the test-car, named the A500 laboratory car, appeared at Jarama in late spring of 1976, and word was then out that Renault was going to join in Formula 1, though at the time nothing was said about when it would be. Doing the test-driving was Jean-Pierre Jabouille, who was also racing a Renault F2 car

> ## "The chassis team developed the car throughout the spring to the point where it was ready for its unveiling to the press and the public, on 10 May 1977 at a gathering in the Renault showrooms in the Champs-Elysées in Paris."

and the turbocharged sports car. All along, the French national petrol and oil company, Elf, has been closely associated with all the Renault-Gordini activities, the cars being called Renault-Elf, as is this new Formula 1 car supported heavily by Elf.

"Almost exactly one year after the prototype test-car A500 was first seen, Renault has laid open the whole project and told us they are ready to go racing. The car shown on 10 May is the first car to full racing specification, RS/01, the RS standing for Renault-Sport, the competition department of Renault. Its construction was started last November and the completed car was put down onto its wheels two days before it was shown to the press. Before it is entered for a race it has a test programme to fulfil, so Larrousse would not commit himself as to which would be their first event. The French, naturally, hope it will be their own Grand Prix at Dijon-Prenois, but logic and reason suggest it is more likely to be in the British GP at Silverstone, a circuit one might think more suited to a turbocharged engine than the Dijon circuit. Whatever happens, Jabouille will be the driver for whatever races they run in 1977, and, if all goes well, they plan to run two cars in 1978, and if it performs well there won't be a shortage of drivers for the second car. The overall impression of the car is that it is very small, compact, and a unified design, clearly designed around two major factors: the

> ## "The French, naturally, hope it will be their own Grand Prix at Dijon-Prenois, but logic and reason suggest it is more likely to be in the British GP at Silverstone, a circuit one might think more suited to a turbocharged engine than the Dijon circuit."

turbocharged 1.5-litre V6 engine and Michelin radial tyres. Many people have been involved in the design and creation of the car, with engine specialists, gearbox specialists, chassis and suspension specialists, aerodynamic specialists, to say nothing of all the tyre specialists at Michelin who have been working exclusively for Renault. The whole project has been under the control of François Castaing, a 31-year-old engineer who is the technical director of Renault-Gordini and who was responsible, among other things, for the original 4 overhead cam V6 Renault-Gordini engine. Older readers who recall Amédée Gordini when he was running his Grand Prix team in the 1950s may be wondering how the old 'Sorcerer' fits into the new set-up. In fact, he doesn't: his company was taken over by Renault in the late 1960s and Amédée has been retired for many years now, leaving his name on Renault competition activities as a sort of symbol of respectability. He still attends Formula 1 races as a spectator, and no doubt will be about the place to see the new Renault make its racing début.

"The heart of the design is the V6 engine, limited to 1.5 litres by Formula 1 rules. It is a 90° vee with bore and stroke of 86 x 42.8mm – 1492cc, with 4 valves per cylinder and two overhead camshafts driven by toothed belt for each cylinder head. The engine block is cast-iron, made in the foundries of

On the left we see the grandmaster of the F1 project from Elf, François Guiter; alongside him is Gérard Larrousse. By the car are Castaing, Sage, Guénard, Marguet and Hubert, with Jabouille in the car.

Régie-Renault, and the heads are aluminium alloy. It is a very short and compact engine and is mounted ahead of a Hewland FGA 400 gearbox/final drive unit, containing six forward speeds. Between the engine and the transmission unit is a fairly long alloy spacer, and above this is the turbocharger unit. To the left is the exhaust-driven turbine, fed by two pipes; one from the left-hand exhaust manifold more or less directly, the other from an exhaust pipe from the right-hand manifold which passes underneath the spacer. The exhaust-driven turbine vents into a single, large-diameter pipe through the adjustable waste-gate and into a large, megaphone-ended tail pipe. Directly over the engine/transmission spacer is the compressor driven by the turbine, and this draws air from a duct on the right-hand side. From the compressor the inlet manifold runs forward along the vee of the engine into an inter-cooler, and then back over the top of the cooler to the six-branch manifold feeding the cylinders, each branch containing a fuel-injection nozzle aimed directly down

The RS01 goes on show.

Smooth lines and a contemporary appearance.

the inlet port onto the backs of the inlet valves. Turbocharging pressure is quoted as about 21psi and, with a compression ratio of 7 to 1, the engine is claimed to develop 510bhp at 11,000rpm running on normal Elf petrol, naturally. It develops its maximum torque at 9600rpm which means that Jabouille will have to keep his eyes on the electric rpm indicator. The only other instrument he has to watch is the boost-gauge; other functions or malfunctions are indicated by coloured lights. The turbocharger is by Garrett and the fuel injection by Kugelfischer, the unit mounted in the vee of the engine and driven by toothed belt from the right-hand inlet camshaft. Between the engine and the inter-cooler is the oil tank for the dry sump lubrication system, this tank being a complicated affair with passageways through

> ## "Turbocharging pressure is quoted as about 21psi and, with a compression ratio of 7 to 1, the engine is claimed to develop 510bhp at 11,000rpm running on normal Elf petrol, naturally."

it for the inlet pipe from the turbocharger and for other various pipes and controls. The whole power unit looks very purposeful and neat, and is a stressed unit attached to the rear of the chassis monocoque, with side-mounted water radiators. Suspension all round is by coil springs with internal Koni dampers, the front ones operated by rocker arms with lower wishbones and the rear layout being conventional double lower links, single top and twin radius rods. Very wide ventilated disc brakes are used, with Lockheed calipers, the rear discs being mounted inboard, and Ferodo supply the brake pads. The overall impression of the car is one of compactness and lightness, especially as regards detail design on such things as suspension joints, drive shafts, hubs, steering parts, and so on. It is not a question of lightness for the sake of weight-saving, but lightness by careful design overall and in detail. Although it is very much a French car and a Renault, it has to turn to suppliers who are specialists with regard to such things as brakes, clutch, body fasteners, sparking plugs, brake pads and clutch linings, life-support system, gearbox, ball-races and batteries, and it's nice to see there are many British firms or British-influenced international firms who are involved. Building a car is one thing; winning races is another matter altogether; but, whatever happens, this appearance of a Renault Formula 1 car, with the backing and responsibility of the Régie-Renault behind it, must be of interest to the overall scene in Formula

1. Of particular interest is the tyre question, with Michelin wholeheartedly behind the project. At the moment, Goodyear has a monopoly in Formula 1, and they dictate the type of tyre that everyone will use for each race, and no one is allowed to use special 'short-life' tyres for practice and grid-position qualifying. This is an unofficial 'gentleman's agreement' among the members of the Constructors' Association, but Renault is not in the association and if Michelin produce some super-sticky tyres for Jabouille to use in practice, no one can stop them. We can foresee the 'gentleman's agreement' going by the board. There are one or two other 'carefully arranged' manipulations within the Formula 1 'circus' that might also get a bit of a jolt when Renault starts entering races, which won't be a bad thing for the sport in general."

Directly after the launch it was time for testing at the Paul Ricard circuit. The car first turned a wheel on the smaller 3.3km circuit on 31 May and on the long 5.8km track on 1 June.

> ## "Goodyear has a monopoly in Formula 1, and it dictates the type of tyre that everyone will use for each race, and no one is allowed to use special 'short-life' tyres for practice and grid-position qualifying."

After these first shakedown runs, a reduced team of F1 personnel returned to Paris to make an assessment of the opening trials; reduced because almost all of the engineers and senior technical people were diverted to concentrate on the forthcoming Le Mans 24 Hours.

As the F1 cars left Paul Ricard they were replaced by the sports-prototype team which had arrived to carry out final testing before the great 24-hour epic. The following week all the operating staff of Renault Sport went to Le Mans for the 45th running of the race on 11 and 12 June. Jean-Pierre Jabouille took pole with 3min 31.07sec, 231.951kmh (144.127mph). Things were looking good.

The A442s were very competitive at Le Mans and very fast, though, unfortunately, did not finish as each of the cars suffered piston failure. This problem took a long time to resolve, entailing many weeks of testing and modification to the sports car engine. Much of the information acquired was transferred to the F1 team for use in engine development. For now, though, the men who were more heavily involved in the F1 team returned to base at Viry-Châtillon, and took the RS01 for tests at the Dijon-

Big rear wing; just how powerful *is* that engine?

Here, there is an engine cover and full-width nose; Jabouille on board.

The famous telegram. (Jean Sage Archives)

Revisions and trials. Note the taped-on panels over the side-pods.
(© Dominique Pascal)

Prenois circuit on 15 and 16 June. It was from Dijon on 16 June that Jean Sage sent his famous telegram to the British Royal Automobile Club, entering the car in the Formula 1 British Grand Prix, due to take place on 16 July 1977 at Silverstone.

This was the official specification of the RS01 as released by Renault just before its first race:

Type:	RS01
Body:	Kevlar, front spoiler aluminium
Chassis:	Light aluminium monocoque with steel and duralumin bulkhead; engine classified as a stressed chassis member.
Dimensions:	Wheelbase 2500mm (98.4 inches)
	Front axle 1425mm (56.1 inches)
	Rear axle 1525mm (60.03 inches)
	Weight 600kg (1322lb)
	Front wheels 13 x 11.5 inches
	Rear wheels 13 x 19.5 inches
Brakes:	Front calipers Lockheed CP 2561-2
	Rear calipers Girling AR6
	Front discs Lockheed diam. 274.4mm (10.8.inches) Ventilated CP2261
	Rear discs Girling diam. 304.8mm (12 inches) Ventilated Brake pads Ferodo DS11
Suspension:	Front inboard pivoting
	Rear double lower parallel arms with reaction rods
Steering:	Rack and pinion with 9-tooth pinion
Fuel tanks:	3 Superflexit FT3, soft-skinned, capacity 200 litres (43.9 imp gallons)
Radiators:	Chausson light alloy water and oil
Gear box:	Hewland FGA 400 6-speed
Clutch:	Borg and Beck bi-disc
Tyres:	Michelin
Engine:	1.5-litre, type EF1 V6 90°
	Cylinder capacity 1492cc bore 86mm (3.38 inches) stroke 42.8mm (1.68.inches), 4 valves per cylinder
	Compression ratio 7.1
	Weight 180kg (396.8lb) with starter mechanism and turbos
	Width 680mm (26.77 inches)
	Height 650mm (25.59 inches)
	Length 480mm (18.89 inches)
	Rpm 12,000
	Bhp 500 at 11,000rpm

Full team attention, practice.

"The engine block is made out of GS cast iron in the Renault foundry. The sleeves are water-cooled suspended type and they are made of nitrided steel. The cylinder head gasket is composite metallic type with viton toric joints for water and oil. The crankshaft, cut from solid steel, is nitrided and runs on four bearings. Con rods are steel and the pistons are of cast-aluminium alloy. The cylinder head is of aluminium alloy and has four valves per cylinder. The angle of the valve to the cylinder head is 10° for the inlet valves and 11.3° for the exhaust valves. Valves are driven by double overhead camshafts.

"The water pumps consist of two centrifugal-type units, each one supplying one bank of cylinders. The lubrication is a dry sump-type with a discharge and pressure pump placed on each side of the engine. The fuel is introduced by an indirect injection system by Kugelfischer driven by a cam. Ignition is by Marelli and is electro-magnetic."

Two weeks prior to the British Grand Prix, the French GP was to be held at Dijon, and Gérard Larrousse and François Castaing had, for a few days, considered giving the RS01 its début at Dijon. They abandoned this idea for several reasons. Gérard Larrousse: "Firstly, in order to avoid taking the risk of failure, which would have been judged too public in France for a car bearing the name Renault; secondly, because the Dijon tests had

Silverstone 1977.

Note the off-the-shelf rear-view mirrors!

For the British Grand Prix of 1977 thirty-seven F1 cars had been entered for just twenty-six places on the starting grid, so the RAC organising committee arranged a pre-qualifying session for Wednesday 13 July with the intention of reducing the field to leave only thirty cars to take part in the two days of official practice.

The first official practice for the Grand Prix was set to take place on Thursday 14 July, with the race being held on its traditional day which, that year, was Saturday 16 July. As it stood, the task facing Jean-Pierre Jabouille and the Renault Sport team was not looking good or easy. However, Bernie Ecclestone considered the Régie and its competition department as a whole entity, capable of playing a very important role in Grand Prix racing for the future and not just a small private team involved only in this British Grand Prix. At that time there were many small private teams who wanted to take part, and these were the teams who frequented the back of the list of thirty-seven entries. Ecclestone applied some pressure and it was decided that Renault Sport would be excused from the Wednesday pre-qualifying to give the fledgling team – which, although small, was in reality supported by an automotive industry giant – a clean start. The F1 'establishment' had played its card.

By the time the team arrived at Silverstone the RS01 had, in fact, run about 2500km (1553 miles), including a number of laps at Silverstone on 6 and 7 July, the week prior to the Grand Prix. It had actually run 84 laps, which was encouraging as the Grand Prix would consist of 68 laps.

> **"By the time the team arrived at Silverstone the RS01 had, in fact, run about 2500km (1553 miles), including a number of laps at Silverstone on 6 and 7 July, the week prior to the Grand Prix."**

With the new nose on the car, some thought the RS01 didn't look as good as it did before, but Jabouille had persuaded the team that functional requirements were more important and good cooling was vital; ironically, the weather was far from warm that weekend at Silverstone. Interestingly, the later RS01/02 which came out in 1978 had identical bodywork to that used at Silverstone, but was finished to a higher quality, and looked more professional.

The results of the first day's practice were not brilliant: the car had a fuel supply problem and the engine was suffocating.

revealed some minor problems which could not be resolved in time, including a feeling by Jean-Pierre [Jabouille] that the car would, as he said: "stay cooler if we did away with the full-width nose." They tried it in the wind tunnel.

Beautiful though it was, with the full-width nose there was a chance that cooling was indeed being compromised, so a modification was made before the car was taken to Silverstone.

British Grand Prix, Silverstone, 16 July 1977

As a brief aside, for those who may be interested, the numbering of the Renault Sport chassis, apart from the A500 prototype designed under the leadership of André de Cortanze, originally foresaw a direct progression: RS01, then RS02 for the second chassis type, RS03, etc. However, the Renault Sport team adopted the usual (at the time) chassis numbering for the RS01s: RS01, then RS01/02, RS01/03, etc, so during the 1977 season and the beginning of 1978, this numbering system was used, although the team did return to the original plan of direct numbering with RS10 for 1979, then RS11, then RS12, etc, for the cars that followed.

A little anecdote here about the team from Jacques Poisson, ex-Renault Public Relations: "I remember a funny moment between unofficial and official practice. Around 12.30pm the whole team was eating quietly at a table prepared for lunch in the pits when all the other teams were very busy preparing their cars! This French idea of eating at lunchtime had to stop!"

"... the later RS01/02 which came out in 1978 had identical bodywork to that used at Silverstone, but was finished to a higher quality, and looked more professional."

After lunch work continued and, finally, Jean-Pierre Jabouille managed to qualify in 21st position during the Friday session, with a time of 1min 20.11sec, only 1.22sec outside the pole position time set by James Hunt in his McLaren-Ford M26. Ecclestone and his supporters had been vindicated; although it was a lowly position for the car on the grid, its performance was more than satisfying. A completely new car powered by this strange engine had arrived. The team was enthusiastic, but one problem remained: the start; the Renault would not get off the line as quickly as its rivals.

Jean-Pierre Jabouille: "We came with a car that was different from everything else in several ways: radial Michelin tyres [these were new to Grand Prix racing]; a turbocharged engine [the first in Formula 1]; and me. OK, I was European Formula 2 champion, but I had driven nothing in F1. So everything was new. We were very realistic about Silverstone. I had a feeling that we would eventually be successful, but first of all I wanted to finish races."

Jean-Pierre continues: "I remember as if it were yesterday that it was cold, because my first concern was the tyres and Michelin, who, by now, had the tendency to make the tyres too hard, too rigid, for reasons of safety because they were always afraid of a burst, and when it was cold I had a lot of difficulty warming them up. It was tricky to drive this car on cold tyres with the turbo engine which was much more brutal when it was cold and the power arrived more suddenly.

"I'll tell you a little story: when at the end of the season another top French driver tested the car he did three or four laps and stopped, saying that it was undrivable. So I had to get in the car and warm up the tyres for him because it was so difficult to drive on the cold tyres!

"Anyway, back to Silverstone: it was a big problem to warm up the tyres, especially in practice, without going off the track.

Waiting ... for Jean-Pierre to return.

More checks ...

A chilly Silverstone race.

Are you serious?

So it all had to be used very delicately – engine, tyres, etc – using third gear instead of second to stop wheel spin, while all the others were revving up on their Goodyears ... I had not yet tried Goodyears on that car. In the end, I managed to qualify in the middle, so reasonably well, but we had lots of little problems and, from time to time, I came back in with the engine smoking,

which made Ken Tyrrell laugh because he said he (now) didn't believe in it at all! It's strange because, originally, he was enthusiastic that Renault should build a turbo."

Come race day, as the lights signalled the start, Jabouille worked wonders, and limited the damage of the slow start by dropping only one place to 22nd position at the end of the first lap. Very soon the power was in evidence and he set about making up the lost time: on lap 5 he was 18th, then 16th on lap 7. It was looking good: a few more laps and they could be in the top 10.

Shortly afterward, however, the engine began to lose power and, on the 12th lap, Jabouille had to make a first visit to the Renault pit: the air box fitted above the engine turbo had cracked and boost pressure was falling. The mechanics made makeshift repairs, but four laps after Jabouille returned to the race the turbocompressor, a Garrett unit designed more for endurance racing and the type used at Le Mans, gave up. It had suffered from the changes in boost pressure before Jabouille's first stop. The fastest race lap the RS01 achieved was not brilliant: 1min 23.01sec, compared with James Hunt's best lap of 1min 19.6sec.

"This was not only Renault's race début: as we see it was also a début for Michelin and its new tyres – radials created specifically for racing – which Jabouille had had great difficulty getting up to temperature so that they worked efficiently."

Jabouille: "Unfortunately, the engine had broken in a huge cloud of smoke. Then everyone, including Ken Tyrrell, did have a good laugh."

This was not only Renault's race début: as we see it was also a début for Michelin and its new tyres – radials created specifically for racing – which Jabouille had had great difficulty getting up to temperature so that they worked efficiently. A team member there at the time explained, "Whatever manufacturer we were working with, we found it quite difficult to get technical information on the Formula 1 tyres. The suppliers were always happy to give us an evaluation of the performance of the tyres' behaviour on the car, but remained extremely secretive about the whys and wherefores of this behaviour. This may be understandable on the part of Michelin who, following the example of our 'turbo' gamble, had done the same to demonstrate to the world that their radial technology, which

Note the tape on the nose!

Gérard Larrousse (r) and François Castaing.

had arrived at the level of F1, could give better results than the conventional solution offered by Goodyear. It was certain, though, that, at this first race for the team, Jabouille just could not get enough heat into his tyres at Silverstone."

Whatever the result for the first outing by the turbo car, the spectators at this 1977 British Grand Prix had a lot more to see. Apart from Renault and Michelin, a future great – Gilles Villeneuve – was driving in F1 in a McLaren for the first time, and Patrick Tambay made his début in an Ensign. Tambay was to drive for Renault in later years.

Although the turbo had become the butt of many jokes (Ken Tyrrell had nicknamed it the 'Yellow Teapot'), Renault, with its revolutionary thinking, had raised eyebrows amongst the F1 fraternity, and, whilst its performance had not given the Cosworth runners any cause for concern, the fact that a company the size of Renault was investing in this route to Grand Prix glory was certainly food for thought.

Little did they know, but those who were there witnessed what was to be the start of a great French team, with a 1500cc, turbocharged V6 engine, a project which – even for the world of Formula 1 – was bordering on extravagance. The Renault turbo

Silverstone race statistics.

STARTING GRID		RESULTS - Silverstone (320,892 km)			
Watson 1'18.77"	Hunt 1'18.49"	1. Hunt	McLaren-Ford	68	1h31'46.06" 209.790 km/h
Scheckter J. 1'18.85"	Lauda 1'18.84"	2. Lauda	Ferrari	68	+ 18.31"
Andretti 1'19.11"	Nilsson 1'18.95"	3. Nilsson	Lotus-Ford	68	+ 19.57"
Brambilla 1'19.20"	Stuck 1'19.16"	4. Mass	McLaren-Ford	68	+ 47.76"
Peterson 1'19.42"	Villeneuve 1'19.32"	5. Stuck	Brabham-Alfa Romeo	68	+ 1'11.73"
Jones 1'19.60"	Mass 1'19.55"	6. Laffite	Ligier-Matra	67	+ 1 lap
Reutemann 1'19.64"	Keegan 1'19.64"	7. Jones	Shadow-Ford	67	+ 1 lap
Tambay 1'19.81"	Laffite 1'19.75"	8. Brambilla	Surtees-Ford	67	+ 1 lap
Depailler 1'19.90"	Merzario 1'19.88"	9. Jarier	ATS-Ford	67	+ 1 lap
Jarier 1'20.10"	Lunger 1'20.06"	10. Neve	March Williams-Ford	66	+ 2 laps
Fittipaldi 1'20.20"	Jabouille 1'20.11"	11. Villeneuve	McLaren-Ford	66	+ 2 laps
Scheckter I. 1'20.31"	Schuppan 1'20.24"	12. Schuppan	Surtees-Ford	66	+ 2 laps
Neve 1'20.36"	Patrese 1'20.35"	13. Lunger	McLaren-Ford	64	+ 4 laps
		14. Reutemann	Ferrari	62	+ 6 laps
		15. Andretti	Lotus-Ford	62	Engine

FASTEST LAP		
Hunt	McLaren-Ford	1'19.60" 213.400 km/h

RETIREMENTS			
Watson	Brabham-Alfa Romeo	60	Fuel feed
Scheckter J.	Wolf-Ford	60	Engine
Fittipaldi	Copersucar-Ford	43	Fuel feed
Merzario	March-Ford	28	Transmission shaft
Patrese	Shadow-Ford	21	Fuel feed
Depailler	Tyrrell-Ford	17	Accident / brakes
Jabouille	Renault	17	Turbo
Scheckter I.	March-Ford	7	Accident
Tambay	Ensign-Ford	4	Fuel pressure
Peterson	Tyrrell-Ford	3	Engine
Keegan	Hesketh-Ford	1	Collision Merzario

had at last raced for the first time, even though it was amid a general feeling of scepticism from other competitors and public alike.

Dutch Grand Prix, Zandvoort, 28 August 1977

Following the British Grand Prix and the first race for the RS01, Gérard Larrousse and François Castaing decided to give themselves time to think and did not enter the next two Grands Prix in Germany and Austria. Castaing, with his team of engine specialists, had several details to correct; at the same time, he had some problems to address with his chassis team. François Castaing: "In those early days, we didn't have four chassis and twenty-five engines in the Renault Sport workshop – nothing like it!"

After the first attempt at Silverstone, it was decided to go next for another open circuit race; for the 1977 season the Dutch Grand Prix looked interesting because it was to be at Zandvoort.

Jean-Pierre Jabouille started the first practice session with the original nose section that had been used at Silverstone, though this time with the engine fitted with a 'racing' turbocompressor from the Renault Sport team workshop, rather than the Le Mans-type production item that was used in the British GP. The new turbo was a 'composition' based on British Garrett turbocharger parts and Renault Sport parts. However, the Renault didn't look convincing with these modifications: engine tuning produced so much black smoke that people were worried, asking what could possibly be burning in there! Jabouille wasn't as familiar with Zandvoort as with other circuits, either, but that

Reverting to the full nose.

On the grid.

wasn't what made his performance suffer: very early on, the turbocompressor had swallowed a stone and, although the turbine didn't break, it lost power. It also looked like a tyre war was looming because, in order to relegate the Michelins of the Renault to the back of the grid, Goodyear had provided some of its 'specials' to several of the smaller teams; these were thought of as qualifying tyres, usually given only to top teams. The pressure was on for Renault and, whilst Jabouille went round in 1min 26.96sec, Mario Andretti, up at the front of the grid in his Lotus-Ford, was doing it in 1min 18.85sec.

In the afternoon session it got worse: the engine suffered the failure of an intercooler, damaged during the morning; it had lost an internal deflector which had been immediately swallowed into the combustion chamber.

The engine and nose cone were changed for the Saturday and, from the first practice session, Jean-Pierre Jabouille was immediately able to get himself in a better position, improving by more than 3 seconds on his time from the day before. In the last hour of qualification he again managed to win another 3 seconds. His quickest laps had been 1min 26.9sec, 1min 23.89sec, and 1min 20.13sec, this last time giving him tenth place on the starting grid; this enormous improvement over the day before was a great relief for the team.

At the start on race day, Jabouille chose to keep out of trouble as the cars left the line and his slow-starting car slipped to 14th at the end of the 1st lap. Undaunted, he did something that was to become his trademark at subsequent races: he set about moving up the placings as the race settled down. On the 20th lap (there were 75 in the Grand Prix) he was up to 9th. He then took advantage of the demise of Alan Jones (Shadow) and took on Emerson Fittipaldi (Copersucar). By mid-race he was 6th behind Lauda (Ferrari) and Laffite (Ligier), shoulder to shoulder with Tambay (Ensign), Scheckter (Wolf), and Fittipaldi. Jabouille was beginning to believe he could have his eye on 1st place when, on the 39th lap, his suspension broke, inducing a spin: the rear left-hand upper arm had failed. He returned to the pits and was out of the race. It was over, but this time the car had shown some serious pace.

Italian Grand Prix, Monza, 11 September 1977

Great Britain, Holland, now Italy: Renault Sport was going to its third Grand Prix. Even more than it had been at Zandvoort, Goodyear was watching Michelin very closely. A few days before the GP at Monza the Renault's performance in private testing had

STARTING GRID	
Laffite 1'19.27"	Andretti 1'18.65"
Lauda 1'19.54"	Hunt 1'19.50"
Reutemann 1'19.66"	Nilsson 1'19.57"
Watson 1'19.93"	Peterson 1'19.85"
Jabouille 1'20.13"	Regazzoni 1'19.93"
Tambay 1'20.23"	Depailler 1'20.14"
Mass 1'20.24"	Jones 1'20.24"
Patrese 1'20.43"	Scheckter J. 1'20.24"
Binder 1'20.84"	Fittipaldi 1'20.53"
Lunger 1'20.87"	Stuck 1'20.86"
Brambilla 1'21.12"	Jarier 1'21.06"
Ribeiro 1'21.16"	Henton 1'21.13"
Keegan 1'21.53"	Scheckter I. 1'21.19"

RESULTS - Zandvoort (316,950 km)

1. Lauda	Ferrari	75	1h41'45.93" 186.186 km/h
2. Laffite	Ligier-Matra	75	+ 1.89"
3. Scheckter J.	Wolf-Ford	74	+ 1 lap
4. Fittipaldi	Copersucar-Ford	74	+ 1 lap
5. Tambay	Ensign-Ford	73	Out of fuel
6. Reutemann	Ferrari	73	+ 2 laps
7. Stuck	Brabham-Alfa Romeo	73	+ 2 laps
8. Binder	ATS-Ford	73	+ 2 laps
9. Lunger	McLaren-Ford	73	+ 2 laps
10. Scheckter I.	March-Ford	73	+ 2 laps
11. Ribeiro	March-Ford	72	+ 3 laps

FASTEST LAP

Lauda	Ferrari	1'19.99" 190.195 km/h

RETIREMENTS

Henton		71	Fuel leak Disqualified
Patrese	Shadow-Ford	68	Ignition
Brambilla	Surtees-Ford	68	Accident
Jabouille	Renault	40	Rear suspension failure
Nilsson	Lotus-Ford	35	Collision Reutemann
Jones	Shadow-Ford	33	Engine
Depailler	Tyrrell-Ford	32	Engine
Peterson	Tyrrell-Ford	19	Fuel feed
Regazzoni	Ensign-Ford	18	Throttle cable
Andretti	Lotus-Ford	15	Engine
Keegan	Hesketh-Ford	9	Accident
Hunt	McLaren-Ford	6	Collision Andretti
Jarier	ATS-Ford	5	Engine
Watson	Brabham-Alfa Romeo	3	Oil sump failure
Mass	McLaren-Ford	1	Collision with Jones

Zandvoort race statistics.

been very impressive. Jabouille had easily beaten Laffite's best official lap time from the year before, as well as the unofficial record of Reutemann with his Ferrari, which was 1min 40.4sec. With this being only the team's third appearance at a race, there was an air of optimism right from the start of the first session on the Friday. The evidence of a huge power advantage was there to be seen: Reutemann got down to 1min 40.2sec; the first official serious time had been recorded. Jabouille immediately replied with a 1min 40.5sec time, which left everyone staggered.

Unfortunately, the V6 turbo immediately broke and Jabouille couldn't defend his place. It was the first break in what was to be an epidemic. The following day, when most competitors were improving, Jabouille did not appear on the circuit until the last half hour of practice; his engine, broken the day before, had taken a lot longer to change than had been hoped. He did improve his time by a few tenths of a second, but the problem was that his rivals were moving away from him in whole seconds. From 7th place, Jabouille went tumbling down to 20th with a time of 1min 40.3sec.

Sunday morning: race day, and during the warm-up, Jabouille again demonstrated the considerable pace of the turbo when it was running properly, ending the session a respectable second fastest, behind Lauda's Ferrari. Smiles all round in the Renault pit – it couldn't last! Indeed, the high hopes of the morning's performance were dashed when he clashed with Ian Scheckter (elder brother of future 1979 World Champion, Jody Scheckter), damaging the turbo's front wing. Jabouille continued driving in an anonymous 13th place before having to abandon the race on the 23rd of the 52 laps, when the engine failed again.

The Renault's chassis had been strengthened by revised suspension, and its engine – although it failed – had the benefit of an updated turbo which stood up better to the operational environment. However, it was now the valves which were making life difficult for the technicians. On the Friday a valve stem had broken, causing considerable damage; then, on the Saturday and Sunday, it was the valves themselves that were burning: it seemed that richness adjustment and the injection pump were the likely culprits.

US East Coast Grand Prix, Watkins Glen, 2 October 1977

The team had decided to try an away Grand Prix, where Jean-Pierre Jabouille could continue his apprenticeship on the circuits; so it was that he discovered Watkins Glen, with a preliminary practice session on the Tuesday before the race.

Having got the hang of the circuit, Jabouille wanted to

STARTING GRID	
Hunt 1'38.08"	Reutemann 1'38.15"
Scheckter J. 1'38.29"	Andretti 1'38.37"
Lauda 1'38.54"	Patrese 1'38.683"
Regazzoni 1'38.684"	Laffite 1'38.77"
Mass 1'38.86"	Brambilla 1'38.92"
Stuck 1'39.05"	Peterson 1'39.17"
Depailler 1'39.18"	Watson 1'39.21"
Giacomelli 1'39.42"	Jones 1'39.50"
Scheckter I. 1'39.62"	Jarier 1'39.63"
Nilsson 1'39.85"	Jabouille 1'40.03"
Tambay 1'40.19"	Lunger 1'40.26"
Keegan 1'40.28"	Neve 1'40.51"

RESULTS - Monza (301,600 km)

1. Andretti	Lotus-Ford	52	1h27'50.30" 206.014 km/h
2. Lauda	Ferrari	52	+ 16.96"
3. Jones	Shadow-Ford	52	+ 23.63"
4. Mass	McLaren-Ford	52	+ 28.48"
5. Regazzoni	Ensign-Ford	52	+ 30.11"
6. Peterson	Tyrrell-Ford	52	+ 1'19.22"
7. Neve	March Williams-Ford	50	+ 2 laps
8. Laffite	Ligier-Matra	50	+ 2 laps
9. Keegan	Hesketh-Ford	48	+ 4 laps

FASTEST LAP

Andretti	Lotus-Ford	1'39.10" 210.696 km/h

RETIREMENTS

Scheckter I.	March-Ford	42	Transmission shaft
Reutemann	Ferrari	40	Accident
Patrese	Shadow-Ford	39	Accident
Giacomelli	McLaren-Ford	39	Engine
Stuck	Brabham-Alfa Romeo	32	Engine
Hunt	McLaren-Ford	27	Brakes
Depailler	Tyrrell-Ford	25	Engine
Scheckter J.	Wolf-Ford	24	Engine
Jabouille	Renault	24	Engine
Jarier	ATS-Ford	19	Engine
Tambay	Ensign-Ford	9	Overheating engine
Brambilla	Surtees-Ford	6	Oil pipe
Lunger	McLaren-Ford	5	Engine
Nilsson	Lotus-Ford	5	Front suspension
Watson	Brabham-Alfa Romeo	4	Support engine

Monza race statistics.

be able to fine-tune the RS01's chassis set-up, but an engine breakage prevented him, so he spent the first official practice session just trying to make progress. On the Friday he eventually qualified in 14th position on the grid, in spite of the Michelin tyres not reacting well to the cold temperature at the track. Friday's grid was to become definitive on the Saturday when it began to rain – persistently – before the last qualifying session.

In the rain, the Renault appeared very slow, though Goodyear staff thought it was a calculated tactic aimed at disguising the exact performance of the Michelin tyres. Working on this idea, the American manufacturer brought out a new compound of super-wet tyre for the race, whilst the Renault was still struggling to get its Michelins up to temperature!

As the race got under way in the rain, the turbo was quickly relegated to the back of the bunch. As the rain eased, the team reasoned that, if it stopped, Jabouille could do the whole race without coming into the pits. Unfortunately, this didn't happen and Jabouille was forced to abandon the race on the 31st of 58 laps with a broken drive belt when he was in 11th position. Renault Sport had had a difficult weekend – much less promising than the earlier events – but the worst was still to come …

STARTING GRID		Results - Watkins Glen (320,665 km)			
Stuck	Hunt	1. Hunt	McLaren-Ford	59	1h58'23.267"
1'41.138"	1'40.863"				162.476 km/h
Andretti	Watson	2. Andretti	Lotus-Ford	59	+ 2.026"
1'41.481"	1'41.193"	3. Scheckter J.	Wolf-Ford	59	+ 1'18.879"
Reutemann	Peterson	4. Lauda	Ferrari	59	+ 1'40.615"
1'41.952"	1'41.908"	5. Regazzoni	Ensign-Ford	59	+ 1'48.138"
Depailler	Lauda	6. Reutemann	Ferrari	58	+ 1 lap
1'42.238"	1'42.089"	7. Laffite	Ligier-Matra	58	+ 1 lap
Laffite	Scheckter J.	8. Keegan	Hesketh-Ford	58	+ 1 lap
1'42.640"	1'42.315"	9. Jarier	Shadow-Ford	58	+ 1 lap
Nilsson	Brambilla	10. Lunger	McLaren-Ford	57	+ 2 laps
1'42.815"	1'42.786"	11. Binder	Surtees-Ford	57	+ 2 laps
Jabouille	Jones	12. Watson	Brabham-Alfa Romeo	57	+ 2 laps
1'43.069"	1'43.019"	13. Fittipaldi	Copersucar-Ford	57	+ 2 laps
Jarier	Mass	14. Depailler	Tyrrell-Ford	56	+ 3 laps
1'43.516"	1'43.242"	15. Ribeiro	March-Ford	56	+ 3 laps
Fittipaldi	Lunger	16. Peterson	Tyrrell-Ford	56	+ 3 laps
1'43.938"	1'43.698"	17. Ashley	Hesketh-Ford	55	+ 4 laps
Keegan	Regazzoni	18. Neve	March Williams-Ford	55	+ 4 laps
1'44.550"	1'44.208"	19. Brambilla	Surtees-Ford	54	+ 5 laps
Ashley	Scheckter I.				
1'45.100"	1'44.702"				
Neve	Ribeiro		**FASTEST LAP**		
1'45.845"	1'45.473"				
Ongais	Binder	Peterson	Tyrrell-Ford		1'51.854"
1'46.070"	1'45.880"				174.924 km/h
			RETIREMENTS		
		Jabouille	Renault	31	Driving belt
		Nilsson	Lotus-Ford	18	Collision Peterson
		Stuck	Brabham-Alfa Romeo	15	Accident
		Scheckter I.	March-Ford	11	Accident
		Mass	McLaren-Ford	9	Engine
		Ongais	Penske-Ford	7	Accident
		Jones	Shadow-Ford	4	Accident

Watkins Glen race statistics.

Canadian Grand Prix, Mosport, 9 October 1977

Things always look better a few days after a failure, as everyone begins to look forward to the next race; not this time, however. Disaster for Renault struck during the first practice day, the Friday. In the morning, when the V6 turbo engine was started, the drive belt providing the distributor drive jumped out of position, and Jabouille was able to do only a few laps with a faltering engine, unaware of the real cause as he drove the ailing car, hoping it might clear itself. However, it soon stopped completely, due to a holed piston caused by the misaligned ignition.

Two accidents marred the Friday session: one in which Ian Ashley, driving the Obex Oil-sponsored Hesketh, survived a monumental crash at around 170mph (273kph); the other less serious from which Jochen Mass emerged uninjured. The teams began to think that the old Mosport circuit, now perceived as dangerous, was no longer a fit place to hold a Formula 1 Grand Prix. At Renault, following the breakage and replacement of his first engine, Jean-Pierre Jabouille was able to go back out on the circuit, but in the near-Siberian cold the car was almost impossible

to drive as its Michelins refused to come up to temperature. Jabouille was forced to approach every corner slowly because of the cold tyres, and his engine was clearly losing the momentum necessary for the correct operation of the turbocharger. Renault Sport was moving inevitably towards disqualification.

Things got worse on Saturday: it was pouring with rain and Jabouille ended with a time of 1min 46.7sec. Mario Andretti achieved 1min 11.85sec, taking pole position! Jabouille didn't qualify. Renault Sport and Michelin returned from Canada with plenty to think about if they were to prepare themselves better.

"Two accidents marred the Friday session: one in which Ian Ashley, driving the Obex Oil-sponsored Hesketh, survived a monumental crash at around 170mph (273kph); the other less serious from which Jochen Mass emerged uninjured."

Gérard Larrousse and François Castaing decided to withdraw from the 17th and last Grand Prix of the 1977 season that was due to be held in Japan.

With hindsight, there were a number of things that the team might have done to ensure a better start. Tyres were certainly one of them, but, as a French team with the French public behind it, and Michelin tyres – two giants of a proud French nation – to use Goodyears would have been considered sacrilegious. With a tyre that worked well enough to get the turbo up to performance, the team might have had a better run in the American and Canadian races.

However much had been learnt, it was only the first year, the engine was new, as was the organisation and logistics of Grand Prix racing. The team would go into 1978 better prepared and with a better strategy. Many other teams, though, were racing ahead design-wise: at Tyrrell, the first signs of a new super-technology were seen in the shape of a computer-controlled active suspension; Lotus was talking a new language called 'ground-effect.'

Unfortunately, the chassis records for the first RS01 car have been lost, though records for chassis RS01/2 do exist. All of the chassis records were to stay with each chassis for its lifetime, written up by the chief mechanic, the engineer, or the driver who carried out the various tests or made adjustments to the car. In the following records – which are from the originals that first appeared in *Les Années Turbo* (in French) – can be seen some of the details

STARTING GRID	
Hunt 1'11.942"	Andretti 1'11.385"
Nilsson 1'12.975"	Peterson 1'12.752"
Depailler 1'13.207"	Mass 1'13.116"
Patrese 1'13.435"	Jones 1'13.347"
Watson 1'13.500"	Scheckter J. 1'13.497"
Reutemann 1'13.890"	Laffite 1'13.739"
Regazzoni 1'13.999"	Stuck 1'13.953"
Tambay 1'14.464"	Brambilla 1'14.222"
Scheckter I. 1'14.855"	Villeneuve 1'14.465"
Lunger 1'14.930"	Fittipaldi 1'14.857"
Ongais 1'15.599"	Neve 1'15.510"
Binder 1'16.568"	Ribeiro 1'15.770"
	Keegan 1'17.000"

RESULTS - Mosport (316,560 km)

1. Scheckter J.	Wolf-Ford	80	1h40'00.000" 187.722 km/h	
2. Depailler	Tyrrell-Ford	80	+ 6.775"	
3. Mass	McLaren-Ford	80	+ 8.989"	
4. Jones	Shadow-Ford	80	+ 30.928"	
5. Tambay	Ensign-Ford	80	+ 1'16.563"	
6. Brambilla	Surtees-Ford	78	Accident	
7. Ongais	Penske-Ford	78	+ 2 laps	
8. Ribeiro	March-Ford	78	+ 2 laps	
9. Andretti	Lotus-Ford	77	Engine	
10. Patrese	Shadow-Ford	76	Accident	
11. Lunger	McLaren-Ford	76	Engine	
12. Villeneuve	Ferrari	76	Transmission	

FASTEST LAP

Andretti	Lotus-Ford	1'13.299" 194.343 km/h

RETIREMENTS

Hunt	McLaren-Ford	62	Collision with Mass
Neve	March Williams-Ford	57	Engine
Peterson	Tyrrell-Ford	35	Fuel leak
Keegan	Hesketh-Ford	33	Collision with Binder
Binder	Surtees-Ford	32	Collision with Keegan
Fittipaldi	Copersucar-Ford	30	Engine
Scheckter I.	March-Ford	30	Engine
Reutemann	Ferrari	21	Engine
Stuck	Brabham-Alfa Romeo	20	Engine
Nilsson	Lotus-Ford	18	Accident
Laffite	Ligier-Matra	13	Transmission
Watson	Brabham-Alfa Romeo	3	Accident
Regazzoni	Ensign-Ford	1	Accident

Mosport race statistics.

Pits, testing at Paul Ricard, November 1977 (new bodywork around the cockpit, rear-view mirror now enclosed).

Jean-Pierre with Jackie Stewart.

Jackie Stewart tries the RS01.

of the tests and races, and the many changes made to the cars. We will follow these records right through the development period up to the end of the year of the first victory: at first they are fairly short, but, as we progress to the years that follow, they become quite important to this study.

10.11.77   First running of the RS01/02, with Jean-Pierre Jabouille, on the Paul Ricard 5.8km circuit. Halted at the end of 18 laps due to loss of compression on a cylinder.

05.12.77   Jabouille, on the Paul Ricard circuit (5.8km), completes 12 laps. Incidents: failure of oil pressure gauge, loss of compression on two cylinders. Best lap: 1min 49.53sec.

06.12.77   Jabouille on the Paul Ricard short circuit (3.3km). Tests with Ferrari. Jabouille does 23 laps. Best lap: 1min 11.39sec. Best lap by Carlos Reutemann in the Ferrari: 1min 11.88sec.

07.12.77   Jabouille, again on the 5.8km circuit. Halted after 18 laps, complete engine failure. Best lap: 1min 49.5sec. In his Ferrari, Gilles Villeneuve's best lap is 1min 49sec. New engine fitted at 3pm. Jabouille does 6 laps and then hands the car to Jackie Stewart who is to test it for a series of articles and for television. Stewart's best lap: 1min 56.1sec. Going round at the same time as Stewart in his Ferrari 312 T3, Reutemann's best lap is 1min 48.9sec.

At 4pm, back on the 3.3km circuit, Stewart does 28 laps, the best of which is timed at 1min 11.12sec.

Re-confirming his thoughts written many years ago, Sir Jackie Stewart says, "I remember that from the beginning of my test I could feel the car was a bit like a dancer, a prima donna. It was a bit difficult to start from the grid due to the delay in the accelerator. Once out on the circuit, the huge push of the turbocharger was immediately very powerful. When the engine came on song and the turbo reached its boost pressure, the combination really worked. It gave a great sensation of abundant horsepower, much more than that of the 3-litre Ford-Cosworth V8. However, the response of the accelerator needed to be improved – I could see I was going to have problems getting used to the delay. It would be difficult to run in a Grand Prix. If I wanted to take advantage of the errors of other drivers it was impossible to seize a chance based on reaction in fractions of a second because of the delay in the response of the throttle.

"The car was designed around Jean-Pierre and it would be difficult for any driver other than him to feel comfortable in the car. In F1 it's important to be able to adjust the steering and

Stewart on the Paul Ricard short circuit. (Jean Sage Archives)

Jackie Stewart during the test. (Jean Sage Archives)

things such as the seat position, since all drivers change their driving position for different circumstances, sometimes in minute details, according to the comfort and variation in speed at certain circuits. But such things were understandable at that stage in the development programme.

"It was also interesting to see the Renault team, comparatively new in F1, up against old soldiers such as the Ferrari stable, who were testing at Paul Ricard at the same time. Their car arrived full of adjustable options in all parts of the vehicle; very impressive. Jean-Pierre took the car out for a few laps with the new turbo before returning to the pits to hand over to me. I went out very briefly before returning for minor adjustments to the seating position. I started out again on the small circuit. The engine was extremely powerful when the turbo cut in and the rise in revs was so fast that I found myself constantly changing gear. I felt as if I was continually trying to run according to the demands of the engine. The Renault had abundant torque, with an exact, pleasant development throughout its peak performance, but the spectrum or usable range of revs was small. On that short circuit I had to use all six gears, while the Ferrari drivers, testing at the same time, used only four. Watching Jean-Pierre driving earlier that day, it seemed as if the engine swallowed a big gulp of air each time he changed gear, like a man who has been running too fast and has trouble breathing in.

"I tried to line up the car to take the radius of a corner and then applied the power afterwards, but nothing happened. No power arrived until I had exited the corner! The basic behaviour of the car was truly exciting, but if I must criticise I would say that it was inclined to be unstable at high speed, which I believe was due to the front aerodynamics. The car generally tended to be very nervous; it seemed to be running on the edge of its tyres round the fast 5th gear turn at the end of the straight. The Michelin tyres had a very level, flat profile with angular grooves. It felt as if I was driving on the edge of the tread, which wasn't very encouraging, and they seemed to lose efficiency slightly after a few laps. The first two fast laps were fairly good, but then the car lost a bit of traction. In general, though, I thought the car and its tyres performed well.

"I never really felt as if I had reached the limit of adherence, and it's true to say it did feel as if it was stuck to the ground. It also seemed to transfer the power to the track very efficiently. On the occasions when I got my timing right I discovered that I could drive it almost in the same way as I had the McLaren M26, and that says a lot about the car. By the end of the afternoon I had been driving the car for 30 laps and was just beginning to feel that I was getting to know it. Despite the inherent problems of the turbo, I also did a lap in 1min 11.1sec, only 2/10ths slower than the best lap recorded by Carlos Reutemann in the Ferrari. I was surprised by my time, considering the inability of the turbo to do what I thought it should in various areas of the circuit. This means that the chassis must have been very good and that this engine 'gets up and goes' when everything is working together. The Renault team was extremely considerate and co-operative, and I would really have liked to drive a few more laps in that car.

The old A500 at the exhibition.

"The V6's power was impressive – exciting, even – but the best way I can describe the sensation of driving the turbo would be by comparing it to riding blindfolded on the pillion of a motorcycle. You would be trying to hold on to the driver without knowing when the 'horseman' was going to brake, accelerate, turn left or right. In truth, I found the experience a little confusing. However, this technology will undoubtedly have an important role in the normal production of cars in the future. Renault is to be applauded for its enterprise and courage."

Profound words, indeed, as if he was seeing into the future, as the R5 Turbo had not turned a wheel at that time and was a complete secret.

17.12.77   More tests at Paul Ricard (3.3km circuit) with Jabouille. Best lap 1min 9.87sec, compared with Niki Lauda (1min 11.2sec in a Brabham-Alfa Romeo), and Alan Jones (1min 12.14sec in a Williams-Ford). Mid-afternoon, Jabouille's tests are halted by engine failure.

18.12.77   The engine was changed during the previous evening and the tests continue. Jabouille's best lap is timed at 1min 9.34sec, in spite of some poor laps at low speed, and this must be compared with Lauda's performance (1min 8.94sec) and Jones' (1min 10.94sec).

Renault Sport finished 1977 with an exhibition in December celebrating Renault's 80 years in the sport.

The 1978 season began on 15 January in Buenos Aires with the Argentine Grand Prix, but Renault Sport had chosen not to take part in that year's South American campaign, which also included the Brazilian Grand Prix in Rio de Janeiro on 29 January. Larrousse planned to return to the championship at the South African Grand Prix on 4 March 1978. Two years previously he had suggested, in response to Bernard Hanon's question, that they might be able to win a Grand Prix at a high-altitude circuit, and Kyalami in South Africa was just the circuit he had in mind. Situated some twenty kilometres north-east of Johannesburg, it is around 1800m (5905ft) above sea level, and the world of F1 knew by then that, in principle, the altitude was less of a handicap for boosted engines than for normally-aspirated ones.

Before we look at the Grand Prix, it's worth considering the problem of racing at high altitude tracks where there is a variation in atmospheric pressure compared with sea level.

Bernard Dudot: "Atmospheric pressure is a function of altitude 'z' and follows this law:

$$p = po \; \frac{(288 - 0.0065z)^{5.255}}{288}$$

In the case of Kyalami, at 1800 metres altitude, the atmospheric pressure is only:

$$p = 1 \times \frac{(288 - 0.0065 \times 1800)^{5.255}}{288} = 0.804 \text{ atmosphere}$$

which gives a density of:
$$\varrho z = 0.838 \; \varrho o$$

From this we can see that the power of an atmospheric engine with 510bhp at sea level will not be more than 427bhp:

$$P = 510 \times 0.838 = 427\text{bhp}$$

"So, at Kyalami the loss of power is 83bhp, which is considerable. This situation is worse in Mexico, at some 2200m (7218ft), where the same atmospheric engine will have no more than 390bhp at its disposal.

"The turbocharged engine can compensate for this loss because of the possibility of re-establishing the same atmospheric pressure experienced at sea level by making the turbocharger blow harder. However, this adjustment does not come without problems, as the compressor must work harder, and the higher the boost pressure, the higher the temperature at the air outlet. The reduction in air density at altitude also has the effect of reducing the capacity of the cooling heat exchangers, since the mass flow of cooling air is reduced. If the air temperature at the engine inlet at sea level is 56°C, it will be 65°C at the altitude of Kyalami for equivalent power conditions. This 9° of difference has a considerable effect on engine performance and, in particular, on pick-up. Moreover, with the engine cycle being hotter, the dreaded pinking conditions are closer, whose destructive effects on this type of engine are well known.

> **"... Kyalami in South Africa ... some twenty kilometres north-east of Johannesburg, it is around 1800m (5905ft) above sea level, and the world of F1 knew by then that, in principle, the altitude was less of a handicap for boosted engines than for normally-aspirated ones."**

"At the time, technology of materials and electronics was not as highly developed as it is today, and the location and arrangement of the turbocharger were important. The engine mechanic had to review his turbocharger arrangement and compressor trim if he wished to maintain the same power level at high altitude as at sea level; he had to check that the new compression ratio chosen for an identical mass throughput didn't work the compressor into a catastrophic situation, which would result not only in excessively high inlet temperatures, but also greatly increased pressure at the turbine inlet, prejudicial

Note the turbo air intake snorkel on the left of the picture, last used on the A500.

to the thermal effects on the engine by a reduction in cooling that is naturally effected by the overlap scavenging of the fuel air mix in the chamber. Generally, one tries to choose a compressor with a weaker trim but a definitive choice could only be decided through testing."

Bernard continues: "For the turbine, because the relaxation rate is higher at altitude due to the bias of the reduction in atmospheric pressure, the throughput of exhaust gas being assumed to be the same since the power is the same, the efficiency will be greater. Under these conditions one can try to reduce the A/R of the turbine housing. Here again, only testing can decide, as it is a matter of compromise between the quality of the pick-up, the response time, and the available power at high speed. This last aspect must be taken seriously into account, as both Kyalami and Mexico circuits have a long straight where power comes to the fore and passing is possible."

Jean-Pierre Boudy: "Also then, we did not have modern electronic injection systems which, later, were sufficiently sophisticated to take into account the absolute value of the inlet pressure and deliver a correct mixture at all speeds and under any conditions."

So now let's look at the race.

Citizen Grand Prix of South Africa, Kyalami, 4 March 1978

After the early failures of that first year when the car didn't qualify for the Canadian Grand Prix at Mosport – as well as the withdrawal from Japan and missing out Buenos Aires and Rio at the start of this year – the entire team was now itching to get started, highly motivated to prove its worth after a winter of hard work and testing.

This motivation intensified when, during the preliminary practice at Kyalami before the Grand Prix, Jabouille recorded the third fastest time of 1min 15.9sec, behind Hunt in his McLaren and Reutemann in a Ferrari. Not only that but he completed 89 laps of the circuit without a problem. Was it a good omen?

Jean-Pierre Jabouille had arrived with the RS01, chassis 02, which had received a more streamlined package with improved aerodynamics. However, during the first day of official practice, he was to fall victim to some of the old engine response time problems; then, once that was sorted out during the second day, he experienced persistent understeer, the cause of which was eventually discovered whilst the car was being checked over between qualifying and the race: it seems a small bracket supporting the front bodywork had twisted while the car was being lifted, causing the nose to be displaced by a tiny amount.

Nevertheless, the car was on the third row of the grid behind Lauda (Brabham-Alfa Romeo), Andretti (Lotus-Ford), and the two McLaren-Fords of Hunt and Tambay. Jabouille's time: 1min 15.36sec; Lauda's: 1min 14.65sec.

> ## "... during the preliminary practice at Kyalami before the Grand Prix, Jabouille recorded the third fastest time of 1min 15.9sec, behind Hunt in his McLaren and Reutemann in a Ferrari."

Once the reason for the problem with the front body was established, the mechanics quickly rectified the situation. In the race day warm-up everything was back in order, and Jabouille recorded the 2nd fastest time behind the unexpectedly quick Arrows-Ford of Patrese. All was looking good; was Larrousse about to be proved right? Sadly, it was not to be. Running in 7th place for quite a while, Jabouille gradually lost ground, retiring on the 38th lap with what was later found to be a vapour-lock.

The Renault Sport team was annoyed, but this time not so much because of the engine but the lack of mechanical grip: the

Amédée Gordini visiting Kyalami.

Michelin tyres were actually found to be picking up the scuffed-off rubber left on the track by the Goodyears! This problem was confirmed by Villeneuve and Reutemann, whose Ferraris, now also Michelin-shod, had both experienced the same problem. All that was left to do was to pack up and head for the USA.

US West Coast Grand Prix, Long Beach, 2 April 1978

Fine, sunny weather greeted the teams at Long Beach, California, but this didn't prevent Renault Sport from experiencing problems. The first day of practice was catastrophic: gearbox ratios were found to be too high, but it was impossible to change them because Renault was using the only ones available to it at the time. Pick-up at low speed was, of course, very difficult.

Despite this ratio problem, between the Friday and Saturday practice sessions the engineers concentrated their talents on trying to improve the smoothness of the engine. They succeeded and Jabouille moved up the grid. But in the first qualifying session on the Friday, Jabouille had recorded only 25th fastest time; more work brought him up to 13th.

Fortunately, on the Saturday the times began to tumble and, at the end of the last hour of qualifying, Jabouille was down to 1min 22.49sec and 7th row of the grid.

STARTING GRID	
Andretti 1'14.90"	Lauda 1'14.65"
Tambay 1'15.30"	Hunt 1'15.14"
Jabouille 1'15.36"	Scheckter 1'15.32"
Villeneuve 1'15.50"	Patrese 1'15.48"
Watson 1'15.62"	Reutemann 1'15.52"
Peterson 1'15.94"	Depailler 1'15.97"
Pironi 1'16.38"	Laffite 1'16.40"
Fittipaldi 1'16.47"	Mass 1'16.60"
Jones 1'17.16"	Jarier 1'17.12"
Lunger 1'17.30"	Brambilla 1'17.32"
Stommelen 1'17.49"	Rebaque 1'17.50"
Rosberg 1'17.62"	Keegan 1'17.57"
Merzario 1'18.15"	Cheever 1'17.83"

RESULTS

1. Peterson	Lotus-Ford	78	1h42'15.767"
2. Depailler	Tyrrell-Ford	78	1h42'16.233"
3. Watson	Brabham-Alfa Romeo	78	1h42'20.209"
4. Jones	Williams-Ford	78	1h42'54.753"
5. Laffite	Ligier-Matra	78	1h43'24.985"
6. Pironi	Tyrrell-Ford	77	+ 1 lap
7. Andretti	Lotus-Ford	77	+ 1 lap
8. Jarier	ATS-Ford	77	+ 1 lap
9. Stommelen	Arrows-Ford	77	+ 1 lap
10. Rebaque	Lotus-Ford	77	+ 1 lap
11. Lunger	McLaren-Ford	76	+ 2 laps
12. Brambilla	Surtees-Ford	76	+ 2 laps

FASTEST LAP

Andretti	Lotus-Ford	1'17.09" 191.649 km/h

RETIREMENTS

Patrese	Arrows-Ford	63	Engine
Scheckter	Wolf-Ford	59	Engine problems…
Tambay	McLaren-Ford	56	Accident
Reutemann	Ferrari	55	Accident
Villeneuve	Ferrari	55	Oil leak
Keegan	Surtees-Ford	52	Oil leak
Lauda	Brabham-Alfa Romeo	52	Engine
Mass	ATS-Ford	43	Engine
Merzario	Merzario-Ford	39	Rear suspension failure
Jabouille	Renault	38	Engine
Rosberg	Theodore-Ford	14	Clutch / engine Fuel leak
Fittipaldi	Copersucar-Ford	8	Half shaft
Cheever	Theodore-Ford	8	Oil leak
Hunt	McLaren-Ford	5	Engine

Snorkel air-box is bottom left of photo.

Kyalami race statistics.

STARTING GRID		RESULTS - Long Beach (261,625 km)			
Villeneuve 1'20.836"	Reutemann 1'20.636"	1. Reutemann	Ferrari	80	1h52'01.301"
Andretti 1'21.188'	Lauda 1'20.937"	2. Andretti	Lotus-Ford	80	1h52'12.362"
Peterson 1'21.474"	Watson 1'21.244"	3. Depailler	Tyrrell-Ford	80	1h52'30.252"
Jones 1'21.935"	Hunt 1'21.738"	4. Peterson	Lotus-Ford	80	1h52'46.904"
Schekter 1'22.163"	Patrese 1'22.006"	5. Laffite	Ligier-Matra	80	1h53'24.185"
Depailler 1'22.414"	Tambay 1'22.234"	6. Patrese	Arrows-Ford	79	1h52'21.327"
Laffite 1'22.630"	Jabouille 1'22.491"	7. Jones	Williams-Ford	79	1h53'02.221"
Mass 1'23.106"	Fittipaldi 1'22.790"	8. Fittipaldi	Copersucar-Ford	79	1h53'06.821"
Stommelen 1'23.291"	Brambilla 1'23.212"	9. Stommelen	Arrows-Ford	79	1h53'08.585"
Regazzoni 1'23.454"	Jarier 1'23.419"	10. Regazzoni	Shadow-Ford	79	1h53'10.681"
Pironi 1'23.792"	Merzario 1'23.589"	11. Jarier	ATS-Ford	75	1h52'50.193"
		12. Tambay	McLaren-Ford	74	Collision with Laffite

FASTEST LAP		
Jones	Williams-Ford	1'22.215" 142.215 km/h

RETIREMENTS			
Scheckter	Wolf-Ford	59	Collision Tambay
Brambilla	Surtees-Ford	50	Mechanical
Jabouille	Renault	43	Supercharger
Villeneuve	Ferrari	38	Collision Regazzoni
Lauda	Brabham-Alfa Romeo	27	Ignition
Pironi	Tyrrell-Ford	25	Gearbox
Merzario	Merzario-Ford	17	Gearbox
Mass	ATS-Ford	11	Brakes
Watson	Brabham-Alfa Romeo	9	Oil tank failure
Hunt	McLaren-Ford	5	Accident suspension failure

Long Beach race statistics.

Monaco, Jabouille — no snorkel here; practice with the raised platform rear bodywork.

Note front wing extensions.

But it was a worrying start, as the car was known to be heavier in relation to the other cars, and the turbo engine wasn't taking kindly to all of the breaks in rhythm on a circuit which contained many twisting corners. The starting grid was away from the pits at the other end of the circuit on Shoreline Drive, so the Grand Prix actually comprised 80½ laps. Jabouille lost two places on the first lap but gradually crept back; he was running in 10th position when a broken turbo caused an oil leak which produced a spectacular fire and inevitable retirement on lap 43.

His comments were: "Difficult beginning to the race with a full tank, but, as it became lighter, the chassis gradually responded much better." It was, in fact, the first time the car had passed the halfway point in a Grand Prix. Maybe Europe would bring better luck ...

Monaco Grand Prix, 7 May 1978

After the trip to the USA the Viry-Châtillon team carried out several modifications to try and improve throttle response, and a test was conducted at the CEV airfield in Brétigny, where a fairly tight circuit was laid out to evaluate the response of the engine and other faults that had materialised at Long Beach.

The first test session at Monaco proved tiresome for Jabouille, as the car was difficult to control, the engine power still arriving too suddenly. Because of this, he couldn't avoid a few close shaves with barriers, though, fortunately, not serious ones. He wasn't confident that he could make full race distance under these conditions.

Jabouille on his way to the team's first race distance finish, 10th place. Note that front wing extensions were not used in the race.

Practice with front wing extensions in place.

Action in the pits. (Jean Sage Archives)

So, it was first time at Monaco for Renault, almost a home Grand Prix, the Principality being on the French mainland. Jabouille was on the 6th row of the grid (12th place), between the McLaren-Ford of Tambay and the Tyrrell-Ford of Pironi. After a laborious start which cost him two places, he gradually moved up: 13th on the 5th lap, 12th on the 15th lap, 11th on the 30th lap, and after a brief stop to attend to a braking problem on the 69th lap, he eventually gave the team its first finish, albeit in 10th position and 4 laps behind the winner, fellow countryman, Patrick Depailler, in a Tyrrell-Ford! It had been physically challenging

103

STARTING GRID		RESULTS - Monaco (248,400 km)			
Watson 1'28.83"	Reutemann 1'28.34"	1. Depailler	Tyrrell-Ford	75	1h55'14.66"
Andretti 1'29.10"	Lauda 1'28.84"	2. Lauda	Brabham-Alfa Romeo	75	1h55'37.11"
Hunt 1'29.22"	Depailler 1'29.14"	3. Scheckter	Wolf-Ford	75	1h55'46.95"
Villeneuve 1'29.40"	Peterson 1'29.23"	4. Watson	Brabham-Alfa Romeo	75	1h55'48.19"
Jones 1'29.51"	Scheckter 1'29.50"	5. Pironi	Tyrrell-Ford	75	1h56'22.72"
Jabouille 1'30.18"	Tambay 1'30.08"	6. Patrese	Arrows-Ford	75	1h56'23.43"
Patrese 1'30.59"	Pironi 1'30.55"	7. Tambay	McLaren-Ford	74	+ 1 lap
Ickx 1'30.72"	Laffite 1'30.60"	8. Reutemann	Ferrari	74	+ 1 lap
Keegan 1'31.31"	Stuck 1'31.30"	9. Fittipaldi	Copersucar-Ford	74	+ 1 lap
Fittipaldi 1'31.36"	Stommelen 1'31.31"	10. Jabouille	Renault	71	+ 4 laps
		11. Andretti	Lotus-Ford	69	+ 6 laps

FASTEST LAP

Lauda	Brabham-Alfa Romeo	1'28.65" 134.649 km/h

RETIREMENTS

Villeneuve	Ferrari	62	Accident
Peterson	Lotus-Ford	56	Gearbox
Hunt	McLaren-Ford	43	Road-holding
Stommelen	Arrows-Ford	38	
Jones	Williams-Ford	29	Driver ill
Ickx	Ensign-Ford	27	Oil leak
Stuck	Shadow-Ford	24	Brakes
			Steering (collision with Keegan)
Lafitte	Ligier-Matra	13	Gearbox
Keegan	Surtees-Ford	8	Engine

Monaco race statistics.

Extended front wings in use again.

for Jean-Pierre, who had even considered retiring around the 15th lap. He had also to overcome another problem apart from turbo lag: his Michelins were failing fast at the end of the race. However, the car had passed the chequered flag, and at Monaco into the bargain. The team was in good spirits.

It was to the Monaco GP that Bernie Ecclestone had asked the new teams not to take motorhomes, so Renault Sport's engineers had stayed back at Viry-Châtillon and Jean Sage had quickly rented a boat in the luxurious harbour for the race team. It goes without saying, of course, that all of the big teams had been allowed to take *their* motorhomes!

Belgian Grand Prix, Zolder, 21 May 1978

Things didn't start off too well for the team when news came through of a delay on the way to the Belgium GP. The Viry-Châtillon race transporter had been stopped by a mobile Customs and Excise team near Valenciennes. The truck had to be completely emptied and the Customs officials slowly made a detailed list of everything on board: cars, parts, engines, tools, etc. The transporter drivers – Francis Breton and Maurice Brosse (both of them excellent mechanics) – were very dejected. Fortunately, nothing was found to be out of order and they were allowed to go on their way.

Before leaving for Zolder, the Renault team had done some private testing at the Folembray circuit, and prior to that there had been preliminary testing at Zolder, though it is recorded that it rained most of the time.

At the Grand Prix on the first day of official practice, Jabouille was back driving the RS01, chassis 02; it was his favourite car, as he thought it ran better than the others. But after three-quarters of an hour on a dry track, the engine seized and he had to climb into chassis 03. Then its engine began to progressively lose power due to a faulty turbo. After modification he went out in the final hour of qualifying on the Saturday, eventually starting from 10th place on the grid.

On race day Jabouille got off the line very well and moved up three places during the 1st lap. However, finding himself at the head of his quicker rivals, he realised that, effectively, he was holding them up, just as he was being held up himself because of the engine response time – still the bane of his life. Eventually, the cars behind got past him and he began falling back, finding himself in 14th position by lap 10. When he stopped for the first time on the 16th lap because of a brake problem, a little queue of the slower – but by now disgruntled – drivers was lined up behind him. He had to stop twice more with the same problem. Despite the lag on the engine, without the brake problem

STARTING GRID		RESULTS - Zolder (298,340 km)			
Andretti 1'20.90"	Reutemann 1'21.69"	1. Andretti	Lotus-Ford	70	1h39'52.02"
Lauda 1'21.70"	Villeneuve 1'21.77"	2. Peterson	Lotus-Ford	70	1h40'01.92"
Schekter 1'22.12"	Hunt 1'22.50"	3. Reutemann	Ferrari	70	1h40'16.36"
Peterson 1'22.62"	Patrese 1'23.25"	4. Villeneuve	Ferrari	70	1h40'39.06"
Watson 1'23.26"	Jabouille 1'23.58"	5. Laffite	Ligier-Matra	69	Collision with Reutemann
Jones 1'23.71"	Brambilla 1'23.78"	6. Pironi	Tyrrell-Ford	69	+ 1 lap
Depailler 1'23.82"	Laffite 1'23.90"	7. Lunger	McLaren-Ford	69	+ 1 lap
Fittipaldi 1'24.11"	Mass 1'24.14"	8. Giacomelli	McLaren-Ford	69	+ 1 lap
Stommelen 1'24.14"	Regazzoni 1'24.18"	9. Arnoux	Martini-Ford	68	+ 2 laps
Arnoux 1'24.22"	Stuck 1'24.47"	10. Jones	Williams-Ford	68	+ 2 laps
Giacomelli 1'24.81"	Ickx 1'24.82"	11. Mass	ATS-Ford	68	+ 2 laps
Pironi 1'24.85"	Lunger 1'24.99"	12. Ickx	Ensign-Ford	64	+ 6 laps
		13. Brambilla	Surtees-Ford	63	Engine

NOT CLASSIFIED

Jabouille	Renault	56	+ 14 laps

FASTEST LAP

Peterson	Lotus-Ford	1'23.13"

RETIREMENTS

Stuck	Shadow-Ford	56	Spun off
Scheckter	Wolf-Ford	53	Accident
Depailler	Tyrrell-Ford	51	Gearbox
Regazzoni	Shadow-Ford	40	Differential
Patrese	Arrows-Ford	31	Rear suspension failure
Stommelen	Arrows-Ford	26	Acident
Watson	Brabham-Alfa Romeo	18	Chassis / engine
Fittipaldi	Copersucar-Ford	1	Collision with Ickx
Hunt	McLaren-Ford	1	Collision with Patrese
Lauda	Brabham-Alfa Romeo	1	Collision with Scheckter

Zolder race statistics.

Jabouille waits.

Jabouille could have hoped to finish because the engine was actually now working perfectly. He did actually finish but too far behind to be classified.

It is worth noting here a prophetic comment made by German driver Rolf Stommelen to Jean Sage, who was standing with François Guiter: "Why doesn't Renault use a twin turbo? It would considerably improve the response time."

Spanish Grand Prix, Jarama, 4 June 1978
A few days before the Grand Prix, Renault Sport decided to carry out private testing on the Jarama circuit. Jabouille was again at the wheel, accompanied on track by René Arnoux in a Martini-Ford and Hector Rebaque in a Lotus-Ford.

The three went on to the first official practice with Jean-Pierre having to deal with constant oversteer. Luckily, he found a way to resolve the problem during the Friday qualifying session and the Renault achieved its best time of the weekend, though nothing too startling as he was to begin from 11th place on the grid. Disaster struck immediately after the start of the race: in turn 2, Depailler's Tyrrell and the Renault collided; Jabouille spun, but recovered to be last of the 24 starters at the end of the 1st lap.

Large crowd in Spain.

STARTING GRID		RESULTS - Jarama (255,300 km)			
Peterson 1'16.68"	Andretti 1'16.39"	1. Andretti	Lotus-Ford	75	1h41'47.06"
Hunt 1'17.66"	Reutemann 1'17.40"	2. Peterson	Lotus-Ford	75	1h42'06.62"
Lauda 1'17.94"	Villeneuve 1'17.76"	3. Laffite	Ligier-Matra	75	1h42'24.30"
Patrese 1'18.14"	Watson 1'17.98"	4. Scheckter	Wolf-Ford	75	1h42'47.12"
Laffite 1'18.42"	Scheckter 1'18.24"	5. Watson Brabham-Alfa Romeo		75	1h42'52.98"
Depailler 1'19.06"	Jabouille 1'18.99"	6. Hunt	McLaren-Ford	74	+ 1 lap
Tambay 1'19.28"	Pironi 1'19.11"	7. Brambilla	Surtees-Ford	74	+ 1 lap
Brambilla 1'19.71"	Fittipaldi 1'19.33"	8. Jones	Williams-Ford	74	+ 1 lap
Jones 1'19.99"	Mass 1'19.98"	9. Mass	ATS-Ford	74	+ 1 lap
Rebaque 1'20.21"	Stommelen 1'20.03"	10. Villeneuve	Ferrari	74	+ 1 lap
Regazzoni 1'20.67"	Ickx 1'20.36"	11. Keegan	Surtees-Ford	73	+ 2 laps
Stuck 1'20.87"	Keegan 1'20.77"	12. Pironi	Tyrrell-Ford	71	+ 4 laps
		13. Jabouille	Renault	71	+ 4 laps
		14. Stommelen	Arrows-Ford	71	+ 4 laps
		15. Regazzoni	Shadow-Ford	67	Fuel pipe

FASTEST LAP

Andretti	Lotus-Ford	1'20.06"
		153.065 km/h

RETIREMENTS

Ickx	Ensign-Ford	64	Engine
Fittipaldi	Copersucar-Ford	62	Throttle control
Reutemann	Ferrari	57	Accident, 1/2 Transmission shaft
Lauda	Brabham-Alfa Romeo	56	Engine
Depailler	Tyrrell-Ford	51	Engine
Stuck	Shadow-Ford	45	Rear suspension failure
Rebaque	Lotus-Ford	21	Exhaust failure
Patrese	Arrows-Ford	21	Engine
Tambay	McLaren-Ford	16	Spun off, clutch failure

Jarama race statistics.

He set about climbing back up, but had to stop on the 58th lap to have his engine checked. Re-entering the race, he finally crossed the finishing line in 13th place, some four laps behind the winner, Mario Andretti, in a Lotus-Ford 79.

Once again the Renault had made it to the finish, but it still wasn't consistently quick enough, leaving Jean-Pierre frustrated that he couldn't put in a better performance.

Swedish Grand Prix, Anderstorp, 17 June 1978

Everyone was in good spirits: at last, Renault was at a high point. The Alpine A442, powered by the turbocharged 2-litre version of the engine, had won the Le Mans 24 Hours the previous weekend; the entire Viry team was in happy mood, as was Renault senior management.

From that day on Renault Sport had only one mission: to win in Formula 1. The potential of the engine and the team was proven: it could be done. This decision was not one the Automobile Club de l'Ouest (ACO) in Le Mans wanted to hear, as it was hoping for Renault to return in 1979. It was not to be: Bernard Hanon had made his decision and F1 was calling. From now on the big effort was to be in that direction.

The day after Le Mans, the full engineering team – which had been called to assist at Le Mans – had to hurry to

Le Mans 1978 winners, Pironi and Jaussaud.

Brabham BT46 fan car on secret testing at Brands Hatch before the Swedish Grand Prix. (© Maureen Magee)

STARTING GRID			RESULTS - Anderstorp (282,170 km)			
Watson	Andretti	1. Lauda	Brabham-Alfa Romeo	70	1h41'00.606"	
1'22.737"	1'22.058"	2. Patrese	Arrows-Ford	70	1h41'36.625"	
Peterson	Lauda	3. Peterson	Lotus-Ford	70	1h41'34.711"	
1'23.120"	1'22.783"	4. Tambay	McLaren-Ford	69	1h41'31.221"	
Scheckter	Patrese	5. Regazzoni	Shadow-Ford	69	1h41'32.070"	
1'23.621"	1'23.369"	6. Fittipaldi	Copersucar-Ford	69	1h41'32.711"	
Reutemann	Villeneuve	7. Laffite	Ligier-Matra	69	+ 1 lap	
1'23.737"	1'23.730"	8. Hunt	McLaren-Ford	69	+ 1 lap	
Jabouille	Jones	9. Villeneuve	Ferrari	69	+ 1 lap	
1'23.963"	1'23.951"	10. Reutemann	Ferrari	69	+ 1 lap	
Depailler	Laffite	11. Stuck	Shadow-Ford	68	+ 2 laps	
1'24.203"	1'24.030"	12. Rebaque	Lotus-Ford	68	+ 2 laps	
Hunt	Fittipaldi	13. Mass	ATS-Ford	68	+ 2 laps	
1'24.761"	1'24.274"	14. Stommelen	Arrows-Ford	67	+ 3 laps	
Regazzoni	Tambay	15. Rosberg	ATS-Ford	63	+ 7 laps	
1'25.007"	1'24.986"					
Brambilla	Pironi	**FASTEST LAP**				
1'26.618"	1'25.813"					
Stuck	Mass	Lauda	Brabham-Alfa Romeo		1'24.836"	
1'27.011"	1'26.787"				171.100 km/h	
Merzario	Rebaque					
1'27.479"	1'27.139"	**NOT CLASSIFIED**				
Stommelen	Rosberg					
1'27.812"	1'27.560"	Merzario	Merzario-Ford	62	+ 8 laps	

RETIREMENTS

Andretti	Lotus-Ford	46	Engine
Jones	Williams-Ford	46	Rolling bearing
Depailler	Tyrrell-Ford	42	Rear brakes
Jabouille	Renault	28	Engine
Watson	Brabham-Alfa Romeo	19	Spin... Throttle blocked
Scheckter	Wolf-Ford	16	Overheating Water jacket failure
Pironi	Tyrrell-Ford	8	Collision Brambilla
Brambilla	Surtees-Ford	7	Collision with Pironi

Anderstorp race statistics.

Anderstorp in Sweden for private tests organised by Michelin. The week before, during Goodyear tests, Ronnie Peterson and his Lotus-Ford had thrown down the gauntlet with a time of 1min 22.3sec. However, to everyone's surprise, Jabouille came up immediately with a lap of 1min 23sec: the Renault may have been heavy but it had a lot of power. In the end, after the two tyre-testing sessions, Jabouille's times showed he was in front of Villeneuve, Reutemann, and Lauda. Contrary to the fears of the Renault-Elf team, the RS01 was happy on the long bends of the Anderstorp circuit, and for once Jean-Pierre Jabouille said he was only bothered by turbo lag in one corner. He confirmed that the tyre-testing performance was no fluke during the first official day of practice, taking 5th fastest time. The second day didn't go so well, though, when a valve spring broke on the RS01/02, then an electrical breakdown hit RS01/03 and Jabouille came to a standstill on the track. After recovering the car he went out again, but there was no improvement and he slipped five places on the grid. There was one positive point: the tests with 14-inch

diameter front wheels (formerly 13) had proved that the Michelin tyres were standing up well in large format.

Come the race, Jabouille started well. He moved from 11th to 7th place, but on lap 29 the engine began to falter – faulty oil pressure was indicated; something had failed. He was out. This race went down in F1 history because of Niki Lauda's victory in the Brabham-Alfa Romeo BT46B. Known as the 'vacuum cleaner,' it was a fan-suction car designed to suck the chassis down onto the ground. It was the only time this ingenious car was seen in action in a Grand Prix; the day after the race, it was outlawed by the international sporting authority.

However, another new development was on the horizon. Lotus was rumoured to have something special; things were about to change, those words 'ground effect' were creeping into the racing vocabulary.

French Grand Prix, Paul Ricard, 2 July 1978

Renault F1 arrived at the Paul Ricard circuit with new bodywork developed in the S4 wind tunnel for better aerodynamic efficiency. It was the new RS01/03. Was the team ready?

STARTING GRID			RESULTS - Le Castellet (313,740 km)			
Watson	Andretti	1. Andretti	Lotus-Ford	54	1h38'51.92"	
1'44.41"	1'44.46"	2. Peterson	Lotus-Ford	54	1h38'54.85"	
Lauda	Hunt	3. Hunt	McLaren-Ford	54	1h39'11.72"	
1'44.71"	1'44.92"	4. Watson	Brabham-Alfa Romeo	54	1h39'28.80"	
Peterson	Tambay	5. Jones	Williams-Ford	54	1h39'33.73"	
1'44.98"	1'45.07"	6. Scheckter	Wolf-Ford	54	1h39'46.45"	
Scheckter	Reutemann	7. Laffite	Ligier-Matra	54	1h39'46.66"	
1'45.20"	1'45.35"	8. Patrese	Arrows-Ford	54	1h40'16.80"	
Villeneuve	Laffite	9. Tambay	McLaren-Ford	54	1h40'18.98"	
1'45.55"	1'45.68"	10. Pironi	Tyrrell-Ford	54	1h40'21.90"	
Jabouille	Patrese	11. Stuck	Shadow-Ford	53	+ 1 lap	
1'45.73"	1'46.32"	12. Villeneuve	Ferrari	53	+ 1 lap	
Depailler	Jones	13. Mass	ATS-Ford	53	+ 1 lap	
1'46.37"	1'46.40"	14. Arnoux	Martini-Ford	53	+ 1 lap	
Fittipaldi	Pironi	15. Stommelen	Arrows-Ford	53	+ 1 lap	
1'46.70"	1'47.12"	16. Rosberg	ATS-Ford	52	+ 2 laps	
Regazzoni	Arnoux	17. Brambilla	Surtees-Ford	52	+ 2 laps	
1'48.55"	1'48.68"	18. Reutemann	Ferrari	49	+ 5 laps	
Brambilla	Stuck					
1'48.68"	1'48.89"	**FASTEST LAP**				
Stommelen	Giacomelli					
1'49.14"	1'49.53"	Reutemann	Ferrari		1'48.56"	
Keegan	Lunger				192.597 km/h	
1'49.54"	1'49.55"					
Mass	Rosberg					
1'49.90"	1'50.09"	**RETIREMENTS**				

Lunger	McLaren-Ford	45	Engine
Fittipaldi	Copersucar-Ford	43	Suspension AR
Keegan	Surtees-Ford	40	Engine
Giacomelli	McLaren-Ford	28	Engine
Depailler	Tyrrell-Ford	10	Engine
Lauda	Brabham-Alfa Romeo	10	Engine
Regazzoni	Shadow-Ford	4	Electrical
Jabouille	Renault	1	Engine

Le Castellet (Paul Ricard) race statistics.

Raised side-pod rear bodywork under trial again (it wasn't used in the race).

Druids corner, Brands Hatch.

The French Grand Prix on home ground, always an important race, looked promising. After twenty minutes of qualifying on the Friday, Jabouille had 3rd fastest time. But then, disaster! At that moment the engine failed, he had to fall back on the RS01/02 with conventional bodywork and was unable to improve his performance. His final time on the Friday was 1min 45.73sec, only good enough for 11th position on the grid. More engine problems on the Saturday meant he was unable to improve his position then, either. It was not looking good and worse was still to come. During the warm-up lap the engine was becoming weaker, and on the starting grid was putting out an abnormal amount of smoke. His retirement is recorded in the records as engine failure lap 1! Jean-Pierre's comments when he got out of the car are unprintable ... Poor Jean-Pierre Boudy bore the brunt, and had a lot on his plate trying to resolve the problems of failing piston rings and pinking. It was back to the drawing board.

British Grand Prix, Brands Hatch, 16 July 1978

After its severe defeat in the French Grand Prix, the Renault-Elf team was somewhat apprehensive upon arrival at Brands Hatch for the first anniversary of the Régie's Formula 1 début. One can imagine that Gérard Larrousse, François Castaing, Jean-Pierre Boudy and Jean-Pierre Jabouille were on tenterhooks, and impatient to see the results of the engine modifications: new liners, new pistons, new piston rings.

The car began the day slowly, four seconds behind the new Lotus, the innovatory ground-effect car of Ronnie Peterson. After some adjustments and new tyres, things were going better, but catastrophe struck – an oil leak between the engine and the tank of the RS01/02 with its new bodywork. Even more serious, it was

STARTING GRID		RESULTS - Brands Hatch (319,732 km)			
Peterson	Andretti	1. Reutemann	Ferrari	76	1h42'12.39"
1'16.80"	1'17.06"	2. Lauda	Brabham-Alfa Romeo	76	1h42'13.62"
Scheckter	Lauda	3. Watson	Brabham-Alfa Romeo	76	1h42'49.64"
1h17.37"	1'17.48"	4. Depailler	Tyrrell-Ford	76	1h43'25.66"
Patrese	Jones	5. Stuck	Shadow-Ford	75	1h42'25.88"
1'18.28"	1'18.36"	6. Tambay	McLaren-Ford	75	1h42'27.51"
Laffite	Reutemann	7. Giacomelli	McLaren-Ford	75	1h42'29.96"
1'18.44"	1'18.45"	8. Lunger	McLaren-Ford	75	1h43'12.60"
Watson	Depailler	9. Brambilla	Surtees-Ford	75	1h43'33.99"
1'18.57"	1'18.73"	10. Laffite	Ligier-Matra	73	1h42'52.32"
Fittipaldi	Jabouille				
1'18.78"	1'18.88"	**FASTEST LAP**			
Villeneuve	Hunt				
1'18.99"	1'19.05"	Lauda	Brabham-Alfa Romeo		1'18.60"
Daly	Giacomelli				192.650 km/h
1'19.13"	1'19.79"				
Regazzoni	Stuck	**RETIREMENTS**			
1'19.83"	1'19.79"				
Pironi	Tambay	Mass	ATS-Ford	66	1h43'08.58"
1'19.99"	1'20.14"	Rosberg	ATS-Ford	59	Front suspension
Rebaque	Rosberg	Regazzoni	Shadow-Ford	49	Gearbox
1'20.24"	1'20.27"	Jabouille	Renault	46	Engine
Merzario	Lunger	Patrese	Arrows-Ford	40	Rear suspension
1'20.35"	1'20.39"	Pironi	Tyrrell-Ford	40	Gearbox
Brambilla	Mass	Scheckter	Wolf-Ford	36	Gearbox
1'20.70"	1'20.71"	Fittipaldi	Copersucar-Ford	32	Engine
		Merzario	Merzario-Ford	32	Fuel pump
		Daly	Ensign-Ford	30	Lost rear wheel
		Andretti	Lotus-Ford	28	Engine
		Jones	Williams-Ford	26	Transmission shaft
		Villeneuve	Ferrari	19	Transmission shaft
		Rebaque	Lotus-Ford	15	Gearbox
		Hunt	McLaren-Ford	7	Accident
		Peterson	Lotus-Ford	6	Fuel leak

Brands Hatch race statistics.

impossible for the mechanics to reach the source of the leak. So Jean-Pierre Jabouille had to change cars. He settled himself in the RS01/03 with the earlier bodywork and had to start again at the beginning as far as set-up was concerned.

> ## "After some adjustments and new tyres, things were going better, but catastrophe struck – an oil leak between the engine and the tank of the RS01/02 with its new bodywork."

He demonstrated his undoubted skill by recording the 6th fastest time – the best of the drivers on Michelin tyres. For Goodyear, which usually supplied only its top teams with super-qualifiers, this meant war, and it immediately also fitted out some of the slower runners on its customer list, as it had done the year before in an effort to get in front of the Renault and move it down the grid. Alan Jones was entrusted with a set of the miracle tyres

to the detriment of Laffite and Regazzoni. A tyre war was openly declared, with Pironi's Tyrrell and Tambay's McLaren all receiving the top Goodyear radial tyres.

Jabouille had got a good result on the first day, but, as had happened in the preceding four Grands Prix, could not improve his performance during the second day of practice. This time, it was a traction problem that couldn't be resolved. Jabouille slipped to 12th, in the middle of the grid, second Michelin runner to Reutemann in the Ferrari.

Reutemann won the race the next day, taking advantage of the retirement of the two Lotuses which had engine problems. Jean-Pierre lost five places in the 1st lap, a victim, yet again, to slow turbo response times and also poor tyre choice. He stopped to change them on the 13th lap but to no avail, as he retired on the 46th lap with a broken turbo. Still no success for Renault; Reutemann won using Michelins, proving that the tyres were fine. By now, Renault management must have been getting nervous ...

German Grand Prix, Hockenheim, 30 July 1978

It was stiflingly hot at the Hockenheim circuit. The Renault-Elf team had carried out some small adjustments to the rear of its RS01s to allow them to carry a new, wider Michelin tyre. However, the ambient heat was causing serious problems for the engine specialists, particularly as regards the dreaded turbo response time. A way had to be found of cooling things down.

Jean Sage: "We had an idea: ice cubes stuffed into the side-pods. But ice cubes don't last long – they melt completely within less than a lap. At the end of the session, with no more ice, I went out and found a local fish supplier and bought a huge quantity of ice. Problem was, the car, the pits and everyone in them smelt of cod all weekend!"

The heat problem on the engine was so bad that, during the second qualifying session, it was decided that Jabouille would get himself in the groove – whilst at the same time warming up the qualifying tyres – by using the spare car, before jumping back into the cockpit of the race car while the mechanics rushed to switch over the tyres. These gymnastics allowed the driver to start with a cold engine, in particular a cold air inlet, necessary in order to achieve a good qualifying time. However, on the second lap the turbo-lag problem reappeared as everything just got too hot. In spite of the fun and games, Jabouille came out of it reasonably well, with a 9th place on the grid, though he was sure that, if it hadn't been for the heat problems, he could have done much better, because the Renault was holding the road perfectly, and, in fact, started in front of the two Ferraris.

In the race Jabouille got off to the usual difficult start and

A hot day in Hockenheim.

Quick, but fighting the gremlins.

Into the Stadium complex, Hockenheim.

STARTING GRID		RESULTS - Hockenheim (305,505 km)			
Peterson 1'51.99"	Andretti 1'51.90"	1. Andretti	Lotus-Ford	45	1h28'00.90"
Scheckter 1'52.68"	Lauda 1'52.29"	2. Scheckter	Wolf-Ford	45	1h28'16.25"
Jones 1'53.50"	Watson 1'52.84"	3. Laffite	Ligier-Matra	45	1h28'28.91"
Hunt 1'53.46"	Laffite 1'53.40"	4. Fittipaldi	Copersucar-Ford	45	1h28'37.78"
Fittipaldi 1'54.03"	Jabouille 1'53.61"	5. Pironi	Tyrrell-Ford	45	1h28'58.16"
Reutemann 1'54.17"	Tambay 1'54.04"	6. Rebaque	Lotus-Ford	45	1h29'38.76"
Patrese 1'54.34"	Depailler 1'54.32"	7. Watson	Brabham-Alfa Romeo	45	1h29'40.43"
Pironi 1'54.63"	Villeneuve 1'54.40"	8. Villeneuve	Ferrari	45	1h29'57.77"
Rebaque 1'55.57"	Stomelen 1'55.18"	9. Patrese	Arrows-Ford	44	+ 1 lap
Brambilla 1'55.86"	Rosberg 1'55.57"	10. Rosberg	Wolf-Ford	42	+ 3 laps
Mass 1'56.21"	Piquet 1'56.15"	11. Ertl	Ensign-Ford	41	Engine
Stuck 1'56.45"	Ertl 1'56.25"				

DISQUALIFIED (Do not respect the regular track)

Stommelen	Arrows-Ford	42	
Hunt	McLaren-Ford	34	

FASTEST LAP

Peterson	Lotus-Ford	1'55.62" 211.354 km/h

RETIREMENTS

Peterson	Lotus-Ford	36	Gearbox
Jones	Williams-Ford	31	Fuel in boiling point
Piquet	Ensign-Ford	31	Engine
Brambilla	Surtees-Ford	24	Fuel in boiling point
Tambay	McLaren-Ford	16	Accident
Reutemann	Ferrari	14	Fuel in boiling point
Lauda	Brabham-Alfa Romeo	11	Engine
Jabouille	Renault	5	Engine
Stuck	Shadow-Ford	1	Collision with Mass
Mass	ATS-Ford	1	Suspension failure … accident
Depailler	Tyrrell-Ford	0	Accident (start)

Hockenheim race statistics.

was 13th at the end of lap 1. But the power was there; he moved up – 10th on the 2nd lap, 8th on the 4th lap, and 7th on the 5th lap after passing Pironi, Fittipaldi, Villeneuve, Reutemann, Laffite, Hunt, and Watson.

It was going well, but then the seemingly inevitable gremlins appeared and, on the 6th lap, the engine failed: piston rings. Nevertheless, although Jabouille had to retire yet again, the German Grand Prix had, in some respects, been a positive experience: firstly, it witnessed some fine, if fleeting, performances from car and driver, and also brought to light what problems high ambient temperatures caused for the turbo engine's performance. This was a new discovery for François Castaing and his team.

Austrian Grand Prix, Zeltweg, 13 August 1978

Zeltweg saw the RS01 arrive with a new, larger heat exchanger and an oil tank situated not in front of the engine but on its right side. Alternative bodywork around the rear part of the car was also tried.

The first practice session saw Jabouille, on the provisional second row of the starting grid, behind Ronnie Peterson and Mario Andretti in their Lotus-Ford ground-effect cars. The Renault was working well, the improvement in temperature reduction immediately noticeable by a drop from 90° to 60°C.

The track stayed dry for only five minutes at the beginning of the second qualifying session on the Saturday, and none of the drivers was to improve his position. At the start of the race, from a good fourth place on the grid in fine drizzle, Jabouille found himself trapped by Peterson and Andretti; he had to brake, losing momentum, and, while the turbo lagged, the rest of the field took advantage, forcing the Renault down to 10th position at the end of the 1st lap. Then, as had been seen many times before, Jabouille went on the attack: 8th on the 2nd lap, 6th on the 3rd, and so on, until he was in 4th place on the 6th lap when the rear wing of the Renault was damaged in an incident with another car. However, Jabouille had a spot of luck when, on the 8th lap, the Grand Prix

STARTING GRID		RESULTS - Zeltweg (320,868 km)			
Andretti 1'37.76"	Peterson 1'37.71"	1. Peterson	Lotus-Ford	54	1h41'21.57"
Reutmann 1'38.50"	Jabouille 1'38.32"	2. Depailler	Tyrrell-Ford	54	1h42'09.01"
Fittipaldi 1'38.77"	Laffite 1'38.71"	3. Villeneuve	Ferrari	54	1h43'01.33"
Hunt 1'39.10"	Scheckter 1'38.85"	4. Fittipaldi	Copersucar-Ford	53	1h42'45.99"
Watson 1'39.35"	Pironi 1'39.23"	5. Laffite	Ligier-Matra	53	1h42'46.57"
Lauda 1'39.49"	Villeneuve 1'39.40"	6. Brambilla	Surtees-Ford	53	1h43'05.46"
Tambay 1'39.59"	Depailler 1'39.51"	7. Watson	Brabham-Alfa Romeo	53	1h43'11.02"
Patrese 1'40.11"	Jones 1'39.81"	8. Lunger	McLaren-Ford	52	1h42'25.99"
Rebaque 1'40.84"	Lunger 1'40.80"	9. Arnoux	Martini-Ford	52	1h43'27.27"
Piquet 1'41.15"	Daly 1'41.02"				
Regazzoni 1'41.42"	Brambilla 1'41.16"				
Ertl 1'41.60"	Stuck 1'41.58"				
Arnoux 1'41.84"	Rosberg 1'41.72"				

DISQUALIFIED

Daly	Ensign-Ford	43	outside assistance after a Spin
Reutemann	Ferrari	27	outside assistance after a Spin

FASTEST LAP

Peterson	Lotus-Ford	1'43.12" 207.40 km/h

RETIREMENTS

Rosberg	Wolf-Ford	47	1h42'11.30"
Regazzoni	Shadow-Ford	47	1h42'13.06"
Tambay	McLaren-Ford	40	Accident
Stuck	Shadow-Ford	33	Accident
Jabouille	Renault	31	Gearbox
Lauda	Brabham-Alfa Romeo	28	Accident
Pironi	Tyrrell-Ford	20	Accident
Hunt	McLaren-Ford	8	Collision with Daly
Jones	Williams-Ford	7	Accident
Ertl	Ensign-Ford	6	Collision with Patrese (2nd start)
Patrese	Arrows-Ford	6	Collision with Ertl (2nd start)
Scheckter	Wolf-Ford	3	Accident
Rebaque	Lotus-Ford	1	Clutch
Andretti	Lotus-Ford	0	Accident
Piquet	McLaren-Ford	2	Accident

Zeltweg race statistics.

It got very wet!

Note different side-pod/rear bodywork on test.

was stopped because of a downpour which had caused a number of cars to go off the track.

The race was restarted and all of the cars were on full wets. The final classification was to be decided by adding together the times of the two stages. Starting from 14th place, Jabouille gradually climbed up to 4th before retiring in frustration with a broken gearbox. In the rain and with a turbo engine, the transmission was found to be under too much stress. Jabouille was disappointed; he felt he could have done very well, because the car ran beautifully and the turbo had behaved itself this time ...

Dutch Grand Prix, Zandvoort, 27 August 1978

Just after the Austrian race, the Renault-Elf team carried out a series of private tests on the Folembray circuit, where one of the RS01s appeared with new bodywork. Known, at that time, as the 'Camel,' it was never used in racing but was characteristic of the direction of developmental thinking and aerodynamic tests done by the team. Unfortunately, we don't have any pictures of the car.

After Folembray it was on to Holland, where the weather was cool and cloudy with only a few sunny periods. Jabouille got off to a bad start; bizarrely, his car was found to be suffering from a faulty sparkplug! Michel Têtu had now joined the team from his previous role of developing A310 rally cars and the R5 Turbo. He decided to try Lexan side-skirts in an attempt at achieving ground-effect on the spare car, but these bent and made the chassis very unstable. Jabouille ended the first practice in 9th place, but thought he could do better – perhaps much better.

However, the second practice day showed no improvement (the same, fortunately, was true of his rivals), and the Renault was to hold on to 9th place on the starting grid.

Jabouille fluffed the start and dropped to 13th position on the 1st lap. Once again, he gradually regained his composure and had moved up to 8th place by the 29th lap, though just 6 laps later had to retire with a broken engine, again the result of piston ring problems.

Italian Grand Prix, Monza, 10 September 1978

It was not as hot as had been forecast at Monza Park, where Renault Sport had taken RS01/02 and RS01/03. Interestingly, both cars were fitted with mixed air/water heat exchangers and a modified engine with new cylinder liners. The old engines – by now less reliable – had become test units. The new engine had

Note the proximity of the photographers to the track!

STARTING GRID		RESULTS - Zandvoort (316,950 km)			
Peterson 1'16.97"	Andretti 1'16.36"	1. Andretti	Lotus-Ford	75	1h41'04.23"
Reutemann 1'17.34"	Lauda 1'17.33"	2. Peterson	Lotus-Ford	75	1h41'04.55"
Laffite 1'17.55"	Villeneuve 1'17.54"	3. Lauda	Brabham-Alfa Romeo	75	1h41'16.44"
Watson 1'17.73"	Hunt 1'17.67"	4. Watson	Brabham-Alfa Romeo	75	1h41'25.15"
Fittipaldi 1'18.30"	Jabouille 1'18.28"	5. Fittipaldi	Copersucar-Ford	75	1h41'25.73"
Depailler 1'18.43"	Jones 1'18.42"	6. Villeneuve	Ferrari	75	1h41'50.18"
Tambay 1'18.50"	Patrese 1'18.50"	7. Reutemann	Ferrari	75	1h42'04.73"
Daly 1'19.39"	Scheckter 1'18.57"	8. Laffite	Ligier-Matra	74	+ 1 lap
Stuck 1'19.62"	Pironi 1'19.59"	9. Tambay	McLaren-Ford	74	+ 1 lap
Rebaque 1'20.02"	Giacomelli 1'19.83"	10. Hunt	McLaren-Ford	74	+ 1 lap
Brambilla 1'20.26"	Lunger 1'20.03"	11. Rebaque	Lotus-Ford	74	+ 1 lap
Rosberg 1'20.26"	Arnoux 1'20.31"	12. Scheckter	Wolf-Ford	73	+ 2 laps
Piquet 1'20.64"	Merzario 1'20.64"				

DISQUALIFIED

Brambilla	Surtees-Ford	37

FASTEST LAP

Lauda	Brabham-Alfa Romeo	1'19.57" 191.198 km/h

RETIREMENTS

Giacomelli	McLaren-Ford	60	Spin, stall
Stuck	Shadow-Ford	56	Differential
Arnoux	Martini-Ford	40	Support rear wing
Merzario	Merzario-Ford	40	Engine
Jabouille	Renault	35	Engine, piston
Lunger	McLaren-Ford	35	Engine
Rosberg	Wolf-Ford	21	Throttle blocked
Jones	Williams-Ford	17	Throttle cable
Piquet	McLaren-Ford	16	Transmission shaft
Depailler	Tyrrell-Ford	13	Engine
Daly	Ensign-Ford	10	Transmission shaft
Patrese	Arrows-Ford	0	Collision with Pironi
Pironi	Tyrrell-Ford	0	Collision with Patrese

Monza Park, a tragic weekend.

Monza race statistics.

Zandvoort race statistics.

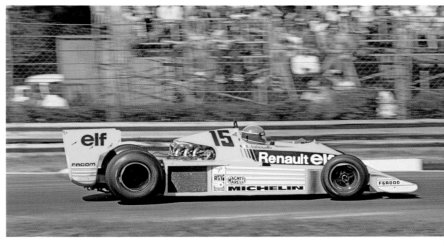

On the front row for a while!

STARTING GRID		RESULTS - Monza (232 km)			
Andretti 1'37.520"	Villeneuve 1'37.866"	1. Lauda	Brabham-Alfa Romeo	40	1h07'04.54"
Jabouille 1'37.930"	Lauda 1'38.215"	2. Watson	Brabham-Alfa Romeo	40	1h07'06.02"
*Peterson 1'38.256"	Jones 1'38.271"	3. Reutemann	Ferrari	40	1h07'25.01"
Watson 1'38.610"	Laffite 1'38.917"	4. Laffite	Ligier-Matra	40	1h07'42.07"
Scheckter 1'38.937"	Hunt 1'38.938"	5. Tambay	McLaren-Ford	40	1h07'44.93"
Reutemann 1'39.959"	Patrese 1'39.179"	6. Andretti	Lotus-Ford	40	1h07'50.87"
Fittipaldi 1'39.421"	*Pironi 1'39.563"	7. Villeneuve	Ferrari	40	1h07'53.02"
Regazzoni 1'39.621"	Depailler 1'39.630"	8. Fittipaldi	Copersucar-Ford	40	1h07'59.78"
*Stuck 1'39.701"	Daly 1'40.075"	9. Piquet	McLaren-Ford	40	1h08'11.37"
Tambay 1'40.163"	Giacomelli 1'40.199"	10. Daly	Ensign-Ford	40	1h08'13.65"
*Lunger 1'40.302"	Merzario 1'40.702"	11. Depailler	Tyrrell-Ford	40	1h08'21.11"
*Brambilla 1'40.805"	Piquet 1'40.846"	12. Scheckter	Wolf-Ford	39	+ 1 lap
		13. Jones	Williams-Ford	39	+ 1 lap
		14. Giacomelli	McLaren-Ford	39	+ 1 lap

* N'a pas pris part au deuxième départ

FASTEST LAP

Andretti	Lotus-Ford	1'38.23" 212.652 km/h

RETIREMENTS

Regazzoni	Shadow-Ford	33	
Patrese	Arrows-Ford	29	Engine
Hunt	McLaren-Ford	19	Allumeur
Merzario	Merzario-Ford	14	Engine
Jabouille	Renault	6	Engine

ELIMINÉS APRÈS LE PREMIER DÉPART

Pironi	Tyrrell-Ford	Accident
Depailler	Tyrrell-Ford	Accident
Peterson	Lotus-Ford	Collision with Hunt fatal crash
Hunt	McLaren-Ford	Accident
Reutemann	Ferrari	Accident
Stuck	Shadow-Ford	Accident
Regazzoni	Shadow-Ford	Accident
Brambilla	Surtees-Ford	Accident
Daly	Ensign-Ford	Accident
Lunger	McLaren-Ford	Accident

been tested during a non-stop, 350km endurance test and had a total of 600km on the clock.

Jabouille's Renault in first practice was to be on the 2nd row of the grid, in 3rd position behind the two ground-effect Lotuses. On the Saturday, for a short time he was even on the front row instead of Peterson, though, in the end, Villeneuve dislodged him by 64/1000th of a second.

History records it was a weekend of tragedy. Just after the race started, a huge pile-up involved many cars, including the Lotus in which Ronnie Peterson was seriously injured; sadly, he died in hospital the next day. Unaware of the true condition of Peterson, the officials restarted the race, but Villeneuve and Andretti jumped the start and were penalised. Jabouille was to restart in 3rd place on the grid, a position he held until the 6th lap, when he again had to retire with a broken engine. Not a good weekend for anyone. The race was won by Niki Lauda in the Brabham-Alfa Romeo.

US East Coast Grand Prix, Watkins Glen, 1 October 1978

Although the Italian Grand Prix had seen the early retirement of Jabouille, morale was quite high in the Renault-Elf team. The optimism was due to a breakthrough in testing and Jabouille had been able to demonstrate the car's true potential. Also, the team had ascertained why the engine broke on the 6th lap at Monza; quite simply, because of a faulty sparkplug again. Monza had taught the Renault-Elf team a great deal, and the solution of mixed heat exchangers tried out in Italy was continued for the American race as it clearly improved things by cooling inlet air temperature. By now, the team was thinking about a new car for the 1979 season, and François Castaing had decided to stay behind at Viry-Châtillon to work on it.

The notoriously heavy RS01 was subjecting its brakes to torture on the Watkins Glen circuit, in spite of oversized discs. Jabouille was in 9th place on the provisional grid, but had to cope with failing brakes as the fluid began to boil. On the other hand, as far as the engine went progress was being made, and, for the first time in the free testing for this Grand Prix, the Renault engine was fitted with new Nikasil linings (aluminium linings with nickel-based coating).

At the green light, Jabouille set off with a typically average start that dropped him a few places, though, as usual he went straight on the attack, moving up from 12th position on the 1st lap to 3rd position halfway through the race. The team in the pits was ecstatic; at last Renault was duelling for podium position, demonstrating after so long how far the team had come.

The engine now had Nikasil linings in the cylinders.

Jabouille on his way to the first points.

STARTING GRID		RESULTS - Watkins Glen (320,665 km)			
Reutemann 1'39.179"	Andretti 1'38.114"	1. Reutemann	Ferrari	59	1h40'48.800"
Villeneuve 1'39.820"	Jones 1'39.742"	2. Jones	Williams-Ford	59	1h41'08.539"
Hunt 1'39.991"	Lauda 1'39.892"	3. Scheckter	Wolf-Ford	59	1h41'34.501"
Jarier 1'40.034"	Watson 1'40.000"	4. Jabouille	Renault	59	1h42'13.807"
Laffite 1'40.228"	Jabouille 1'40.136"	5. Fittipaldi	Copersucar-Ford	59	1h42'16.889"
Depailler 1'40.828"	Scheckter 1'40.762"	6. Tambay	McLaren-Ford	59	1h42'30.010"
Stuck 1'41.681"	Fittipaldi 1'41.007"	7. Hunt	McLaren-Ford	58	+ 1 lap
Pironi 1'41.815"	Rosberg 1'41.773"	8. Daly	Ensign-Ford	58	+ 1 lap
Tambay 1'41.974"	Regazzoni 1'41.855"	9. Arnoux	Surtees-Ford	58	+ 1 lap
Rahal 1'42.429"	Daly 1'42.179"	10. Pironi	Tyrrell-Ford	58	+ 1 lap
Stommelen 1'42.741"	Arnoux 1'42.541"	11. Laffite	Ligier-Matra	58	+ 1 lap
Lunger 1'43.067"	Rebaque 1'43.028"	12. Rahal	Wolf-Ford	58	+ 1 lap
Merzario 1'44.286"	Bleekemolen 1'43.572"	13. Lunger	Ensign-Ford	58	+ 1 lap
		14. Regazzoni	Shadow-Ford	56	+ 3 laps
		15. Jarier	Lotus-Ford	55	Out of fuel
		16. Stommelen	Arrows-Ford	54	+ 5 laps

FASTEST LAP

Jarier	Lotus-Ford	1'39.557"
		196.474 km/h

RETIREMENTS

Merzario	Merzario-Ford	46	Oil leak Gearbox
Bleekemolen	ATS-Ford	43	Oil pump leak
Lauda	Brabham-Alfa Romeo	28	Engine
Andretti	Lotus-Ford	27	Engine
Watson	Brabham-Alfa Romeo	25	Engine
Depailler	Tyrrell-Ford	23	Rolling bearing
Villeneuve	Ferrari	22	Engine
Rosberg	ATS-Ford	21	Gear selector
Stuck	Shadow-Ford	1	Fuel pump
Rebaque	Lotus-Ford	0	Clutch

Watkins Glen race statistics.

Busy in the pits.

Reutemann (Ferrari) and Jones (Williams-Ford) were too far ahead to catch, but a third place was a possibility. Suddenly, alarm bells began to ring: the car was starting to exhibit fuel starvation problems.

The team was almost resigned to another retirement, and, for the tenth time, just 8 laps from the end. Jabouille slowed, going round all the bends in a higher gear, desperately trying not to make demands on the engine. In fact, the reason for the fuel starvation was that he had forgotten to switch over one of the fuel pumps! Once this was done, the brakes, which were wearing due to overheating, began to recover just a little, though, try as he might, he could not hold off Scheckter in the Wolf-Ford, who slipped by to take third place. Jabouille held on in those last few laps to pass the chequered flag a reasonably happy man, as well he might be: it was the first real result, the first points scored. So near a podium, but still a case of 'close but no cigar ...'

Canadian Grand Prix, Ile-Notre-Dame, Montreal, 8 October 1978

The old and dangerous Mosport circuit had been abandoned, and

Partners with a dream.

A chat with the boss: Gérard Larrousse and Renault president,
Bernard Vernier-Palliez

the Formula 1 Grand Prix circus had moved to the new Ile-Notre-Dame circuit in Montreal, subsequently re-named Circuit Gilles Villeneuve in memory of the great and inspirational driver who was to lose his life a few years later.

Initially, Montreal didn't suit Jabouille or the Renault. It rained the whole day on the Friday and the Saturday morning, the track drying out only during the last hour of qualifying. Jean-Pierre did not have time to get his car sorted and was beset by problems. The six-speed gearbox had been modified to only five speeds (more practical, it was thought at the time), but the first gear pinion broke. Then, in the timed session the engine failed due to a loss of compression. A fresh engine allowed him to take part in the second session only to have the gearbox break again; this time the second gear pinion of the RS01/02. However, he *had* qualified the car – just – on the last row of the grid, in 22nd place.

In the race, the car was very temperamental because the tyres were simply not warming sufficiently. Jabouille was in 15th position when he made a stop on the 47th lap to attend to faulty brakes and add 4mm of downforce to the front wing. He finally finished in 12th position, some five laps down on the winner, the aforementioned Gilles Villeneuve, who was celebrating his first F1 victory.

CHASSIS RECORDS FOR 1978 ON RS01/2

07.01.78   Testing. Jabouille on the Paul Ricard circuit (3.3km). Halted after 18 laps. Broken turbo.

08.01.78   Testing starts again and Jabouille does 82 laps in the day, the best of which is timed at 1min 8.64sec.

09.01.78   Tests continue, this time on the 5.8km circuit. Jabouille does 82 laps, the best of which is 1min 46.14sec "with an almost perfect car," says the French driver.
The result of these two days of tests must be compared with that of those in mid-December 1977. Improvements were coming.

23.02.78   Preliminary tests at the South African Grand Prix on the Kyalami circuit. Jabouille does 88 laps with a best lap of 1min 15.92sec on the 83rd.

24.02.78   New tests at Kyalami, and, with an engine with a total of 648km, Jabouille does his best lap in 1min 15.6sec. Before the Grand Prix, the total distance run by the RS01/02 is 1095km.

STARTING GRID

Jarier 1'38.015"	Scheckter 1'38.026"
Villeneuve 1'38.230"	Watson 1'38.471"
Jones 1'38.861"	Fittipaldi 1'38.930"
Lauda 1'39.020"	Stuck 1'39.081"
Andretti 1'39.236"	Laffite 1'39.381"
Reutemann 1'39.455"	Patrese 1'39.491"
Depailler 1'39.619"	Piquet 1'39.624"
Daly 1'40.042"	Arnoux 1'40.515"
Tambay 1'40.669"	Pironi 1'40.959"
Hunt 1'40.970"	Rahal 1'40.983"
Rosberg 1'41.611"	Jabouille 1'41.689"

RESULTS - Montréal (326,900 km)

1. Villeneuve	Ferrari	70	1h57'49.196"
2. Scheckter	Wolf-Ford	70	1h58'02.568"
3. Reutemann	Ferrari	70	1h58'08.604"
4. Patrese	Arrows-Ford	70	1h58'13.863"
5. Depailler	Tyrrell-Ford	70	1h58'17.754"
6. Daly	Ensign-Ford	70	1h58'43.672"
7. Pironi	Tyrrell-Ford	70	1h59'10.446"
8. Tambay	McLaren-Ford	70	1h59'15.756"
9. Jones	Williams-Ford	70	1h59'18.138"
10. Andretti	Lotus-Ford	69	1h58'00.933"
11. Piquet	Brabham-Alfa Romeo	69	1h58'38.151"
12. Jabouille	Renault	65	1h59'01.186"

FASTEST LAP

Jones	Williams-Ford	1'39.077" 169.686 km/h

RETIREMENTS

Rosberg	ATS-Ford	58	1h58'57.209"
Laffite	Ligier-Matra	52	Transmission
Hunt	McLaren-Ford	51	Accident
Jarier	Lotus-Ford	49	Brakes liquid leak
Arnoux	Surtees-Ford	37	Oil pipe
Rahal	Wolf-Ford	16	Fuel feed
Watson	Brabham-Alfa Romeo	8	Collision Andretti
Lauda	Brabham-Alfa Romeo	5	Accident
Stuck	Shadow-Ford	1	Collision Fittipaldi
Fittipaldi	Copersucar-Ford	0	Collision with Stuck

Montreal race statistics.

13.03.78   Endurance tests on the Paul Ricard circuit 3.3km. Jabouille does 90 laps.

14.03.78   Endurance tests continue and, between 9.45am and 6.20pm, Jabouille does 162 laps. During these two days, the French driver has therefore done a total of 252 laps, ie: 831km.

15.03.78   Last of the planned 3 days of tests. Jabouille stops on the 52nd lap with a broken brake disc mounting.

16.03.78   From the Paul Ricard circuit, Jabouille and the test team return directly to Clermont-Ferrand to Michelin's private circuit for tyre testing on the 'canard' (duck) circuit. Jean Sage is in charge of recording not only Jabouille's performance in the RS01 but also that of Reutemann in a Ferrari T2. Assisted by Michelin's technicians, the two drivers have the job of testing a selection of rain tyres. Jabouille stops with a broken sparkplug.

17.03.78   Tests continue, still on the 'duck,' but are halted by snow! Air temperature: 1°C.

31.03.78   Official practice for the west coast US Grand Prix at Long Beach. Incidents: faulty battery connection and broken turbo. Although the ignition module is changed, Jabouille complains that the engine keeps cutting out.

02.05.78   Rolling tests on the Paul Ricard circuit racing school (2.2km) before the Monaco Grand Prix. Running-in of the new gearbox shows a torque of 8.31.

26.06.78   Preliminary tests at the French Grand Prix on the Paul Ricard circuit (5.8km). Jabouille does 19 laps.

27.06.78   39 laps.

30.06.78   First official practice session for the French Grand Prix – broken engine and gearbox. The first gearbox breakage for Renault Sport.

11.08.78   Official practice for the Austrian Grand Prix at the Österreichring in Zeltweg. The Renault Sport technicians use a mixed cooling exchanger for the first time. During the race, the gearbox fails.

25.08.78   Official practice for the Dutch Grand Prix at Zandvoort. Engine fails due to a twisted valve.

08.09.78   Official practice for the Italian Grand Prix at Monza. Jabouille goes off the road.

28.09.78   Official practice for the east coast US Grand Prix at Watkins Glen. A burnt-out valve during the second session. First use in tests of new cylinder liners made of Nikasil (aluminium with a nickel-base coating). The RS01/02 takes part in the race using these liners.

06.10.78   Official practice for the Canadian Grand Prix in Montreal. Engine failure during the first day: three cylinders lose compression. Jabouille says he is finding it impossible to warm up the tyres. Also a gearbox failure. The RS01/02 is repaired and takes part in the race.

01.11.78   Jabouille on the Paul Ricard circuit (3.3km). Testing of brakes and telemetry measurements. Jabouille's best lap is recorded at 1min 10.26sec with new tyres. Gilles Villeneuve does 1min 7.01sec in the same conditions with his Ferrari.

02.11.78   191km for Jabouille and a best lap of 1min 8.10sec. Villeneuve does 1min 8.61sec.

03.11.78   Jabouille does an endurance test, running 346km.

04.11.78   Tests of various differentials specially modified for the Renault gearbox unit. Jabouille runs 158km. He completes a total of 153 laps in four days with no problem except for the failure of a drive belt caused by a stone. The repair takes three hours.

27.11.78   Back again on the 3.3km Paul Ricard circuit. Jabouille does a 56km proving test.

28.11.78   Another proving session for the following day; 82km.

29.11.78   On this day, a small group of journalists is to watch testing of the RS01/02. Before they arrive at 10am, René Arnoux, Jabouille's future team-mate for the 79 season, gets into the car for the first time and does one 15-lap run, not timed, for the photographers, the TV and film cameras.

30.11.78   Still on the 3.3km circuit, Arnoux does a second test session. He does 40 laps per session, with 70 litres of fuel, and his best lap is timed at 1min 10.21sec on the 21st lap. It is cold and very dry. Arnoux's first remarks concern his position and installation in the cockpit of the RS01/02.

This third chassis RS01/03 was first driven by Jabouille during the 1978 season, then by Arnoux at the beginning of the 1979 season.

30.01.78   First run at the 3.3km Paul Ricard circuit then on the 5.8km. The settings chart contains this comment: "The engine does not smoke on start-up. A good sign, but also worrying." Any new fact could be analysed as a symptom of future failure. Jean-Pierre Jabouille does his first laps.

02.02.78   Jean-Pierre Jaussaud, known as 'Papy,' takes over from Jabouille. Endurance test on the 5.8km Paul Ricard circuit. He does 116 laps in total, interrupted by two engine cut-outs on the 10th lap and a disconnected fuse wire. Jabouille replaces him but goes off the track: rear wing broken off. Overfeed pressure: 1.750 bar.

03.02.78   Tests continue. An anomaly has been recorded: a sudden rise in the boost pressure above 10,000rpm.

21.02.78   Preliminary testing at Kyalami for the South African Grand prix. Session halted by rain. Jabouille at the wheel.

22.02.78   Tests continue. Halted due to a broken turbo. Compressor and turbine changed. 26 laps, then halted with a blocked waste-gate.

23.02.78   Tests soon halted by an engine failure at 118km.

24.02.78   Still at Kyalami. Aerodynamic tests.

25.02.78   Tyre testing. Jabouille back at low speed. Air inlet flattened after 42 laps. Air boxes (snorkels) fitted for the first time. Last used on A500.

31.03.78   Practice for the west coast US Grand Prix at Long Beach. The A500 engine air inlet snorkel removed. The engine is also fitted with Marelli ignition.

01.05.78   Tests on the Paul Ricard circuit 3.3km for the Monaco Grand Prix.

02.05.78   Continued preliminary testing for Monaco but this time on the 2.2km Paul Ricard circuit.

19.05.78   Practice for the Belgian Grand Prix at Zolder. Oil too

hot. Jabouille says that the engine take-up at low speed is very average. Finally, the engine breaks.

29.05.78   Preliminary testing at Jarama for the Spanish Grand Prix. Aerodynamics and tyres. Jabouille does 87 laps. Consumption: 55 litres/100 km.

30.05.78   Preliminary testing at Jarama continues. 11 laps.

15.06.78   Official practice for the Swedish Grand Prix. The RS01/03 stops when an intake becomes detached and a turbo burns out. Jabouille's comment: "Brakes are borderline."

26.06.78   Preliminary testing for the French Grand Prix at the 5.8km Paul Ricard circuit. Engine and tyre tests. Jabouille does 260km.

27.06.78   Preliminary testing for France continues. Jabouille does 40km.

30.06.78   Official practice for the French Grand Prix, Paul Ricard circuit 5.8km.

01.07.78   2nd day of practice for the French Grand Prix. Jabouille does 9 laps before withdrawing the 03. The car has lost its balance, oversteering on left-hand corners.

14.07.78   Official practice for British Grand Prix at Brands Hatch. The adjustments record states, "Rear tyres scuffed."

16.07.78   Warm-up for the British Grand Prix. Faulty injection. Jabouille races in the Grand Prix with the RS01/02.

28.07.78   First day of practice for the German Grand Prix at Hockenheim. 108°C at the air inlet.

11.08.78   First day of practice for the Austrian Grand Prix at Zeltweg. Air inlet temperature 100°C.

05.09.78   Preliminary tests at Monza for the Italian Grand Prix. Jabouille does 34 laps.

06.09.78   Preliminary tests at Monza continue. Endurance test: 50 laps first, then a second series of 21 laps. Temperature: 26°C in the shade. The engine runs a total of 643km without missing a beat. The distance of the Grand Prix is 40 laps, 232km.

09.09.78   4th qualifying session for Italian Grand Prix. Jabouille goes off the track on the 23rd lap and the engine fails on the 26th.

28.09.78   Preliminary tests at Watkins Glen for the east-coast US Grand Prix. Fine weather, but no grip.

08.10.78   Warm-up for the Canadian Grand Prix in Montreal. 18 laps.

04.12.78   Private testing in Brazil on the Rio-Jacarepagua circuit, the Interlagos circuit being unavailable. 31°C in the shade, 44°C on the ground. Suffocating heat in the cockpit, according to Jabouille. Water temperature 100°C. Alarming temperature in the ignition chamber, but 70°C inlet temperature. Jabouille does 67 laps, 335km. One incident: broken pneumatic starter motor. Incomprehensible drop in engine performance; variations in top speed and acceleration.

05.12.78   40°C in the shade, 55°C on the ground. Water temperature 100°C. Cockpit ventilated by small, semi-dynamic lateral air inlets. Large diameter front tyres tested. Incidents: breakage of the rear wing support. Jamming of one of the pistons of the Kugelfischer injection system. 52 laps during the day, 261km. The result is therefore satisfactory: 119 laps in total. Consumption 50 litres/100km.

06.12.78   The Renault Sport team, the cars and the equipment go by truck to Interlagos, near to São Paulo.

07.12.78   Private testing continues at Interlagos. 12 laps during the afternoon.

08.12.78   Engine testing, with new butterflies on the admission inlet and new Marelli module. 15 laps only. "The engine growls above 9500rpm."

09.12.78   Testing of engine and then of wings, aerodynamics, top speed and lastly tyres. Jabouille completes 66 laps without incident. Best lap: 2min 28.4sec.

10.12.78   The sheet shows the comment: "Sunday: rest day."

Tests continue. Planned to begin at 8am, the session doesn't start until 10am because the duty firemen have overslept! The Ferrari stable with Scheckter has joined Renault Sport. Jabouille does 49 laps before stopping at 4.15pm with a broken engine (valve spring). His best lap is timed at 2min 27.9sec, with new tyres and ambient temperature of 22°C. Comment: "Play in the steering." Consumption: 55 litres/100km. Total for engine before breakage: 351km.

For Renault Sport it had been a year of joy and disappointment in equal measure. It was clear that the car had potential; it could be very fast but also suffered due to its weight and the many component failures. Something would have to be done to improve things for 1979. But the talented Michel Têtu was to come on board for the chassis design improvements, and there were also some new ideas going into the engines. Têtu, ex-Ligier and Alfa Romeo, had joined the Renault Sport team in 1976, having been brought in by Gérard Larrousse to develop the R5 Turbo as a car rather than just an idea. He was to continue with this until his workload became too great to cope with both F1 and R5 Turbo projects; he then concentrated on Formula 1. In addition, Bernard Dudot and Jean-Pierre Boudy were now able to concentrate on Formula 1 after the Le Mans success and the decision to cease sports car racing.

An RS01/04 would be developed for the start of 1979, while the new RS10 chassis was being created – initially in much the same way as the RS01 – by constructing a mock-up and designing the components as they went along. The designers were principally Hervé Guilpin and Marc Bande (de Cortanze had left the team), with considerable input from Jabouille and Guénard. But this time, as well as designing from a mock-up, detailed calculations were used as early programmable calculators and the first commercially usable computers appeared on the scene. Wind tunnel use was to assume even greater importance.

It was at a tyre-testing session at Dijon that the late Harvey Postlethwaite, who was working with the Wolf team at the time, was watching the Renault speed-trap times. "I will never forget it. Suddenly, the trap recorder read out a speed about 20mph faster than anything we'd ever seen before. That was it: the Renault was coming good. Soon we will all need turbos."

So, too, the world was to see the new RS10 Renault ground-effect car developed from the design by Guilpin and Bande, as Michel Têtu, who had moved down from Dieppe and the R5 Turbo work, became involved. Ss design team leader he was to take over the work that had begun in 1978 on the new chassis. Here, in pictures, is the construction of the RS10.

The car was ready for testing but not yet for racing. The season would start using the RS01 design, now updated to chassis RS03 and 04.

Rear chassis checks. Calculations now play a greater role than the 'suck it and see' approach of previous years.

Monocoque.

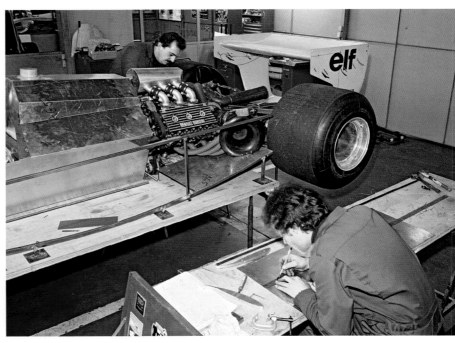

Car coming together.

Mock-up.

Shaping the moulds.

Body moulding commences February 1979.

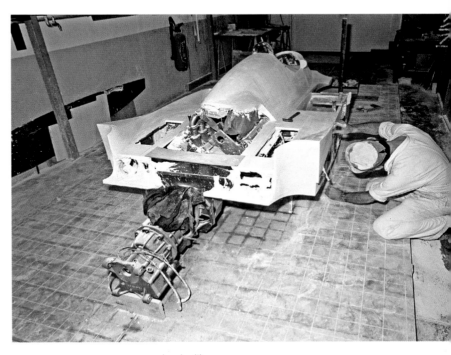

Looks like a car now.

Final touches.

Arnoux and Jabouille at the presentation in Viry-Châtillon, 30 March 1979.

Argentine Grand Prix, Buenos Aires, 21 January 1979

When Formula 1 returned to the Buenos Aires circuit, Carlos Reutemann had left Ferrari for Lotus, replaced by Jody Scheckter, and there had also been some changes within the two French teams of Renault and Ligier.

Renault was about to make its presence felt. For 1979, two Renault turbo cars would appear, demonstrating maturity as a serious team. Maybe the turbo was about to cause some concern among the British Cosworth-powered teams? René Arnoux was brought on board to support Jean-Pierre Jabouille: nobody was surprised at this, as René had been crowned European Formula 2 Champion in 1977 at the wheel of a Martini powered by the normally-aspirated V6 2-litre Renault, his efforts fully supported as a product of the team's sister-company, Elf. Didier Pironi had been approached by Renault but decided to stay with Tyrrell.

For the first practice at Renault, the engines were found to be running too hot, affecting performance. Another problem was that Jean-Pierre Jabouille did not know the circuit, so was just bedding himself in and was down in 10th place on the grid beside Emerson Fittipaldi. But Jean-Pierre's difficulties were nothing compared with those of team newcomer René Arnoux. Having had three engine failures, Arnoux had only managed to complete 14 laps in the two days of practice! Disaster, and in his first race within the Renault stable he did not manage to qualify.

Race day dawned and there would be plenty of upsets. During the warm-up on the Sunday morning, Ricardo Patrese collided with Nelson Piquet; his Arrows was destroyed and the Italian driver had to withdraw. His place would normally have gone to Hans Stuck, who was the first of the non-qualifiers to come in as substitute, but the German team didn't think his car, the ATS, was up to speed and decided to withdraw. The next non-qualifier was René Arnoux, who was duly invited to take the start.

> ## "Having had three engine failures, Arnoux had only managed to complete 14 laps in the two days of practice! Disaster, and in his first race within the Renault stable he did not manage to qualify."

As the lights went green and they left the line, a collision between Jody Scheckter and John Watson marred proceedings. Immediately behind these two, Tambay's McLaren ploughed into Andretti's Lotus and the race had to be stopped. The re-start saw Jacques Laffite dominate the situation just in front of Depailler.

STARTING GRID		RESULTS - Buenos Aires (316,304 km)			
Depailler 1'45.24"	Laffite 1'44.20"	1. Laffite	Ligier-Ford	53	1h36'03.21"
Jarier 1'45.36"	Reutemann 1'45.34"	2. Reutemann	Lotus-Ford	53	1h36'18.15"
Watson 1'45.76"	Scheckter 1'45.58"	3. Watson	McLaren-Ford	53	1h37'32.02"
Pironi 1'46.43"	Andretti 1'45.96"	4. Depailler	Ligier-Ford	53	1h37'44.93"
Villeneuve 1'46.88"	Tambay 1'46.56"	5. Andretti	Lotus-Ford	52	+ 1 lap
Jabouille 1'47.46"	Fittipaldi 1'47.15"	6. Fittipaldi	Copersucar-Ford	52	+ 1 lap
Jones 1'48.44"	Mass 1'48.34"	7. De Angelis	Shadow-Ford	52	+ 1 lap
Regazzoni 1'48.64"	De Angelis 1'48.51"	8. Mass	Arrows-Ford	51	+ 2 laps
Rebaque 1'49.36"	Hunt 1'48.77"	9. Jones	Williams-Ford	51	+ 2 laps
Lammers 1'49.51"	Piquet 1'49.49"	10. Regazzoni	Williams-Ford	51	+ 2 laps
Lauda 1'50.29"	Merzario 1'50.26"	11. Daly	Ensign-Ford	51	+ 2 laps
Arnoux 1'51.52"	Daly 1'51.05"				

FASTEST LAP

Laffite	Ligier-Ford	1'46.91" 200.968 km/h

RETIREMENTS

Villeneuve	Ferrari	48	Engine
Rebaque	Lotus-Ford	46	Suspension
Lammers	Shadow-Ford	42	Transmission shaft
Hunt	Wolf-Ford	41	Electrical
Jarier	Tyrrell-Ford	15	Engine
Jabouille	Renault	15	Engine
Lauda	Brabham-Alfa Romeo	8	Fuel pressure
Arnoux	Renault	6	Engine

Buenos Aires race statistics.

Changed bodywork again over the side-pods. (© DPPI/Ren)

"Physically, it was a demanding circuit for the drivers and fitness was a vital element, the driver's neck taking the most stress to the extent that some attached a tie cord to the side of their helmets and fixed to the cockpit sides to help resist the g-forces ..."

The two Ligier JS11s were invincible and crushed the competition the way the Lotus 79s had the season before. The Renaults didn't get a glimpse of the chequered flag. The heat, which was even worse than during practice, was troubling the engines, added to which the V6 turbos did not like the Argentine fuel supply. Both engines were to fail early on – one on the 6th lap (Arnoux), Jabouille on the 15th. Not a good start to the season ...

Brazilian Grand Prix, Interlagos, 4 February 1979
Interlagos was regarded as one of the most demanding of championship circuits. Laid out in natural surroundings – including lakes – the track constantly rises and falls, offering the spectator an unimpeded view of almost the whole circuit. The drivers appreciate the technical nature of the course, but had complained about the bumpy surface which had been remade in parts, leading to variations in mechanical grip which they could well do without. Physically, it was a demanding circuit for the drivers and fitness was a vital element, the driver's neck taking the most stress to the extent that some attached a tie cord to the side of their helmets and fixed to the cockpit sides to help resist the g-forces that caused the neck muscles to become so tired towards the end of a race that the driver would find it difficult to hold his head in position.

Once again the Ligiers proved untouchable. Laffite broke all the records during his first day of practice, giving himself the luxury of sitting quietly, watching his rivals fighting to try to beat his time. For Renault, things were looking better than in Argentina. The turbos were behaving well, thanks to the weather, which was cloudy and not as hot as in Buenos Aires, and to updates to the oil cooling system. Jean-Pierre Jabouille was a happier man, and in the early practice managed to qualify on the 7th row of the unofficial grid. René Arnoux, in only his second Grand Prix, put his car on the provisional sixth row.

Final qualifying was hectic and, despite the efforts of Reutemann and Andretti, both in Lotuses, Jacques Laffite started in pole position, on 2min 23.7sec, just 92/100th better than

Arnoux.

team-mate Patrick Depailler. Jabouille was on 7th and Arnoux had slipped back to 11th.

At the start, Depailler spun the Ligier's wheels too much and Laffite tore off in front – the race was won and no one saw him again as he led from start to finish.

For Jabouille there was a problem: his engine had stalled. Fortunately, he was able to get his car going again, though, by then, right at the back. Not to be discouraged, the king of fight-back showed his tenacious spirit again and launched a superb recovery, to the delight of the 50,000+ spectators. By the 10th lap 8 places had been taken and he set off in pursuit of the two Arrows of Patrese and Mass; a further ten laps and he was with them. Just over halfway through the race, Jean-Pierre moved the

Renault up another place when Gilles Villeneuve had to stop in the pits to change a wheel. The crowd's delight at watching Jabouille's progress from the back turned to despair as their hero, Fittipaldi, retired; then Scheckter had to pit, also for a wheel change. This put the Renault in the points. But its tyres were giving problems and, on lap 30 of the 40-lap race, Jabouille had to pit for new ones. René Arnoux's luck had run out two laps before, on lap 28, when he had lost control of his Renault in turn 1. Jabouille rejoined the race in 11th place and, though he managed to make up one place before the flag fell, could do no more. It had been a good race; the engines worked well – definitely an improvement over Argentina, but still a case of 'not quite.'

STARTING GRID	
Laffite	Depailler
2'23.07"	2'23.99"
Reutemann	Andretti
2'24.15"	2'24.28"
Villeneuve	Scheckter
2'24.34"	2'24.48"
Jabouille	Pironi
2'24.85"	2'25.16"
Fittipaldi	Hunt
2'26.35"	2'26.37"
Arnoux	Lauda
2'26.43"	2'27.57"
Jones	Watson
2'27.67"	2'27.82"
Patrese	
2'28.08"	
Regazzoni	Tambay
2'28.88"	2'29.39"
Mass	De Angelis
2'29.42"	2'30.29"
Lammers	Piquet
2'31.60"	2'31.64"
Daily	Stuck
2'31.78"	2'32.27"

RESULTS - Interlagos (318,400 km)

1. Laffite	Ligier-Ford	40	1h40'09.64"
2. Depailler	Ligier-Ford	40	1h40'14.92"
3. Reutemann	Lotus-Ford	40	1h40'53.78"
4. Pironi	Tyrrell-Ford	40	1h41'35.52"
5. Villeneuve	Ferrari	39	+ 1 lap
6. Scheckter	Ferrari	39	+ 1 lap
7. Mass	Arrows-Ford	39	+ 1 lap
8. Watson	McLaren-Ford	39	+ 1 lap
9. Patrese	Arrows-Ford	39	+ 1 lap
10. Jabouille	Renault	39	+ 1 lap
11. Fittipaldi	Copersucar-Ford	39	+ 1 lap
12. De Angelis	Shadow-Ford	39	+ 1 lap
13. Daly	Ensign-Ford	39	+ 1 lap
14. Lammers	Shadow-Ford	39	+ 1 lap
15. Regazzoni	Williams-Ford	38	+ 2 laps

FASTEST LAP

Laffite	Ligier-Ford	2'28.76"
		190.548 km/h

RETIREMENTS

Jones	Williams-Ford	33	Fuel pressure
Stuck	ATS-Ford	31	Steering wheel broken
Arnoux	Renault	28	Spin
Tambay	McLaren-Ford	7	Accident
Hunt	Wolf-Ford	7	Steering
Piquet	Brabham-Alfa Romeo	5	Accident
Lauda	Brabham-Alfa Romeo	5	Gear selector
Andretti	Lotus-Ford	2	Fuel leak

Interlagos race statistics.

South African Grand Prix, Kyalami, 3 March 1979

Kyalami circuit – back to the rarefied atmosphere which caused problems for the normally-aspirated cars. Could the turbo do better this time? The team had some experience from the previous year. This race was the first Grand Prix that Michel Têtu had attended in his new role. He took it all in as his mind was on the RS10.

Weather conditions were mild for the Thursday practice, and Jean-Pierre Jabouille made full use of the turbo by clocking up best time on the first practice day. Turbo power was definitely an advantage – but would it be reliable? Local hero, Jody Scheckter, was just behind the Renault in his new Ferrari T4, with Gilles Villeneuve in 3rd position. Michelin, who supplied both Ferrari and Renault, was happy, and having a field day, even if it was only Thursday. Satisfied with his car's performance, Jabouille hopefully forgot about the fragility of the engines, despite the fact that in private testing the day before he had been stopped in his tracks by two failures!

Friday dawned with near-perfect conditions; the clouds had disappeared from Kyalami, though, in the sun, the temperature had jumped about ten degrees. Try as they might, however, Thursday's times could not be beaten.

Suddenly, it was realised that Jean-Pierre Jabouille and Renault had put the new turbo car, the RS01 – the one that everybody had laughed at just 18 months before – on pole position in a Formula 1 Grand Prix! Arnoux, with the other Renault, was a little further down the grid.

Saturday morning again dawned with beautiful weather, but the forecast was not good; as heavy grey clouds began covering the sky, the track darkened, along with everyone's optimism. The start of the race, at least, was dry and all got away without problem, Villeneuve and Scheckter quicker off the line than Jabouille, their Ferraris in front of the Renault as they rounded Crowthorne, the first corner, for the first time. The three cars were wheel-to-wheel, and, going out of Leeukop, the corner before the long straight, the Renault's power really began to come to the fore, as it blasted past the Ferraris to lead at the end of the 1st lap. On lap two, however, the nimbler Villeneuve returned the favour to Jabouille. Pierre Dupasquier of Michelin was jumping for joy as the three Michelin-shod cars were already beginning to drop their rivals. But then a violent storm suddenly broke over the circuit and the race had to be stopped, and it was fifty minutes before it could restart. Villeneuve and Jabouille chose to go out on rain tyres, but a brave Scheckter took a chance on

A furious start, but the Turbo was on pole!

STARTING GRID		RESULTS - Kyalami (320,112 km)			
Scheckter 1'12.04"	Jabouille 1'11.80"	1. Villeneuve	Ferrari	78	1h41'49.96"
Lauda 1'12.12"	Villeneuve 1'12.07"	2. Scheckter	Ferrari	78	1h41'53.38"
Laffite 1'12.26"	Depailler 1'12.15"	3. Jarier	Tyrrell-Ford	78	1h42'12.07"
Andretti 1'12.36"	Pironi 1'12.33"	4. Andretti	Lotus-Ford	78	1h42'17.84"
Arnoux 1'12.69"	Jarier 1'12.55"	5. Reutemann	Lotus-Ford	78	1h42'56.93"
Piquet 1'13.07"	Reutemann 1'12.75"	6. Lauda	Brabham-Alfa Romeo	77	+ 1 lap
Watson 1'14.44"	Hunt 1'14.21"	7. Piquet	Brabham-Alfa Romeo	77	+ 1 lap
Patrese 1'14.54"	De Angelis 1'14.44"	8. Hunt	Wolf-Ford	77	+ 1 lap
Fittipaldi 1'14.61"	Tambay 1'14.58"	9. Regazzoni	Williams-Ford	76	+ 2 laps
Mass 1'15.00"	Jones 1'14.64"	10. Tambay	McLaren-Ford	75	+ 3 laps
Regazzoni 1'15.68"	Lammers 1'15.35"	11. Patrese	Arrows-Ford	75	+ 3 laps
Stuck 1'16.31"	Rebaque 1'16.15"	12. Mass	Arrows-Ford	74	+ 4 laps
		13. Fittipaldi	Copersucar-Ford	74	+ 4 laps

FASTEST LAP			
Villeneuve	Ferrari	1'14.41" 198.540 km/h	

RETIREMENTS			
Rebaque	Lotus-Ford	71	Engine
Arnoux	Renault	67	Puncture
Jones	Williams-Ford	63	Rear suspension
Watson	McLaren-Ford	61	Ignition
Stuck	ATS-Ford	57	Accident
Jabouille	Renault	47	Engine
Laffite	Ligier-Ford	45	Accident
Pironi	Tyrrell-Ford	25	Accélérateur
De Angelis	Shadow-Ford	16	Accident
Depailler	Ligier-Ford	4	Accident
Lammers	Shadow-Ford	2	Collision Rebaque

Kyalami race statistics.

slicks, which proved a good choice. Jabouille could not repeat his exploits of the two first laps in the dry; his Renault struggled on the wets and he dropped a long way back before being obliged to stop for slicks to be fitted. All to no avail, however, as the Renault's engine failed on the 47th lap, just as he had come to terms with the grip and was about to pass Andretti for 4th place.

Renault hopes turned to Arnoux. He was going well when Alan Jones violently left the track; arriving just behind the Australian, René could not avoid driving over the debris left by the Williams. This looked bad: when he braked hard at the end of the straight, the left rear tyre of the Renault burst. It was to take all of René's expertise to maintain control of his wildly steering projectile and bring it to a stop intact. Not the finish the team had hoped for, but at least the Renault had demonstrated that it had the capability by taking pole in front of the Ferraris.

US West Coast Grand Prix, Long Beach, 8 April 1979

At the request of Goodyear, supposedly in the interests of economy, it was decided that the first morning session of practice on the first day would no longer be officially timed but would be free practice, and only the second session would count for

the grid. Everyone seemed happy with this and the drivers didn't complain.

Used by everyday traffic, the Long Beach circuit has to be created for the race, which means that the surface is very slippery for an F1 car. It is therefore essential for the drivers to generate grip by driving round and putting down a layer of rubber on the

"Whilst the Renault was being driven at some 270kmh (167.7mph), a transmission halfshaft snapped and came out of its housing, destroying the car's left rear suspension in the process ... "

track. There were always plenty of spins and skids when this was going on, and Villeneuve struggled with the lack of mechanical grip in the morning, before eventually qualifying his Ferrari T4 on the 1st row in the afternoon.

STARTING GRID		RESULTS - Long Beach (261,625 km)			
Reutemann 1'18.886"	Villeneuve 1'18.825"	1. Villeneuve	Ferrari	80	1h50'25.40"
Depailler 1'19.025"	Scheckter 1'18.911"	2. Scheckter	Ferrari	80	1h50'54.78"
Andretti 1'19.454	Laffite 1'19.032"	3. Jones	Williams-Ford	80	1h51'25.09"
Hunt 1'19.643"	Jarier 1'19.580"	4. Andretti	Lotus-Ford	80	1h51'29.73"
Jones 1'19.910"	Patrese 1'19.727"	5. Depailler	Ligier-Ford	80	1h51'48.92"
Piquet 1'20.456"	Lauda 1'20.041"	6. Jarier	Tyrrell-Ford	79	+ 1 lap
Lammers 1'20.740"	Mass 1'20.608"	7. De Angelis	Shadow-Ford	78	+ 2 laps
Fittipaldi 1'21.033"	Regazzoni 1'20.768"	8. Piquet	Brabham-Alfa Romeo	78	+ 2 laps
Watson 1'21.304"	Pironi 1'21.192"	9. Mass	Arrows-Ford	78	+ 2 laps
De Angelis 1'21.961"	Tambay 1'21.411"				
Merzario 1'22.938"	Stuck 1'22.828"				
Daly 1'23.888"	Rebaque 1'22.990"				

DISQUALIFIED (pushed during the start)			
Pironi	Tyrrell-Ford	72	
Stuck	ATS-Ford	49	

FASTEST LAP			
Villeneuve	Ferrari	1'21.2" 144.133 km/h	

RETIREMENTS			
Rebaque	Lotus-Ford	71	Collision with Daly
Daly	Ensign-Ford	69	Collision Rebaque
Watson	McLaren-Ford	62	Injection system
Regazzoni	Williams-Ford	48	Engine
Lammers	Shadow-Ford	47	Suspension
Patrese	Arrows-Ford	40	Brakes
Reutemann	Lotus-Ford	21	Transmission shaft
Fittipaldi	Copersucar-Ford	19	Transmission shaft
Merzario	Merzario-Ford	13	Engine
Laffite	Ligier-Ford	8	Brakes
Hunt	Wolf-Ford	0	Half shaft
Lauda	Brabham-Alfa Romeo	0	Collision with Tambay
Tambay	McLaren-Ford	0	Collision with Lauda

Long Beach race statistics.

For Renault it was a disaster, causing Jean Sage to decide to withdraw after the two practice days. So what happened? On the Friday Jabouille had transmission problems and spent more time in the pits than on the track. The next day it was even worse. Whilst the Renault was being driven at some 270kmh (167.7mph), a transmission halfshaft snapped and came out of its housing, destroying the car's left rear suspension in the process. Jabouille could do nothing to control what was, by then, a mobile accident waiting to happen. He collided violently with the protective wall along the track, though, fortunately, escaped with just a small injury to his wrist. René Arnoux fared no better: his car caught fire when a loose pipe dripped oil onto the engine exhaust. Despite these problems, both drivers managed to qualify on the grid. On the Sunday morning during the warm-up, Arnoux fell victim to the broken halfshaft malady in similar conditions to his team-mate. "Too dangerous for the race," declared Jean Sage. The decision was made to withdraw.

The race was dominated from start to finish by Gilles Villeneuve. With Scheckter in 2nd, it was the Scuderia's second one-two in two races, and on Michelins.

Spanish Grand Prix, Jarama, 29 April 1979

Ground-effect technology was what everyone was talking about. After the successful (but banned) Gordon Murray fan car from Brabham, Lotus had taken the lead with a legal ground-effect system, and the technology that, by now, was familiar to Lotus was, after a few races, beginning to be adopted by the other teams. Williams had created the FW07 which had already been seen at Long Beach, although it didn't race. There was talk about the Renault RS10 but no one had seen it, so it was an entirely unknown quantity.

On a chilly Friday morning, excitement mounted as competing teams watched the Williams and Renault trucks unload their new cars. Ground effect had arrived.

Renault had just one RS10 in Spain for Jean-Pierre Jabouille, who, at the end of the two practice days, was in 9th position on the grid. The Michel Têtu-influenced chassis was very new and not yet fully developed; Jabouille felt he thought it would take a couple of races to get it up to full potential.

The RS10 displayed a sharp, slippery-bodied image, with excellent-looking aerodynamics, proven immediately as it was the quickest on the straight at Jarama. Jean-Pierre suffered from some teething troubles on the Friday when he had to stop with continual breakages of the throttle cable, and on the Saturday morning with a broken turbo. Just behind him on the grid was René Arnoux, still driving the old and much-modified RS01.

First outing for the new RS10: Jabouille. (© DPPI/Ren)

Arnoux kept the old car. (© DPPI/Ren)

Arnoux ahead of Villeneuve.

René began his weekend by recording the 7th fastest time in the now well-used old car on the Friday, but his second timed session was plagued by an injector problem; by the time the mechanics had identified the fault it was too late for René to improve his position. He had nearly thrown it all away on the Friday morning when he damaged his suspension against the barrier by setting off too quickly on cold tyres. The Goodyear-shod cars were taking advantage of the rubber being laid down by the Michelin runners and, in the end, it was Laffite who took pole from Depailler.

During the Saturday night heavy rain washed clean the track, and on race day it was in the same condition as the drivers had started with on the Friday morning, meaning that all of the teams had a level playing field and had to think hard during warm-up about what tyre choice to make.

At the start, Andretti in row 2 managed to get past the front row cars to set off ahead of everyone else, though wasn't able to keep his advantage and the two Ligiers flew by, off to fight a memorable duel from which Patrick Depailler was to emerge victorious, while Laffite had to retire after over-revving his engine, causing it to fail. Behind the two Ligiers and Reutemann's Lotus, Villeneuve was getting impatient, believing that the Argentinian was slowing him down, so he tried an overtaking manoeuvre by braking as late as possible. But the rear wheels locked and the T4 went into a spin that left the Canadian face-to-face with the bunch. Trying to avoid him, Jabouille also went into a spin. With its engine stalled, the RS10 had to be pushed by the marshals to get it going again. The inevitable disqualification proved superfluous as Jabouille had to retire anyway on the 21st lap, with the Renault V6 losing fuel pressure. As for Arnoux in the old RS01, he finished the race in 9th place, despite a bad choice of tyres; the chosen compound was too soft.

"Villeneuve was getting impatient ... so he tried an overtaking manoeuvre by braking as late as possible. But the rear wheels locked and the T4 went into a spin that left the Canadian face-to-face with the bunch. Trying to avoid him, Jabouille also went into a spin."

Jean-Pierre Jabouille: "I remember an argument over the chassis of the RS10 and the use of the engine, whether to put a twin turbo in it and modify the chassis to a ground-effect car.

STARTING GRID			RESULTS - Jarama (255,300 km)			
Depailler	Laffite	1.	Depailler	Ligier-Ford	75	1h39'11.84"
1'14.79"	1'14.50"	2.	Reutemann	Lotus-Ford	75	1h39'32.78"
Andretti	Villeneuve	3.	Andretti	Lotus-Ford	75	1h39'39.15"
1'15.07"	1'14.82"	4.	Scheckter	Ferrari	75	1h39'40.52"
Lauda	Scheckter	5.	Jarier	Tyrrell-Ford	75	1h39'42.23"
1'15.45"	1'15.10"	6.	Pironi	Tyrrell-Ford	75	1h40'00.27"
Reutemann	Piquet	7.	Villeneuve	Ferrari	75	1h40'04.15"
1'15.67"	1'15.61"	8.	Mass	Arrows-Ford	75	1h40'26.68"
Pironi	Jabouille	9.	Arnoux	Renault	74	1h39'34.49"
1'16.04"	1'15.78"	10.	Patrese	Arrows-Ford	74	1h39'43.86"
Jarier	Arnoux	11.	Fittipaldi	Copersucar-Ford	74	1h40'19.73"
1'16.08"	1'16.06"	12.	Lammers	Shadow-Ford	73	1h39'18.20"
Regazzoni	Jones	13.	Tambay	McLaren-Ford	72	1h40'26.41"
1'16.61"	1'16.23"	14.	Stuck	ATS-Ford	69	1h40'25.55"
Patrese	Hunt					
1'16.92"	1'16.88"		**FASTEST LAP**			
Watson	Mass					
1'17.11"	1'17.04"	Villeneuve		Ferrari		1'16.44"
Tambay	Fittipaldi					160.329 km/h
1'17.45"	1'17.35"					
De Angelis	Stuck		**RETIREMENTS**			
1'17.85"	1'17.57"					
Lammers	Rebaque	Lauda	Brabham-Alfa Romeo	63	Water leak	
1'18.79"	1'18.42"	Rebaque	Lotus-Ford	58	Engine	
		Jones	Williams-Ford	54	Gear selector	
		De Angelis	Shadow-Ford	52	Engine	
		Regazzoni	Williams-Ford	32	Engine	
		Hunt	Wolf-Ford	26	Brakes	
		Watson	McLaren-Ford	21	Engine	
		Jabouille	Renault	21	Fuel pressure	
		Laffite	Ligier-Ford	15	Engine	
		Piquet	Brabham-Alfa Romeo	15	Fuel feed	

Jarama race statistics.

The single-turbo RS10 struggled.

"I thought it was obvious, because of the Lotus – they were doing it already. Some people at the time in the aerodynamics department at Renault Sport thought we could achieve greater efficiency going out of the corners, but there were others who were against the twin turbo and the ground-effect system. I was in favour of a ground-effect car with twin turbo, but some were not convinced. So we found a happy medium and we made a ground-effect car with a single turbo. I was certain that it wasn't a good idea after I had run a race with a single turbo and ground-effect. I said I wanted a twin turbo with the ground-effect car. Gradually, it became clear to everyone that the twin turbo and ground-effect were super-efficient, and from that moment on René and I were very soon winning races."

Belgian Grand Prix, Zolder, 13 May 1979

Friday morning started wet, much to the drivers' displeasure. Then, Jean-Pierre Jabouille surprised everyone by making the second fastest time in front of Jacques Laffite. But the last word went to Laffite, who got the final pole position the next day in better weather, and, once again, Patrick Depailler was lined up with his team-mate, despite going off the track during the session. After a brave performance in the previous practice sessions, Jabouille's morale took a nosedive. He went from 2nd place to 17th on the grid as he was stuck in the pits with a leak in his fuel system.

RS01 in the background; RS10 in the foreground.

STARTING GRID	
Laffite 1'21.13"	Depailler 1'21.20"
Piquet 1'21.35"	Jones 1'21.59"
Andretti 1'21.83"	Villeneuve 1'22.08"
Scheckter 1'22.08"	Regazzoni 1'22.40"
Hunt 1'22.55"	Reutemann 1'22.56"
Jarier 1'22.68"	Pironi 1'22.85"
Lauda 1'22.87"	Giacomelli 1'23.15"
Rebaque 1'23.63"	Patrese 1'23.92"
Jabouille 1'24.02"	Arnoux 1'24.33"
Watson 1'24.37"	Stuck 1'24.62"
Lammers 1'24.76"	Mass 1'25.08"
Fittipaldi 1'25.18"	De Angelis 1'25.48"

RESULTS - Zolder (298,340 km)

1. Scheckter	Ferrari	70	1h39'59.53"
2. Laffite	Ligier-Ford	70	1h40'14.89"
3. Pironi	Tyrrell-Ford	70	1h40'34.70"
4. Reutemann	Lotus-Ford	70	1h40'46.02"
5. Patrese	Arrows-Ford	70	1h41'03.84"
6. Watson	McLaren-Ford	70	1h41'05.38"
7. Villeneuve	Ferrari	69	+ 1 lap
8. Stuck	ATS-Ford	69	+ 1 lap
9. Fittipaldi	Copersucar-Ford	68	+ 2 laps
10. Lammers	Shadow-Ford	67	+ 3 laps
11. Jarier	Tyrrell-Ford	67	+ 3 laps

FASTEST LAP

Scheckter	Ferrari	1'22.39" 186.226 km/h

RETIREMENTS

Depailler	Ligier-Ford	46	Accident
Hunt	Wolf-Ford	40	Accident
Jones	Williams-Ford	39	Electrical system
Andretti	Lotus-Ford	27	Brakes
Piquet	Brabham-Alfa Romeo	23	Engine
Lauda	Brabham-Alfa Romeo	23	Engine
Arnoux	Renault	22	Supercharger
Giacomelli	Alfa Romeo	21	Collision De Angelis
De Angelis	Shadow-Ford	21	Collision Giacomelli
Mass	Arrows-Ford	17	Spin, stall
Rebaque	Lotus-Ford	13	Transmission shaft
Jabouille	Renault	13	Supercharger
Regazzoni	Williams-Ford	1	Collision with Scheckter and Villeneuve

Zolder race statistics.

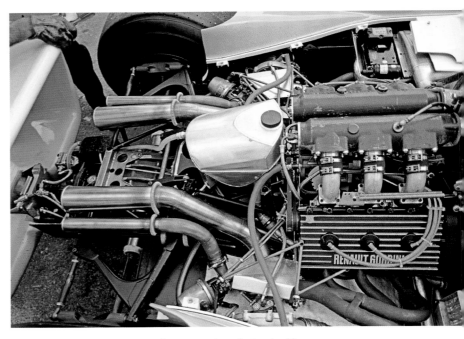

RS10 twin-turbo engine installation for Monaco.

In spite of differences of opinion in the team, Renault had begun to develop a twin-turbo engine and the RS10 was modified for that unit, but the engine was not ready and this chassis required a lot of DIY when the single turbo was fitted. Renault started on the ninth row of the grid. However, the race proved similar to many that had gone before when both cars retired with turbocharger problems, Jabouille on the 2nd lap and Arnoux on the 22nd.

The frustration was palpable: would they ever find the reliability and consistency they searched for? The power was there – South Africa had proved that, albeit at altitude – but the cars were just not consistent enough. Maybe the twin turbo would prove better?

For the record, the race was won by Scheckter from Laffite.

Monaco Grand Prix, 27 May 1979

Nobody was too worried by the turbo cars yet; after all, the Cosworths were still winning and Ferrari had not yet gone turbo, so maybe it wasn't such a good idea after all. But that did not stop the teams from closely examining the Renaults as they arrived at Monaco. For the first time everyone would see the new Renault twin-turbo engine! Maybe this was going to be the turning point?

From its beginnings, and up to 1979 for the RS10's first Grand Prix races, the engine was boosted by a single turbocompressor. However, the design construction of the V6 easily lent itself to modification. Viry engineers had, for some time, been investigating the possibility of twin turbos, and in all the tests it was seen that fitting two small turbocompressors – one per row of cylinders – created very few and often no problems at all. The thermal aspects of the RS10's engine compartment also benefited (Rolf Stommelen had been right!). The first comparative tests of the twin turbo in the car had taken place at Dijon on a private track equipped with chicanes, in order to demonstrate the differences between the two solutions of behaviour in acceleration and response time.

Every possible version was tested and compared with the original single-turbo set-up. Garrett and KKK were tried against each other. In all, seven different types or brands were tested, including a hybrid turbocharger based on a Garrett turbine and a KKK compressor. It's worth noting here that the Renault Sport engine design office had, after four years of development, become specialist in the field of turbocharging. It found that the twin-turbo versions provided results which clearly favoured this type of installation compared with the single-turbo version it had been using up until this time.

Availability of components and the time in which they could be prepared, as well as performance, played a major part in the final choice, and the Viry team settled on a KKK twin-turbocharger because this manufacturer had the advantage of having within its commercial range the product it needed. This, of course, provided considerable advantages in terms of cost and delivery time.

After much testing carried out in secret it was decided that the Monaco 1979 Grand Prix would witness the first appearance of the RS10 fitted with the twin-turbo. Renault believed from experience that the Monaco track had the ideal layout to put the engine to good use, and, despite the fact that not all of the testing had been completed by the time of the GP, confidence was high. All of the system components were new: not only the turbos themselves but also the exhaust system, the inlet manifolds, the heat exchanger intercoolers, the accelerator controls, and the air filters.

> ## "... it was decided that the Monaco 1979 Grand Prix would witness the first appearance of the RS10 fitted with the twin-turbo. Renault believed from experience that the Monaco track had the ideal layout to put the engine to good use ..."

Renault had brought two vehicles, so René Arnoux at last had a ground-effect car – the RS10 – while Jabouille was given a lighter, updated version – the RS11 – with a new rear wing. The car's performance was so much better that Jabouille and Arnoux no longer recognised their V6 power units from the considerably faster throttle-response time. Even so, the practice sessions weren't easy for the team, which was lucky even to qualify, but it did – just – on the back row. Both drivers had rear wheel troubles on the Thursday, Arnoux had a problem with the fuel feed circuit on the Saturday, and Jabouille even had to abandon his car at the Casino when a transmission halfshaft broke. Scheckter was to take pole from Villeneuve, going on to win from Regazzoni after Villeneuve went out on lap 54 with transmission problems.

RS10. (© ETAI)

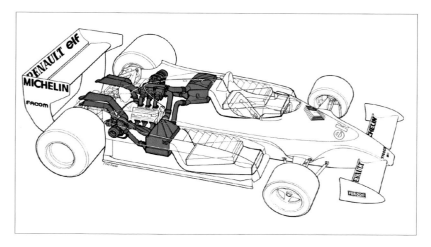

Location of turbos in RS10. (© ETAI)

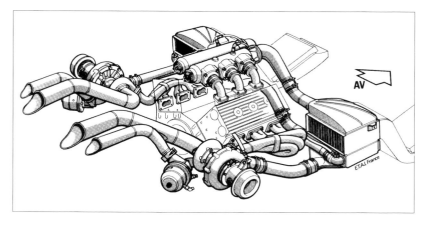

Turbo layout. (© ETAI)

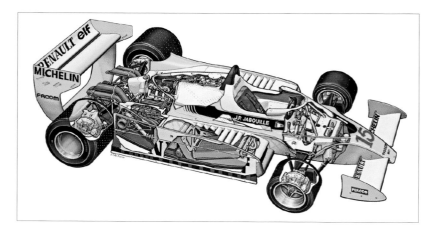

Would they ever win? Monaco was a low point.

First try with a twin-turbo.

At Renault the new engine's hoped-for glory didn't materialise. Arnoux collided with Piquet on the 8th lap and had to retire. Jabouille did his best, stopping several times in the pits to try to remedy a fuel feed problem, but without success. Then, one of the exchangers of Jabouille's car sprang a leak and the engine progressively lost power. Although he eventually came in 7th, Jean-Pierre was not classified as he didn't complete a sufficient distance. François Guiter: "It was a difficult time; Gérard was thinking it was not going to work and for the first time looked depressed. I walked over to him and tried to give him some words of encouragement. I told him, 'Go on! Keep going! It's going to work.'"

After the Monaco Grand Prix an infuriated François Castaing and Jean-Pierre Boudy set up a systematic testing programme to determine component reliability. There was clear progress in performance, undoubtedly due to the new boost system, but the cars were still let down by faulty components.

A few words here from Jean-Pierre Boudy on the new engines: "The big advantage of the twin turbocompressors was the much improved response time they gave the engine, the throughput of gas treated by each of the turbocompressors being half of the engine's requirements; also the sizes of the compressors and the turbines were proportionally smaller. Thus, the gain in inertia of the mobile components of the turbocompressors – the rotors – was substantial.

"... one of the exchangers of Jabouille's car sprang a leak and the engine progressively lost power. Although he eventually came in 7th, Jean-Pierre was not classified as he didn't complete a sufficient distance."

"The acceleration of the turbocompressor's rotating components will be greater, inasmuch as the moment of inertia of the rotor wheels is less, hence the dimension of the rotor wheels and their mass is smaller. It was from this position that the new smaller turbos improved performances. It also became clear that the higher the surplus energy from the turbine, the lower the compression force. This was how the notion of compressor efficiency was calculated. To obtain maximum efficiency, for aerodynamic reasons, the smaller the dimension of the compressor the faster they can run. For example, a single TV61-T04 turbo ran at 80,000rpm on the test bench, while the KKK 3070GD twin turbos ran at 150,000rpm under the same conditions. The only limiting factor is the temperature of the turbine at high speeds, which can restrict even higher rpm."

Tests relating to the metallurgy of the turbine wheels were conducted with the greatest care, because the mechanical constraints of the vanes due to the combination of speed and temperature, often higher than 1100°C, represented a very difficult problem for the turbine engineers. All the turbo manufacturing companies kept very quiet about their metallurgical solutions. In general, they used super-alloys with a very high proportion of nickel, chrome and cobalt, whose essential characteristics lay in their excellent resistance to fatigue at high temperatures.

Jean-Pierre Boudy again: "For the same turbine speed [150,000rpm at 1100°C], the time before breakage can be anywhere between half an hour and three hours, depending on the type of steel chosen within the range offered by KKK, for example. At 180,000rpm in the same temperature conditions and with the same materials, this time can vary from a few minutes to half an hour. In the light of this example, one can see the importance of the technological choice of components and the pressures to which the team subjected their turbocompressor supplier at the time to get him to try to keep abreast of the

STARTING GRID		RESULTS - Monaco (251,712 km)			
Scheckter 1'26.45"	Villeneuve 1'26.52"	1. Scheckter	Ferrari	76	1h55'22.48"
Depailler 1'27.11"	Lauda 1'27.21"	2. Regazzoni	Williams-Ford	76	1h55'22.92"
Laffite 1'27.26"	Jarier 1'27.42"	3. Reutemann	Lotus-Ford	76	1h55'31.05"
Pironi 1'27.42"	Mass 1'27.47"	4. Watson	McLaren-Ford	76	1h56'03.79"
Jones 1'27.67"	Hunt 1'27.96"	5. Depailler	Ligier-Ford	74	+ 2 laps
Reutemann 1'27.99"	Stuck 1'28.22"	6. Mass	Arrows-Ford	69	Engine
Andretti 1'28.23"	Watson 1'28.23"				
Patrese 1'28.30"	Regazzoni 1'28.48"	**NOT CLASSIFIED**			
Fittipaldi 1'28.49"	Piquet 1'28.52"	Jabouille	Renault	68	+ 8 laps
Arnoux 1'28.57"	Jabouille 1'28.68"				

FASTEST LAP			
Depailler	Ligier-Ford	1'28.82" 134.240 km/h	

RETIREMENTS			
Piquet	Brabham-Alfa Romeo	68	Transmission shaft
Laffite	Ligier-Ford	55	Gearbox
Villeneuve	Ferrari	54	Differential
Jones	Williams-Ford	43	Accident Front suspension
Jarier	Tyrrell-Ford	34	Drive shaft
Stuck	ATS-Ford	30	Wheel broken
Lauda	Brabham-Alfa Romeo	21	Collision with Pironi
Pironi	Tyrrell-Ford	21	Collision with Lauda
Andretti	Lotus-Ford	21	Rear suspension
Fittipaldi	Copersucar-Ford	17	Engine
Arnoux	Renault	8	Collision with Piquet
Hunt	Wolf-Ford	4	Transmission
Patrese	Arrows-Ford	4	Suspension

Monaco race statistics.

technological development of Formula 1 engines, and to persuade him to design a turbocompressor specifically for the Renault cars."

The team only partially succeeded in getting the manufacturer to play ball, in that a great deal of work was done on the compressor rotor wheel, but all of the design and fine tuning to perfection was undertaken by the Renault Sport design office. Unfortunately, the lack of cooperation in these confidential areas, where materials were needed from the supplier in quick time, caused problems, and it is still thought by those involved that, a few years later in 1983, this was one of the factors (along with the use of an illegal fuel by another team) that cost them victory in the Italian and South African Grands Prix at the very least, and the possibility of becoming world champion.

French Grand Prix, Dijon, 1 July 1979

After two years Renault Sport had still not overcome the difficulty of competing against the V8, normally-aspirated Ford-Cosworth engine (launched in 1967), or the fine, 12-cylinder Ferrari 'boxer' (created in 1970) with a small, 1500cc boosted engine. So far, in almost two years of effort, a 4th place (US Grand Prix 1978)

133

Jabouille, Larrousse, Arnoux.

Arnoux in full flight. (© DPPI/Ren)

Very efficient rear wing.

was all there was to show on the records of the turbocharged car. At times the performance had been there, but reliability was still uncertain. The little V6 Renault engine, operated at high temperatures, had gurgling hiccups when started, and long flames spat out of the enormous exhaust pipe when the power came in under acceleration. The RS10 was startling: it had a spectacular appearance, sounded different, and looked fast even standing still. It seemed unbeatable, though so far had not delivered.

Inspired by the Lotus of the previous year, its narrow cockpit squeezed between two side-pods, aerodynamically designed to cause a depression which increased downforce, it came with the important modification to the power unit of twin turbocompressors, not dissimilar, in fact, to that on the Porsche 935, which had shown greatly improved performance. The turbos themselves had also been developed further since the Monaco race.

Cancellation of the Swedish Grand Prix that year, originally planned for June, had given the team nearly a month's extra development time before the French Grand Prix. It made the most of it and the RS10 and RS11 immediately proved easier to control, as Jabouille and Arnoux both commented at the time.

Jean-Pierre Jabouille: "I remember the new engine was no more powerful than the old one but it was much less brutal. The throttle pick-up was more progressive and came in earlier at 5500-6000rpm instead of 6500-7000."

Progress had occurred in leaps and bounds during private testing in early June at Dijon-Prenois, with its many big corners and high-speed sections that played to the aerodynamic efficiency of the new car and helped the team make the most of the engine, which, with its new flexibility, was giving a 'velvety' sound to the exhaust note.

The grip of the RS10 was so good now that Jabouille had to interrupt a 300km (186 mile) test because his neck muscles couldn't take the forces they were subjected to in the corners, the centrifugal force now so great because of the ground-effect. He only managed to complete the test after the installation of a lateral headrest.

Both drivers came to the French Grand Prix in high spirits, a new state of affairs for them. Jabouille remembers: "I needed to go 5/10 th quicker in qualifying than in our private testing." His optimism was unaffected by two years of so much effort, so far in vain.

On Friday 29 June, only fifteen minutes into the official practice at the French Grand Prix, the Renault was already down to 1min 8sec, pulverising the previous lap record. The weather, unusually cool for the time of year, was helping by improving the performance of the exchangers cooling the inlet air. After only half an hour on the track, Jabouille was down to 1min 7.41sec, which only he managed to beat the following morning with a brilliant 1min 7.19sec that confirmed his pole position. The RS10 was truly flying.

René Arnoux was also having a great practice and qualifying, getting down to 1min 7.45sec on the Friday. Even though

> **"70,000 fervently patriotic spectators thronged the Dijon-Prenois circuit on a weekend that was to change the face of Grand Prix racing. Given the dominance of the yellow cars in practice, the Renault team and the whole of France took a deep breath ..."**

he suffered a broken valve spring on the Saturday, that time guaranteed a place on the front row.

For the first time in Grand Prix history, the starting grid for the French race had two of the yellow cars, mockingly called the 'Yellow Teapots' only two years previously, dominating the weekend's qualifying. Would they be reliable? Ferrari, Ligier, Lotus, and all the Cosworth teams were looking on in amazement

Jabouille goes into the lead. (© DPPI/Ren)

at the speed of the new cars, but were not afraid because they knew that reliability had always been a problem for the Renaults. All the British teams were saying that one swallow does not a summer make, so would this be that swallow or was this the start of summer? They were about to find out.

70,000 fervently patriotic spectators thronged the Dijon-Prenois circuit on a weekend that was to change the face of Grand Prix racing. Given the dominance of the yellow cars in practice, the Renault team and the whole of France took a deep breath. The crowd, of course, was enthusiastic, though well aware of the failures of the past; there was still a question mark about the reliability of an engine which had so far proved exceedingly vulnerable. Also of concern were the physical effects on the drivers: the new cars were very fast, nearly half a second faster per lap than anyone else, according to qualifying. The lateral headrest tested during practice offered a good solution in this area.

But there were also tyre worries, particularly the left front, which was showing signs of wearing quickly when subjected to merciless torture on the interminable corners of the clockwise Prenois circuit. Michelin had offered two types of tyre; Jabouille chose the softer ones, basing his choice on a logical theory: "My thinking was that as the more resistant tyres gripped slightly less,

Arnoux in a fierce battle for second. (© DPPI/Ren)

Victory 1.

they would cause an understeer which would become greater as the race progressed. With softer tyres, I could control the wear of my front left tyre by saving it in the early stages of the race. If I could do that, it should be in perfect condition for the second half." Renault and Michelin technicians knew better than to contradict him ...

The cars still had some turbo lag, even with twin turbos, so it couldn't be taken for granted that they would get off to a good

"Arnoux caught up with the Ferrari on the 75th lap. So began a stunning duel during which both took considerable risks in their battle for 2nd place, attacking each other from all possible positions ..."

start. For the Ferraris it was the opposite: they could be virtually guaranteed to start fast. At the green light Villeneuve slipped his Ferrari between the Renaults, towing along in his slipstream his team-mate Scheckter. Arnoux found himself surrounded on all sides, but Jabouille managed to limit his initial setback by getting between Villeneuve and Scheckter at the first corner. He and

Victory 2.

Villeneuve finished the 1st lap slightly in front of Scheckter, with Piquet (Brabham-Alfa), Jarier (Tyrrell-Ford), Lauda (Brabham-Alfa), Laffite (Ligier-Ford), Jones (Williams-Ford), and Arnoux, now in 9th position, following on.

Scheckter couldn't keep up the pace and Jabouille was soon able to concentrate on his strategy without fear of an attack from the rear. After 10 of the 80 laps it was Villeneuve, Jabouille, Scheckter, and Arnoux close behind. Could Villeneuve maintain this determined pace? Jabouille didn't worry. His only concern was to keep his tyres in good condition; if he managed to do this, he would have time to worry about the Ferrari in the second half of the Grand Prix, whether or not Villeneuve had worn his tyres out.

Ten laps before halfway, Villeneuve seemed to be fading a little. Jabouille forced his pace slightly, coming within sight of the leader. The two then had 19 seconds over Arnoux, behind whom Scheckter was in trouble: the South African had stopped for a few seconds to check the slide of his bodywork skirts, on which the ground-effect depended. Jabouille, close to the Ferrari, made an error: braking too harshly, he touched the verge and his distance behind Villeneuve increased to 3 seconds. Jabouille forced the pace again and, on lap 44, the Ferrari and the Renault were once more wheel-to-wheel. The Ferrari was starting to understeer but its engine picked up much better going out of the corners. All of the cars were having trouble with their brakes but, with an additional 60 litres of fuel on board, the Renaults were hampered by the considerable extra weight which put an additional strain on the steel discs (carbon had not yet been introduced).

However, it was under braking that Jabouille attacked Villeneuve on the outside, at the end of the straight. The Renault managed to gain a slight advantage coming into the corner and held it so that, at the beginning of the 47th of 80 laps, Jabouille had taken the lead in his home Grand Prix. An ecstatic crowd roared its approval as he refused to let it go.

10 laps later his lead was 5 seconds. Villeneuve could not respond and had to watch Jabouille's lead steadily increase. Worse still, Arnoux was now within sight behind the Ferrari. The distance between them 20 laps from the finish was 20 seconds. Ten more laps and it was just 5.5 seconds! Arnoux caught up with the Ferrari on the 75th lap. So began a stunning duel during which both took considerable risks in their battle for 2nd place, attacking each other from all possible positions. As soon as one of them seized the 2nd place, he was immediately harassed by the other. Wheels came together violently several times, but the two drivers were always in control of the situation, even if it meant going off the track and driving on the verge. The performance is

Jabouille and Arnoux on the podium. (© DPPI/Ren)

remembered by all who saw that race: it was unforgettable, and almost eclipsed the fine victory of Jabouille, who knew nothing of the struggle going on behind him between Villeneuve and Arnoux.

Jabouille again: "Everything was going well in the car, but the last few kilometres seemed to take for ever. Each time I went

"The Renault, with its new twin-turbo engine and Michelin 'soft' tyres, driven with rigorous precision by Jean-Pierre Jabouille, took the chequered flag for a well-deserved and historic victory."

past the pits, I could see the whole Renault-Elf team standing behind the crash barrier with our pit boards. Somehow I realised how impatient the mechanics must be. After two years of struggle, victory was close. Among the faces turned towards me was my chief mechanic, Jean-Claude Guénard, a man who had made such great sacrifices to achieve what we were about to see become reality. I extended my safety margin as far as I could …"

The Renault, with its new twin-turbo engine and Michelin 'soft' tyres, driven with rigorous precision by Jean-Pierre Jabouille, took the chequered flag for a well-deserved and historic victory.

Jean-Pierre again: "Why were we able to win here? Well, we had done a huge amount of work with the Michelin people because, at the end of the day, we knew the fastest car was really the Ferrari, also on Michelin tyres. So we had decided to do a Grand Prix simulation at Dijon. As you know it was I who did the test and we had finished more than the length of a Grand Prix. What had seemed difficult to me was the g-force in the Pouas corner which we were now going round flat-out with ground-effect ... and I remember that when we did this simulation my head was squashed on my shoulders and I couldn't straighten it ... I didn't want to stop because I wanted to complete the simulation, but in the end I had to. This was the first time we had this problem, because now the car was well balanced, the tyres were good, and we were quite satisfied and it was now that bit faster. I had known for some time that if the car could stay reliable we could win because the team and I had prepared well.

"On the day of the race, I was getting ready, and obviously there was a change in weather conditions since the testing ... but everything was going well. I knew it could go fast but you had to drive the car in a certain way because, in the quicker parts of the circuit, it put a lot of demands on that left-hand front tyre, and it actually began to have problems at the start, especially starting with 230 litres of fuel; it wasn't the same as now, when they set off with 80 litres. So, for the cornering, the brakes, the tyres, everything, it was still a difficult balance. As you know, a turbo engine is a delicate thing and, in general, our starts were getting better and better, but it was still difficult. Gilles was going very fast – I could have followed him, but I knew that if I followed I would have a problem with my left front tyre. I improved my

"Jean Sage ... asked the official technical marshals to take the engines out of Jabouille's and Arnoux's cars so that they could check the conformity of the two V6 Renaults and especially their 1500cc capacity ... They were perfect."

rhythm and realised that I could move up closer. The rest you know: I got past Gilles and pulled away, leaving René to have that monumental battle. For Michelin, for the turbo engine, I was happy because it was all French equipment winning in France.

STARTING GRID	
Arnoux 1'07.45"	Jabouille 1'07.19"
Piquet 1'08.13	Villeneuve 1'07.65"
Lauda 1'08.20"	Scheckter 1'08.15"
Laffite 1'08.55"	Jones 1'08.23"
Jarier 1'08.80"	Regazzoni 1'08.65"
Andretti 1'09.35"	Pironi 1'08.95"
Ickx 1'09.68"	Reutemann 1'09.36"
Rosberg 1'10.15"	Watson 1'09.97"
Fittipaldi 1'10.61"	Giacomelli 1'10.59"
Tambay 1'10.92"	Patrese 1'10.70"
Mass 1'11.14"	Lammers 1'11.14"
De Angelis 1'12.23"	Rebaque 1'11.97"

RESULTS - Dijon-Prénois (304 km)

1. Jabouille	Renault	80	1h35'20.42"
2. Villeneuve	Ferrari	80	1h35'35.01"
3. Arnoux	Renault	80	1h35'35.25"
4. Jones	Williams-Ford	80	1h35'57.03"
5. Jarier	Tyrrell-Ford	80	1h36'24.93"
6. Regazzoni	Williams-Ford	80	1h36'25.93"
7. Scheckter	Ferrari	79	+ 1 lap
8. Laffite	Ligier-Ford	79	+ 1 lap
9. Rosberg	Wolf-Ford	79	+ 1 lap
10. Tambay	McLaren-Ford	78	+ 2 laps
11. Watson	McLaren-Ford	78	+ 2 laps
12. Rebaque	Lotus-Ford	78	+ 2 laps
13. Reutemann	Lotus-Ford	77	Accident
14. Patrese	Arrows-Ford	77	+ 3 laps
15. Mass	Arrows-Ford	75	+ 5 laps
16. De Angelis	Shadow-Ford	75	+ 5 laps
17. Giacomelli	Alfa Romeo	75	+ 5 laps
18. Lammers	Shadow-Ford	73	+ 7 laps

FASTEST LAP

Arnoux	Renault	1'09.16" 197.802 km/h

RETIREMENTS

Pironi	Tyrrell-Ford	71	Suspension
Fittipaldi	Copersucar-Ford	53	Oil leak
Piquet	Brabham-Alfa Romeo	52	Accident
Andretti	Lotus-Ford	51	Brakes, suspension, puncture
Ickx	Ligier-Ford	45	Engine
Lauda	Brabham-Alfa Romeo	23	Spin, stall

Dijon race statistics.

"So, we won our first Grand Prix with turbo technology which, of course, was totally different from what the other teams were using – tyres as well as the other stuff – all within 2 years."

The gamble taken by Bernard Hanon and Gérard Larrousse on behalf of Renault had paid off at last. Renault had won a Grand Prix and established a new type of engine technology in Formula 1. Gilles Villeneuve finally took the advantage over Arnoux to finish in 2nd place. A good sportsman, he saluted Jabouille with a friendly joke: "At last he's won with the flamethrower!" But it would be two years more before he was to drive the first Ferrari turbo to victory. In a smart move to prevent any rumours, as spiteful gossip is not unknown in the pits of the Formula 1 teams, Jean Sage, sports director of Renault Sport, immediately asked the official technical marshals to take the engines out of Jabouille's and Arnoux's cars so that they could check the conformity of the two V6 Renaults and especially their 1500cc capacity. This was done within the few minutes following the end of the race. They were perfect.

Part 4

THE GRAND PRIX YEARS

INTERESTING ASIDES: FUELS, AERODYNAMICS, AND TYRES

It had taken a lot of thought, effort, investmen, and a belief in the project. As we have seen, in the beginning everyone laughed. However, now it had achieved that first victory, the turbo principle was beginning to be taken seriously; the thinking in the pit lane was that, having done it once, they might just do it again.

Little did the world of Formula 1 realise that, at the beginning of 1979, a sea change was about to take place. The turbo years had arrived and in the seasons to come huge power outputs from some incredibly complex engines would be the norm. By 1981, the use of a turbocharged engine had changed thinking completely, and the 3-litre Cosworth cars were under great pressure as the major manufacturers switched to turbo power. In 1982, the Constructors' Championship would be won with a turbo. Effectively, to win in F1 now, a team needed a turbo car.

> **"By 1981, the use of a turbocharged engine had changed thinking completely, and the 3-litre Cosworth cars were under great pressure as the major manufacturers switched to turbo power."**

The title of this book indicates that it is about the development of the Renault turbo car; in fact, it had taken three designs to arrive at that first victory: the A500, the RS01, and the RS10. The history of the development is virtually complete: the story of the power years of the turbo period has been covered many times, and was never intended to be the prime subject of this book. However, it is interesting to learn what happened to the Renault team in the years that followed up to 1985, at which point it was decided to withdraw from F1. By this date, Renault had won 15 times and achieved 30 pole positions. Race statistics show the performances race-by-race in comparison with the other teams, and the following pages describe the epoch of the turbo through the eyes of Renault – years of peaks and troughs – and how close it came to being world champion. Whilst not definitive, the story is told pictorially with a few notes on each race.

Before we start this section on the Grand Prix years, however, it might be useful to look at three most important influences on the Renault turbo cars and indeed all the cars of the period, for this was a time of great change in fuels, aerodynamics, and tyres, when all three were to play a bigger part than ever before.

FUELS AND LUBRICANTS: THE INFLUENCE OF ELF

Some of the fuels that had to be developed for the cars were incredible. In what follows we hear from François Guiter, who masterminded Elf's involvement, and Jean-Claude Fayard, technical specialist at Elf at the time.

In 1967, the French government decided to create a brand name for its national oil interest under the moniker Société Nationale des Pétroles d'Aquitaine (SNPA). François Guiter, whose story is legendary – much of it with Renault, but also with Matra in the early days – was to join that new company from Caltex. The chosen brand name was Elf.

François Guiter: "In 1966, I was given the task of launching Elf the following year. I asked Jean Prada, my boss, to tell me what should be the image of our new brand. His reply was, 'Young, dynamic, French; we will have to talk about the method.' We were looking for something that would excite the public at large and link their use of oil to us, and we hit on motor sport. We knew nothing about it. I had never seen a race in my life! The first was Monaco in 1967.

"In French rallying there was only Alpine, contracted to Shell at that time, but in circuit racing there was nothing much at all. Alpine had some small single-seaters, as did Matra, and Matra had recently bought out René Bonnet. Most drivers were casuals, with few on permanent contracts. So we decided, very pretentiously, that we would put France back at the highest level. We knew about Matra – at the time it was mostly known for armaments for the military, but they were looking to expand their portfolio and image. It also helped that Jean Prada knew Jean-Luc Lagardère, the boss of Matra – they got on well together.

"This was the time when F3s and F2s were very popular. We went out to find some famous drivers and we found Beltoise,

Servoz-Gavin, Henri Pescarolo, and Jean-Pierre Jaussaud. We came to an agreement and, a few months before the launch of the team, decided to reveal our ambitions at a press conference during the Monte Carlo Rally. We declared:

We are going to win in Formula 3 this year. (That aim was achieved – Pescarolo was champion of France with 11 victories.)

We are going to win in Formula 2. (Aim achieved with Beltoise the second year.)

We are going to win in F1 and build an F1 engine. (Everyone smiled, but the third year we won with Jackie Stewart, albeit with a Ford-Cosworth.)

Lastly, we are going to win Le Mans. (This one we didn't achieve – at least not at first, as the 5-litre Porsche 917s were still there. Our turn came with Renault in 1978.)"

François Guiter continues: "Marketing-wise, when we started there was only Renault and their publicity machine involved in French motor sport. Renault's man was, of course, Jean Terramorsi; he was crazy about car racing. In the end our publicity annoyed some of the people at Renault and they asked us what we might do together. We agreed a contract for all cars leaving Renault to be lubricated by Elf (this contract is still valid). In 1968, we got involved in the Coupe Gordini and then Formula France which became Formula Renault. We also continued for four years with Matra. But in 1970 Matra had an agreement with Simca which involved Chrysler and Shell. We could see a problem ahead. Two drivers came to see me – Depailler and Jabouille – saying, 'We have a super F3 chassis with new rules on the engines, the 1600 of the Renault 16.' We made the decision to go with Renault 100 per cent.

"We won the championship in 1971: 1st Depailler, 2nd Jabouille. We wanted to go forward into something bigger. However, Renault wouldn't build a special racing engine, so we threatened to cancel our racing budget to them, a lot of which was taken at that time by Alpine, mostly for rallying. As you already know, their reply was: 'You want an engine? Then order it from us, and you pay!' Thus was born the 2-litre V6, fruit of the collaboration between Castaing and Moteur Moderne. The price: 300,000 francs – not very expensive. That engine won all the 2-litre sports proto races in Europe, then two years in F2 and, with the turbo (Terramorsi's idea), eventually Le Mans in 1978.

"We wanted to do F1; initially we got the same unenthusiastic response from Renault, but put up another 500,000 francs. They built the engines; we supplied the fuels to run in them, and those fuels became very special."

Jean-Claude Fayard: "Well, it was in 1971 when François

Guiter asked the Elf research centre at Solaize, near Lyon, to supply better lubricants to Renault and the other teams sponsored by Elf in order to improve the reliability of their engines. Alain Robinet, a young engineer responsible for lubricants, decided to develop a new one on a polyglycol base which possessed particularly interesting properties, naturally anti-wear, which allowed us to improve appreciably the reliability of racing-car engines.

"However, an attempt at marketing the product, named 13000TR, in the outside world was a fiasco. Our young team had badly underestimated all the problems that a commercially available oil could face in the public's everyday cars, which, of course, are completely different from racing cars. This lubricant had a high level of viscosity; that is, its variation of viscosity with temperature was less than conventional lubricants (VI> 200). We continued to improve it, and its use in all the competition cars sponsored by Elf was proven to be successful. It was, in fact, the lubricant which was used in the victorious Pironi and Jaussaud car at the Le Mans 24 Hours in 1978.

"... the 2-litre V6, fruit of the collaboration between Castaing and Moteur Moderne ... 300,000 francs – not very expensive. That engine won all the 2-litre sports proto races in Europe, then two years in F2 and, with the turbo (Terramorsi's idea), eventually Le Mans in 1978."

"I had been put in charge of the development of the fuels that year and we worked very closely with the Renault team to develop the products further and provide something special for the turbo engine, which, up to that time, was using standard high-octane fuel. Up to this point André Duval, our engineer responsible for the commercial fuels, had selected the best chemistry for our product from the refinery at Feyzin to meet the regulations in force in F1 as regards octane limits, but, unfortunately, the turbo cars seemed to have a problem, with many failures, burnt pistons, etc.

"I made my first attempt to formulate a special fuel when I managed to convince the various people in charge in Elf and Renault that by carrying out an analysis of how the octane levels affected an engine, I found a way of improving the octane rating within the limits of the rules, and improving detonation within the combustion chambers while alleviating the dreaded 'pinking'

Wind tunnels were quite basic, then! This is the open Eiffel wind tunnel.

points. Bernard [Dudot] went on to use this technology in later engines. However, in 1984, the authorities in charge of Formula 1 decided to ban water injection, so we had to return to chemistry to formulate our fuels, which began to contain high percentages of aromatics. We found a new family of hydrocarbons which, with these aromatics, again allowed us to adjust the octane rating to suit the regulations. These fuels contained a strong proportion of mesitylene [trimethyl-benzene] and they had a boiling point of 150°C, but with a combustion capability even higher than that of toluene.

"We had found the ultimate weapon, a RON that met the regulations (102) but which would be the equivalent in a conventional fuel of more than 110 RON. The engines liked it! We improved it even further with a heat exchanger which warmed the incoming fuel with the water of the cooling system. It is with this type of fuel that the engines at the end of the turbo years had such enormous power outputs. We called it Formulation No. 99!"

Jean-Claude continues: "I was lucky to be supported by a great team. We were young and François [Guiter] was a driving force. They were great days of enormous horsepower outputs and very fast cars, but crazy now when we look back on it, though it's true to say I loved it!"

that was so common in the turbocharged engine. I eventually found a solution which consisted of adding a small proportion of toluene to the fuel. This was within the regulations and Renault gave its agreement to proceed with this modification. Regrettably, the development took time and many engines were to break before we could be certain of the correct chemistry.

"In 1980, I was asked to take complete responsibility for the supply of the Renault team's lubricants and fuels and we created a small specialist team at the research centre in Solaize. From 1978 to 1983, we developed about forty formulations of fuel which were tried or used in the Renault turbo cars. We evolved the product using more and more toluene, along with other hydrocarbons whilst keeping within the regulations of 102 RON, in the knowledge that with pure toluene we could get a RON of more than 120.

"While working on the fuel formulations I also experimented with water injection and discovered its incredible influence on the reduction of the requirement in octane rating of the engine. At some percentages this injection of water into the air intake just before the fuel jets, and after the turbo had compressed the air, reduced the requirement for higher octane by more than ten

AERODYNAMICS AND THE GROUND-EFFECT ERA

A black art? It certainly was in the early 1970s, but, towards the end of the decade, cars were becoming faster and more powerful, so aerodynamics became extremely important, not least 'ground-effect,' which became vital for a short period in determining parameters in the performance of an F1 car.

Aerodynamics was and still is one of the most important factors in the road-holding qualities of a chassis. Michel Têtu: "The overall drag of an F1 car is the sum of the drag of the following:
– the body, which amounts to very little unless it is a brick;
– the wheels, whose front surfaces are such that the drag induced represents 40 to 50 per cent of the total;
– the wings, which are the element by which the aerodynamics of the assembly are adjusted, and whose drag can vary between 50 and 60 per cent of the total, according to the adjustment chosen."

Michel Têtu, with the Renault Sport aerodynamics engineer, Marcel Hubert, and, later on, Jean-Claude Migeot, were responsible for the development of aerodynamics on the Renault turbo cars. During that period of the late 1970s and early 1980s, side-pods played a key role in the general aerodynamics of the car.

Technical regulations within Formula 1 were consistently against ground-effect, first of all by forbidding mobile skirts, then by imposing a flat bottom. That period can, in fact, be divided into three sections, each with its own influence on the aerodynamic performance of the cars:

- 1977-1980: the lower side-pods were designed with a profile similar to an inverted aeroplane wing and were edged laterally with sliding skirts;
- 1981: the side-pods kept their profile but the mobile skirts were forbidden;
- 1983: developments in the shape of the side-pods were forbidden and the flat bottom was imposed, leading to the final disappearance of the skirts.

The first period is the one that interests us as regards our story of the development of the turbo car, and it was, of course, what was eventually called the ground-effect era. Colin Chapman's Lotus 78 was the first F1 ground-effect car to be raced. This car had a different construction compared with its competitors, and its performance caused a lot of consternation amongst the technicians of the rival teams. Adherence to the track was so much better than that of the competition that the Lotus easily won the 1978 championship. The fantastic road-holding was achieved by the venturi effect of the side-pod, and worked by increasing air movement speed in the small narrow section, thus lowering the pressure in this area and accelerating extraction of air from the ground. The whole thing worked like an inverted aeroplane wing, the downforce created by the difference in pressure between the lower part of the side-pod, which was in depression relative to the atmosphere, and the upper part of the side-pod exposed to the static pressure of the air.

Michel Têtu: "The width of a side-pod was not much more than 40cm. To recreate the length necessary for correct operation, it was a matter of edging the outside of the side-pods with guard plates to fill the space between the bottom of the bodywork and the ground as efficiently as possible. This is where Colin Chapman's intuitive mind was working; he was the first to understand the importance of the air tightness of the lower edges of the side-pods.

"This led to the creation of sliding skirts, whose correct operation had such an effect on the car's road-holding ability. However, any defect, even temporary, in the tightness of the skirt to the road produced immediate variations in force which quickly

The sliding skirt. (© Maureen Magee)

made the car unstable. The worst situation for the driver was the case of a skirt with excellent tightness but which didn't absorb the bumps when the sliding mechanism was not working perfectly. This situation produced a surging effect at high speed, due to the sudden variations in pressure under the side-pods, making the car virtually undrivable."

Like all the teams, Renault Sport had experience of these defects in operation, particularly with the RS10 and the RE20. It was often preferable to sacrifice some tightness and accept a slightly lower level of adherence overall in favour of consistency. Constructors were to invest huge sums of money in the design of lightweight honeycomb panels sliding in side-pod edges fitted with Teflon strips, or even with channels fitted with special bearings, as was the case with the RE20, where the panel assembly ensured contact with the ground by a very sophisticated spring system. On the RE20, there were springs with carbon leaves to reduce the weight of the mobile assembly and improve the dynamic response of the skirt.

The parts in contact with the ground were studied very carefully. Usually, they consisted of aluminium or Teflon runners covered in ceramic to reduce wear and maintain as consistent an operation as possible during the extended length of a Grand Prix.

Within the operating budgets of an F1 car at this time,

skirts were an horrendous financial burden. Because of the cost involved, test skirts for the Friday and Saturday often came from a previous Grand Prix, carefully repaired to give the car the required performance during practice. Then, specially chosen qualifying skirts were fitted, meticulously prepared to reduce operational play and ensure ground contact and tightness. In qualifying, it was not unusual to change the skirts at the same time as the tyres, in order to try for pole position in the best possible conditions.

The aerodynamic operation of a ground-effect car with sliding skirts depends entirely on the airflow under the side-pods. To ensure the most constant air circulation possible at a given speed, the height of the body in relation to the ground had to be checked and the trim had to be constant. In the absence of automatic trim-correction suspension (which would have been the best solution to this problem) the next best policy was to lock the suspension. This resulted in the cars of that time behaving like karts, as suspension movement was reduced to the minimum in order to control the behaviour of the car.

Michel Têtu again: "The interaction of side-pods and ground, or, if you like, the movement of the ground in relation to the side-pods, has the effect of increasing the sensitivity of the coefficient of lift and the moment of pitch on the trim and the height of the body in relation to the ground. Moreover, the effect of the rear wings is not so much to create downforce by deflection of the air circulation, as in the classic case, but rather to generate it by the induction effect of modifying the speed of the air circulation under the side-pod. The front wing was used only to ensure the general aerodynamic balance of the car. In some configurations on the RE20 we were able to do without the front wing, as many others did. These cars with low-angle wings or none at all were very efficient. With 600bhp, 300kmh was possible on the straight on the 5.8km Paul Ricard circuit."

At the end of the 1979 season, the sport's authorities, aware of the dangers facing drivers of cars with locked suspension and phenomenal but uncertain downforce, changed the technical rules by forbidding sliding skirts, in addition to which there had to be a 6cm gap between the ground and the side-pods with the car stationary. But the teams found that by shaping the sides of the body downward, air flow could still be controlled, and, whilst maintaining the 6cm gap, ground-effect was still impressive. The venturi effect came in as the speed increased, setting up a downforce which pushed the car down on its suspension.

Michel Têtu: "It was sufficient at the time to have suspension stiffness at two levels in order to bring the car quickly closer to the ground and reduce the required 6cm gap down to 1 or

2cm, or even less. Locking of the suspension, at whatever rating was needed, was obtained by inserting blocks at the required height; this was to be a major concern for the designers. Using the suspension in this way caused a lot of problems, above all, instability of the suction effect. This was to manifest itself dramatically on an uneven road surface, where any lightening of the chassis over a bump resulted in a sudden reduction in aerodynamic efficiency."

Michel continues: "All the teams experienced more or less the same thing when the cars were locked on a fixed suspension setting, placing extreme demands on the mounting points and making driving the cars over bumps and in fast corners very delicate. This was the cause of much concern to us at Renault Sport; I had to reinforce the suspension mounting points after meticulous testing in the workshop. In spite of all this, we had a serious accident with Jean-Pierre Jabouille at Montreal in 1980 following the breakage of a hub-carrier joint, and again with René Arnoux at Zandvoort in 1981. Jean-Pierre broke a leg; René was luckier and escaped unhurt, but we realised that, in spite of all the precautions, we were not immune from catastrophe.

"The balance of those cars varied considerably between high and low speeds to the point where any adjustment was the result of a very poor compromise. Then came the 1981 season, when Brabham raced one of its cars fitted with a pneumatic control, allowing the height of the car to be adjusted while it was in motion. They could, therefore, present a compliant vehicle when it was stationary, the 6cm gap being respected, but once it got up to a certain speed it lowered itself more or less automatically, thus reducing the space between the bodywork and the ground to the minimum. This system gave Brabham a decisive advantage in the first three races and then, although the device was not strictly within the letter of the law, we all followed suit." The advantage of this solution lay in the control of the height of the car which made it behave much more consistently at whatever speed it was travelling.

Throughout that season the cars were uncomfortable from the drivers' point of view, and really quite dangerous because of the mechanical demands made on them. Halfway through the year they were back to more or less the same downforce level as the previous season. Things had to change and the governing body decided to ban those systems for the following year.

Here we will leave the ground-effect story, which was indeed a period of intense and futuristic development that, though exciting, was proving very costly, with budgets spiralling almost out of control.

TYRES

Finally, before we move on, let's look at the part played by Michelin and a remarkable man by the name of Pierre Dupasquier.

Pierre Dupasquier joined Michelin's research division in 1962 after serving in the French Air Force as a pilot. In 1967, he was assigned to the department that handled technical relationships with car manufacturers, moving to the competition department in 1973, where he was to become doyen of the tyre scene in F1 for nearly 30 years. He was awarded the Légion d'Honneur in 2006 for services to French motor sport. Jean-Jacques Lachaze was in charge of the commercial department and dealt directly with the manufacturers when Pierre Dupasquier joined Michelin. Pierre: "He was a great guy and it was my good fortune to work directly with this brilliant, experienced man whose integrity was absolute."

Bernard Hanon had contacted Jean-Jacques in late 1975 to ask for Michelin's assistance in a new project that Renault had in mind. But it had been in 1973 that Mr Cau, then head of personnel at Michelin, had suggested to Pierre that, if Michelin was to follow motor sport more closely, he would be more useful to the company if he looked after it from Clermont-Ferrand rather than in Paris. At the time the technical service department for motor sport had not been created but, in effect, Pierre was now going to be responsible for the group's sporting activity. In 1976 Lachaze agreed with Renault that Michelin would be prepared to supply Renault with tyres suitable for a new secret Formula 1 project.

Pierre: "In fact, André de Cortanze had already told me about it, and we even arranged a very secret series of tests at Ferrari to judge Michelin's technical potential."

Michelin, therefore, had some knowledge of Formula 1 through the tests done with Ferrari and world champion, Niki Lauda, and other drivers; namely Beltoise, Cevert, Laffite, and Depailler, who had been or still were acting as valuable consultants. Pierre: "Michelin was rather nervous of the Renault turbo engine idea and the prototype versions were not that promising from a tyre supplier's point of view. A lot of racing car manufacturers had told us that the disadvantage was too great and that the turbo would never be competitive in Formula 1. Stick to rallying, they said! [Michelin, of course, had created the XAS radial-ply tyre that was to play such an important part in many of the top rally teams.] We were certainly concerned about it but we didn't share this opinion, even if it did come from the likes of Porsche. We even had to reassure our directors on the subject, as François Michelin himself had read the technical analysis of the turbo from the design department. Monsieur François was the professional and moral authority of our company. He listened very carefully to everything and he told me, 'It's a gamble that's already lost; they won't be able to do it.' However, he was an astute businessman, and once he had seen reports from Renault we reasoned that there were some solid arguments in their favour: they had already achieved huge horsepower outputs on the test bench. The rest was going to be a matter of materials and technology, time and money."

Michelin's Michel de Reynal, a brilliant and passionate engineer colleague of Dupasquier, prepared some initial tyres for testing in 1976. The first ones were not so good but they learnt quickly and, in the end, Michelin decided to do it and came to Formula 1 officially in 1977 – first with Renault, then with Ferrari, too. The radial-ply tyre was designed with ply cords which were set at 90° to the direction of travel: that is, on a line following the wheel and tyre radius and passing through its centre. The treaded part of the tyre section was braced by a steel or textile band moulded into the rubber with the tread on top of that. The radial-ply tyre offered less tread distortion under load than a cross-ply tyre; its sidewalls were far more flexible, generating higher cornering force, better traction under power and braking, and better straight-line stability. The radial racing tyre, like its sister then in use on the road, offered greater grip at its limits than did a cross-ply tyre. To run radial tyres, suspension settings with more camber change became important as the suspension rose and fell through its arc. It was found that radial-ply tyres also ran cooler and had better wall-flexing characteristics than a cross-ply tyre, so softer, stickier construction compounds could be used. One disadvantage remained. Jean-Pierre Jabouille: "The change from grip to letting go was quite sudden and its characteristics had to be learnt."

From the Renault point of view, the turbo began to win over all the technicians in the design department. Michelin then supplied Renault and Ferrari and, in 1983 and 1984, it was turbo engines that gave Michelin two world championships in the turbo cars before it decided to withdraw from Formula 1 at the end of the 1984 season. In 1981, Pirelli, too, had arrived on the scene with radial-ply tyres, although it had little impact on the Grand Prix landscape, and lacked commitment compared with the big boys – Goodyear and Michelin. A brief Goodyear withdrawal from racing in early 1981 caused many of the smaller teams to complain, and Avon tyres were also allowed. However, Goodyear was to return with a radial-ply Formula 1 tyre of its own with which to compete against Michelin.

Pierre: "It was a hard fight, you know; during tests in South

Big trucks to carry hundreds of tyres.

No! I think we brought the wrong ones! (Argentina 1980).

America between 1979 and the start of the 1980 season, for example, we tested about 40 prototype tyres. A Formula 1 tyre is designed to function within a fairly narrow temperature range, say, between 70°C and 100°C. Below that level, the mixture is not hot enough to give the rubber the stickiness it needs for adherence. Above the upper temperature, the chemical

components of the rubber begin to degrade, causing the rubber to break down and form bubbles which destroy the tread. All the skill of the engineer and driver is directed towards finding the correct association between the settings of the car and the choice of rubber, which must be as soft as possible to allow the four tyres to function within this temperature range.

"The technicians have several means of achieving this decisive compromise at their disposal. Downforce plays the most important part. By increasing it one increases the vertical load on the tyre and thus its adherence. Moreover, the flattening produced by the load makes the rubber work harder and raises its temperature. The technician will therefore adjust the front and rear downforce to keep the temperature within the desired range. This is the first step to be taken, but it is not enough because, in general, the tyres on the outside when cornering will be more subject to the downforce and will be warmer; moreover, part of the increase in the temperature of the rear tyres was gained by spinning under acceleration.

"Then there is the mechanical adjustment of the suspension, which can also play a part. The camber angle of the wheel is an important element, too, as it allows a certain amount of limitation of the distribution of temperature on the tread. The amount of camber can also be reduced or increased as the rigidity of the suspension springs is reduced or increased.

"It is therefore clear that even a brief list of the elements of adjustment which permit the best operation of a tyre is a long one, and most of the time they interact with each other. For example, reducing the stiffness of the rear suspension changes the trim of the car in relation to the speed, and so modifies the aerodynamic distribution between front and rear. Temperature readings had to be taken into account. Observation of the appearance of the tread aspect was also very important. This was all a matter of experience, and the engineers sent to Renault Sport by Michelin and Goodyear were a valuable source of assistance to the Renault team in this analysis. The condition of the rubber was always carefully examined. The position of the most used area on the width of the tread, wear in relation to lap times and their development, the tuning of the car, the quantity of fuel taken on board, the number of laps carried out, and the condition of the road surface at any given moment – all these were continually monitored. The intellectual gymnastics required by this analysis demand wide experience on the part of those involved, and perfect understanding with technicians like Georges Bresson from our team, whose contribution was essential.

"The driver's assessment is, of course, of utmost importance, as his analysis complements that of the technicians. He is the only one in a position to judge the 'comfort' aspect and variations in behaviour according to his driving style and the demands he puts on the car. When we speak of comfort, we mean the ease or difficulty experienced by the driver in replicating a time under racing conditions."

Léo Mehl was Pierre Dupasquier's opposite number at Goodyear, and he knew very well that, to claim victory, a tyre manufacturer needed at least two of the five best teams. Competition was fierce and Léo also knew that Michelin had a special relationship with Ferrari. Goodyear had tried to obtain an original equipment contract from Maranello, but in the USA the company was sticking to conventional cross-ply carcasses and had not been able to find a product to match Michelin's XWX. It was for these reasons that Goodyear had begun to prepare its special qualifying tyres. After the first showing by the Renault turbo at Silverstone in 1977, Léo Mehl saw the progress of Michelin and began to consider a change to radials: the tyre war had begun.

Pierre: "I had a call from Ferrari: 'Can you come to Maranello tomorrow? The Commendatore wants to see you.' I was unofficially told that it was about the possibility of using Michelins on their cars. Ferrari, of course, was well established, and the early showing of Renault and lack of results brought doubts to some of the team about the efficiency of our product. Also, from Michelin's side, we were concerned that with Renault as sole partner we were taking a big risk."

Pierre continues: "Ferrari's move came just at the right moment and we had to take advantage of it. 'I asked you to come for the following reason,' began the Commendatore. 'Up to now you were absent from the circuits, but now that you are supplying Renault you are officially in Formula 1. How can I get your tyres?' François Michelin's decision to say yes to Renault was part of our relationship with the French compatriot constructor and not an official participation in Formula 1. 'Our participation with Renault is based on the technical cooperation that we have with a large constructor,' I told him."

But Michelin knew that, having agreed to help Renault, there was every chance it could do the same with this other partner – Ferrari – and Fiat, which now owned Ferrari. Jean-Jacques Lachaze gave his agreement, and so Michelin was to start the 1978 season with three cars: the Ferraris of Reutemann and Villeneuve, and Jabouille's Renault.

Pierre: "But before 1978, we had to finish the 1977 season with the Canadian Grand Prix at Mosport. We knew the track as we had run a prototype there. We tried many things but it was a disaster. I don't know by whom or at what level the decision

was made, but Gérard Larrousse, in charge of the team, came to warn us: 'I've booked the circuit for Monday; we're going to try Goodyears.' They were worried sick at Renault that they couldn't have Goodyears like everybody else, and there were so many rumours now flying about regarding the poor behaviour of radial tyres at that level of competition. I was very annoyed, especially as it was quite possible that the car would be quicker on the Monday: better knowledge of the circuit, more grip on the track, good weather forecast, better engine, and Lord knows what else. I didn't think that this testing session, especially in North America, was a good idea and, on the Sunday evening, I wrote a note to Larrousse saying that his initiative was 'industrially irresponsible.' We packed up our stuff and set off back to France, but took care to leave an observer in the woods, Pierre Blanchet, who later agreed with Renault that the car would not qualify any faster on Goodyears."

At the same time, assured of the support of Ferrari, Michelin prepared for the 1978 season with new weapons. The Ferrari team was at its highest point: Lauda was champion and the Argentinian, Carlos Reutemann, fourth in the 1977 Drivers' World Championship, was to be the new lead driver, seconded by a young man from Quebec, Gilles Villeneuve.

"Competition was fierce and Léo also knew that Michelin had a special relationship with Ferrari ... After the first showing by the Renault turbo at Silverstone in 1977, Léo Mehl saw the progress of Michelin and began to consider a change to radials: the tyre war had begun."

Pierre: "Our first complete year in Formula 1 with Ferrari and Renault started off with all of us excited – learning about the formula, the circuits, dealing with real problems, the thrill of the search. But the previous season had produced an event that would have determining consequences for the life of Formula 1: at Zolder, for the Belgian Grand Prix, Colin Chapman had revealed the first version of his 'ground-effect' concept car. I was like a fascinated tourist arriving at Zolder on the Saturday morning. This was certainly going to be the future. I wondered if we could meet the new challenge.

"Georges Bresson, in charge of racing tyre development, was confident, and over the years we got better and better. We turned to our chemists when things got tough. The chemistry department tried many different mixtures and several original combinations which gave us efficiency and consistency, culminating in the impressive demonstration of the two Renaults and Ferraris in the early 1980s. Things weren't always perfect, however: on one occasion Carlos Reutemann had had trouble sorting his car and was to start the race a long way back. Mauro Forghieri sent for me and asked me to meet him in the Ferrari caravan. There was also Piero Lardi-Ferrari, the Commendatore's son, and Tomaini, their loyal second engineer. For a quarter of an hour Mauro explained to me that our tyres didn't stand up in comparison with the Goodyears, that our rate of progress was too slow, that we were bad engineers, and lots more kind things of the sort. I just took notes and when I thought he had finished I said, 'I understand, Mauro. Ferrari is a team that wants to win the World Championship and can't waste its time with a team such as you have just described. The next Grand Prix will be in Germany in a fortnight and I believe you must get in touch with Goodyear immediately.' Piero Lardi was very upset: 'No, Pierre, that wasn't what Mauro meant, but you have to understand ...' The next day, after a splendid race, Reutemann brought us a wonderful third victory. That conversation was never mentioned again.

"Renault had quickly understood the principle of ground-effect during that period, but inconsistency of their engines prevented them from concentrating on aerodynamics as they would have wished. We, on the other hand, were always more interested in ground surfaces, and after a while established the following list of things we needed to know to get the right tyre for the right circuit:

– The granulometry of tarmac tracks varies in contact surface area from small pieces of gravel to large pieces with big spaces between them; we needed to know what those spaces were;

– We needed to know the nature of the gravel, as it can be rough or polished, round or flat;

– The temperature that concerned us most was the temperature of the track and not the air;

– When the tyre is placed on the ground, it is distorted; it makes contact with the surface without reaching the bottom of the gaps in the tarmac. We needed to find a way of calculating the surface that the tyre effectively occupied;

– On long corners in which the car has time to stabilise, the drift of the tyres is the essential limiting factor on the rubber mixture. So what was the surface like in those corners?

"The most important point in tyre design was to avoid introducing the wrong tension between the ground and our mixture, which could cause loss of adhesion. You know, at one point we even used a bottle of printing ink, a little brush, a packet of Kleenex, and a student's eraser with the same hardness they were researching (35 Shore hardness)! This highly sophisticated equipment allowed us to create a bench mark to establish a complete file on the different surfaces. Then we used all sorts of tests and procedures to reach an evaluation for any given circuit based on a coefficient linked to the size of the 'gaps' in the surface, a coefficient based on the number of corners of more than 120°, a 'micro'-factor characterising the 'glass paper' nature of the surface of the track, and a factor relating to temperature."

The Michelin development team created a circuit rating, which featured a severity test related to the stress applied to the tread and came up with a chart which noted that the lowest values were for the least 'severe' circuits – Brands Hatch, Long Beach, and Montreal – while the highest were Ricard, Dijon, and São Paulo. These ratings proved correct and reflected the results obtained.

Pierre: "One of our main interests in this approach was to show our chemists the parameters governing the good performance of a tyre, ie: the parameters which they should take into account, such as deformability, internal consumption of energy, and resistance to tearing. In fact, it is the combined forms of the ground surface and the tyre that must allow water evacuation on a wet track and produce a positive contact between surface and tyre, without knowing which of the two surfaces is responsible for it; in other words, if the granulometry of the circuit is sufficient, there is no need for the tyre to be cut. We applied this information to Scheckter's Ferrari and in 1979 he won the championship – Michelin's first in F1.

"It's a pity Renault never won the championship: they came close twice in the 1980s, and it was always a case that they seemed to be let down by component suppliers. There was no doubt that they tried hard. In that period our tyres were pretty much the best around in Formula 1. We had come a long way and so had Renault."

From this overview of developments in the fuel, aerodynamics and tyre game that existed at that time, we now turn to the period that followed the first two years of Grand Prix and the longed-for first victory.

We will start with an afterthought on the Dijon race and a look at the qualifying times. Only two years previously, Mario Andretti had taken pole in the Lotus 78 with 1min 12.21sec; now Jabouille had shaved an incredible 5 seconds off that time. In Grand Prix racing 5 seconds is almost a light year.

FOR THE RECORD: THE REMAINDER OF 1979

British Grand Prix, Silverstone, 14 July 1979
The next race was the British Grand Prix on Bastille Day, and
Jabouille put the car on the front row; Arnoux was back on P6.

Renault had arrived at Silverstone in confident mood, and
all the teams were watching to see if the French Grand Prix win
had been a fluke or a sign of things to come. At that time the
circuit – with its long, fast bends – did not have a really slow
section, and it was thought that it would favour cars with perfect
mastery of ground-effect. All was looking good for Williams and
Renault. On the Thursday afternoon, third fastest was none other
than René Arnoux, backing up his team-mate, Jabouille, who was
confirming his performance at Dijon with a time just 2/100ths of
a second slower. Alan Jones with the Williams was on pole.

During the warm-up session before the Grand Prix, the
Renault mechanics were unpleasantly surprised to find that
Jabouille's gearbox had seized. After some checks he went out
onto the track, but no luck; they had to change the gearbox. Even
more serious, Jean-Pierre could not complete his practice run or a
practice start with a full tank and had to start the race with tuning
and tyre choice decided by guesswork.

As the cars left the line Regazzoni got away well, and was
leading at Copse in front of his team-mate. Jabouille, 3rd and
driving a car fitted with soft tyres, felt ready to attack Regazzoni,
which he did, then suddenly both drivers found themselves
passed by Jones. Jabouille managed to squeeze into 2nd place
and kept up the pace for 6 or 7 laps until he began having
problems with his tyres; on the 17th lap he had to go into the
pits to change them. Unfortunately, leaving the pit he caught the
pneumatic wheel-gun pipe, which wound itself round the front
wing and broke it clean off. Jean-Pierre did another lap, stopped
again, set off again. His engine didn't like the incident and, a few
minutes later on lap 21, it expired with a broken valve spring.

On lap 38, the leading Williams had disappeared – the
engine's water pump had failed. On lap 42, Laffite stopped with
his engine in a mess. Regazzoni gave Frank Williams his first
victory in the British Grand Prix, but in second place was the
Renault of René Arnoux, the Frenchman proving both his own
maturity and that of the Renault turbo. Now they knew that Dijon
was no fluke win.

Arnoux. (© DPPI/Ren)

Arnoux (left) celebrates his second place.

STARTING GRID		RESULTS - Silverstone (320,89 km)			
Jabouille	Jones	1. Regazzoni	Williams-Ford	68	1h26'11.17"
1'12.48"	1'11.88"	2. Arnoux	Renault	68	1h26'35.45"
Regazzoni	Piquet	3. Jarier	Tyrrell-Ford	67	+ 1 lap
1'13.11"	1'12.65"	4. Watson	McLaren-Ford	67	+ 1 lap
Lauda	Arnoux	5. Scheckter	Ferrari	67	+ 1 lap
1'13.44"	1'13.29"	6. Ickx	Ligier-Ford	67	+ 1 lap
Reutemann	Watson	7. Tambay	McLaren-Ford	66	Out of fuel
1'13.87"	1'13.57"	8. Reutemann	Lotus-Ford	66	+ 2 laps
Laffite	Andretti	9. Rebaque	Lotus-Ford	66	+ 2 laps
1'14.37"	1'14.20"	10. Pironi	Tyrrell-Ford	66	+ 2 laps
De Angelis	Scheckter	11. Lammers	Shadow-Ford	65	+ 3 laps
1'14.87"	1'14.60"	12. De Angelis	Shadow-Ford	65	1' penalty
Rosberg	Villeneuve				Stolen start
1'14.96"	1'14.90"	13. Gaillard	Ensign-Ford	65	+ 3 laps
Jarier	Pironi	14. Villeneuve	Ferrari	63	Fuel vapour
1'15.63"	1'15.28"				
Tambay	Ickx		**FASTEST LAP**		
1'15.67"	1'15.63"				
Mass	Patrese	Regazzoni	Williams-Ford	1'14.40"	
1'16.19"	1'15.77"			228.32 km/h	
Fittipaldi	Lammers				
1'16.68"	1'16.66"		**RETIREMENTS**		
Rebaque	Gaillard				
1'17.32"	1'17.07"	Mass	Arrows-Ford	36	Gearbox
		Patrese	Arrows-Ford	45	Gearbox
		Rosberg	Wolf-Ford	44	Fuel feed
		Laffite	Ligier-Ford	44	Engine sparking plugs
		Jones	Williams-Ford	38	Engine
		Fittipaldi	Copersucar-Ford	25	Engine
		Jabouille	Renault	21	Engine
		Lauda	Brabham-Alfa Romeo	12	Brakes
		Andretti	Lotus-Ford	3	Rear rolling bearing
		Piquet	Brabham-Alfa Romeo	1	Spin, stall

Silverstone race statistics.

German Grand Prix, Hockenheim, 29 July 1979

Jean-Pierre Jabouille made no secret of the fact that he loved Hockenheim because of the success he had had there in other disciplines, especially F2. Fully confident in the afternoon qualifying period, he went straight off in pursuit of pole position and, with his first flying lap, clocked an astonishing time of 1min 48.48sec, which would not be equalled over the whole weekend.

René Arnoux wasn't as fortunate, though things had started well for him on the Friday morning with a second fastest lap. On the Friday afternoon, a leak in the engine's turbo boost system pushed him back into 4th place, then, on the Saturday, he dropped back to the 5th row next to Gilles Villeneuve. It was Alan Jones who was to start on the front row beside Jabouille.

In the suffocating heat of the Hockenheim stadium, Jones took advantage at the start and moved his Williams ahead of Jabouille. The two men quickly pulled away in front of the pursuers, led by Laffite. It looked as if Jabouille, employing his usual tactics, was waiting for his car to become lighter, as it used fuel, before starting to push hard. It did not go his way, however, as the heat was affecting the engine, which was not working

Arnoux waits for adjustments. (© DPPI/Ren)

at full power. Forced to race out of his comfort zone, Jabouille spun off on the 7th lap at the Sachs curve. His engine stalled and he couldn't get it going again. Jones finished in first place, but slowing dramatically with a puncture. Without the spin, Jabouille could have carried off his second Grand Prix. It was not to be Renault-Elf team's weekend, as it ended worse than it had begun when René Arnoux also went off the track with a burst tyre. Despite this, the cars had once again shown pace and reliability.

STARTING GRID

Jones 1'48.75"	Jabouille 1'48.48"
Piquet 1'49.50"	Laffite 1'49.43"
Regazzoni 1'50.12"	Scheckter 1'50.00"
Pironi 1'50.40"	Lauda 1'50.37"
Arnoux 1'50.48"	Villeneuve 1'50.41"
Watson 1'50.86"	Andretti 1'50.68"
Ickx 1'51.07"	Reutemann 1'50.94"
Lees 1'51.50"	Tambay 1'51.47"
Mass 1'52.74"	Rosberg 1'52.01"
Lammers 1'53.59"	Patrese 1'52.93"
Fittipaldi 1'54.01"	De Angelis 1'53.73"
Rebaque 1'55.86"	Stuck 1'54.47"

RESULTS - Hockenheim (305,505 km)

1. Jones	Williams-Ford	45	1h24'48.83"
2. Regazzoni	Williams-Ford	45	1h24'51.74"
3. Laffite	Ligier-Ford	45	1h25'07.22"
4. Scheckter	Ferrari	45	1h25'20.03"
5. Watson	McLaren-Ford	45	1h26'26.63"
6. Mass	Arrows-Ford	44	+ 1 lap
7. Lees	Tyrrell-Ford	44	+ 1 lap
8. Villeneuve	Ferrari	44	+ 1 lap
9. Pironi	Tyrrell-Ford	44	+ 1 lap
10. Lammers	Shadow-Ford	44	+ 1 lap
11. De Angelis	Shadow-Ford	43	+ 2 laps
12. Piquet	Brabham-Alfa Romeo	42	Engine

FASTEST LAP

Villeneuve	Ferrari	1'51.69" 218.400 km/h

RETIREMENTS

Patrese	Arrows-Ford	34	Pneu
Tambay	McLaren-Ford	30	Rear suspension
Rosberg	Wolf-Ford	29	Engine
Lauda	Brabham-Alfa Romeo	27	Engine
Ickx	Ligier-Ford	24	Pneu
Rebaque	Lotus-Ford	22	Road-holding
Andretti	Lotus-Ford	16	Transmission shaft
Arnoux	Renault	9	Tyres
Jabouille	Renault	7	Spin, stall
Fittipaldi	Copersucar-Ford	4	Electrical
Reutemann	Lotus-Ford	1	Accident
Stuck	ATS-Ford	0	Front suspension

Hockenheim race statistics.

Jabouille.

Austrian Grand Prix, Zeltweg, 12 August 1979

Two weeks after the concrete and scenery of Hockenheim, the natural surroundings of Zeltweg heartened the Renault-Elf team drivers: this was an altitude circuit, where the turbo V6s could easily compensate for the lack of oxygen required for the V12s and V8s.

On the Friday morning, on a wet track, Arnoux was steadfast, spirited and masterful. In the afternoon, he attained third fastest time, even though handicapped by a small leak in the turbo. On the Saturday, he improved on his time of the previous day by more than a second, and treated himself to a magnificent first pole position. Beside him on the grid he found not his team-mate but the inevitable Alan Jones, whose Williams was performing well on this fast circuit. Jean-Pierre Jabouille was third fastest.

At the start Jones got away quicker than Arnoux and expected to see the Renault in his rear-view mirrors, but it was a red car that passed him. Taken aback, the Australian had to watch Villeneuve claim the lead. Arnoux was having problems and was overtaken by Lauda. Jabouille had messed up his start and found himself in 9th after the 1st lap, though, in typical fashion,

STARTING GRID

Jones 1'34.28"	Arnoux 1'34.07"
Lauda 1'35.51"	Jabouille 1'34.45"
Regazzoni 1'35.82"	Villeneuve 1'35.70"
Laffite 1'35.92"	Piquet 1'35.85"
Pironi 1'36.26"	Scheckter 1'36.10"
Rosberg 1'36.67"	Daly 1'36.42"
Tambay 1'36.72"	Patrese 1'36.71"
Watson 1'37.16"	Andretti 1'37.11"
Stuck 1'37.93"	Reutemann 1'37.32"
Mass 1'38.85"	Fittipaldi 1'38.38"
De Angelis 1'39.44"	Ickx 1'39.31"
Gaillard 1'41.10"	Lammers 1'39.45"

RESULTS - Zeltweg (320,868 km)

1. Jones	Williams-Ford	54	1h27'38.01"
2. Villeneuve	Ferrari	54	1h28'14.06"
3. Laffite	Ligier-Ford	54	1h28'24.78"
4. Scheckter	Ferrari	54	1h28'25.22"
5. Regazzoni	Williams-Ford	54	1h28'26.93"
6. Arnoux	Renault	53	+ 1 lap
7. Pironi	Tyrrell-Ford	53	+ 1 lap
8. Daly	Ensign-Ford	53	+ 1 lap
9. Watson	McLaren-Ford	53	+ 1 lap
10. Tambay	McLaren-Ford	53	+ 1 lap

FASTEST LAP

Arnoux	Renault	1'35.77" 223.378 km/h

RETIREMENTS

Lauda	Brabham-Alfa Romeo	45	Oil leak
Gaillard	Ensign-Ford	42	Front suspension
De Angelis	Shadow-Ford	34	Engine
Patrese	Arrows-Ford	34	Rear suspension
Piquet	Brabham-Alfa Romeo	32	Engine
Stuck	ATS-Ford	28	Engine
Ickx	Ligier-Ford	26	Engine
Reutemann	Lotus-Ford	22	Road-holding
Jabouille	Renault	16	Clutch + Gearbox
Fittipaldi	Copersucar-Ford	15	Brakes
Rosberg	Wolf-Ford	15	Electrical
Lammers	Shadow-Ford	3	Accident
Mass	Arrows-Ford	1	Engine
Andretti	Lotus-Ford	0	Clutch

Zeltweg race statistics.

on the 4th lap was up to 4th behind Arnoux, who had re-passed Lauda. All to no avail, however, as a few laps later Jabouille was out – the clutch was broken and the gearbox useless. From a third of the way in the race, Jones went on to win from Villeneuve. Arnoux finished in 6th after having to stop for fuel. François Castaing didn't understand how his driver could have run out of fuel with nearly 20 litres' margin, but found the answer when the fuel tank was removed: the foam used in the fuel tank to contain the movement of the fluid had broken up and blocked the inlet ...

Dutch Grand Prix, Zandvoort, 26 August 1979
Seeking to improve safety at the fast Zandvoort circuit, Lauda and Scheckter – the two influential champions on the drivers' committee – insisted that the Dutch organisers build a chicane just before the east tunnel. This request, made in Austria, was pretty much an ultimatum, since the pair were threatening outright to refuse to drive there. So it was that, with the help of Lauda and Scheckter, the Zandvoort promoters got to work – only to find that nobody liked the new chicane when they got there!

This time, Arnoux found himself totally free of mechanical problems. Réné took full advantage to claim his 2nd pole position. Jean-Pierre took 3rd position, but found his car suffering

In the pits. (© TVA)

> **"For a brief moment, four cars were side-by-side, with Regazzoni – squeezed between Arnoux and the pit wall – trying to overtake. The front wheel of the Williams hit the rear of the Renault, tearing the wheel off the Williams; he went round Tarzan on three wheels and came to a halt."**

from constant understeer. As a last resort he took the wheel of the old RS01 car at the same time as a rainstorm broke over the circuit. He had just the Sunday morning session, therefore, to get his original car properly sorted. Nevertheless, he managed to get 4th fastest time, just behind Clay Regazzoni.

Dutch law prohibited noise on Sunday mornings, so the half-hour warm-up began at 1pm in a mood of general anxiety. Jabouille tried the mule RS, then decided on the RS11 for the race, as it was thought to be more reliable. At the start, Villeneuve on P5 was fast off the line and managed to catch up with Jabouille, Regazzoni, and Arnoux. For a brief moment, four cars were side-by-side, with Regazzoni – squeezed between Arnoux and the pit wall – trying to overtake. The front wheel of

Jabouille gets his feet wet.

Arnoux.

STARTING GRID	
Jones	Arnoux
1'15.646"	1'15.461"
Jabouille	Regazzoni
1'16.304"	1'16.288"
Villeneuve	Scheckter
1'16.939"	1'16.392"
Rosberg	Laffite
1'17.280"	1'17.129"
Pironi	Lauda
1'17.625"	1'17.495"
Watson	Piquet
1'17.750"	1'17.667"
Tambay	Reutemann
1'18.147"	1'18.001"
Jarier	Stuck
1'18.430"	1'18.256"
Mass	Andretti
1'18.606"	1'18.452"
Ickx	Patrese
1'18.706"	1'18.629"
De Angelis	Fittipaldi
1'20.709"	1'19.433"
Rebaque	Lammers
1'21.344"	1'21.084"

RESULTS - Zandvoort (318,900 km)

1. Jones	Williams-Ford	75	1h41'19.775"
2. Scheckter	Ferrari	75	1h41'41.558"
3. Laffite	Ligier-Ford	75	1h42'23.028"
4. Piquet	Brabham-Alfa Romeo	74	+ 1 lap
5. Ickx	Ligier-Ford	74	+ 1 lap
6. Mass	Arrows-Ford	73	+ 2 laps
7. Rebaque	Lotus-Ford	73	+ 2 laps

FASTEST LAP

Villeneuve	Ferrari	1'19.43" 192.713 km/h

RETIREMENTS

Pironi	Tyrrell-Ford	51	Rear suspension
Villeneuve	Ferrari	49	Tyre, suspension
De Angelis	Shadow-Ford	40	Drive shaft
Rosberg	Wolf-Ford	33	Engine
Jabouille	Renault	26	Clutch
Watson	McLaren-Ford	22	Engine
Jarier	Tyrrell-Ford	20	Throttle
			Spin
Stuck	ATS-Ford	19	Transmission shaft
Lammers	Shadow-Ford	12	Gearbox
Andretti	Lotus-Ford	9	Rear suspension
Patrese	Arrows-Ford	7	Accident, brakes
Tambay	McLaren-Ford	6	Engine
Lauda	Brabham-Alfa Romeo	4	Retirement, pains
Fittipaldi	Copersucar-Ford	2	Electrical
Reutemann	Lotus-Ford	1	Collision
Arnoux	Renault	1	Collision Regazzoni
Regazzoni	Williams-Ford	0	Collision Arnoux

Zandvoort race statistics.

the Williams hit the rear of the Renault, tearing the wheel off the Williams; he went round Tarzan on three wheels and came to a halt. A furious Regazzoni climbed out. Arnoux managed another lap before retiring, the rear suspension of the Renault buckled from the impact. Villeneuve was now in 2nd place behind Jones, followed by Jabouille, Pironi, and Laffite. Jabouille was watching the struggle in front with interest, but not for long as he had to retire with clutch failure. Jones, in the Williams, took the win from Scheckter and Laffite. Just 7 cars finished out of the 24 starters.

Italian Grand Prix, Monza, 9 September 1979

As at Zandvoort, Jabouille's RS11 was struggling for grip. It understeered, and everyone had to confess that they didn't understand why they couldn't control the problem, so, on the Saturday, Jean-Pierre was blowing hot and cold in the pits. He had achieved fastest time on only his 6th lap, but then, making a braking error at the first chicane, damaged the body of the RS10, so was forced to start the race at the wheel of the RS11, in which he no longer felt confident. Although fastest on the Friday, René

Arnoux was unable to fight for pole position on the Saturday because of an engine oil leak. But luck was on his side and the incredible time he had put up the day before meant he still kept his place on the front row. Outclassed, Villeneuve could not hold onto his 2nd place and moved back a row, leaving his team-mate and Alan Jones in front of him.

When the lights turned to green Jabouille paused momentarily, allowing Scheckter and Villeneuve to pull away, along with Arnoux, who had got off to a good start. At the end of the first chicane, the order was Scheckter, Arnoux, Villeneuve, Laffite, Jabouille. Coming out of the Parabolica, Arnoux's Renault was right behind Scheckter's Ferrari. He attacked the South African on braking for the chicane, sure that he would make it. Scheckter did not want to risk losing a title and so let him go past. Behind, Laffite was fighting back and, if he was to have a chance to win the championship, mustn't let Scheckter win. Behind this leading quartet, Jabouille wasn't very optimistic: given the RS11's understeer problem, he couldn't hope to keep up the pace for very long.

A dramatic turn of events occurred on the 13th lap, in the second Lesmo corner, when Arnoux felt his engine cut out. His

Jean-Pierre confers with Alan Jones. (© DPPI/Ren)

three pursuers passed him as he tried to restart, but the V6 had lost a lot of power, and René stopped in the pits on the 16th lap with broken valve springs. His first F1 victory would have to wait for another occasion. Jabouille trailed in 14th and last, 5 laps down. At Monza, on Italian soil, Ferrari and Scheckter were crowned world champions.

Canadian Grand Prix, Montreal, 30 September 1979

It was a strange weekend, and unsuccessful for Renault.

Niki Lauda decided to hang up his helmet right in the middle of the first practice day; by the time the first timed session began, he was on his way to Los Angeles airport, replaced by Argentinian, Ricardo Zunino. On the 10th lap of the race, Jabouille came into the pits with brake trouble. The pads were too hard and had seized. He set off again but had to retire on the 24th lap – it was impossible to drive under these conditions.

STARTING GRID		RESULTS - Monza (290 km)			
Jabouille	Arnoux	1. Scheckter	Ferrari	50	1h22'00.22"
1'34.580"	1'34.704"	2. Villeneuve	Ferrari	50	1h22'00.68"
Scheckter	Jones	3. Regazzoni	Williams-Ford	50	1h22'05.00"
1'34.830"	1'34.914"	4. Lauda Brabham-Alfa Romeo		50	1h22'54.62"
Villeneuve	Regazzoni	5. Andretti	Lotus-Ford	50	1h22'59.92"
1'34.989"	1'35.333"	6. Jarier	Tyrrell-Ford	50	1h23'01.77"
Laffite	Piquet	7. Reutemann	Lotus-Ford	50	1h23'24.36"
1'35.443"	1'35.587"	8. Fittipaldi	Copersucar-Ford	49	+ 1 lap
Lauda	Andretti	9. Jones	Williams-Ford	49	+ 1 lap
1'36.219"	1'36.655"	10. Pironi	Tyrrell-Ford	49	+ 1 lap
Ickx	Pironi	11. Stuck	ATS-Ford	49	+ 1 lap
1'37.114"	1'37.181"	12. Brambilla	Alfa Romeo	49	+ 1 lap
Reutemann	Tambay	13. Patrese	Arrows-Ford	47	+ 3 laps
1'37.202"	1'37.231"	14. Jabouille	Renault	45	Engine
Stuck	Jarier				
1'37.297"	1'37.581"	**FASTEST LAP**			
Patrese	Giacomelli				
1'37.674"	1'38.053"	Regazzoni	Williams-Ford		1'35.60"
Watson	Fittipaldi				218.14 km/h
1'38.093"	1'38.136"				
Mass	Brambilla	**RETIREMENTS**			
1'38.163"	1'38.601"				
Rosberg	De Angelis	Laffite	Ligier-Ford	41	Engine
1'38.854"	1'39.149"	Rosberg	Wolf-Ford	41	Engine
		Ickx	Ligier-Ford	40	Engine
		De Angelis	Shadow-Ford	33	Clutch
		Giacomelli	Alfa Romeo	28	Spin, stall
		Watson	McLaren-Ford	13	Collision with Jarier
		Arnoux	Renault	13	Engine problems
		Tambay	McLaren-Ford	3	Engine
		Mass	Arrows-Ford	3	Suspension
		Piquet	Brabham-Alfa Romeo	1	Accident

Monza race statistics.

Familiar colours. (© DPPI/Ren)

Team-mate René Arnoux had the same problem but didn't have time to stop. Arnoux tangled with Hans Stuck on lap 14: Stuck missed a braking point and managed to push the Renault off into the scenery. Another retirement.

US East Coast Grand Prix, Watkins Glen, 7 October 1979

Toyota sponsored the US GP at Watkins Glen, the last race of the season. It was wet and cold, and both cars had problems heating their tyres sufficiently. Arnoux, starting from P7, was to come through to take 2nd at the chequered flag, whilst Jabouille from P8 got caught up in an accident on lap 28 that brought an end to his race.

Reliability was the problem again; power was not – they had plenty, and Ferrari, for one, was to look very closely at its turbo programme during the coming winter months.

So, 28 starts from the 14 Grands Prix that were attended. The great first win at Dijon was supported by second places in Britain and USA, but Renault had finished only 8 times! It would need better reliability the following year.

The following set of 1979 chassis records includes the victory at Dijon. These records continue for all the Grand Prix years that followed, but, as our story is primarily concerned with the development phase, we will conclude with these.

STARTING GRID	
Jones 1'29.892"	Villeneuve 1'30.554"
Regazzoni 1'30.768"	Piquet 1'30.775"
Laffite 1'30.820"	Pironi 1'31.941"
Jabouille 1'32.103"	Arnoux 1'32.116"
Scheckter 1'32.280"	Andretti 1'32.651"
Reutemann 1'32.682"	Stuck 1'32.858"
Jarier 1'33.065"	Patrese 1'33.090"
Fittipaldi 1'33.297"	Ickx 1'33.355"
Watson 1'33.362"	Brambilla 1'33.378"
Zunino 1'33.511"	Tambay 1'33.603"
Lammers 1'34.102"	Rebaque 1'34.129"
De Angelis 1'34.256"	Daly 1'34.301"

RESULTS - Montréal (317,520 km)

1. Jones	Williams-Ford	72	1h52'06.892"
2. Villeneuve	Ferrari	72	1h52'07.972"
3. Regazzoni	Williams-Ford	72	1h53'20.548"
4. Scheckter	Ferrari	71	+ 1 lap
5. Pironi	Tyrrell-Ford	71	+ 1 lap
6. Watson	McLaren-Ford	70	+ 2 laps
7. Zunino	Brabham-Ford	68	+ 4 laps
8. Fittipaldi	Copersucar-Ford	67	+ 5 laps
9. Lammers	Shadow-Ford	67	+ 5 laps
10. Andretti	Lotus-Ford	66	Out of fuel

FASTEST LAP

Jones	Williams-Ford	1'31.272" 173.942 km/h

RETIREMENTS

Piquet	Brabham-Ford	61	Gearbox
Brambilla	Alfa Romeo	52	Fuel feed
Ickx	Ligier-Ford	47	Engine
Jarier	Tyrrell-Ford	33	Engine
Daly	Tyrrell-Ford	28	Engine
Rebaque	Lotus-Ford	26	Engine support
De Angelis	Shadow-Ford	24	Rotor broken
Jabouille	Renault	24	Brakes
Reutemann	Lotus-Ford	23	Rear suspension
Patrese	Arrows-Ford	20	Spin, stall
Tambay	McLaren-Ford	19	Engine
Arnoux	Renault	14	Collision with Stuck
Stuck	ATS-Ford	14	Collision Arnoux
Laffite	Ligier-Ford	10	Engine

Montreal race statistics.

Arnoux. (© DPPI/Ren)

155

STARTING GRID		RESULTS - Watkins Glen (320,665 km)			
Jones 1'35.615"	Piquet 1'36.914"	1. Villeneuve	Ferrari	59	1h52'17.734"
Villeneuve 1'36.948"	Laffite 1'37.066"	2. Arnoux	Renault	59	1h53'06.521"
Regazzoni 1'37.128"	Reutemann 1'37.872"	3. Pironi	Tyrrell-Ford	59	1h53'10.933"
Arnoux 1'38.195"	Jabouille 1'38.218"	4. De Angelis	Shadow-Ford	59	1h53'48.246"
Zunino 1'38.509"	Pironi 1'38.823"	5. Stuck	ATS-Ford	59	1h53'58.993"
Jarier 1'38.945"	Rosberg 1'39.035"	6. Watson	McLaren-Ford	58	+ 1 lap
Watson 1'39.233"	Stuck 1'39.329"	7. Fittipaldi	Copersucar-Ford	54	+ 5 laps
Daly 1'39.468"	Scheckter 1'39.576"	**FASTEST LAP**			
Andretti 1'40.144"	Giacomelli 1'40.277"	Piquet	Brabham-Ford		1'40.054"
Patrese 1'40.337"	De Angelis 1'40.625"				195.490 km/h
Surer 1'40.635"	Tambay 1'40.731"	**RETIREMENTS**			
Fittipaldi 1'40.741"	Ickx 1'40.745"	Piquet	Brabham-Ford	53	
		Daly	Tyrrell-Ford	52	Transmission shaft
		Scheckter	Ferrari	48	Accident
		Patrese	Arrows-Ford	44	Puncture
		Jones	Williams-Ford	36	Rear suspension
		Surer	Ensign-Ford	32	Lost rear wheel
		Regazzoni	Williams-Ford	29	Engine
		Zunino	Brabham-Ford	25	Collision
		Jabouille	Renault	24	Accident
		Tambay	McLaren-Ford	20	Driving belt
		Rosberg	Wolf-Ford	20	Engine
		Jarier	Tyrrell-Ford	18	Collision with Daly, Spin, stall
		Andretti	Lotus-Ford	16	Gearbox
		Reutemann	Lotus-Ford	6	Accident
		Laffite	Ligier-Ford	3	Accident
		Ickx	Ligier-Ford	2	Accident
		Giacomelli	Alfa Romeo	0	Accident

Watkins Glen race statistics.

CHASSIS RECORDS FOR 1979

18.01.79   The RS01/02 takes part in practice for the Argentine Grand Prix at the Almirante Brown circuit in Buenos Aires as a mule. It is fitted with RS01/03 bodywork.

20.01.79   Front brake problem. Engine failure on the 3rd lap.

02.02.79   Official practice for the Brazilian Grand Prix at Interlagos. The air temperature is very high. Notes: water temperature 95°C, overfeed pressure 2.650 bar, engine speed 10,800rpm in 6th.

18.02.79 to 26.02.79   A week of preliminary testing at Kyalami for the South African Grand Prix. Jabouille and Arnoux do a series of high-speed tests to compare with Villeneuve's Ferrari, Lauda's Brabham, and Andretti's Lotus. The operation record comprises 45 pages of speed recordings in a week.

02.03.79   Official practice for the South African Grand Prix with Jabouille. At the exit of the engine, the water temperature is 116°C. The car takes part in the race the following day. Jabouille retires after 49 laps with a broken valve spring. The inlet of the water radiator is blocked with tyre debris. The fuel tank is emptied: 108 litres.

06.04.79   Official practice for the west coast American Grand Prix at Long Beach. Renault Sport withdraws after worrying transmission breakages, one of them causing Jabouille to leave the track dramatically.

22.05.79   Rolling tests before the Monaco Grand Prix on the Paul Ricard circuit. The RS01/02, used as a mule, does 7 laps – its last 7 laps before retirement. Jabouille was driving for the occasion.

RECORDS FOR RS01/03

18.01.79   Preliminary day for Argentine Grand Prix, 21 January, in Buenos Aires. Arnoux at the wheel. Fuel supply problem. It has to be injected with a spray can before the engine will start.

19.01.79   Official practice. Broken engine: there are two more on the same day. Water temperature 160°C after 3 laps.

20.01.79   More problems with engine and fuel temperature after 9 laps.

01.02.79   Preliminary day for Brazilian Grand Prix, 4 February, Interlagos. Arnoux gets to know the 7.960km circuit. Water 100°C. Overfeed pressure: 2.6 bar. Consumption: 4 litres per lap.

02.02.79.1   Free testing (tyres).

03.02.79.1.1   Arnoux in qualifying. Testing of new Salisbury differential. After 7 laps, the gearbox seizes. Gearbox dismantled during qualifying. Afternoon: Arnoux's second session: broken segments after 8 laps.

04.02.79   Warm-up. With 200 litres of fuel, the car is bottoming out all round the circuit. Grand Prix: Arnoux goes off the track on the 29th lap.

28.02.79   Preliminary day for African Grand Prix, 3 March, at

Kyalami. Arnoux at the wheel. His engine is still fitted with a supplementary water circuit in the exchanger. The engine cuts out at 10,800rpm. The limiter is disconnected. 50km without the limiter.

01.03.79   First official practice. Arnoux at the wheel. 35 laps in total. The engine cuts out after 33 laps.

02.03.79   Engine and turbo changed. After 16 laps, the engine blows up.

03.03.79   Warm-up. Engine running on 5 cylinders and cutting out. Sparkplugs changed. First start and rain. René takes the second start in 15th position with re-cut rain tyres. 5th and 6th ratios too short. 64th lap: Alan Jones goes off the track. 66th lap: Arnoux bursts a tyre on the debris of Jones' Williams.

06.04.79   Practice for the west coast American Grand Prix at Long Beach. Arnoux at the wheel. Several problems: broken starter motor, engine rough. Sparkplugs changed. Delayed response time. Total 39 laps.

07.04.79   Arnoux does 6 laps. Turbo mounting gasket fails.

08.04.79   Warm-up. New engine, new gearbox, new transmissions. 10th lap: car stops on the circuit. The two racing cars, 01/03 for Arnoux and 01/04 for Jabouille, are withdrawn following a transmission breakage resulting in Jabouille dramatically going off the track the previous day.

18.04.79   Private testing at Jarama, Spain. First day: tyres. 69 laps, 235km. Arnoux at the wheel.

19.04.79   66 laps, 225km, also without incident.

20.04.79   Engine blowing water after 37 laps. Overheating, cylinder head gasket. Engine total: 620km.

27.04.79   First day of qualifying for the Spanish Grand Prix at Jarama. 32 laps for Arnoux. Electrical breakdown.

28.04.79   René goes off the track on the 14th lap, in the morning. In the afternoon, 24 laps in qualifying. The engine not picking up at low speed. 11th place on the grid.

29.04.79   Nothing of note during the warm-up. During the race,

Arnoux finishes 9th, 1 lap behind the winner, Patrick Depailler, in a Ligier.

03.05.79   Private testing at Zolder. Arnoux does 51 laps without incident.

11.05.79   Official practice for the Belgian Grand Prix at Zolder. Arnoux at the wheel: 8 laps in the morning, stopped because of rain. Qualifying at 1pm. The circuit is beginning to dry out. Arnoux does 20 laps. Rain again.

12.05.79   Cloudy weather, track damp. A lot of oversteer in the morning. Afternoon: qualifying: track dry. The car understeers in the slow corners! 37 laps, 18th position for Arnoux.

13.05.79   Warm-up. Fine weather. 14 laps. Grand Prix: "The two Renaults hamper each other," notes Gérard Larrousse. (In the French records there is a question mark replacing the next part.) Arnoux retires on the 23rd lap with a broken turbo.

22.05.79   Running tests on the Paul Ricard circuit (3.3km) preceding the Monaco Grand Prix, where the RS01/03 is to be used as a mule. Arnoux does 7 laps on the 3.3km course.

RS01, CHASSIS 04
Primarily Jabouille's car at the beginning of the 1979 season – the last chassis of the RS01 type before the ground-effect cars.

18.01.79   Preliminary test day in Buenos Aires for the Argentine Grand Prix, the first race of the 1979 season. Jean-Pierre Jabouille gives the RS01/04, which will be his racing car, its first run.

19.01.79   First official practice for the Argentine Grand Prix. 9 laps. Engine displays symptoms of vapour lock, but found to be merely a blocked fuel filter.

20.01.79   20 laps in the morning, 21 in the afternoon in qualifying. 12th place for Jabouille.

21.01.79   Warm-up. 14 laps. Vibration in the rear wing. During the race, broken engine on the 15th lap.

26.01.79   Private testing at Interlagos, Brazil, before the Grand Prix. The engine blows. Car very rigid in the hairpins. 34 laps total for this day. 100°C water temp.

27.01.79   Installation of Chausson radiators. 33 laps, 105°C water temp.

01.02.79   Preliminary day for Brazilian Grand Prix. 14 laps, engine broken.

02.02.79   The RS01/04 becomes the mule. It doesn't run.

28.02.79   Preliminary testing at Kyalami for South African Grand Prix on 3 March. 13 laps: engine failure. Water temp. 116°C.

14.03.79   Private testing at Dijon-Prenois where a Long Beach-type chicane has been installed. 23 laps for Jabouille. Wet track.

16.03.79   Still at Dijon. Only 4 laps in the morning, then return to Viry.

06.04.79   Testing for the west coast American Grand Prix at Long Beach. 12 laps: Jabouille stops with a broken gearbox outlet (left-hand side).

Jabouille does 19 laps before leaving the track violently due to a transmission problem which proves insoluble. Renault Sport withdraws from the race to avoid pointless risks. The RS01/04 is completely destroyed.

RS10

Beginning with the RS10, which was Renault Sport's first ground-effect car, the competition department of the Régie changed the numbering system for its chassis. Instead of giving each chassis the same name but a different number, eg: RS01/01, RS01/02, etc, Renault Sport decided to change the name; ie: RS10, then RS11, etc. This had been the system for three years, after which the conventional system was re-adopted. Some traditional journalists refused to call the RS11 by its name, and referred to it as the RS10/02!

05.04.79   First run for the RS10 at 3.20pm, Jean-Pierre Jaussaud at the wheel. The ceremony takes place on the outside Canard ('duck') test circuit at Michelin, which is 1.982km long. Weather: rain, slushy snow, hail. A succession of spins. Jaussaud comments: "The skirts need lowering." 26 laps before stopping.

06.04.79   Still Jaussaud at the wheel, going out at 11.55am. After 5 laps, a turbo breaks. After the turbo is changed, he goes out

again. Jaussaud does some return trips on the number 1 'duck.' Comment: "The skirts need lifting again." Left-hand front skirt destroyed – it has become wedged at the back. More spins.

10.04.79   Jaussaud, on the Paul Ricard 3.3km circuit. Tests of different ceramic skirts edged in Teflon. Aerodynamic telemetry. 31 laps, then the car stops with a jammed throttle. Best lap: 1min 12.3sec. The same day at 5.40pm, Jean-Pierre Jabouille takes over from Jaussaud. 15 laps. Best lap: 1min 11.4sec.

11.04.79   Jabouille at the wheel. 8 laps.

19.04.79   Preliminary testing at Jarama in Spain. Skirts as defined at Ricard. 6 laps. Mixture too weak.

20.04.79   Testing of gearbox ratios and suspension springs. 26 laps in total for Jabouille. Best lap: 1min 21.8sec. Maximum speed recorded: 270kmh.

21.04.79   Last day of testing. 39 laps. Big clutch problems.

27.04.79   First practice day for Spanish Grand Prix at Jarama. 13 laps. Stop: broken injection butterfly cable. Qualifying in the afternoon: adjustments only. Jabouille's comment: "General lack of performance."

28.04.79   Free testing. 1 lap. Broken turbo. Skirts modified. Qualifying: 34 laps after changing the turbo. 1min 15.78sec: 9th position. Jabouille: "The car brakes badly, suspension too supple at the rear, lack of power but good aerodynamic balance."

29.04.79   Warm-up. 17 laps after modifying skirts. Spin on the 4th lap of the race. Jabouille retires on the 21st lap, overfeed pressure zero. Jabouille: "Steering much too heavy. I couldn't have finished the Grand Prix in these conditions."

03.05.79   Preliminaries for the Belgian Grand Prix in Zolder. Adjustments, 35 laps. Track damp or wet: "Brakes vibrating but power not bad," says Jabouille. Stop: turbine wheel broken. Special note: "Noise behind me." Jabouille had noticed a 'boom' noise when he cornered.

11.05.79   First day of practice for the Belgian Grand Prix in Zolder. Free testing: wet track. The car understeers in the slow corners, oversteers in the quick ones. Qualifying: 18 laps.

12.05.79   Free practice. Jabouille leaves the pits with the camera of film-maker Alain Boisnard fixed to his roll bar. 19 laps. Qualifying: 12 laps. Engine losing power; waste-gate changed. 17th position: 1min 24.2sec.

13.05.79   Warm-up. 5 laps. Turbo joint broken and fire begins to break out. During race: 8th lap, tyre change, Jabouille in 17th place; retires on 13th lap with a broken turbo. "The car is very heavy, not good under braking and acceleration. Too heavy at the front, too light at the rear."

20.05.79   On the way to the Monaco Grand Prix, which will take place on 27 May; first stop at Dijon. 76 laps with many problems including a very slippery track. One incident: rupture of the left-hand waste-gate pipe. For the first time, the Renault engine is fitted with twin turbocompressors. Jabouille has decided the gearbox ratios for Monaco. They call it a day at 5pm.

21.05.79   After Dijon, Paul Ricard. Running tests before Monaco on the 3.3km circuit. Jabouille begins at 5pm and stops at 8pm. 63 laps, best lap 1min 8.58sec. Several engine tests.

22.05.79   Jabouille does 23 laps in the RS10 before handing over to René Arnoux, who is driving it for the first time. Jabouille spends the day around the RS11; its first run will be in the evening. Arnoux stops at 9pm after several series of laps to get used to the twin turbos and ground-effect. Best lap: 1min 9.66sec.

24.05.79   First day of practice for the Monaco Grand Prix. Arnoux does 9 laps then stops: the lower ball joint of one of the wheel hub supports is touching the brake disc. The centring spigot pin of the rear left wheel is broken. Qualifying: 19 laps, then the centring pin breaks again. Arnoux says the car understeers.

26.05.79   Tests continue at Monaco. In the morning, air sleeves torn off and no brakes. Qualifying: 26 laps, but the engine breaks down on the 9th lap (best time: 1min 28.57sec on the 3rd lap). Right exchanger split.

27.05.79   Warm-up. Rainy weather. 14 laps. Oil leak. Arnoux says the chassis is behaving well. Race: 8th lap, collision with Piquet; suspension damaged.

27.06.79   Suspension tests at Montlhéry. Jabouille does 6 laps.

03.07.79   Private testing at Hockenheim. Jabouille at the wheel.

Stops after 48 laps: water leak on the left-hand side. "Car fine in the big corner at the end," says Jean-Pierre. Boost pressure: 2.6 bar, 10,800rpm in 5th.

04.07.79   First installation of a small dry battery. Boost pressure: 2.65 bar. 35 laps. Engine problem. Normal battery refitted.

12.07.79   First qualifying session for the British Grand Prix at Silverstone. Jabouille uses the car as a mule. 8 laps. Engine response time too long.

13.07.79   3 laps during the morning's free practice to carry the camera of film-maker Alain Boisnard.

30.07.79   Private testing at Zandvoort in Holland the day following the German Grand Prix at Hockenheim. Jabouille does 2 laps of testing after the truck arrives.

31.07.79   32 laps for Jabouille. Engine problems and "more and more understeering."

10.08.79   First practice day of the Austrian Grand Prix on the Österreichring at Zeltweg. Mule: Jabouille uses it for 7 laps in the free practice. Fine rain. He also uses it in the afternoon's qualifying: 11 laps, best lap 1min 36.2sec.

11.8.79   Jabouille uses the car again. 7 laps in the morning's free practice; 5 laps in qualifying. 1min 34.45sec, 3rd position.

24.8.79   First day of practice at the Dutch Grand Prix at Zandvoort. Mule for Jabouille. Free practice: 20 laps. Qualifying: 50 laps. Jabouille is on 2nd place on the provisional grid, 1min 16.338sec.

25.08.79   Mule. Jabouille: 6 laps in qualifying; stops for rain.

07.09.79   First day of practice for Italian Grand Prix at Monza. Mule for Jean-Pierre Jabouille. 10 laps in qualifying. Accelerator jams down and the turbo swallows a foreign body.

08.09.79   Practice continues. Mule: 20 laps in the morning for Jabouille in free practice. Jabouille on pole with 1min 34.58sec.

20.09.79   Private testing at Folembray. 52 laps for Jabouille who is testing an engine fitted with a water injection system. [This is the first time we hear this system tested.]

29.09.79   Second day of practice for Canadian GP in Montreal. Mule used by Jabouille in qualifying. 32 laps, 1min 32.103sec. 7th position on the starting grid.

04.10.79   Preliminaries at Watkins Glen for the east coast American GP on 7 October. Jabouille in the mule, 12 laps, nothing of note.

06.10.79   Free testing on Saturday morning. Mule, 16 laps.

17.10.79   Private testing on the Dijon-Prenois circuit. The car report doesn't give the driver's name. Probably Jean-Pierre Jabouille, given the importance of the tests. Drizzle. 75 laps. New fuel circuit, new water radiator. Stops on the track with broken accelerator.

18.10.79   Modified injection system and new turbos tested. 16 laps, then accelerator cable breaks again. 11 laps, then accelerator cable breaks for the third time. 50 laps in total. Test driver's comments: steering lighter, the skirts jump on the straight.

24.10.79   Private testing on the 3.3km Paul Ricard circuit. Jabouille at the wheel. New injection pump, named a 3P, tested. 103 laps in total. Best lap: 1min 6.27sec.

25.10.79   Testing continues, still with Jabouille. New brake pads tested. 67 laps. Wet, cold weather. 4 laps. New gearbox and engine.

29.10.79   Wet, cold weather. Difficult track with mud on the Méjanes S. 38 laps for Jabouille, skirt problem.

30.10.79   Testing continues at Paul Ricard. Carbon right-hand skirts fitted. 40 laps. One spin. Engine broken.

27.11.79   Private testing on the Paul Ricard circuit with Arnoux. New 6-speed gearbox tested. 105 laps in total on the 2.2km training circuit. 49th lap: burst tyre. From 1st to 28th lap with a chicane: best lap 51.71sec. From 29th to 105th lap, without chicane: best lap 47.33 sec. With 6-speed box, Arnoux does a lot of brake testing.

28.11.79   Testing continues, particularly of brakes, still with Arnoux. New pads, discs, calipers. 77 laps of the 2.2km circuit. Best lap: 47.61sec.

29.11.79   Testing continues and completed. Brakes and tyres tested on the 3.3km circuit. Stops on 34th lap with left drive shaft broken.

11.12.79   Private testing on the 5 km 'small' circuit at Interlagos, Brazil. Arnoux at the wheel. Weather cloudy with intermittent rain, temperature 35°C. 30 laps. René goes off the track in the wet. "Some damage," says the log.

12.12.79   Testing continues. Subject: suspension and engine with new valve-springs. Sudden increase in response time.

13.12.79   Engine changed. Overfeed pressure 2.3bar. Exchanger collars changed; pressure 2.6 bar.

RS11

Jabouille's racing car during the 1979 season. It was perhaps the most famous chassis of them all; the one with which Renault achieved its first Grand Prix success.

22.05.79   First run for the car with Jabouille at the 3.3km Paul Ricard circuit. 9.12pm. Fuel: 20 litres. Jabouille does 6 laps; best: 1min 22.44sec; total about 20km.

23.05.79   First tests of RS11 continue. Jabouille goes out onto the 3.3km track and does series of 3 or 4 laps. 60 litres fuel, brakes purged, undershield adjusted. "Steering too hard, slight understeer," notes Jabouille. After 3 series, a Kyalami-type rear wing is fitted: gain of 200rpm at maximum speed. Best lap: 1min 7.71sec. New seat fitted and position of steering wheel on stem inverted. Total of 132km today and 66 litres fuel consumption.

24.05.79   First day of practice at Monaco Grand Prix. Various problems and adjustments during free practice for Jabouille: poor functioning of fuel pump, accelerator in contact with rear hood, poor speed pickup of engine and lack of acceleration. Additional flap fitted. Fuel consumption 38 litres for 24 laps. Best lap 1min 30.09sec, 22nd fastest. For qualifying: gearbox ratios changed, left front skirt repaired. Jabouille notes vibration under braking at front. Flat tyre front right. Breakdown on 15th lap: last lap 1min 29.87sec.

26.05.79   Practice for Monaco Grand Prix continues. Free practice: trying to improve cooling of the surface of the brake discs. AP discs fitted to front. New rear wheel spigots fitted.

Engine mixture too lean. Rear wing lowered. Angle bracket removed from front despite 'small fence' wing. 46 litres for 23 laps. Last series with rear wing lowered to maximum. Qualifying: general increase in downforce. 3 laps. Engine breakdown. 1min 28.68sec, slowest time.

27.05.79 Monaco Grand Prix. Warm-up: adjustments as defined on Saturday; new gearbox; new skirt runners; waste-gate adjusted. 180 litres fuel. 14 laps (47km), best lap 1min 32.6sec. Jabouille requests displacement of gear lever 5/6mm to left. Race: pit stop on 42nd lap to adjust engine and on 44th to lean the mixture off. Tyre change. Total of 68 laps out of 76. Jabouille not classified.

02.06.79 Private testing at Dijon. Torque ratio 8 x 33 and gearbox 13 x 35, 15 x 33, 17 x 31, 18 x 28, 20 x 27, 24 x 29. Jabouille goes out on the track at 10.11am and does short series of laps. Comments: "Bad vibration under braking; response time too long; slight understeer; too much downforce at front; more precise at front." And underlined: "Too much play in the steering."
    The engineer present at these tests is Michel Têtu, who, with his attention to detail, notes all Jabouille's comments. For example: "Jabouille sees no difference in the behaviour of the engine, easier to drive, better at the front, hits limiter," etc. For the 46 laps today, there are exactly 3 pages of notes on the car log. Total 46 laps, 117 litres of fuel, consumption 66.9 litres/100km. Fastest time on 43rd lap: 1min 9.38sec. 267kmh at maximum speed. Stopped on track on 45th lap with fuel leak.

03.06.79 Private testing continues at Dijon, still with Jabouille. Fine weather; 15°C on the track. Testing of tyres and suspension. Jabouille starts at 8.10am. After 4 stops and 4 tyre changes (12 laps in all), he does an endurance test. 63 laps; best time 1min 11.3sec, 282km and 186 litres, or 66 litres/100km. 10,200rpm on the straight. Engine consumes 1 litre of oil. Jabouille's comments: "6th gear jumps. Increasing vibration at front." After this test, Jabouille does 5 more laps to test the tyres. Stops with a broken exhaust at entry of waste-gate. Total for the day 80 laps, 304km – the distance of the French Grand Prix at Dijon.

05.06.79 Private testing at Silverstone. Fine weather, 18°C on the track. Car with Dijon configuration but engine with short trumpets, different setting for fuel pump, new richness adjustment and overfeed pressure at 2.75 bar. Jabouille on the track at 10.20am. 3 laps, then stops. 3 more laps and stops again.

Jabouille has heard an explosion behind him (see also 3.5.79 at Zolder with the RS10). This explosion came from the tank, as shown by the body panels which suddenly take on a dent at this location. This will not be the last incident of this type, and it will take the Renault Sport technicians several weeks to find the cause. They even find one body totally distorted. The problem is an accumulation of static electricity between the tank and the body. Tests are suspended at Silverstone.

20.06.79 Private testing at Dijon. Jabouille at the wheel. 6th gear lengthened by 400 revs. Tyres and brakes tested. Jabouille carries a remote control camera fixed to a frame. On the track at 10.56am: 34 laps, fastest 1min 10.47sec, 276kmh on the straight. Comments: Skirts jammed? Stops at 12.50 and starts again at 3.55pm. New brake master cylinders; new Scotch-Teflon to cover skirts and make them slide better; new turbine casings. After the tyres, aerodynamic testing. Maxi-Dijon configuration determined in wind tunnel, ie: front wing with Gurney strip, side-pods type Zolder or Monaco, rear wing type Kyalami with Gurney strip, undershield adjusted accordingly. Results: 9900rpm, braking distance reduced by 20 to 30 per cent. 5.29pm: Jabouille stops, having difficulty keeping his head steady on the corners. Left headrest bar fitted. Finally stops 6.50pm. Total for the day 95 laps, 361km, quickest lap: 1min 8.38sec on the 82nd lap.

21.06.79 Tests at Dijon continue, still with Jabouille. On the track at 11.35am. Engine testing (sparkplugs, injection). 4 series of 24 laps; fastest lap 1min 10.3sec, 271kmh on the straight. 1.56pm: start of endurance test; temperature 25°C. Stops on 50th lap of test for tyre change. Stops on 67th lap for tyre change and fitting of run-in tyres. Jabouille stops on the 72nd lap. Total for the day: 96 laps, 364km, consumption 237 litres or 2.4 litres per lap. Overfeed pressure: 2.55 bar, or a loss of pressure of 100g with no apparent cause. Exhaust darker than before test; oil leak in left side-pod, steering very heavy, headrest essential. Left skirt runner missing. Note in a box and heavily underlined: "Fitting of rear wheel catastrophic."

27.06.79 Running at Montlhéry. 12 laps, 30km. Broken screw on rear brake caliper. Jabouille's comment: "Too high at the front."

29.06.79 First day of practice for the French Grand Prix in Dijon. Jabouille goes out with 60 litres. 27 laps; best lap 1min 7.41sec (fastest lap). Additional fuel 30 litres. Engine rather rich, 10,700rpm on the straight. Leaned off by ¼ turn. Jabouille's comments: "Car good, braking OK. Understeers slightly." A large anti-roll bar is fitted to the rear but after 4 laps the original one is refitted. Fuel emptied: 30 litres. Consumption: 60 litres. Afternoon: same adjustments but rear wing raised to the last hole. Note: consider intermediary adjustment of rear wing. Jabouille's comments: "Car almost perfect, 23 laps, 48 litres consumed." Fastest lap: 1min 7.88sec on 21st lap, ie: 2nd fastest behind Arnoux.

30.06.79   Practice continues at French Grand Prix. Untimed session. Long steering levers fitted. Negative camber increased front and rear left, 1 turn of waste-gate. Different tyres tested on Gotti and Dymag rims. Jabouille goes out with 180 litres on board. He comments: "Tyres too hard, take too long to warm up. Car not bad, steering good, pitches slightly on the straight. 215/216 tyres tested but final preference for 180/181. 1 more turn of waste-gate. Pads fitted for running-in. Rear downforce increased to 135 (from 130). Fuel emptied: 130 litres. 100 litres consumed for 49 laps. Fastest lap: 1min 9.8sec, 270kmh maximum. Last qualifying session: 34 laps in 6 series, one with Michelin 215/216, one with 174/175, three with 200/208. Rear downforce reduced from 135 to 132. Jabouille's comment: "Car almost perfect." He secures pole position at 2.32pm: 1min 7.19sec. Consumption: 71 litres for 34 laps. Engine: 315km total.

01.07.79   Warm-up. Ratios changed: 14 x 46, 14 x 32, 16 x 31, 18 x 28, 20 x 17, 21 x 26. New skirts, high rear brake air inlets, headrest tube fitted. 180 litres, tyres 215/216 run in but seem "a bit too tight," says Jabouille; replaced by 180/181: "Not bad, but slow to warm up." Overfeed pressure: 2.65, ¾ turn of waste-gate. 21 laps. Best lap: 1min 9.79sec. Race: Dymag rims. No other notes on operating log except for an arrow meaning "takes the lead on the 47th lap." First F1 victory for the Renault turbo engine and Jean-Pierre Jabouille. Engine total: 103 laps (80 for the race, 2 for grid formation and lap of honour, 21 for warm-up), or 392km.

05.07.79   Private testing at Silverstone (4.719km) a week before the British Grand Prix. Gearbox ratios: 12 x 35, 14 x 34, 16 x 34, 18 x 30, 19 x 27, 21 x 20. Expected consumption: 3.06 litres/lap. Aerodynamic tests: different widths and heights of wing, double rear flap, but interrupted by engine problems. "Plugs 505, engine s**t; plugs 503, distribution noise." Finally, "Angular adjustment Dijon for rear wing" and engine broken on 31st lap at 12.20pm. Loss of compression in number 6. Restart 4.50pm with new engine and skirt runners. Jabouille does 3 laps to check, or 34 laps in all for today, Thursday.

06.07.79   Private testing continues at Silverstone. Still aerodynamics but also suspension and engine "which seems to be tightening." Jabouille on the track at 10.10am. Bendix feed "exterior detached." Ceramics broken on left skirt and skirt damaged. 76th lap: "Still understeering a little, not good under braking, engine weak." At the end of the afternoon, after testing new wings, Jabouille gets out. 69 laps on Friday and total of 103 laps for these two days of testing. "Jabouille's best lap: 1min 13.3sec on the 102nd with 261kmh max speed," notes engineer François Castaing.

12.07.79   First official practice for British Grand Prix at Silverstone. Non-qualifying session. Jabouille does 22 laps; best lap: 1min 14.26sec. Comments: "Seat needs modifying, tyres not warm enough on the right, can't pick up speed soon enough. Wing better." Consumption: 61 litres for 22 laps, or 2.77 litres/lap. Qualifying session Thursday afternoon. Type F2 rear wing with Gurney strip, bodywork height adjusted, 2 notches compression and 2 notches release added to rear shock absorbers, engine less satisfactory, vibration under braking. Jabouille does 24 laps including 1min 13.27sec on 16th (fastest time on the grid). Consumption: 2.82 litres/lap.

13.07.79   Second day of practice, non-qualifying session. New rear bearings. General check: nothing significant. "Car not bad," says Jabouille. Incidents: rear caliper screw broken, front left runner completely worn, left skirt trapped. Best lap: 1min 15.72sec on the 16th with 180 litres at start. 19 laps in all. Maximum speed registered in front of pit 14: Piquet 242kmh, Scheckter 240, Villeneuve and Jabouille 239, Lauda 238, Reutemann 237, Arnoux 236, Jones 235, Andretti 234. Last qualifying session in the afternoon. Old model front skirt springs; springs reconditioned, ½ turn for waste-gate. Jabouille goes out with 60 litres. Comments: "Track not very quick; too long in 6th with 10,400rpm, less grip than yesterday." 1min 12.83sec on the 8th lap at around 1.50pm. Left-hand tyre pressures changed; front and rear wings changed; 30 litres fuel loaded; engine OK. 30th lap: 1min 12.48sec, pole position. 37th lap: stops on the track – distribution drive belt sprung. 56 laps in all; 265km. Jabouille's comment: "Better with this wing position – easier to drive." Max. speeds in front of pit 14: Jabouille 250kmh, Arnoux 246, Scheckter and Piquet 245, Lauda and Jones 244, Villeneuve 243, Andretti and Reutemann 240.

14.07.79   Warm-up. Engine changed, run-in pads, skirts with 20mm runners, gearbox ratios No. 2: 12 x 35, 14 x 34, 16 x

32, 17 x 29, 19 x 27, 24 x 29. 200 litres fuel. Jabouille doesn't take part in warm-up: gearbox 1st bearing seized; bearing and pinion of 1st changed; seizes again. Gearbox changed. Race: 2nd behind Jones until 16th lap and stops on 17th lap: engine. Restarts twice from pits and finally stops on 21st lap.

27.07.79   First day of practice for German Grand Prix. Untimed session on Friday morning. Only 4 laps for Jabouille; goes off track on 5th lap. Driver's comments: "Car a little slow going into the corner, oversteers on exit." Skirts changed; left inside and outside panels changed; engine made richer. Best lap: 1min 48.48sec on 6th lap with Michelin 200s. "Car almost perfect," says Jabouille, "in spite of a slight lack of grip." Consumption: 4 litres/lap.

28.07.79   Second day of practice. Non-qualifying session. 'Long' rear Koni shock absorbers fitted. Gearbox ratios changed: 12 x 35, 14 x 34, 17 x 31, 19 x 29, 20 x 27, 22 x 26. Front skirt springs 10 spirals. Jabouille: "Not bad; brakes OK; car understeering more as laps progress. Seems to be a skirt problem." 23 laps, 96 litres, lack of overfeed pressure (2.6 instead of 2.650). Best lap: 1min 51.92sec on the 21st. Qualifying session: overfeed pressure checked, 1.5 turns more on the waste-gate, 0.5 less of richness. Brake pedal problem on 2nd lap; car not very good. Master-cylinder? Best lap: 1min 49.77sec on 3rd. Stops at 3.24pm: track not as fast. Jabouille therefore maintains his pole position from the day before.

29.07.79   Warm-up. Skirt panels reinforced. Front disk tracks cooled with Folembray air inlets. Dynamic air inlets for rear brakes. Pads run-in, circuit purged. Front wing lowered 1mm. General check of brake assembly. 200 litres fuel. 13 laps and 1min 51.71sec on 8th. Race: 2nd place behind Jones until 7th lap; spin and stall on 8th.

01.08.79   Private testing on the Österreichring at Zeltweg in Austria. Jabouille at the wheel. Circuit: 5.942km. Tyres and aerodynamics tested. Stop on the 4th lap: rear right-hand hood has blown off. Incorrectly attached? Skirts not working at rear. Jabouille's comments after change of skirts: "Surprising grip; car understeering slightly." Gearbox ratios changed because 10,200rpm in front of the pits and 10,500rpm behind. In the afternoon, tyres, suspension and brakes tested. Serious vibration from R3 pads but better on braking attack. 37 laps in total for the day. Consumption: 3.35 litres/lap. Sparkplug cable disconnected on 24th lap.

02.08.79   Private testing continues, still with Jabouille. Temperature 28°C, 38°C on track. After changing skirts, shock absorbers adjusted, brakes checked (new disks at front), endurance test. Jabouille on track at 9.24am. 12 laps perfecting. 1min 35.7sec on 11th, best time so far: Pironi in Tyrrell-Ford 1min 38.49sec. After this, several problems for Jabouille: left rear-view mirror detached; sparkplug cable disconnected for the second time on cylinder 3; serious understeer. Finally, the endurance test becomes a tyre test, but more problems: air is getting in at the exhaust panel notch and lifting the undershield; tachometer broken, burnt by exhaust; emergency tachometer also broken; battery has come out of casing; fixing Rylsans broken as well as the cable at exit of lead connection; undershield crushed and worn. "Difficult to judge the car; speed at exit of corners impossible to estimate without tachometer," says Jabouille. 39 laps in total today. Best lap: 1min 35.3sec.

10.08.79   First official day of practice for the Austrian Grand Prix at Österreichring. Track very wet. Jabouille stops on 8th lap after time of 2min 0.3sec. Qualifying: 25 laps; best lap: 1min 34.45sec on 12th. Ignition box changed. Goes slightly off the track on 21st lap. Skirts checked. Day's total 33 laps.

11.08.79   Practice continues for Austrian Grand Prix. Jabouille goes out with 180 litres. Stops on 7th lap of the non-qualifying session: turbo blades broken. Rear bottoming after 5 laps. Qualifying: 1min 34.49sec on 15th lap after changing downforce and emptying tank. Jabouille holds on to his best time of the previous day (1min 34.45sec) which gives him 3rd place on the grid. François Castaing's note: "Cannot explain why front wing, which was better on the RS12, makes the RS11 understeer." Consumption: 3.69 litres/lap.

12.08.79   Warm-up. Damp track. 13 laps. Best time on 12th: 1min 36.8sec. Note: numerous changes in brake air inlets throughout the two days of practice and warm-up. Race: 4mm more rear wing. Jabouille 2nd behind Jones (Williams-Ford) on the 15th lap but retires on 16th with seized clutch.

25.08.79   Second official day of practice for Dutch Grand Prix at Zandvoort. Jabouille spent Friday in the mule (the RS10). Damp track on Saturday morning when he goes out in the RS11. New brakes; wings adjusted. Too much overfeed pressure: the black box shows 2.8. 24 laps; best 1min 18.7sec on the 21st and 23rd laps. Qualifying: Jabouille goes out with 60 litres of fuel. 20 laps, best time on the 17th lap: 1min 16.304sec – 4th place on grid.

26.08.79 Warm-up. 16 laps. 5mm less rear wing. Nothing of note. Race: 3rd on the 25th lap behind Villeneuve (Ferrari) and Jones (Williams-Ford) and retires on 26th lap with broken clutch.

07.09.79 First day of practice at Italian Grand Prix in Monza. Tyre tests. Two much understeer. Tests of different brake scoops. Jabouille does 20 laps. Best lap: 1min 36.7sec. 22 laps qualifying in afternoon and tests of narrow rear rims during first two series of laps. For the three other series, normal rims replaced. Best lap: 1min 35.665sec on 21st. Problem with brake wear.

09.09.79 Warm-up for Italian Grand Prix. Jabouille uses the mule (RS10) during the Saturday and it is with this car that he obtains pole position. 13 laps during warm-up, configuration of RS11 identical to RS10 except for triple disc clutch, large rear brake calipers and new pads. "Pedal long but temperature too high," notes engineer, Castaing. The car is loaded with 200 litres of fuel. Race: fine, very warm weather. Jabouille is in 4th place on 45th lap but retires on the 46th with a broken engine. "It was a bit soft," notes Jabouille. The valve springs were new.

In total, after the 1979 Italian Grand Prix, chassis RS11 had done 6,058km since its first run.

RS12

Arnoux's racing car in which he fought his legendary duel with Gilles Villeneuve at the French Grand Prix.

28.06.79 First run for RS12 at Montlhéry with René Arnoux at the wheel. It is 5.56pm. Arnoux does just one lap before stopping for routine checks. At 6.10pm, he goes out again for a series of 4 fast laps. Rev limiter at 10,400rpm; overfeed pressure raised to 2.7 bar before being lowered again to 2.65 bar. Brakes OK; steering "very good," maximum turning OK. Problem to use gears. Adjustment of clutch and clearance. Limiter at 10,700rpm but there is still a problem with changing gear during the second series of runs. 6.51pm: one fast lap. The car bottoms a lot at high speed (10,000rpm in 6th). The undershield is removed, the gearbox bolts softened and the limiter set at 10,800rpm. This first test finishes at 7pm. The Renault Sport truck leaves immediately for Dijon.

29.06.79 First day of official practice for French Grand Prix in Dijon. Arnoux goes out with 60 litres of fuel. Wings adjusted and tests of various anti-roll bars during 30 laps, all with Michelin

106s. Serious understeer towards the end of the session, but after a pit stop it is noted that the right-hand rear wheel is flat. Brakes drained, engine checked, waste-gate altered and three more notches on the rear shock absorbers before the afternoon's qualifying. Still on Michelin 106s. 18 laps; 1min 7.45sec on 17th lap which gives Arnoux pole position for the time being. Fuel consumption much improved: 2.22 litres/lap.

30.06.79 Second practice day; this Saturday morning session is not qualifying. 35 laps for Arnoux who starts with 180 litres of fuel. He does 10 laps. Incidents: battery and rev counter changed; oil leak from right turbo. Brake pads have to be changed and rear-view mirrors refitted. Last qualifying session Saturday afternoon. Engine problems for Arnoux whose pole position is spirited away by Jabouille.

01.07.79 Warm-up for the French Grand Prix. 180 litres fuel. According to Arnoux, nothing of note. Boost pressure 2.7 bar. 14 laps; best lap: 1min 10.34sec on 8th. Race: Arnoux 3rd after historic duel with Gilles Villeneuve. Engine: 357km in total.

12.07.79 First day of practice for British Grand Prix at Silverstone. Cloudy and cool. Arnoux does 21 laps, soon noting that the car jumps at high speed. After a check of the body height, the behaviour of the RS12 is unchanged. Worse: in spite of the adjustments, the movement is increasing. [They have discovered 'pumping' (porpoising) – typical fault of ground-effect cars.] Finally, after adjusting the shock absorbers, the car's behaviour improves. 21 laps; best lap 1min 15.6sec on the 19th. Qualifying: 47 laps in all. Slight electrical problem, but "Car OK, except for slight persistent understeer," says Arnoux. Runs out of fuel on 43rd lap. 30 litres quickly loaded and Arnoux does 1min 13.29sec on the 45th lap. Comments: "Skirts lifting going into chicane; brake pads need replacing; gear selection difficult; fuel consumption to be checked; move gear lever towards driver; steering wheel to be changed; bodywork screws to be tightened."

13.07.79 Second day of practice for British Grand Prix – non-qualifying session. 13 laps only for Arnoux who has road-holding problems. The car loses traction suddenly when cornering and vibrates a lot. Worn skirts? Last qualifying session early afternoon. Arnoux does 45 laps but can't improve on his time. Rear wing at 130. Arnoux's comments: "Car OK in corners but slow on the straight. Brake pedal hard down on last laps."

14.07.79 Warm-up. "Slight understeer; brakes borderline but

engine adjustment excellent. Otherwise nothing of note," says Arnoux. Race: Arnoux in 2nd place behind Clay Regazzoni on the 39th lap and the two drivers finish the Grand Prix in this order.

19.07.79   Private testing on the Folembray circuit (2.33km). The driver's name is not mentioned on the log. The subject of these tests is important: to try a new AP braking system (discs, pads, air inlets) together with an assistance system with two master-cylinders. The car is fitted with a Magneti Marelli battery and has no undershield. Comments of drivers and Renault Sport mechanics: "Adjustment of pads and discs seems very easy. But no play on the pedal. 15 laps in total from 10.01am to 11.24am; stops on 15th lap; engine failure. Engine changed and test continues at 4.13pm with "increased operating pressure in AP assistance system." Various braking distributions tested; endurance test of brakes; various cooling air inlets fitted on discs and clips. 53 laps in total during the day and testing stops at 7.09pm. Fastest lap: 48.9sec on the 38th. Incidents: one missed chicane; gearbox casing changed after adjustment of gearbox ratios; a brake assistance cable disconnected; front left brake air inlet torn off. Driver's comments: "The brake pedal travel gets longer as the laps progress."

20.07.79   Private testing continues at Folembray; still AP brakes with assistance system. Front discs are fitted with autoventilation by identical double channels and pads. 38 laps, after which the comments are: "Not bad; no more vibration, but brake pedal travel gets longer after 30 laps." From 39th lap, endurance test begins (11.46am) which finishes on the 86th lap (fastest time: 47.28sec). General comments: "The brake pedal goes down to 5 or 6mm after the first 10 laps, then remains constant. With these discs, braking is a bit late. The 'AP boys' think that the front pad temperatures are 90°C lower in operation than with the other discs. They should therefore wear better."

From the 87th lap, the brake assistance system is removed; testing to 103rd lap. Comments: "Much harder on the pedal; impossible to lock the wheels." From the 104th lap (2.35pm) up to the 144th lap, wheel-changing training for the whole Renault Sport team. The car leaves the pits and stops again after one or two laps. This makes 16 pit stops, of which the best is 22sec "with locking pins removed and replaced," preceded by a 22sec "with locking pins not replaced" and followed by a 23sec "with locking pins but without the driver's foot on the brake pedal," then a 34sec "with change of position of operators." After the wheel changes, tests continue from 145th lap (4.32pm) to 170th (towards 6pm); brake pads run in. Total for these two days at

Folembray: 453km. Final remarks: "Start with a small air tank tested; didn't work. Underside of front hood torn off. Clutch pedal and footrest to be moved forward by 10 to 15mm." This leads one to suppose that, since the RS12 was to be Arnoux's car, only he could have requested such adjustments. It would seem, therefore, that Arnoux was the test driver for these two days.

27.07.79   First official day of practice for the German Grand Prix at Hockenheim; session not officially timed. Arnoux: 18 laps. Slight understeer everywhere through track and chicanes. Consumption: 4.1 litres/lap.Qualifying: fine, hot weather. Arnoux: 20 laps: "Balance OK." Boost pressure: less than 2.6; "tends to fall." 10,800-10,900rpm at start of session. 15th lap: stop: steering wheel broken. Comment: "Spare steering wheel to be provided in case of breakage or theft." Consumption: 3.95 litres/lap, or 58.15 litres/100km. Arnoux: 1min 50.48sec on 7th lap.

28.07.79   Second day of practice for German Grand Prix. Non-qualifying session on Saturday morning. Arnoux does 15 laps: "Balance OK; tends to understeer; too much clutch clearance; in all, no improvement." Fastest lap: 1min 53.99sec. Arnoux doesn't take part in the 2nd qualifying session due to a valve spring broken when he takes to the track. His time from the day before puts him in 10th place on the grid.

29.07.79   Warm-up. Fine, hot weather. Large Folembray-type front brake scoops fitted, as well as at the rear above the side-pod. Pressure: 2.650 bar; 10,700rpm. Arnoux's comments: "Clutch clearance very strange. Vibration from rear brakes." 14 laps; fastest lap: 1min 52.52sec. Race: Arnoux is 6th on the 9th lap but stops on the track on the 10th lap with a burst tyre.

10.08.79   First official day of practice for the Austrian Grand Prix at the Österreichring (Zeltweg). It is raining during the first untimed session. Arnoux: 11 laps; "2nd a bit long." Aerodynamic grip: "Ditto dry." Qualifying: dry track; Arnoux does 31 laps with a few problems. "Slight understeer; reactions in the steering; brake pedal soft; boost pressure manometer broken and no more boost pressure; burst inlet pipe." Fastest lap: 1min 35.53sec on the 18th lap with new Michelin 200s.

11.08.79   Second practice day. First session non-qualifying. Arnoux: 15 laps; severe vibration at the front and bad understeer. Brake discs and pads changed (DS11 tested) and rear downforce reduced as well as "strip retracted." Best lap: 1min 36.4sec on the 14th. 1 turn of camber front left; ½ turn on rear brakes. Final comment: "Car OK," although still understeering slightly. Arnoux clocks 1min 34.7sec on the 14th lap giving the Grenoble driver his first pole position.

12.08.79   Warm-up for the Austrian Grand Prix. Arnoux: 12 laps. Still some vibration from the brakes and pedal a bit soft. Consumption: 3.41 litres/lap. Race: Arnoux starts with 210 litres, giving the permitted consumption over 52 laps of 4 litres/lap. Then on the 50th lap he runs out of fuel and stops. Jean Sage has 15 litres put in and Arnoux restarts, but he has dropped from 2nd to 6th place at the finish.

24.08.79   First official day of practice for the Dutch Grand Prix at Zandvoort. Arnoux at the wheel. Faulty turbo connection; oil leak. The connection is changed but he stops again; "2 connections fitted." Arnoux's comments: "Slight understeer on big corner. Oil on tight ones. Wait for track to dry." Afternoon: qualifying. Track drying out. "Car OK," says Arnoux. 44 laps in 1 hour. Consumption: 2.76 litres/lap. In the last few laps, "The rear hangs out."

25.08.79   Second day of practice. Fine, cool weather. Adjusted front downforce (+5mm), the car, which "still understeers going into the corners," "turns in better." Best lap: 1min 18.54sec with 142 litres of fuel. Last qualifying session in afternoon: Arnoux fits Michelin 229s. Comment: "On the limiter all the time with these tyres." But on the 12th lap he takes pole position from Alan Jones. 1min 15.44sec according to Renault timekeeping; 1min 15.461sec officially. After this, Arnoux puts Michelin 200s on the car: "Car less efficient." One spin. Stops after 25 laps: rain.

26.08.79   Warm-up for Dutch Grand Prix. Arnoux does 15 laps: tyres constant; "engine better." Additional 3mm downforce. Note: "Prepare re-cut qualifying tyres for race if it rains." Race: shortly after the beginning he collides with Regazzoni and retires.

07.09.79   First official day of practice for the Italian Grand Prix at the Monza circuit. Still the same problem: understeer going into wide corners; oversteer coming out of tight corners. Arnoux: "The car bottoms." 19 laps: consumption 3.8 litres/lap. Qualifying: small rear wing; angle bracket 5mm; bi-convex at front without flap; 100rpm more on the limiter. Arnoux's comments: "Brakes not too good; car OK but a bit slow." Engineer's note: "Speed almost 11,000rpm. NB: Michelin increases pressure of rear tyres." 36 laps for Arnoux; 1min 34.7sec on 28th – fastest time of the day.

08.09.79   Second day; still fine weather. Balance OK, but small water leak from engine and right front tyre "a bit worn; gearbox better with full tank." Total of 17 laps with 180 litres. Afternoon qualifying session: 60 litres fuel; large brake calipers at front. Stops after 5 laps: "Serious engine oil leak." Arnoux has time to comment: "The car jumps a lot." Engineer's note: "Check shock absorbers."

09.09.79   Warm-up for Italian Grand Prix. 200 litres fuel. Car good but "touches a bit at the front ; brakes very hot (change pads); 6th difficult to exit." Arnoux does 12 laps; best 1min 38.66sec. Race: 11 laps in front but retires on 14th lap; engine problem.

28.09.79   First official day of practice for Canadian Grand Prix on the Île-Notre-Dame circuit at Montreal. Arnoux at the wheel: "The car bottoms; engine not clean; 10,500rpm in 5th." Limiter changed to 10,900. Afternoon: cloudy weather. "Car OK; slight understeer; brake pedal too long; 3rd jumps." 35 laps in all; 1min 33.38 on the 27th. At the end of the session, he comments: "Better at entry but almost too fine on exit; not good in the fast ones."

29.09.79   Second day of practice; cloudy weather. 180 litres fuel in the morning. Car good; brake pedal a bit soft. 26 laps; best lap: 1min 33.8sec. Qualifying: "Car good but lazy on entry; engine OK." 31 laps for Arnoux and 1min 31.8sec (officially 1min 32.1sec) – 8th place on the grid. End of session: engine out. Consumption: 3.175 litres/lap.

30.09.79   Warm-up for Canadian Grand Prix. 200 litres fuel. Arnoux does 15 laps: "Car understeers too much; engine strong." Limiter adjustment checked. Race: collision with Hans Stuck (ATS-Ford) on 15th lap.

04.10.79   Preliminary testing at Watkins Glen for east-coast American Grand Prix. Cool weather. Arnoux does 24 laps: "Not much grip." Boost pressure: 2.55 bar. Then: "Boost pressure falls: remove foam in front of turbo." Best lap: 1min 41.38sec.

05.10.79   First official day of practice for east-coast American Grand Prix at Watkins Glen. Heavy rain. 9 laps in the morning for Arnoux ("Car good"); only 3 laps in the afternoon because of rain.

06.10.79   Second practice day; fine cold weather. Arnoux: 23 laps; 1min 40.25sec on 20th. "Slight understeer." Incident: rev counter broken. Qualifying: 39 laps; 1min 38.19sec on 36th. Engineer's note: "Shock absorbers overheating; car bottoms a bit less when downforce is increased; brake pedal goes right down; 10,300rpm in 5th with new rev counter."

07.10.79   Warm-up for American Grand Prix. Arnoux goes out with 200 litres of fuel on board. 13 laps in all; 1min 41.42sec on 11th. "Car bottoms slightly at front; brakes better with water injection." (Race: the log page has disappeared.) Arnoux finishes the race in second place behind Villeneuve.

29.10.79   Private testing on the Paul Ricard 3.3km circuit. Ambient temperature 17°C. Arnoux at the wheel. Subject of testing: tyres. Arnoux does series of 4 to 5 fast laps. Maximum speeds measured. 51 laps in all; best lap: 1min 5.96sec on the 43rd; speed 260.5kmh with Michelin 136 at front, 147 rear.

30.10.79   Testing continues, still with Arnoux on 3.3km circuit. Starts at 9.33am and does 79 laps during the day, trying a dozen types of tyres with different rubber, carcass and dimensions. Incidents: broken skirt runner; sparkplug cable disconnected; gear level jammed and finally engine water leak (engine out).

In total, at the end of these private tests at the Paul Ricard circuit, chassis RS12 has done 6807km since its first run.

RS14

Through superstition, the number 13 is rarely used in motor sport. Renault Sport respects this tradition: chassis RS12 was followed by chassis RS14.

21.09.79   First run for the RS14 at Montlhéry. Strangely, the RS14 log doesn't give the name of the driver who did this first 8-lap run with 60 litres of fuel. It could be Jean-Pierre Jabouille, who was to race the RS14. The modifications carried out also indicate that it was Jabouille. These were as follows: "Cut brake pedal low down; foam to be fitted next to left knee; windscreen to be manufactured; rear-view mirror; cover tube on brake pedal; move gear lever 10mm towards steering wheel; inside side-pod screw missing; left brake noise."

28.09.79   First official day of practice for Canadian Grand Prix at Île-Notre-Dame circuit, Montreal. Shakedown testing by Jabouille. 25 laps; fastest 1min 53.3sec on 15th. Comments: "Lean-off the engine; deglaze brakes; connect water injection." Qualifying session: rear downforce changed; rear anti-roll bar softened. 32 laps: 1min 33.4sec twice by Jabouille. Gearbox

ratios: 13 x 35, 15 x 33, 17 x 30, 20 x 28, 22 x 26, 22 x 25. Consumption: 3 litres/lap. Water consumption for brake water injection cooling: "1 can/32 laps."

29.09.79   Second practice day at Canadian Grand Prix. Jabouille and engineer Castaing work mainly on brakes. 18 laps in total then stops with broken valve spring. Fastest lap: 1min 34.2sec. Jabouille uses the mule (RS10) to qualify in the afternoon.

30.09.79   Warm-up. Jabouille does 15 laps. Aerodynamic adjustments and again problems with the brakes, of which two front discs cracked. Race: stops with accelerator cable jammed on 9th lap; rear brakes drained on 18th lap and all brakes drained on 22nd; retires on 14th with insoluble brake problem.

04.10.79   Preliminary test day at Watkins Glen in America, mainly for tyre testing, but François Castaing and Jean-Pierre Jabouille want to solve different problems. Suspension: "Touches at the front." Brakes: drained several times; AP discs used. Incident: rev counter out of action.

05.10.79   First official day of practice at Watkins Glen for east coast American Grand Prix. Rain in morning. Jabouille spins and stops. Shock absorbers: tests of different types, first Koni then de Carbon, titanium springs and different types of shock absorbers. Jabouille does 14 laps in all; he doesn't go out on the track in the afternoon during the qualifying session because of rain.

06.10.79   Second practice day. 6 laps in the morning for Jabouille; wings, bars and body height changed. Comments: "Doesn't understeer but pumps and jumps a lot." 33 laps in qualifying; perfection adjustments. 1min 38.1sec on 25th lap – 8th on the starting grid.

07.10.79   Warm-up. 200 litres fuel. Jabouille does 15 laps; 1min 42.6 on the 10th. Rear and front downforce increased.

(The log for the American Grand Prix is not available. We only know that Jabouille was 3rd on the 24th lap when his engine died with a broken camshaft drive belt.)
Total distance for RS14 since its first run: 1159km.

RS20A – NEW DEVELOPMENT CAR FOR 1980

29.11.79   First run with Jean-Pierre Jabouille on the 3.3km Paul

167

Ricard circuit. 5.17pm: leaves pit and returns. 60 litres fuel. Shortened front air inlets; normal at rear. "Engine not running well. Too rich or too poor? Lean-off 1 turn." 5.26pm: goes out for 2 fast laps: 1min 20.99sec and 1min 17.3sec. "Engine better but not OK yet."

30.11.79   First tests continue, still with Jabouille. 'Le Grand' (nickname for Jean-Pierre) does short series of laps. 10.07am; 5 laps; fastest 1min 14.44sec (still on the 3.3km circuit). Front shock absorbers: 12 notches less; new DS11 728 pads. "Clutch doesn't return quickly enough. Front suspension too hard. Continual understeer." Asbestos lining under rear hood; engine leaned-off; Koni shock absorbers fitted. 11.08am: 4 laps; fastest 1min 10.24sec. "Engine still not OK; front shock absorbers not as hard, but still too much understeer." 11.30am: 3 laps; 1min 23.6sec. "Engine vibrates at 9000rpm; front anti-roll bar softened; rear anti-roll bar softened." 11.48am: 3 laps; 1min 9.85sec. Koni shock absorbers changed front and rear as well as bars. 4.12pm: 5 laps; fastest 1min 9.32sec. 4.27pm: 5 laps; fastest 1min 11.26sec. Battery changed; engine enriched 2 turns. 4.24pm: 4 laps; fastest 1min 16.89sec. Shock absorbers changed again.

01.12.79   Private testing continues at 3.3km Paul Ricard circuit with Jabouille. Engine and tyre tests. Jabouille does a series of laps, of which longest series is 10 laps. He begins at 9.42am and ends at about 5pm after 89 laps; fastest lap 1min 6.45sec in the 6th series which began at 10.23am. The progression of driver's comments is interesting: "Goes better than yesterday but engine doesn't work between 9000 and 10,000rpm. Seems too rich towards 7000. Car understeers." Then: "Car good. Engine better. On the limiter in the straight." 2 more turns of the waste-gate. Incident: cannot restart without adding fuel. Left skirt fitted with carbon spring. After 48th lap: new skirts fitted. "Better on

big corners but less grip on tight corners." Then: "More even between fast and slow corners. Rear springs better: they make car understeer less." And finally: "Tyres better; better progressivity going out of corners." New skirts with helical springs; gradual increase in downforce, "But still understeers a little."

12.12.79   Private testing in Brazil at the small 5km circuit at Interlagos with Jean-Pierre Jabouille.

From the point of view of development, these chassis records (courtesy of *Les Années Turbo* 1991), whilst not complete, do give an in-depth insight to the many changes, adjustments and component failures on the cars, as well as the efforts made by the drivers to refine the balance and performance in conjunction with the engineers. It is interesting to note that later records, from the beginning of 1979, are much more detailed and, perhaps, demonstrate a more meticulous approach to testing than in the beginning. One thing is for sure, though: they prove the huge effort by the team as a group and also by the drivers in giving feedback, before the advent of sophisticated telemetry and pit-to-car communication.

You have now seen the progress and development of the first turbocharged F1 car up to that victory in 1979, a victory that was to change the world of Grand Prix racing; the history of the companies involved – Renault, Alpine, Gordini – the early attempts, the failures, the joys, and the heartaches of developing something revolutionary.

Bernard Hanon had asked in July 1976 if Renault could win in a Grand Prix. Gérard Larrousse had replied, "Yes!" Mission accomplished.

Our story of the development of the turbocharged F1 car is now complete. But it is a well known fact that Formula 1 never stands still. Could Renault win a championship?

NEARLY, BUT NOT QUITE! WHAT CAME AFTER

Renault reached the end of 1979 on a reasonably high note; the team had gone from the birth of an idea in 1975 to achieving its target – a victory in a Grand Prix. From the faltering steps of 1977, when, with three starts and no finishes, things had not looked promising, to 1978 with 4 finishes from 14 starts, came a glimmer of hope. Moreover, Jabouille had scored 3 points at the US Grand Prix at Watkins Glen, although still had 9 failures and one finish when he was so far behind as to be unclassified. However, there was cause for optimism and Renault started 1979 with two cars and a new design, with the result that, not only did it take that first victory, but also scored 26 points in the Constructors' Championship, with both drivers scoring – Arnoux on 17 points and Jabouille on 9. In addition, Renault gained 6 pole positions.

The Viry-Châtillon plant, originally built in 1969, had been increased in size during 1978, and, by 1979, now officially named Usine A Gordini, the expanded plant occupied 3.1 acres of ground (12,545m²). The unit itself contained 60,000ft² (5574m²) of workshops employing 130 people split between four main departments: engine (with 5 test beds), chassis, gearbox, purchasing department and manufacture, with sales and administrative sections. Having won a Grand Prix, now it was time to see if Renault could win a championship. In a period when the ground-effect cars would rule, Renault Sport had become a serious contender.

For 1980 a new structure was in place.

THE RE20 – 1980
The new RE20 chassis had revised side-pods and a new mechanism for operating the skirts. The engine had new intercoolers and a modification to the cooling system. Renault had now switched to the RE title for its cars as opposed to the RS, reflecting the relationship between Renault and Elf. Renault also began to supply Lotus with engines which later powered Ayrton Senna's first victories.

Top right: Têtu, Sage, Larrousse, Dudot.

The reorganised team management as at 1 January 1980.

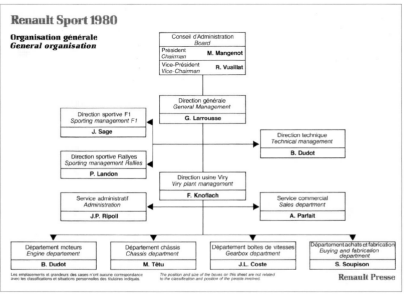

169

RE22: Jabouille.

STARTING GRID	
Jones 1'44.17"	Laffite 1'44.44"
Pironi 1'44.64"	Piquet 1'45.02"
De Angelis 1'45.46"	Andretti 1'45.78"
Patrese 1'46.01"	Villeneuve 1'46.07"
Jabouille 1'46.15"	Reutemann 1'46.19"
Scheckter 1'46.28"	Prost 1'46.75"
Rosberg 1'46.97"	Mass 1'47.05"
Regazzoni 1'47.18"	Zunino 1'47.41"
Watson 1'47.70"	Jarier 1'47.83"
Arnoux 1'48.24"	Giacomelli 1'48.44"
Surer 1'48.86"	Daly 1'48.95"
Depailler 1'49.20"	Fittipaldi 1'49.42"

RESULTS - Buenos Aires (316,304 km)

1. Jones	Williams-Ford	53	1h43'24.38"
2. Piquet	Brabham-Ford	53	1h43'48.97"
3. Rosberg	Fittipaldi-Ford	53	1h44'43.02"
4. Daly	Tyrrell-Ford	53	1h44'47.86"
5. Giacomelli	Alfa Romeo	52	+ 1 lap
6. Prost	McLaren-Ford	52	+ 1 lap
7. Zunino	Brabham-Ford	51	+ 2 laps

NOT CLASSIFIED

Regazzoni	Ensign-Ford	44	+ 9 laps
Fittipaldi	Fittipaldi-Ford	37	+ 16 laps

FASTEST LAP

Jones	Williams-Ford	1'50.45" 194.527 km/h

RETIREMENTS

Depailler	Alfa Romeo	46	Engine
Scheckter	Ferrari	45	Engine
Villeneuve	Ferrari	36	Accident/steering
Laffite	Ligier-Ford	30	Engine
Surer	ATS-Ford	27	Fire
Patrese	Arrows-Ford	27	Engine
Mass	Arrows-Ford	20	Gearbox
Andretti	Lotus-Ford	20	Fuel pump
Reutemann	Williams-Ford	12	Engine
De Angelis	Lotus-Ford	7	Suspension
Watson	McLaren-Ford	5	Gearbox leak
Jabouille	Renault	3	Clutch/Gearbox
Arnoux	Renault	2	Suspension
Pironi	Ligier-Ford	1	Engine
Jarier	Tyrrell-Ford	1	Collision

Buenos Aires race statistics.

Argentine Grand Prix, Buenos Aires, 13 January 1980

For the race in Argentina the team had two new cars: the RE22 for Jabouille and the RE21 for Arnoux, with the earlier RE20 available as the spare car.

Both cars went out early on – Arnoux on lap 2, and Jabouille on lap 3.

Brazilian Grand Prix, Interlagos, 27 January 1980

Success came for the second time in Brazil with Arnoux winning, having started on P6. The victory could have been Jabouille's, starting from pole position, but for a broken turbo on lap 25.

South African Grand Prix, Kyalami, 1 March 1980

For the South African race both cars had a new light clutch linkage. Jabouille again started from pole position, but this time it

Opposite left: Arnoux and Jabouille lead the way.

Opposite right: Kyalami race statistics.

Interlagos race statistics.

Réné Arnoux victorious.

STARTING GRID	
Jabouille 2'21.40"	Pironi 2'21.65"
Villeneuve 2'22.17"	Reutemann 2'22.26"
Laffite 2'22.30"	Arnoux 2'22.31"
De Angelis 2'22.40"	Scheckter 2'23.02"
Piquet 2'23.16"	Jones 2'23.38"
Andretti 2'23.46"	Regazzoni 2'24.85"
Prost 2'24.95"	Patrese 2'25.06"
Rosberg 2'25.74"	Mass 2'25.75"
Giacomelli 2'25.80"	Zunino 2'26.53"
Fittipaldi 2'26.86"	Surer 2'27.10"
Depailler 2'27.11"	Jarier 2'27.15"
Watson 2'27.29"	Daly 2'28.21"

RESULTS - INTERLAGOS (318,400 KM)

1. Arnoux	Renault	40	1h40'01.33"
2. De Angelis	Lotus-Ford	40	1h40'23.19"
3. Jones	Williams-Ford	40	1h41'07.44"
4. Pironi	Ligier-Ford	40	1h41'41.46"
5. Prost	McLaren-Ford	40	1h42'26.74"
6. Patrese	Arrows-Ford	39	+ 1 lap
7. Surer	ATS-Ford	39	+ 1 lap
8. Zunino	Brabham-Ford	39	+ 1 lap
9. Rosberg	Fittipaldi-Ford	39	+ 1 lap
10. Mass	Arrows-Ford	39	+ 1 lap
11. Watson	McLaren-Ford	39	+ 1 lap
12. Jarier	Tyrrell-Ford	39	+ 1 lap
13. Giacomelli	Alfa Romeo	39	+ 1 lap
14. Daly	Tyrrell-Ford	38	+ 2 laps
15. Fittipaldi	Fittipaldi-Ford	38	+ 2 laps
16. Villeneuve	Ferrari	36	Accelerator

FASTEST LAP

Arnoux	Renault	2'27.31" 192.421 km/h

RETIREMENTS

Depailler	Alfa Romeo	33	Electrical
Jabouille	Renault	25	Turbo
Piquet	Brabham-Ford	14	Accident, suspension
Regazzoni	Ensign-Ford	13	Road-holding
Laffite	Ligier-Ford	13	Electrical
Scheckter	Ferrari	10	Engine
Reutemann	Williams-Ford	1	Half shaft
Andretti	Lotus-Ford	1	Spun off

STARTING GRID	
Jabouille 1'10.00"	Arnoux 1'10.21"
Piquet 1'11.87"	Laffite 1'11.88"
Pironi 1'12.11"	Reutemann 1'12.15"
Depailler 1'12.16"	Jones 1'12.23"
Scheckter 1'12.32"	Villeneuve 1'12.38"
Patrese 1'12.50"	Giacomelli 1'12.51"
Jarier 1'12.70"	De Angelis 1'12.74"
Andretti 1'12.93"	Daly 1'13.04"
Zunino 1'13.05"	Fittipaldi 1'13.23"
Mass 1'13.25"	Regazzoni 1'13.25"
Watson 1'13.61"	Cheever 1'13.83"
Rosberg 1'13.84"	Lees 1'14.46"

RESULTS - Kyalami (320,112 km)

1. Arnoux	Renault	78	1h36'52.54"
2. Laffite	Ligier-Ford	78	1h37'26.61"
3. Pironi	Ligier-Ford	78	1h37'45.03"
4. Piquet	Brabham-Ford	78	1h37'53.56"
5. Reutemann	Williams-Ford	77	+ 1 lap
6. Mass	Arrows-Ford	77	+ 1 lap
7. Jarier	Tyrrell-Ford	77	+ 1 lap
8. Fittipaldi	Fittipaldi-Ford	77	+ 1 lap
9. Regazzoni	Ensign-Ford	77	+ 1 lap
10. Zunino	Brabham-Ford	77	+ 1 lap
11. Watson	McLaren-Ford	76	+ 2 laps
12. Andretti	Lotus-Ford	76	+ 2 laps
13. Lees	Shadow-Ford	70	Accident, suspension

NOT CLASSIFIED

Depailler	Alfa Romeo	53	+ 25 laps

FASTEST LAP

Arnoux	Renault	1'13.15" 201.960 km/h

RETIREMENTS

Giacomelli	Alfa Romeo	69	Engine
Jabouille	Renault	61	Puncture
Daly	Tyrrell-Ford	61	Puncture
Rosberg	Fittipaldi-Ford	58	Accident
Jones	Williams-Ford	34	Gearbox, radiator
Villeneuve	Ferrari	31	Transmission
Scheckter	Ferrari	14	Engine/electrical
Patrese	Arrows-Ford	10	Accident
Cheever	Osella-Ford	8	Accident
De Angelis	Lotus-Ford	1	Accident

Arnoux waits patiently. (© DPPI/Ren)

STARTING GRID	
Piquet 1'17.694"	Arnoux 1'18.689"
Depailler 1'18.719"	Lammers 1'18.783"
Jones 1'18.819"	Giacomelli 1'18.924"
Reutemann 1'18.964"	Patrese 1'19.071"
Pironi 1'19.276"	Villeneuve 1'19.285"
Jabouille 1'19.316"	Jarier 1'19.318"
Laffite 1'19.455"	Daly 1'19.744"
Andretti 1'19.763"	Scheckter 1'20.151"
Mass 1'20.410"	Zunino 1'20.419"
Cheever 1'20.808"	De Angelis 1'20.830"
Watson 1'20.868"	Rosberg 1'20.911"
Regazzoni 1'20.984"	Fittipaldi 1'21.350"

RESULTS - Long Beach (261,625 km)

1. Piquet	Brabham-Ford	80	1h50'18.550"
2. Patrese	Arrows-Ford	80	1h51'07.762"
3. Fittipaldi	Fittipaldi-Ford	80	1h51'37.113"
4. Watson	McLaren-Ford	79	+ 1 lap
5. Scheckter	Ferrari	79	+ 1 lap
6. Pironi	Ligier-Ford	79	+ 1 lap
7. Mass	Arrows-Ford	79	+ 1 lap
8. Daly	Tyrrell-Ford	79	+ 1 lap
9. Arnoux	Renault	78	+ 2 laps
10. Jabouille	Renault	71	+ 9 laps

FASTEST LAP

Piquet	Brabham-Ford	1'19.83" 147.570 km/h

RETIREMENTS

Rosberg	Fittipaldi-Ford	58	Overheating
Regazzoni	Ensign-Ford	50	Accident
Giacomelli	Alfa Romeo	49	Collision
Jones	Williams-Ford	47	Collision
Villeneuve	Ferrari	46	Transmission shaft
Depailler	Alfa Romeo	40	Rear suspension
Laffite	Ligier-Ford	36	Puncture
Cheever	Osella-Ford	11	Transmission shaft
Reutemann	Williams-Ford	3	Transmission shaft
Jarier	Tyrrell-Ford	3	Accident
De Angelis	Lotus-Ford	3	Accident
Zunino	Brabham-Ford	0	Accident
Andretti	Lotus-Ford	0	Accident
Lammers	ATS-Ford	0	Transmission shaft

Long Beach race statistics.

was a puncture that deprived him of the victory, allowing Arnoux to win from P2 on the grid with the RE21.

US West Coast Grand Prix, Long Beach, 30 March 1980

At Long Beach a new car, the RE24, was provided for Arnoux. He was put into P2 on the grid by a charging Piquet. Jabouille now had the RE23, which had a wider track at the rear to try to improve traction, but he only managed a grid position of P11. In the race he was to come in 10th and last, with Arnoux just in front, both cars suffering brake problems.

Belgian Grand Prix, Zolder, 4 May 1980

Back in Europe for the race at Zolder, larger discs and bigger Girling calipers instead of Lockheeds were fitted, along with 15-inch as opposed to 13-inch front wheels. Jabouille started on P5 with Arnoux on P6. Jabouille's clutch broke at the start but Arnoux managed to finish in 4th place.

Monaco Grand Prix, 18 May 1980

In the principality both cars went out after starting way down the grid.

STARTING GRID		RESULTS - Zolder (306,864 km)			
Jones 1'19.12"	Pironi 1'19.35"	1. Pironi	Ligier-Ford	72	1h38'46.51"
Laffite 1'19.69"	Reutemann 1'19.79"	2. Jones	Williams-Ford	72	1h39'33.88"
Jabouille 1'19.89"	Arnoux 1'19.89"	3. Reutemann	Williams-Ford	72	1h40'10.63"
Piquet 1'20.23"	De Angelis 1'20.96"	4. Arnoux	Renault	71	+ 1 lap
Jarier 1'21.36"	Depailler 1'21.45"	5. Jarier	Tyrrell-Ford	71	+ 1 lap
Daly 1'21.51"	Villeneuve 1'21.54"	6. Villeneuve	Ferrari	71	+ 1 lap
Mass 1'21.55"	Scheckter 1'21.58"	7. Rosberg	Fittipaldi-Ford	71	+ 1 lap
Lammers 1'21.72"	Patrese 1'21.75"	8. Scheckter	Ferrari	70	+ 2 laps
Andretti 1'22.07"	Giacomelli 1'22.20"	9. Daly	Tyrrell-Ford	70	+ 2 laps
Prost 1'22.26"	Watson 1'22.57"	10. De Angelis	Lotus-Ford	69	Accident
Rosberg 1'22.97"	Zunino 1'23.18"	11. Laffite	Ligier-Ford	68	+ 4 laps
Needell 1'23.50"	Fittipaldi 1'24.22"				

NOT CLASSIFIED

Watson	McLaren-Ford	61	+ 11 laps

FASTEST LAP

Laffite	Ligier-Ford	1'20.88" 189.653 km/h

RETIREMENTS

Lammers	ATS-Ford	64	Engine
Patrese	Arrows-Ford	58	Accident
Andretti	Lotus-Ford	41	Gearbox selector
Depailler	Alfa Romeo	38	Exhaust failure
Piquet	Brabham-Ford	32	Accident
Prost	McLaren-Ford	29	Transmission
Fittipaldi	Fittipaldi-Ford	16	Electrical
Needell	Ensign-Ford	12	Engine
Giacomelli	Alfa Romeo	11	Suspension
Zunino	Brabham-Ford	5	Clutch/boîte
Jabouille	Renault	1	Clutch
Mass	Arrows-Ford	1	Accident

Zolder race statistics.

Arnoux. (© DPPI/Ren)

Arnoux roars through the tunnel.

STARTING GRID		RESULTS - Monaco (251,712 km)			
Pironi 1'24.813"	Reutemann 1'24.882"	1. Reutemann	Williams-Ford	76	1h55'34.365"
Jones 1'25.202"	Piquet 1'25.358"	2. Laffite	Ligier-Ford	76	1h56'47.994"
Laffite 1'25.510"	Villeneuve 1'26.104"	3. Piquet	Brabham-Ford	76	1h56'52.091"
Depailler 1'26.210"	Giacomelli 1'26.227"	4. Mass	Arrows-Ford	75	+ 1 lap
Jarier 1'26.369"	Prost 1'26.826"	5. Villeneuve	Ferrari	75	+ 1 lap
Patrese 1'26.828"	Daly 1'26.838"	6. Fittipaldi	Fittipaldi-Ford	74	+ 2 laps
Lammers 1'26.883"	De Angelis 1'26.930"	7. Andretti	Lotus-Ford	73	+ 3 laps
Mass 1'26.956"	Jabouille 1'27.099"	8. Patrese	Arrows-Ford	73	+ 3 laps
Scheckter 1'27.182"	Fittipaldi 1'27.495"	9. De Angelis	Lotus-Ford	68	Accident
Andretti 1'27.514"	Arnoux 1'27.524"	10. Lammers	ATS-Ford	64	+ 12 laps

FASTEST LAP

Pironi	Ligier-Ford	1'27.40" 136.421 km/h

RETIREMENTS

Pironi	Ligier-Ford	54	Accident
Arnoux	Renault	53	Collision Patrese
Depailler	Alfa Romeo	50	Engine
Scheckter	Ferrari	27	Road-holding
Jabouille	Renault	25	Gearbox
Jones	Williams-Ford	24	Differential
Jarier	Tyrrell-Ford	0	Accident Sᵗᵉ Devote
Giacomelli	Alfa Romeo	0	Accident Sᵗᵉ Devote
Prost	McLaren-Ford	0	Accident Sᵗᵉ Devote
Daly	Tyrrell-Ford	0	Accident Sᵗᵉ Devote

Monaco race statistics.

Spanish Grand Prix, 1980

This became the centre of the organisational battle between FOCA/FIA, and many teams opted out of racing, including Renault. No race.

French Grand Prix, Paul Ricard, 29 June 1980

For the French Grand Prix Arnoux started on P2 after fellow countryman Jacques Laffite had just outpaced him. Jabouille was on P6. Arnoux managed to finish 5th whilst Jabouille didn't complete a lap, due to transmission failure.

British Grand Prix, Brands Hatch, 13 July 1980

The Renaults featured a huge new rear wing which served to show how much power the turbo was now producing to allow so much downforce to be applied.

Both cars started in lowly grid positions, however. Come the race, Arnoux kept running to the end but was not classified. Jabouille went out on lap 6th with engine failure.

Dudot contemplates!

STARTING GRID					
Laffite	Arnoux				
1'38.88"	1'39.49"				
Pironi	Jones				
1'39.49"	1'39.50"				
Reutemann	Jabouille				
1'39.60"	1'40.18"				
Prost	Piquet				
1'40.63"	1'40.67"				
Giacomelli	Depailler				
1'40.85"	1'40.89"				
Surer	Andretti				
1'41.03"	1'41.56"				
Watson	De Angelis				
1'41.63"	1'41.66"				
Mass	Jarier				
1'41.71"	1'41.78"				
Villeneuve	Patrese				
1'41.99"	1'42.07"				
Scheckter	Daly				
1'42.38"	1'42.77"				
Cheever	Zunino				
1'42.85"	1'43.14"				
Rosberg	Fittipaldi				
1'43.16"	1'43.21"				

RESULTS - Le Castellet (313,740 km)

1. Jones	Williams-Ford	54	1h32'43.42"
2. Pironi	Ligier-Ford	54	1h32'47.94"
3. Laffite	Ligier-Ford	54	1h33'13.68"
4. Piquet	Brabham-Ford	54	1h33'58.30"
5. Arnoux	Renault	54	1h33'59.57"
6. Reutemann	Williams-Ford	54	1h34'00.16"
7. Watson	McLaren-Ford	53	+ 1 lap
8. Villeneuve	Ferrari	53	+ 1 lap
9. Patrese	Arrows-Ford	53	+ 1 lap
10. Mass	Arrows-Ford	53	+ 1 lap
11. Daly	Tyrrell-Ford	52	+ 2 laps
12. Scheckter	Ferrari	52	+ 2 laps
13. Fittipaldi	Fittipaldi-Ford	50	+ 4 laps
14. Jarier	Tyrrell-Ford	50	+ 4 laps

FASTEST LAP

Jones	Williams-Ford	1'41.45"
		206.171 km/h

RETIREMENTS

Cheever	Osella-Ford	43	Engine
Surer	ATS-Ford	26	Gearbox
Depailler	Alfa Romeo	25	Road-holding
Andretti	Lotus-Ford	18	Gearbox
Rosberg	Fittipaldi-Ford	8	Accident
Giacomelli	Alfa Romeo	8	Road-holding
Prost	McLaren-Ford	6	Transmission
De Angelis	Lotus-Ford	3	Clutch
Zunino	Brabham-Ford	0	Clutch
Jabouille	Renault	0	Transmission

Paul Ricard race statistics.

STARTING GRID		RESULTS - Brands Hatch (319,732 km)			
Pironi 1'11.00"	Laffite 1'11.39"	1. Jones	Williams-Ford	76	1h34'49.228"
Jones 1'11.60"	Reutemann 1'11.62"	2. Piquet	Brabham-Ford	76	1h35'00.235"
Piquet 1'11.63"	Giacomelli 1'12.12"	3. Reutemann	Williams-Ford	76	1h35'02.513"
Prost 1'12.63"	Depailler 1'13.18"	4. Daly	Tyrrell-Ford	75	+ 1 lap
Andretti 1'13.40"	Daly 1'13.46"	5. Jarier	Tyrrell-Ford	75	+ 1 lap
Jarier 1'13.66"	Watson 1'13.71"	6. Prost	McLaren-Ford	75	+ 1 lap
Jabouille 1'13.74"	De Angelis 1'13.85"	7. Rebaque	Brabham-Ford	74	+ 2 laps
Surer 1'13.95"	Arnoux 1'13.96"	8. Watson	McLaren-Ford	74	+ 2 laps
Rebaque 1'14.22"	Keegan 1'14.23"	9. Patrese	Arrows-Ford	73	+ 3 laps
Villeneuve 1'14.29"	Cheever 1'14.51"	10. Scheckter	Ferrari	73	+ 3 laps
Patrese 1'14.56"	Fittipaldi 1'14.58"	11. Keegan	Williams-Ford	73	+ 3 laps
Scheckter 1'15.37"	Mass 1'15.42"	12. Fittipaldi	Fittipaldi-Ford	72	+ 4 laps
		13. Mass	Arrows-Ford	69	+ 5 laps

NOT CLASSIFIED

Arnoux	Renault	67	+ 9 laps

FASTEST LAP

Pironi	Ligier-Ford	1'12.368" 209.280 km/h

RETIREMENTS

Pironi	Ligier-Ford	63	Wheel
Surer	ATS-Ford	59	Engine
Andretti	Lotus-Ford	57	Gearbox
Giacomelli	Alfa Romeo	42	Accident
Villeneuve	Ferrari	35	Engine
Laffite	Ligier-Ford	30	Accident
Depailler	Alfa Romeo	27	Engine
Cheever	Osella-Ford	17	Rear suspension
De Angelis	Lotus-Ford	16	Rear suspension
Jabouille	Renault	6	Engine

Brand Hatch race statistics.

Opposite: Brands Hatch, big wings in the pit lane. (© DPPI/Ren)

German Grand Prix, Hockenheim, 10 August 1980

A new car specified as the RE25 came out at Hockenheim to be driven by Arnoux, who started on P3 with Jabouille one position higher, but valve spring failure brought both cars to a halt on laps 26 and 27 respectively.

Austrian Grand Prix, Zeltweg, 17 August 1980

By complete contrast, at the Zeltweg circuit, Jabouille was to win from P2 on the grid, with Arnoux 9th.

Dutch Grand Prix, Zandvoort, 31 August 1980

Having qualifed in the same positions as in Austria, at Zandvoort, Jabouille went out on lap 23 with differential problems, though Arnoux was to go on to take second place.

Italian Grand Prix, Imola, 14 September 1980

At Imola, the Renaults again took the front two places on the grid

Jean-Pierre in the new RE25. No front wings this time.

Left to right: Patrick Head, Jean Sage, Michel Têtu; lunch ...

STARTING GRID		RESULTS - Hockenheim (305,505 km)			
Jones 1'45.85"	Jabouille 1'45.89"	1. Laffite	Ligier-Ford	45	1h22'59.73"
Arnoux 1'46.00"	Reutemann 1'46.14"	2. Reutemann	Williams-Ford	45	1h23'02.92"
Laffite 1'46.78"	Piquet 1'46.90"	3. Jones	Williams-Ford	45	1h23'43.26"
Pironi 1'47.20"	Rosberg 1'47.64"	4. Piquet	Brabham-Ford	45	1h23'44.21"
Andretti 1'48.45"	Patrese 1'48.58"	5. Giacomelli	Alfa Romeo	45	1h24'16.22"
De Angelis 1'48.59"	Fittipaldi 1'48.70"	6. Villeneuve	Ferrari	45	1h24'28.45"
Surer 1'48.72"	Prost 1'48.75"	7. Andretti	Lotus-Ford	45	1h24'32.74"
Rebaque 1'48.78"	Villeneuve 1'48.86"	8. Mass	Arrows-Ford	45	1h24'47.48"
Mass 1'48.93"	Cheever 1'49.06"	9. Patrese	Arrows-Ford	44	+ 1 lap
Giacomelli 1'49.11"	Watson 1'49.26"	10. Daly	Tyrrell-Ford	44	+ 1 lap
Scheckter 1'49.35"	Daly 1'49.51"	11. Prost	McLaren-Ford	44	+ 1 lap
Jarier 1'49.52"	Lammers 1'50.30"	12. Surer	ATS-Ford	44	+ 1 lap
		13. Scheckter	Ferrari	44	+ 1 lap
		14. Lammers	Ensign-Ford	44	+ 1 lap
		15. Jarier	Tyrrell-Ford	44	+ 1 lap
		16. De Angelis	Lotus-Ford	43	Rolling bearing

FASTEST LAP

Jones	Williams-Ford	1'48.49" 225.278 km/h

RETIREMENTS

Watson	McLaren-Ford	39	Engine
Jabouille	Renault	27	Valves
Arnoux	Renault	26	Valves
Cheever	Osella-Ford	23	Gearbox
Pironi	Ligier-Ford	18	Transmission shaft
Fittipaldi	Fittipaldi-Ford	18	Aerodynamics
Rosberg	Fittipaldi-Ford	8	Rolling bearing
Rebaque	Brabham-Ford	4	Gearbox

Hockenheim race statistics.

Jabouille, back on top, takes the laurels.

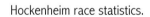

Legendary English journalist, the late Denis Jenkinson, takes a look. (© TVA)

STARTING GRID		RESULTS - Zeltweg (320,868 km)			
Arnoux 1'30.27"	Jabouille 1'31.48"	1. Jabouille	Renault	54	1h26'15.73"
Jones 1'32.95"	Reutemann 1'33.07"	2. Jones	Williams-Ford	54	1h26'16.55"
Laffite 1'33.16"	Pironi 1'33.22"	3. Reutemann	Williams-Ford	54	1h26'35.09"
Piquet 1'33.39"	Giacomelli 1'33.64"	4. Laffite	Ligier-Ford	54	1h26'57.75"
De Angelis 1'33.76"	Daly 1'34.17"	5. Piquet	Brabham-Ford	54	1h27'18.54"
Rosberg 1'34.33"	Prost 1'34.35"	6. De Angelis	Lotus-Ford	54	1h27'30.70"
Jarier 1'34.63"	Rebaque 1'34.86"	7. Prost	McLaren-Ford	54	1h27'49.14"
Villeneuve 1'34.87"	Surer 1'35.10"	8. Villeneuve	Ferrari	53	+ 1 lap
Andretti 1'35.21"	Patrese 1'35.29"	9. Arnoux	Renault	53	+ 1 lap
Cheever 1'35.40"	Keegan 1'35.53"	10. Rebaque	Brabham-Ford	53	+ 1 lap
Watson 1'35.56"	Scheckter 1'35.61"	11. Fittipaldi	Fittipaldi-Ford	53	+ 1 lap
Fittipaldi 1'35.67"	Mansell 1'35.71"	12. Surer	ATS-Ford	53	+ 1 lap
		13. Scheckter	Ferrari	53	+ 1 lap
		14. Patrese	Arrows-Ford	53	+ 1 lap
		15. Keegan	Williams-Ford	52	+ 2 laps
		16. Rosberg	Fittipaldi-Ford	52	+ 2 laps

FASTEST LAP

Arnoux	Renault	1'32.53" 231.197 km/h

RETIREMENTS

Mansell	Lotus-Ford	40	Engine
Watson	McLaren-Ford	34	Engine
Giacomelli	Alfa Romeo	28	Rear suspension
Jarier	Tyrrell-Ford	25	Engine
Pironi	Ligier-Ford	25	Road-holding
Cheever	Osella-Ford	23	Rolling bearing
Daly	Tyrrell-Ford	12	Brakes failure, accident
Andretti	Lotus-Ford	6	Engine

Zeltweg race statistics.

Arnoux on a charge.

STARTING GRID		RESULTS - Zandvoort (306,144 km)			
Arnoux 1'17.44"	Jabouille 1'17.74"	1. Piquet	Brabham-Ford	72	1h38'13.83"
Reutemann 1'17.81"	Jones 1'17.82"	2. Arnoux	Renault	72	1h38'26.76"
Piquet 1'17.85"	Laffite 1'18.15"	3. Laffite	Ligier-Ford	72	1h38'27.26"
Villeneuve 1'18.40"	Giacomelli 1'18.52"	4. Reutemann	Williams-Ford	72	1h38'29.12"
Watson 1'18.53"	Andretti 1'18.60"	5. Jarier	Tyrrell-Ford	72	1h39'13.85"
De Angelis 1'18.74"	Scheckter 1'18.87"	6. Prost	McLaren-Ford	72	1h39'36.45"
Rebaque 1'18.89"	Patrese 1'18.90"	7. Villeneuve	Ferrari	71	+ 1 lap
Pironi 1'18.94"	Mansell 1'18.97"	8. Andretti	Lotus-Ford	70	Out of fuel
Jarier 1'18.98"	Prost 1'19.07"	9. Scheckter	Ferrari	70	+ 2 laps
Cheever 1'19.38"	Surer 1'19.44"	10. Surer	ATS-Ford	69	+ 3 laps
Fittipaldi 1'19.57"	Brambilla 1'19.60"	11. Jones	Williams-Ford	69	+ 3 laps
Daly 1'19.68"	Lees 1'19.72"				

FASTEST LAP

Arnoux	Renault	1'19.35" 192.907 km/h

RETIREMENTS

Daly	Tyrrell-Ford	60	Disque de brakes cassé, accident
Giacomelli	Alfa Romeo	58	Aerodynamics
Cheever	Osella-Ford	38	Engine
Patrese	Arrows-Ford	29	Engine
Jabouille	Renault	23	Road-holding differential
Lees	Ensign-Ford	21	Accident Brambilla
Brambilla	Alfa Romeo	21	Collision Lees
Watson	Williams-Ford	18	Engine
Fittipaldi	Fittipaldi-Ford	16	Brakes
Mansell	Lotus-Ford	15	Brakes and accident
Pironi	Ligier-Ford	2	Accident De Angelis
De Angelis	Lotus-Ford	2	Collision Pironi
Rebaque	Brabham-Ford	1	Gearbox

Zandvoort race statistics.

STARTING GRID		RESULTS - Imola (300 km)			
Arnoux 1'33.988"	Jabouille 1'34.339"	1. Piquet	Brabham-Ford	60	1h38'07.52"
Reutemann 1'34.686"	Giacomelli 1'34.912"	2. Jones	Williams-Ford	60	1h38'36.45"
Piquet 1'34.960"	Jones 1'35.109"	3. Reutemann	Williams-Ford	60	1h39'21.19"
Patrese 1'35.618"	Villeneuve 1'35.751"	4. De Angelis	Lotus-Ford	59	+ 1 lap
Rebaque 1'35.872"	Andretti 1'36.084"	5. Rosberg	Fittipaldi-Ford	59	+ 1 lap
Rosberg 1'36.091"	Jarier 1'36.181"	6. Pironi	Ligier-Ford	59	+ 1 lap
Pironi 1'36.422"	Watson 1'36.450"	7. Prost	McLaren-Ford	59	+ 1 lap
Fittipaldi 1'36.758"	Scheckter 1'36.827"	8. Scheckter	Ferrari	59	+ 1 lap
Cheever 1'36.884"	De Angelis 1'36.919"	9. Laffite	Ligier-Ford	59	+ 1 lap
Brambilla 1'36.929"	Laffite 1'36.927"	10. Arnoux	Renault	58	+ 2 laps
Keegan 1'37.169"	Daly 1'37.215"	11. Keegan	Williams-Ford	58	+ 2 laps
Surer 1'37.270"	Prost 1'37.284"	12. Cheever	Osella-Ford	57	+ 3 laps

FASTEST LAP

Jones	Williams-Ford	1'36.089" 187.326 km/h

RETIREMENTS

Jarier	Tyrrell-Ford	54	Brakes
Jabouille	Renault	53	Gearbox
Surer	ATS-Ford	45	Engine
Andretti	Lotus-Ford	40	Engine
Patrese	Arrows-Ford	38	Engine
Daly	Tyrrell-Ford	33	Accident
Watson	McLaren-Ford	20	Brakes Rolling bearing
Rebaque	Brabham-Ford	18	Rear suspension
Fittipaldi	Fittipaldi-Ford	17	Accident
Villeneuve	Ferrari	5	Accident/puncture
Giacomelli	Alfa Romeo	5	Accident/puncture
Brambilla	Alfa Romeo	4	Accident

Imola race statistics.

Jabouille. (© DPPI/Ren)

STARTING GRID		RESULTS - Montréal (308,700 km)			
Piquet 1'27.328"	Jones 1'28.164"	1. Jones	Williams-Ford	70	1h46'45.53"
Pironi 1'28.322"	Giacomelli 1'28.575"	2. Reutemann	Williams-Ford	70	1h47'01.07"
Reutemann 1'28.663"	Rosberg 1'28.720"	3. Pironi	Ligier-Ford	70	1h47'04.60"
Watson 1'28.755"	De Cesaris 1'29.026"	4. Watson	McLaren-Ford	70	1h47'16.51"
Laffite 1'29.130"	Rebaque 1'29.377"	5. Villeneuve	Ferrari	70	1h47'40.76"
Patrese 1'29.400"	Prost 1'29.804"	6. Rebaque	Brabham-Ford	69	+ 1 lap
Jabouille 1'29.932"	Cheever 1'29.937"	7. Jarier	Tyrrell-Ford	69	+ 1 lap
Jarier 1'30.070"	Fittipaldi 1'30.294"	8. Laffite	Ligier-Ford	68	Out of fuel
De Angelis 1'30.316"	Andretti 1'30.559"	9. Rosberg	Fittipaldi-Ford	68	+ 2 laps
Lammers 1'30.668"	Daly 1'30.791"	10. De Angelis	Lotus-Ford	68	+ 2 laps
Mass 1'30.831"	Villeneuve 1'30.855"	11. Mass	Arrows-Ford	67	+ 3 laps
Arnoux 1'30.912"	Thackwell 1'31.036"	12. Lammers	Ensign-Ford	66	+ 4 laps

FASTEST LAP

Pironi	Ligier-Ford	1'28.76" 178.860 km/h

RETIREMENTS

Prost	McLaren-Ford	41	Suspension failure ... accident
Arnoux	Renault	39	Brakes and gearbox
Jabouille	Renault	25	Suspension failure ... accident
Piquet	Brabham-Ford	23	Engine
Andretti	Lotus-Ford	11	Engine
De Cesaris	Alfa Romeo	8	Engine
Cheever	Osella-Ford	8	Fuel pressure
Fittipaldi	Fittipaldi-Ford	8	Gearbox
Giacomelli	Alfa Romeo	7	Aerodynamics
Patrese	Arrows-Ford	6	Collision Prost

Île-Notre-Dame race statistics.

Arnoux. (© DPPI/Ren)

with the cars carrying large cooling ducts for the brakes, but to no avail. Arnoux did get a finish, in 10th, but Jabouille suffered gearbox failure on lap 53.

Canadian Grand Prix, Île-Notre-Dame, 28 September 1980

Montreal was a bad memory, as, unfortunately, Jean-Pierre Jabouille had a very serious crash caused by a breakage brought about by the need for rigid suspension in the RE23. Badly breaking a leg, he was unable to take part for many months. Arnoux went out on lap 39 with brake problems.

US East Coast Grand Prix, Watkins Glen, 5 October 1980

Arnoux was entered alone for Watkins Glen, the last race of the season, in the RE25. He managed to finish 7th after experiencing a problem with the side-pod skirts.

In 1980, the Renault RE20 series had made 27 starts, with 3 wins, 12 finishes, 5 pole positions and 3 fastest laps. The turbos were proving competitive on a regular basis, certainly in qualifying. The Cosworth teams began to worry.

STARTING GRID		RESULTS - Watkins Glen (320,665 km)			
Giacomelli 1'33.291"	Piquet 1'34.080"	1. Jones	Williams-Ford	59	1h34'36.05"
Reutemann 1'34.111"	De Angelis 1'34.185"	2. Reutemann	Williams-Ford	59	1h34'40.26"
Jones 1'34.216"	Arnoux 1'34.839"	3. Pironi	Ligier-Ford	59	1h34'48.62"
Pironi 1'34.971"	Rebaque 1'35.166"	4. De Angelis	Lotus-Ford	59	1h35'05.74"
Watson 1'35.202"	De Cesaris 1'35.235"	5. Laffite	Ligier-Ford	58	+ 1 lap
Andretti 1'35.343"	Laffite 1'35.421"	6. Andretti	Lotus-Ford	58	+ 1 lap
Prost 1'35.988"	Rosberg 1'36.332"	7. Arnoux	Renault	58	+ 1 lap
Keegan 1'36.750"	Cheever 1'36.908"	8. Surer	ATS-Ford	57	+ 2 laps
Surer 1'37.001"	Villeneuve 1'37.040"	9. Keegan	Williams-Ford	57	+ 2 laps
Fittipaldi 1'37.088"	Patrese 1'37.405"	10. Rosberg	Fittipaldi-Ford	57	+ 2 laps
Daly 1'37.923"	Jarier 1'37.966"	11. Scheckter	Ferrari	56	+ 3 laps
Scheckter 1'38.149"	Mass 1'38.526"	**NOT CLASSIFIED**			
Lammers 1'38.532"		Watson	McLaren-Ford	50	+ 9 laps
		Jarier	Tyrrell-Ford	40	+ 19 laps

FASTEST LAP			
Jones	Williams-Ford		1'34.068" 207.998 km/h

RETIREMENTS			
Villeneuve	Ferrari	49	Accident
Mass	Arrows-Ford	36	Transmission shaft
Giacomelli	Alfa Romeo	31	Electrical
Piquet	Brabham-Ford	25	Spin, outside assistance
Cheever	Osella-Ford	21	Suspension failure
Rebaque	Brabham-Ford	20	Engine
Patrese	Arrows-Ford	16	Accident
Lammers	Ensign-Ford	16	Steering
Fittipaldi	Fittipaldi-Ford	15	Rear suspension
Daly	Tyrrell-Ford	3	Suspension failure collision with De Cesaris
De Cesaris	Alfa Romeo	2	Accident/collision with Daly

Watkins Glen race statistics.

1981: RE20 SERIES B AND RE30

Going into 1981, the ground-effect side-pod skirts – which had also enabled the Cosworth teams to remain competitive with the turbocharged cars – were banned. The RE20 series, the development of the RS10, was now called the RE20B; though Renault started the season with what was, in fact, the 26B. Also, after diligent work back at Renault Sport, the team arrived at the

> **"This car featured many changes to the chassis and bulkhead; not only was the lighter chassis new, but the RE30 also utilised lighter bodywork and a new Renault gearbox that housed the Hewland FG400 internals, giving the car a shorter wheelbase."**

Zolder round with the new RE30. This car featured many changes to the chassis and bulkhead; not only was the lighter chassis new, but the RE30 also utilised lighter bodywork and a new Renault gearbox that housed the Hewland FG400 internals, giving the car a shorter wheelbase. To counter the rule changes, Brabham brought out a hydro-pneumatic, suspension-lowering device. The other teams were sure the authorities would ban it, but, in April, it was declared legal.

Unfortunately, Renault Sport was not ready for this decision: RE30 had been designed as an unskirted car, so, for the first few races, it was playing catch-up. The cars had effectively become like very high-speed go-karts, developing huge loads on structures and drivers alike. Alain Prost was to join the team to partner René Arnoux, replacing the injured Jabouille.

US West Coast Grand Prix, Long Beach, 15 March 1981

Driving the RE26B, Alain Prost started mid-grid, while Arnoux, in the RE27B, started from near the back. Arnoux finished 8th and last, while Prost went out on the first lap after a collision with de Cesaris.

STARTING GRID		RESULTS - Long Beach (261,625 km)			
Patrese 1'19.39"	Jones 1'19.40"	1. Jones	Williams-Ford	80	1h50'41.33"
Reutemann 1'20.14"	Piquet 1'20.28"	2. Reutemann	Williams-Ford	80	1h50'50.52"
Villeneuve 1'20.46"	Andretti 1'20.47"	3. Piquet	Brabham-Ford	80	1h51'16.25"
Mansell 1'20.57"	Cheever 1'20.64"	4. Andretti	Alfa Romeo	80	1h51'30.64"
Giacomelli 1'20.66"	Jarier 1'20.78"	5. Cheever	Tyrrell-Ford	80	1h51'48.03"
Pironi 1'20.90"	Laffite 1'20.92"	6. Tambay	Theodore-Ford	79	+ 1 lap
De Angelis 1'20.92"	Prost 1'20.98"	7. Serra	Fittipaldi-Ford	78	+ 2 laps
Rebaque 1'21.00"	Rosberg 1'21.00"	8. Arnoux	Renault	77	+ 3 laps
Tambay 1'21.29"	Serra 1'21.40"	**FASTEST LAP**			
Surer 1'21.52"	Arnoux 1'21.54"	Jones	Williams-Ford		1'20.901" 144.621 km/h
Lammers 1'21.75"	De Cesaris 1'22.02"				
Watson 1'22.18"	Gabbiani 1'22.21"				

RETIREMENTS			
Surer	Ensign-Ford	70	Electrical
Pironi	Ferrari	67	Engine
Jarier	Ligier-Matra	64	Fuel pump
Rebaque	Brabham-Ford	49	Accident
Laffite	Ligier-Matra	41	Collision Cheever
Giacomelli	Alfa Romeo	41	Collision Lammers
Lammers	ATS-Ford	41	Collision Giacomelli
Rosberg	Fittipaldi-Ford	41	Ignition
Patrese	Arrows-Ford	33	Fuel pump
Gabbiani	Osella-Ford	26	Accident, front suspension
Mansell	Lotus-Ford	25	Accident
Villeneuve	Ferrari	17	Transmission shaft
Watson	McLaren-Ford	16	Engine
De Angelis	Lotus-Ford	13	Accident
Prost	Renault	0	Collision with De Cesaris
De Cesaris	McLaren-Ford	0	Collision Prost

Long Beach race statistics.

STARTING GRID	
Piquet 1'35.079"	Reutemann 1'35.390"
Jones 1'36.377"	Patrese 1'36.667"
Prost 1'36.670"	Giacomelli 1'37.283"
Villeneuve 1'37.497"	Arnoux 1'37.561"
Andretti 1'37.597"	De Angelis 1'37.734"
Rebaque 1'37.777"	Rosberg 1'37.981"
Mansell 1'38.003"	Cheever 1'38.160"
Watson 1'38.263"	Laffite 1'38.273"
Pironi 1'38.565"	Surer 1'38.570"
Tambay 1'38.726"	De Cesaris 1'38.780"
Stohr 1'39.190"	Serra 1'39.326"
Jarier 1'39.398"	Zunino 1'39.798"

RESULTS - Jacarepagua (311,922 km)

1. Reutemann	Williams-Ford	62	2:00'23.66"
2. Jones	Williams-Ford	62	2:00'28.10"
3. Patrese	Arrows-Ford	62	2:01'26.74"
4. Surer	Ensign-Ford	62	2:01'40.69"
5. De Angelis	Lotus-Ford	62	2:01'50.08"
6. Laffite	Ligier-Matra	62	2:01'50.49"
7. Jarier	Ligier-Matra	62	2:01'53.91"
8. Watson	McLaren-Ford	61	+ 1 lap
9. Rosberg	Fittipaldi-Ford	61	+ 1 lap
10. Tambay	Theodore-Ford	61	+ 1 lap
11. Mansell	Lotus-Ford	61	+ 1 lap
12. Piquet	Brabham-Ford	60	+ 2 laps
13. Zunino	Tyrrell-Ford	57	+ 5 laps

NOT CLASSIFIED

Cheever	Tyrrell-Ford	49	+ 13 laps
Giacomelli	Alfa Romeo	40	Electrical

FASTEST LAP

Surer	Ensign-Ford	1'54.30" 158.456 km/h

RETIREMENTS

Villeneuve	Ferrari	25	Turbo
Rebaque	Brabham-Ford	22	Rear suspension
Stohr	Arrows-Ford	20	Collision Tambay
Prost	Renault	20	Collision with Pironi
Pironi	Ferrari	19	Collision with Prost
De Cesaris	McLaren-Ford	9	Electrical
Serra	Fittipaldi-Ford	0	Collision (start)
Arnoux	Renault	0	Collision (start)
Andretti	Alfa Romeo	0	Collision (start)

Jacarepagua race statistics.

Brazilian Grand Prix, Jacarepagua, 29 March 1981

Brazil produced no better results, with both cars involved in race collisions.

Argentine Grand Prix, Buenos Aires, 12 April 1981

Renault flew a new monocoque to Buenos Aires to replace Arnoux's damaged tub. Official practice saw Alan Prost and Piquet fastest. It was here that Brabham was running with a pneumatic system on the suspension which allowed it to get around the 6cm rule (the required distance between the ground and the edge of the side-pods) at high speed. With this system, Brabham was able to recreate ground-effect comparable to that achieved with the now-forbidden mobile skirts. Prost finished 3rd and Arnoux 5th.

Below: New boy!

STARTING GRID

Piquet	Prost
1'42.665"	1'42.981"
Jones	Reutemann
1'43.638"	1'43.935"
Arnoux	Rebaque
1'43.997"	1'44.100"
Villeneuve	Rosberg
1'44.132"	1'44.191"
Patrese	De Angelis
1'45.008"	1'45.065"
Watson	Pironi
1'45.073"	1'45.108"
Cheever	Tambay
1'45.117"	1'45.297"
Mansell	Surer
1'45.369"	1'45.734"
Andretti	De Cesaris
1'46.059"	1'46.387"
Stohr	Serra
1'46.444"	1'46.706"
Laffite	Giacomelli
1'46.854"	1'46.918"
Lammers	Zunino
1'47.174"	1'47.464"

RESULTS - Buenos Aires (326,304 km)

1.	Piquet	Brabham-Ford	53	1h34'32.74"
2.	Reutemann	Williams-Ford	53	1h34'59.35"
3.	Prost	Renault	53	1'35'22.72"
4.	Jones	Williams-Ford	53	1h35'40.62"
5.	Arnoux	Renault	53	1h36'04.59"
6.	De Angelis	Lotus-Ford	52	+ 1 lap
7.	Patrese	Arrows-Ford	52	+ 1 lap
8.	Andretti	Alfa Romeo	52	+ 1 lap
9.	Stohr	Arrows-Ford	52	+ 1 lap
10.	Giacomelli	Alfa Romeo	51	Out of fuel
11.	De Cesaris	McLaren-Ford	51	+ 2 laps
12.	Lammers	ATS-Ford	51	+ 2 laps
13.	Zunino	Tyrrell-Ford	51	Penalty (1 lap)

FASTEST LAP

Piquet	Brabham-Ford	1'45.287" 204.059 km/h

RETIREMENTS

Villeneuve	Ferrari	40	Transmission shaft
Tambay	Theodore-Ford	36	Oil leak
Watson	McLaren-Ford	36	Engine
Rebaque	Brabham-Ford	32	Ignition
Serra	Fittipaldi-Ford	28	Gearbox
Laffite	Ligier-Matra	19	Front vibrations Road-holding
Surer	Ensign-Ford	14	Engine
Rosberg	Fittipaldi-Ford	4	Fuel pump
Mansell	Lotus-Ford	3	Engine
Pironi	Ferrari	3	Engine
Cheever	Tyrrell-Ford	1	Clutch

Buenos Aires race statistics.

San Marino Grand Prix, Imola, 3 May 1981

Back in Europe for the San Marino Grand Prix, Arnoux finished 8th from a grid place of P3, while Prost, from P4, went out on lap 3 with gearbox problems.

Belgian Grand Prix, Zolder, 17 May 1981

Zolder was a disaster, as Arnoux failed to qualify after numerous problems; Prost, who started a low P12 driving the old RE22, had clutch failure on lap 2 after a stop-start race. Renault stayed on to test the two new cars, RE31 and RE32, to prepare for the next race at Monaco.

Monaco Grand Prix, 31 May 1981

The cars were now using servo brakes, with seven new engines available. Prost's RE32 had the new hydro-pneumatic suspension, which the team fitted to Arnoux's car during practice but removed for the race. It was to no purpose, though, as both cars retired – lap 32 for Arnoux and 45 for Prost. Gérard Larrousse remembers: "A problem here was the weight of the servo chamber for the brakes!"

The great Gilles Villeneuve. (© TVA)

STARTING GRID

Villeneuve	Reutemann
1'34.523"	1'35.229"
Arnoux	Prost
1'35.281"	1'35.579"
Piquet	Pironi
1'35.733"	1'35.868"
Watson	Jones
1'36.241"	1'36.280"
Patrese	Laffite
1'36.390"	1'36.477"
Giacomelli	Andretti
1'36.776"	1'36.919"
Rebaque	De Cesaris
1'37.264"	1'37.382"
Rosberg	Tambay
1'37.459"	1'37.545"
Alboreto	Jabouille
1'37.771"	1'38.140"
Cheever	Gabbiani
1'38.266"	1'38.302"
Surer	Guerra
1'38.341"	1'38.773"
Salazar	Borgudd
1'38.827"	1'39.079"

RESULTS - Imola (302,400 km)

1.	Piquet	Brabham-Ford	60	1h51'23.97"
2.	Patrese	Arrows-Ford	60	1h51'28.55"
3.	Reutemann	Williams-Ford	60	1h51'30.31"
4.	Rebaque	Brabham-Ford	60	1h51'46.86"
5.	Pironi	Ferrari	60	1h51'49.84"
6.	De Cesaris	McLaren-Ford	60	1h52'30.58"
7.	Villeneuve	Ferrari	60	1h53'05.94"
8.	Arnoux	Renault	59	+ 1 lap
9.	Surer	Ensign-Ford	59	+ 1 lap
10.	Watson	McLaren-Ford	58	+ 2 laps
11.	Tambay	Theodore-Ford	58	+ 2 laps
12.	Jones	Williams-Ford	58	+ 2 laps
13.	Borgudd	ATS-Ford	57	+ 3 laps

FASTEST LAP

Villeneuve	Ferrari	1'48.06" 167.900 km/h

NOT CLASSIFIED

Jabouille	Ligier-Matra	45	+ 15 laps

RETIREMENTS

Salazar	March-Ford	38	Oil pressure
Alboreto	Tyrrell-Ford	31	Collision Gabbiani
Gabbiani	Osella-Ford	31	Collision Alboreto
Giacomelli	Alfa Romeo	28	Collision Cheever
Cheever	Tyrrell-Ford	28	Collision Giacomelli
Andretti	Alfa Romeo	26	Gearbox
Rosberg	Fittipaldi-Ford	14	Engine
Laffite	Ligier-Matra	7	Collision Arnoux
Prost	Renault	3	Gearbox
Guerra	Osella-Ford	0	Accident

San Marino, Imola race statistics.

Zolder race statistics.

Alain Prost.

Alain Prost.

STARTING GRID	
Reutemann 1'22.28"	Piquet 1'23.13"
Pironi 1'23.47"	Patrese 1'23.67"
Watson 1'23.73"	Jones 1'23.82"
Villeneuve 1'23.94"	Cheever 1'24.38"
Laffite 1'24.41"	Mansell 1'24.44"
Rosberg 1'24.46"	Prost 1'24.63"
Stohr 1'24.66"	De Angelis 1'24.96"
Surer 1'25.19"	Jabouille 1'25.28"
Giacomelli 1'25.31"	Andretti 1'25.56"
Alboreto 1'25.91"	Serra 1'25.93"
Rebaque 1'26.52"	Gabbiani 1'26.69"
De Cesaris 1'26.95"	Ghinzani 1'27.48"

RESULTS - Zolder (230,148 km)

1. Reutemann	Williams-Ford	54	1h16'31.61"
2. Laffite	Ligier-Matra	54	1h17'07.67"
3. Mansell	Lotus-Ford	54	1h17'15.30"
4. Villeneuve	Ferrari	54	1h17'19.25"
5. De Angelis	Lotus-Ford	54	1h17'20.81"
6. Cheever	Tyrrell-Ford	54	1h17'24.12"
7. Watson	McLaren-Ford	54	1h17'33.27"
8. Pironi	Ferrari	54	1h18'03.65"
9. Giacomelli	Alfa Romeo	54	1h18'07.19"
10. Andretti	Alfa Romeo	53	+ 1 lap
11. Surer	Ensign-Ford	52	+ 2 laps
12. Alboreto	Tyrrell-Ford	52	+ 2 laps
13. Ghinzani	Osella-Ford	50	+ 4 laps

FASTEST LAP

Reutemann	Williams-Ford	1'23.30" 184.192 km/h

RETIREMENTS

Rebaque	Brabham-Ford	39	Accident
Jabouille	Ligier-Matra	35	Transmission
Serra	Fittipaldi-Ford	29	Engine
Gabbiani	Osella-Ford	22	Engine
Jones	Williams-Ford	19	Accident
De Cesaris	McLaren-Ford	11	Gearbox
Piquet	Brabham-Ford	10	Collision Jones
Rosberg	Fittipaldi-Ford	10	Gear lever
Prost	Renault	2	Clutch

STARTING GRID	
Piquet 1'25.710"	Villeneuve 1'25.788"
Mansell 1'25.815"	Reutemann 1'26.010"
Patrese 1'26.040"	De Angelis 1'26.259"
Jones 1'26.538"	Laffite 1'26.704"
Prost 1'26.953"	Watson 1'27.058"
De Cesaris 1'27.122"	Andretti 1'27.512"
Arnoux 1'27.513"	Stohr 1'27564"
Cheever 1'27.594"	Tambay 1'27.939"
Pironi 1'28.266"	Giacomelli 1'28.323"
Surer 1'28.339"	Alboreto 1'28.358"

RESULTS - Monaco (251,712 km)

1. Villeneuve	Ferrari	76	1h54'23.38"
2. Jones	Williams-Ford	76	1h55'03.29"
3. Laffite	Ligier-Matra	76	1h55'52.62"
4. Pironi	Ferrari	75	+ 1 lap
5. Cheever	Tyrrell-Ford	74	+ 2 laps
6. Surer	Ensign-Ford	74	+ 2 laps
7. Tambay	Theodore-Ford	72	+ 4 laps

FASTEST LAP

Jones	Williams-Ford	1'27.47" 136.311 km/h

RETIREMENTS

Piquet	Brabham-Ford	53	Accident
Watson	McLaren-Ford	53	Engine
Alboreto	Tyrrell-Ford	50	Spin, collision with Giacomelli
Giacomelli	Alfa Romeo	50	Collision Alboreto
Prost	Renault	45	Engine
Reutemann	Williams-Ford	34	Gearbox
Arnoux	Renault	32	Accident
De Angelis	Lotus-Ford	32	Engine
Patrese	Arrows-Ford	29	Gearbox
Mansell	Lotus-Ford	16	Rear suspension
Stohr	Arrows-Ford	15	Ignition
De Cesaris	McLaren-Ford	0	Collision Prost
Andretti	Alfa Romeo	0	Collision De Cesaris

Monaco race statistics.

STARTING GRID		RESULTS - Jarama (264,970 km)			
Laffite 1'13.754"	Jones 1'14.024"	1. Villeneuve	Ferrari	80	1h46'35.01"
Reutemann 1'14.342"	Watson 1'14.657"	2. Laffite	Ligier-Matra	80	1h46'35.23"
Prost 1'14.669"	Giacomelli 1'14.897"	3. Watson	McLaren-Ford	80	1h46'35.59"
Villeneuve 1'14.987"	Andretti 1'15.159"	4. Reutemann	Williams-Ford	80	1h46'36.02"
Piquet 1'15.355"	De Angelis 1'15.399"	5. De Angelis	Lotus-Ford	80	1h46'36.25"
Mansell 1'15.562"	Patrese 1'15.627"	6. Mansell	Lotus-Ford	80	1h47'03.59"
Pironi 1'15.715"	De Cesaris 1'15.850"	7. Jones	Williams-Ford	80	1h47'31.59"
Rosberg 1'15.924"	Tambay 1'16.355"	8. Andretti	Alfa Romeo	80	1h47'35.81"
Arnoux 1'16.406"	Rebaque 1'16.527"	9. Arnoux	Renault	80	1h47'42.09"
Jabouille 1'16.559"	Cheever 1'16.641"	10. Giacomelli	Alfa Romeo	80	1h47'48.66"
Serra 1'16.782"	Daly 1'16.979"	11. Serra	Fittipaldi-Ford	79	+ 1 lap
Stohr 1'17.294"	Salazar 1'17.822"	12. Rosberg	Fittipaldi-Ford	78	+ 2 laps
		13. Tambay	Theodore-Ford	78	+ 2 laps
		14. Salazar	Ensign-Ford	77	+ 3 laps
		15. Pironi	Ferrari	76	+ 4 laps
		16. Daly	March-Ford	75	+ 5 laps

FASTEST LAP

Jones	Williams-Ford	1'17.818" 153.220 km/h

NOT CLASSIFIED

Cheever	Tyrrell-Ford	61	+ 19 laps

RETIREMENTS

Jabouille	Ligier-Matra	52	Brakes
Rebaque	Brabham-Ford	46	Gearbox
Piquet	Brabham-Ford	43	Accident
Stohr	Arrows-Ford	43	Engine
Prost	Renault	28	Accident
Patrese	Arrows-Ford	21	Engine
De Cesaris	McLaren-Ford	9	Accident

Jarama race statistics.

Arnoux tussles with Reutemann's Williams. (© DPPI/Ren)

Spanish Grand Prix, Jarama, 21 June 1981

At Jarama Arnoux was in a new RE33, finishing 9th. Prost's RE32 was involved in a crash on lap 28.

French Grand Prix, Dijon, 5 July 1981

The damaged car was repaired in time for Arnoux to put it on pole at Dijon, all three cars (two race, one spare) having modified side-pods and rear wings of a new design. Prost, starting on P3 in RE32, took victory in a split race, winning on aggregate after a rainstorm that stopped proceedings.

British Grand Prix, Silverstone, 19 July 1981

At the British Grand Prix, Arnoux took pole and Prost second. Both started well, but Prost had engine failure on lap 17. Arnoux managed to finish in 9th.

German Grand Prix, Hockenheim, 2 August 1981

At Hockenheim Prost took pole with Arnoux second, but in the race Arnoux's rear tyre was punctured by another car's nose wing,

STARTING GRID		RESULTS - Dijon-Prenois (304 km)			
Arnoux 1'05.95"	Watson 1'06.36"	1. Prost	Renault	80	1h35'48.13"
Prost 1'06.36"	Piquet 1'06.91"	2. Watson	McLaren-Ford	80	1h35'50.42"
De Cesaris 1'07.03"	Laffite 1'07.09"	3. Piquet	Brabham-Ford	80	1h36'12.35"
Reutemann 1'07.42"	De Angelis 1'07.52"	4. Arnoux	Renault	80	1h36'30.43"
Jones 1'07.53"	Andretti 1'07.56"	5. Pironi	Ferrari	79	+ 1 lap
Villeneuve 1'07.60"	Giacomelli 1'07.63"	6. De Angelis	Lotus-Ford	79	+ 1 lap
Mansell 1'07.72"	Pironi 1'08.09"	7. Mansell	Lotus-Ford	79	+ 1 lap
Rebaque 1'08.21"	Tambay 1'08.47"	8. Andretti	Alfa Romeo	79	+ 1 lap
Rosberg 1'09.35"	Patrese 1'09.37"	9. Rebaque	Brabham-Ford	78	+ 2 laps
Cheever 1'09.88"	Daly 1'09.94"	10. Reutemann	Williams-Ford	78	+ 2 laps
Surer 1'10.21"	Salazar 1'10.50"	11. De Cesaris	McLaren-Ford	78	+ 2 laps
Alboreto 1'10.64"	Serra 1'10.86"	12. Surer	Theodore-Ford	78	+ 2 laps
		13. Cheever	Tyrrell-Ford	77	+ 3 laps
		14. Patrese	Arrows-Ford	77	+ 3 laps
		15. Giacomelli	Alfa Romeo	77	+ 3 laps
		16. Alboreto	Tyrrell-Ford	77	+ 3 laps
		17. Jones	Williams-Ford	76	+ 4 laps

FASTEST LAP

Prost	Renault	1'09.14" 197.859 km/h

RETIREMENTS

Laffite	Ligier-Matra	57	Front suspension
Daly	March-Ford	55	Engine
Villeneuve	Ferrari	41	Electrical
Tambay	Ligier-Matra	30	Rolling bearing
Rosberg	Fittipaldi-Ford	11	Rear suspension
Salazar	Ensign-Ford	6	Rear suspension
Serra	Fittipaldi-Ford		Spin (warm-up)

Dijon race statistics.

Engineer Daniel Champion with Prost and Jean Ragnotti.

STARTING GRID

Arnoux	Prost
1'11.000"	1'11.046"
Piquet	Pironi
1'11.925"	1'12.644"
Watson	De Cesaris
1'12.712"	1'12.728"
Jones	Villeneuve
1'12.998"	1'13.311"
Reutemann	Patrese
1'13.371"	1'13.762"
Andretti	Giacomelli
1'13.928"	1'14.119"
Rebaque	Laffite
1'14.542"	1'14.798"
Tambay	Rosberg
1'14.976"	1'15.165"
Daly	Stohr
1'15.189"	1'15.304"
Alboreto	Jarier
1'15.850"	1'15.898"
Borgudd	De Angelis
1'15.959"	1'15.971"
Cheever	Surer
1'16.099"	1'16.155"

RESULTS - Silverstone (320,892 km)

1. Watson	McLaren-Ford	68	1h26'54.80"
2. Reutemann	Williams-Ford	68	1h27'35.45"
3. Laffite	Ligier-Matra	67	+ 1 lap
4. Cheever	Tyrrell-Ford	67	+ 1 lap
5. Rebaque	Brabham-Ford	67	+ 1 lap
6. Borgudd	ATS-Ford	67	+ 1 lap
7. Daly	March-Ford	66	+ 2 laps
8. Jarier	Osella-Ford	65	+ 3 laps
9. Arnoux	Renault	64	Engine
10. Patrese	Arrows-Ford	64	Engine
11. Surer	Theodore-Ford	61	Oil pressure

FASTEST LAP

Arnoux	Renault	1'15.067" 226.309 km/h

RETIREMENTS

Andretti	Alfa Romeo	59	Throttle cable
Rosberg	Fittipaldi-Ford	56	Rear suspension
De Angelis	Lotus-Ford	25	Black flag
Prost	Renault	17	Engine
Tambay	Ligier-Matra	15	Ignition
Pironi	Ferrari	13	Engine
Piquet	Brabham-Ford	11	Accident/puncture
Giacomelli	Alfa Romeo	5	Gearbox
Villeneuve	Ferrari	4	Accident
Jones	Williams-Ford	3	Accident Villeneuve
De Cesaris	McLaren-Ford	3	Accident Villeneuve
Alboreto	Tyrrell-Ford	0	Clutch
Stohr	Arrows-Ford	0	Accident

Silverstone race statistics.

and skirt damage unsettled the car's handling. He finished 13th, with Prost in second.

Austrian Grand Prix, Zeltweg, 16 August 1981
At Zeltweg it was Arnoux who took pole to Prost's second. In the race, Arnoux finished second this time, but Prost retired with suspension problems on lap 26.

Dutch Grand Prix, Zandvoort, 30 August 1981
On to Zandvoort in Holland, where a revision called the RE34 was provided for Prost, who put it on pole and went on to victory, while Arnoux, also starting from the front row, went out in an accident on lap 21.

Italian Grand Prix, Monza, 13 September 1981
Arnoux was to put the RE33 on pole at Monza but crashed out in

STARTING GRID

Prost	Arnoux
1'47.50"	1'47.96"
Reutemann	Jones
1'48.43"	1'48.49"
Pironi	Piquet
1'49.00"	1'49.03"
Laffite	Villeneuve
1'49.28"	1'49.44"
Watson	De Cesaris
1'49.52"	1'49.58"
Tambay	Andretti
1'50.00"	1'50.64"
Patrese	De Angelis
1'50.65"	1'50.74"
Mansell	Rebaque
1'50.86"	1'51.17"
Jarier	Cheever
1'52.19"	1'52.19"
Giacomelli	Borgudd
1'52.21"	1'52.54"
Daly	Surer
1'52.65"	1'52.85"
Salazar	Stohr
1'53.16"	1'53.19"

RESULTS - Hockenheim (305,505 km)

1. Piquet	Brabham-Ford	45	1h25'55.60"
2. Prost	Renault	45	1h26'07.12"
3. Laffite	Ligier-Matra	45	1h27'00.20"
4. Rebaque	Brabham-Ford	45	1h27'35.29"
5. Cheever	Tyrrell-Ford	45	1h27'46.12"
6. Watson	McLaren-Ford	44	+ 1 lap
7. De Angelis	Lotus-Ford	44	+ 1 lap
8. Jarier	Osella-Ford	44	+ 1 lap
9. Andretti	Alfa Romeo	44	+ 1 lap
10. Villeneuve	Ferrari	44	+ 1 lap
11. Jones	Williams-Ford	44	+ 1 lap
12. Stohr	Arrows-Ford	44	+ 1 lap
13. Arnoux	Renault	44	+ 1 lap
14. Surer	Theodore-Ford	43	+ 2 laps
15. Giacomelli	Alfa Romeo	43	+ 2 laps

FASTEST LAP

Jones	Williams-Ford	1'52.42" 217.403 km/h

NOT CLASSIFIED

Salazar	Ensign-Ford	39	+ 6 laps

RETIREMENTS

Borgudd	ATS-Ford	35	Engine
Reutemann	Williams-Ford	27	Engine
Patrese	Arrows-Ford	27	Engine
Tambay	Ligier-Matra	27	Rolling bearing
Daly	March-Ford	15	Steering
Mansell	Lotus-Ford	12	Fuel leak
De Cesaris	McLaren-Ford	4	Spin
Pironi	Ferrari	1	Engine

Hockenheim race statistics.

Arnoux and Larrousse. (© TVA)

STARTING GRID	
Prost 1'18.176"	Arnoux 1'18.255"
Piquet 1'18.625"	Jones 1'18.672"
Reutemann 1'18.844"	Laffite 1'19.018"
Andretti 1'19.040"	Watson 1'19.312"
De Angelis 1'19.738"	Patrese 1'19.864"
Tambay 1'19.979"	Pironi 1'20.248"
Giacomelli 1'20.384"	Rebaque 1'20.547"
Villeneuve 1'20.595"	
Mansell 1'20.663"	Jarier 1'21.086"
Daly 1'21.391"	Surer 1'21.454"
Stohr 1'21.568"	Cheever 1'21.698"
Borgudd 1'21.760"	Salazar 1'22.024"

RESULTS - Zandvoort (306,144 km)

1. Prost	Renault	72	1h40'22.43"
2. Piquet	Brabham-Ford	72	1h40'30.67"
3. Jones	Williams-Ford	72	1h40'57.93"
4. Rebaque	Brabham-Ford	71	+ 1 lap
5. De Angelis	Lotus-Ford	71	+ 1 lap
6. Salazar	Ensign-Ford	70	+ 2 laps
7. Stohr	Arrows-Ford	69	+ 3 laps
8. Surer	Theodore-Ford	69	+ 3 laps
9. Alboreto	Tyrrell-Ford	68	Engine
10. Borgudd	ATS-Ford	68	+ 4 laps

FASTEST LAP

Jones	Williams-Ford	1'21.83" 186.832 km/h

RETIREMENTS

Andretti	Alfa Romeo	62	Accident, puncture
Watson	McLaren-Ford	50	Electrical
Cheever	Tyrrell-Ford	46	Accident suspension
Jarier	Osella-Ford	29	Gearbox
Arnoux	Renault	21	Accident
Giacomelli	Alfa Romeo	19	Accident
Laffite	Ligier-Matra	18	Collision Reutemann
Reutemann	Williams-Ford	18	Collision Laffite
Patrese	Arrows-Ford	16	Suspension failure
Daly	March-Ford	5	Suspension failure
Pironi	Ferrari	4	Accident
Mansell	Lotus-Ford	1	Electrical
Tambay	Ligier-Matra	0	Collision Pironi
Villeneuve	Ferrari	0	Collision with Giacomelli and Patrese

Zandvoort race statistics.

STARTING GRID	
Arnoux 1'32.018"	Prost 1'32.321"
Villeneuve 1'33.334"	Laffite 1'34.398"
Reutemann 1'34.531"	Jones 1'34.654"
Piquet 1'34.871"	Pironi 1'35.037"
De Angelis 1'35.294"	Patrese 1'35.442"
Mansell 1'35.569"	Watson 1'35.977"
Andretti 1'36.079"	Jarier 1'36.117"
Rebaque 1'36.150"	Giacomelli 1'36.216"
Tambay 1'36.233"	De Cesaris 1'36.657"
Daly 1'37.230"	Salazar 1'37.631"
Borgudd 1'37'709"	Alboreto 1'38.084"
Surer 1'38.522"	Stohr 1'38.546"

RESULTS - Zeltweg (314,926 km)

1. Laffite	Ligier-Matra	53	1h27'36.47"
2. Arnoux	Renault	53	1h27'41.64"
3. Piquet	Brabham-Ford	53	1h27'43.81"
4. Jones	Williams-Ford	53	1h27'48.51"
5. Reutemann	Williams-Ford	53	1h28'08.32"
6. Watson	McLaren-Ford	53	1h29'07.61"
7. De Angelis	Lotus-Ford	52	+ 1 lap
8. De Cesaris	McLaren-Ford	52	+ 1 lap
9. Pironi	Ferrari	52	+ 1 lap
10. Jarier	Osella-Ford	51	+ 2 laps
11. Daly	March-Ford	47	+ 6 laps

FASTEST LAP

Laffite	Ligier-Matra	1'37.62" 219.127 km/h

RETIREMENTS

Andretti	Alfa Romeo	46	Engine
Borgudd	ATS-Ford	44	Brakes
Patrese	Arrows-Ford	43	Engine
Salazar	Ensign-Ford	43	Engine
Alboreto	Tyrrell-Ford	40	Engine
Giacomelli	Alfa Romeo	35	Engine
Rebaque	Brabham-Ford	31	Clutch
Stohr	Arrows-Ford	27	Spin
Prost	Renault	26	Front suspension
Tambay	Ligier-Matra	26	Engine
Mansell	Lotus-Ford	23	Engine
Villeneuve	Ferrari	11	Accident
Surer	Theodore-Ford	0	Gearwheel

Zeltweg race statistics.

Life in the pits! (© TVA)

Prost: victory at Monza.

STARTING GRID		RESULTS - Monza (301,600 km)			
Arnoux 1'33.467"	Reutemann 1'34.140"	1. Prost	Renault	52	1h26'33.897"
Prost 1'34.374"	Laffite 1'35.062"	2. Jones	Williams-Ford	52	1h26'56.027"
Jones 1'35.359"	Piquet 1'35.449"	3. Reutemann	Williams-Ford	52	1h27'24.484"
Watson 1'35.557"	Pironi 1'35.596"	4. De Angelis	Lotus-Ford	52	1h28'06.799"
Villeneuve 1'35.627"	Giacomelli 1'35.946"	5. Pironi	Ferrari	52	1h28'08.419"
De Angellis 1'36.158"	Mansell 1'36.210"	6. Piquet	Brabham-Ford	51	Engine
Andretti 1'36.296"	Rebaque 1'36.472"	7. De Cesaris	McLaren-Ford	51	Puncture/accident
Tambay 1'36.515"	De Cesaris 1'37.019"	8. Giacomelli	Alfa Romeo	50	+ 2 laps
Cheever 1'37.160"	Jarier 1'37.264"	9. Jarier	Osella-Ford	50	+ 2 laps
Daly 1'37.303"	Patrese 1'37.355"	10. Henton	Toleman-Hart	49	+ 3 laps
Borgudd 1'37.807"	Alboreto 1'37.912"				
Henton 1'38.012"	Salazar 1'38.053"				

FASTEST LAP			
Reutemann	Williams-Ford		1'37.528" 214.092 km/h

RETIREMENTS			
Andretti	Lotus-Ford	41	Engine
Daly	March-Ford	37	Gearbox
Tambay	Ligier-Matra	22	Puncture
Mansell	Lotus-Ford	21	Road-holding
Watson	McLaren-Ford	19	Accident
Patrese	Arrows-Ford	19	Gearbox
Alboreto	Tyrrell-Ford	16	Accident
Salazar	Ensign-Ford	13	Puncture
Arnoux	Renault	12	Accident
Cheever	Tyrrell-Ford	11	Spin
Laffite	Ligier-Matra	11	Puncture
Borgudd	ATS-Ford	10	Spin
Villeneuve	Ferrari	6	Turbo
Rebaque	Brabham-Ford	0	Electrical

Monza race statistics.

STARTING GRID		RESULTS - Montréal (277,830 km)			
Piquet 1'29.211"	Reutemann 1'29.359"	1. Laffite	Ligier-Matra	63	2:01'25.205"
Jones 1'29.728"	Prost 1'29.908"	2. Watson	McLaren-Ford	63	2:01'31.438"
Mansell 1'29.997"	Rebaque 1'30.182"	3. Villeneuve	Ferrari	63	2:03'15.480"
De Angelis 1'30.231"	Arnoux 1'30.232"	4. Giacomelli	Alfa Romeo	62	+ 1 lap
Watson 1'30.566"	Laffite 1'30.705"	5. Piquet	Brabham-Ford	62	+ 1 lap
Villeneuve 1'31.115"	Pironi 1'31.350"	6. De Angelis	Lotus-Ford	62	+ 1 lap
De Cesaris 1'31.507"	Cheever 1'31.547"	7. Andretti	Alfa Romeo	62	+ 1 lap
Giacomelli 1'31.600"	Andretti 1'31.740"	8. Daly	March-Ford	61	+ 2 laps
Tambay 1'31.747"	Patrese 1'31.969"	9. Surer	Theodore-Ford	61	+ 2 laps
Surer 1'32.253"	Daly 1'32.305"	10. Reutemann	Williams-Ford	60	+ 3 laps
Borgudd 1'32.652"	Alboreto 1'32.709"	11. Alboreto	Tyrrell-Ford	59	+ 4 laps
Jarier 1'33.432"	Salazar 1'33.848"	12. Cheever	Tyrrell-Ford	56	Engine

FASTEST LAP		
Watson	McLaren-Ford	1'49.475" 145.019 km/h

RETIREMENTS			
De Cesaris	McLaren-Ford	51	Spin
Prost	Renault	48	Collision Mansell
Mansell	Lotus-Ford	45	Collision Prost
Borgudd	ATS-Ford	39	Spin
Rebaque	Brabham-Ford	35	Spin
Jarier	Osella-Ford	26	Collision with Rebaque
Pironi	Ferrari	24	Engine
Jones	Williams-Ford	24	Road-holding
Salazar	Ensign-Ford	8	Spin
Tambay	Ligier-Matra	6	Spin
Patrese	Arrows-Ford	6	Spin
Arnoux	Renault	0	Accident

Montreal race statistics.

the race on lap 12. Prost, in the RE34, started from P3 and went on to win.

Canadian Grand Prix, Montreal, 27 September 1981
Over to Canada, and changes included new injectors, intercoolers, lightweight honeycomb side-pods, 13-inch front wheels, different brake ducts, and new carbon-fibre front and rear wings, all of which still kept the weight to below 600kg (1320lb). Prost's RE34 weighed-in at 595kg (1311.6 lb), and Arnoux's RE33 at 59kg (1318.4lb). Both cars, though, went out due to accidents; Arnoux on the 1st lap and Prost on lap 48.

US Las Vegas Grand Prix, Caesar's Palace, 18 October 1981
At the final race of the season at Caesar's Palace in Las Vegas, the RE30 replaced Arnoux's RE33 which had crashed in Montreal. Prost was to finish 2nd after starting from P5, while an electrical problem put Arnoux out on lap 10.

The season ended with 14 finishes, including 3 wins, 3 seconds, and 6 pole positions. The RE30 was quick, but still not

A wet Montreal. (© DPPI/Ren)

as reliable as was wanted. However, Renault Sport could look forward to 1982 in a positive frame of mind; a fresh challenge was to come from Ferrari and the new 126C2 turbo car.

1982: RE30B

South African Grand Prix, Kyalami, 23 January 1982
In 1982, Prost and Arnoux began with updated 1981 cars – now called the RE30B – at Kyalami. Arnoux took pole with Prost on P5, but it was Prost who went on to win the race, with Arnoux also on the podium in 3rd. The cars featured lighter panels; carbon discs were also tried on the T (training) car.

Brazilian Grand Prix, Jacarepagua, 21 March 1982
In Brazil it was Prost who took pole and Arnoux P4. Prost won again, but Arnoux went out in an accident on lap 21, colliding with Reutemann.

US West Coast Grand Prix, Long Beach, 4 April 1982
This time, water ballast was added to a hollow seat moulding because the cars were underweight. Arnoux started on P3 and Prost on P4, but both were to go out in accidents – Arnoux on lap 5 and Prost on lap 10.

San Marino Grand Prix, Imola, 25 April 1982
It was back to Europe for the San Marino event. Prost had new

Prost in Vegas.

STARTING GRID		RESULTS - Las Vegas (273,750 km)			
Reutemann 1'17.821"	Jones 1'17.995"	1. Jones	Williams-Ford	75	1h44'09.077"
Vileneuve 1'18.060"	Piquet 1'18.161"	2. Prost	Renault	75	1h44'29.125"
Prost 1'18.433"	Watson 1'18.617"	3. Giacomelli	Alfa Romeo	75	1h44'29.505"
Tambay 1'18.681"	Giacomelli 1'18.792"	4. Mansell	Lotus-Ford	75	1h44'56.550"
Mansell 1'19.044"	Andretti 1'19.068"	5. Piquet	Brabham-Ford	75	1h45'25.515"
Patrese 1'19.152"	Laffite 1'19.167"	6. Laffite	Ligier-Matra	75	1h45'27.252"
Arnoux 1'19.197"	De Cesaris 1'19.217"	7. Watson	McLaren-Ford	75	1h45'27.574"
De Angelis 1'19.562"	Rebaque 1'19.571"	8. Reutemann	Williams-Ford	74	+ 1 lap
Alboreto 1'19.774"	Pironi 1'19.89"	9. Pironi	Ferrari	73	+ 2 laps
Cheever 1'20.475"	Rosberg 1'20.729"	10. Rosberg	Fittipaldi-Ford	73	+ 2 laps
Jarier 1'20.781"	Warwick 1'21.294"	11. Patrese	Arrows-Ford	71	+ 4 laps
Surer 1'21.430"	Salazar 1'21.629"	12. De Cesaris	McLaren-Ford	69	+ 6 laps

NOT CLASSIFIED

Alboreto	Tyrrell-Ford	67	+ 8 laps
Salazar	Ensign-Ford	61	+ 14 laps

DISQUALIFIED

Villeneuve	Ferrari		

FASTEST LAP

Pironi	Ferrari	1'20.156" 163.930 km/h

RETIREMENTS

Warwick	Toleman-Hart	43	Gearbox
Andretti	Alfa Romeo	29	Rear suspension
Rebaque	Brabham-Ford	20	Spin
Surer	Theodore-Ford	19	Rear suspension
Cheever	Tyrrell-Ford	10	Engine
Arnoux	Renault	10	Electrical
Tambay	Ligier-Matra	2	Accident
De Angelis	Lotus-Ford	2	Water leak
Jarier	Osella-Ford	0	Transmission

STARTING GRID		RESULTS - Kyalami (316,008 km)			
Arnoux 1'06.351"	Piquet 1'06.625"	1. Prost	Renault	77	1h32'08.401" 205.779 km/h
Villeneuve 1'07.106"	Patrese 1'07.398"	2. Reutemann	Williams-Ford	77	1h32'23.347"
Prost 1'08.133"	Pironi 1'08.360"	3. Arnoux	Renault	77	1h32'36.301"
Rosberg 1'08.892"	Reutemann 1'09.306"	4. Lauda	McLaren-Ford	77	1h32'40.514"
Watson 1'09.736"	Alboreto 1'10.037"	5. Rosberg	Williams-Ford	77	1h32'54.540"
Laffite 1'10.241"	Salazar 1'10.624"	6. Watson	McLaren-Ford	77	1h32'59.394"
Lauda 1'10.681"	Warwick 1'10.685"	7. Alboreto	Tyrrell-Ford	76	+ 1 lap
De Angelis 1'10.685"	De Cesaris 1'10.952"	8. De Angelis	Lotus-Ford	76	+ 1 lap
Cheever 1'11.005"	Mansell 1'11.227"	9. Salazar	ATS-Ford	75	+ 2 laps
Giacomelli 1'11.285"	Winkelhock 1'11.808"	10. Winkelhock	ATS-Ford	75	+ 2 laps
Boesel 1'12.077"	Mass 1'12.100"	11. Giacomelli	Alfa Romeo	74	+ 3 laps
Borgudd 1'12.366"	Daly 1'13.418"	12. Mass	March-Ford	74	+ 3 laps
Serra 1'13.467"	Jarier 1'13.834"	13. De Cesaris	Alfa Romeo	74	+ 3 laps
		14. Daly	Theodore-Ford	73	+ 4 laps
		15. Boesel	March-Ford	72	+ 5 laps
		16. Borgudd	Tyrrell-Ford	72	+ 5 laps
		17. Serra	Fittipaldi-Ford	72	+ 5 laps
		18. Pironi	Ferrari	71	Engine

FASTEST LAP

Prost	Renault	1'08.278" 216.386 km/h

RETIREMENTS

Laffite	Ligier-Matra	54	Engine
Warwick	Toleman-Hart	44	Accident
Patrese	Brabham-BMW	18	Turbo/Oil pressure
Cheever	Ligier-Matra	11	Ignition
Villeneuve	Ferrari	6	Turbo
Piquet	Brabham-BMW	3	Accident
Mansell	Lotus-Ford	0	Electrical/accident
Jarier	Osella-Ford	0	Accident

Kyalami race statistics.

An ecstatic Renault team. (© DPPI/Ren)

Caesar's Palace race statistics.

RE30B with the team. (© DPPI/Ren)

STARTING GRID		RESULTS - Long Beach (258,738 km)			
De Cesaris 1'27.316"	Lauda 1'27.436"	1. Lauda	McLaren-Ford	75	1h58'25.318" 131.093 km/h
Arnoux 1'27.763"	Prost 1'27.979"	2. Rosberg	Williams-Ford	75	1h58'39.978"
Giacomelli 1'28.087"	Piquet 1'28.276"	3. Patrese	Brabham-Ford	75	1h59'44.461"
Villeneuve 1'28.476"	Rosberg 1'28.576"	4. Alboreto	Tyrrell-Ford	75	1h59'46.265"
Pironi 1'28.680"	Jarier 1'28.708"	5. De Angelis	Lotus-Ford	74	+ 1 lap
Watson 1'28.885"	Alboreto 1'29.027"	6. Watson	McLaren-Ford	74	+ 1 lap
Cheever 1'29.336"	Andretti 1'29.468"	7. Mansell	Lotus-Ford	72	+ 3 laps
Laffite 1'29.587"	De Angelis 1'29.694"	8. Mass	March-Ford	72	+ 3 laps
Mansell 1'29.758"	Patrese 1'29.948"	9. Boesel	March-Ford	70	+ 5 laps
Guerrero 1'30.186"	Henton 1'30.474"	10. Borgudd	Tyrrell-Ford	68	+ 7 laps
Mass 1'30.476"	Daly 1'30.919"				
Boesel 1'30.977"	Borgudd 1'31.033"				
Winkelhock 1'31.593"	Salazar 1'31.825"				

DISQUALIFIED (unconform front wing)

(3) Villeneuve	Ferrari	63	1h43'53.760"

FASTEST LAP

Lauda	McLaren-Ford	1'30.831" 135.826 km/h

RETIREMENTS

Cheever	Ligier-Matra	59	Gearbox
De Cesaris	Alfa Romeo	33	Accident
Henton	Arrows-Ford	32	Accident
Guerrero	Ensign-Ford	27	Accident
Laffite	Ligier-Matra	26	Engine
Jarier	Osella-Ford	26	Engine
Piquet	Brabham-Ford	25	Accident
Daly	Theodore-Ford	22	Accident, engine
Andretti	Williams-Ford	19	Accident, front suspension
Prost	Renault	10	Accident, brakes
Pironi	Ferrari	6	Accident
Arnoux	Renault	5	Collision Giacomelli
Giacomelli	Alfa Romeo	5	Collision with Arnoux
Salazar	ATS-Ford	3	Accident
Winkelhock	ATS-Ford	1	Accident

Long Beach race statistics.

STARTING GRID		RESULTS - Jacarepagua (316,953 km)			
Prost 1'28.808"	Villeneuve 1'29.173"	1. Prost	Renault	63	1h44'33.134" 181.800 km/h
Rosberg 1'29.358"	Arnoux 1'30.121"	2. Watson	McLaren-Ford	63	1h44'36.124"
Lauda 1'30.152"	Reutemann 1'30.183"	3. Mansell	Lotus-Ford	63	1h45'09.993"
Piquet 1'30.281"	Pironi 1'30.655"	4. Alboreto	Tyrrell-Ford	63	1h45'23.895"
Patrese 1'30.967"	De Cesaris 1'31.229"	5. Winkelhock	ATS-Ford	62	+ 1 lap
De Angelis 1'31.790"	Watson 1'31.906"	6. Pironi	Ferrari	62	+ 1 lap
Alboreto 1'31.991"	Mansell 1'32.228"	7. Borgudd	Tyrrell-Ford	61	+ 2 laps
Winkelhock 1'32.524"	Giacomelli 1'32.769"	8. Mass	March-Ford	61	+ 2 laps
Boesel 1'34.050"	Salazar 1'34.262"	9. Jarier	Osella-Ford	60	+ 3 laps
Baldi 1'34.380"	Daly 1'34.413"	10. Baldi	Arrows-Ford	57	+ 6 laps
Borgudd 1'35.020"	Mass 1'35.039"				
Jarier 1'35.081"	Laffite 1'35.084"				
Serra 1'35.246"	Cheever 1'35.288"				

DISQUALIFIED (unconform weight)

(1) Piquet	Brabham-Ford	63	1h43'53.760"
(2) Rosberg	Williams-Ford	63	1h44'05.737"

FASTEST LAP

Prost	Renault	1'37.016" 186.687 km/h

RETIREMENTS

Salazar	ATS-Ford	38	Engine
Serra	Fittipaldi-Ford	36	Accident
Patrese	Brabham-Ford	34	Driver tired
Villeneuve	Ferrari	29	Spun off
Lauda	McLaren-Ford	22	Collision Reutemann
Arnoux	Renault	21	Collision Reutemann
Reutemann	Williams-Ford	21	Collision Arnoux
De Angelis	Lotus-Ford	21	Collision Baldi
Cheever	Ligier-Matra	19	Water leak
Giacomelli	Alfa Romeo	16	Engine
Laffite	Ligier-Matra	15	Water leak
De Cesaris	Alfa Romeo	14	Jupes
Daly	Theodore-Ford	12	Puncture/spin
Boesel	March-Ford	11	Puncture/spin

Jacarepagua race statistics.

Tight racing at the start.

More garage life! (© TVA)

STARTING GRID				RESULTS - Imola (302,400 km)			
Arnoux	Prost		1. Pironi	Ferrari	60	1h36'38.887"
1'29.765"	1'30.249"					187.700 km/h
Villeneuve	Pironi		2. Villeneuve	Ferrari	60	1h36'39.253"
1'30.717"	1'32.020"		3. Alboreto	Tyrrell-Ford	60	1h37'46.571"
Alboreto	Giacomelli		4. Jarier	Osella-Ford	59	+ 1 lap
1'33.209"	1'33.230"		5. Salazar	ATS-Ford	57	+ 3 laps
De Cesaris	Warwick					
1'33.397"	1'33.503"			**FASTEST LAP**		
Jarier	Fabi					
1'34.336"	1'34.647"		Pironi	Ferrari		1'35.030"
Henton	Winkelhock					190.917 km/h
1'35.262"	1'35.790"					
Paletti	Salazar			**NOT CLASSIFIED**		
1'36.228"	1'36.434"					
			Fabi	Toleman-Hart	52	+ 8 laps

DISQUALIFIED (unconform weight)

Winkelhock	ATS-Ford	54	+ 6 laps

RETIREMENTS

Arnoux	Renault	44	Engine
Giacomelli	Alfa Romeo	24	Engine
Paletti	Osella-Ford	18	Suspension
Prost	Renault	7	Engine
De Cesaris	Alfa Romeo	4	Fuel pump
Henton	Tyrrell-Ford	0	Clutch
Warwick	Toleman-Hart	0	Electrical

Imola race statistics.

STARTING GRID			RESULTS - Zolder (298,340 km)			
Prost	Arnoux		1. Watson	McLaren-Ford	70	1h35'41.995"
1'15.701"	1'15.730"					187.047 km/h
Rosberg	Lauda		2. Rosberg	Williams-Ford	70	1h35'49.263"
1'15.847"	1'16.049"		3. Cheever	Ligier-Matra	69	+ 1 lap
Alboreto	De Cesaris		4. De Angelis	Lotus-Ford	68	+ 2 laps
1'16.308"	1'16.575"		5. Piquet	Brabham-BMW	67	+ 3 laps
Mansell	Piquet		6. Serra	Fittipaldi-Ford	67	+ 3 laps
1'16.944"	1'17.124"		7. Surer	Arrows-Ford	66	+ 4 laps
Patrese	Watson		8. Boesel	March-Ford	66	+ 4 laps
1'17.126"	1'17.144"		9. Laffite	Ligier-Matra	66	+ 4 laps
De Angelis	Winkelhock					
1'17.762"	1'17.879"			**NOT CLASSIFIED**		
Daly	Cheever					
1'18.194"	1'18.301"		Baldi	Arrows-Ford	51	+ 19 laps
Giacomelli	Jarier					
1'18.371"	1'18.403"			**DISQUALIFIED (unconform weight)**		
Laffite	Salazar					
1'18.565"	1'18.967"		(3) Lauda	McLaren-Ford	70	1h36'50.132"
Warwick	Henton					
1'18.985"	1'19.150"			**FASTEST LAP**		
Fabi	Surer					
1'19.300"	1'19.584"		Watson	McLaren-Ford		1'20.214"
Serra	Boesel					191.278 km/h
1'19.598"	1'19.621"					
Mass	Baldi			**RETIREMENTS**		
1'19.777"	1'19.815"					

Daly	Williams-Ford	60	Accident
Mass	March-Ford	60	Engine
Prost	Renault	59	Accident
Patrese	Brabham-BMW	52	Accident
Jarier	Osella-Ford	37	Rear wing failure
De Cesaris	Alfa Romeo	34	Gearbox
Henton	Tyrrell-Ford	33	Engine
Alboreto	Tyrrell-Ford	29	Engine
Warwick	Toleman-Hart	29	Transmission
Fabi	Toleman-Hart	13	Brakes
Mansell	Lotus-Ford	9	Clutch
Arnoux	Renault	7	Throttle cable
Winkelhock	ATS-Ford	0	Clutch
Salazar	ATS-Ford	0	Accident (start)
Giacomelli	Alfa Romeo	0	Accident (start)

chassis RE30B/08, the designation of the cars having changed yet again! Arnoux took pole with Prost on P2, but both cars had engine failure in the race.

Belgian Grand Prix, Zolder, 9 May 1982

Renault fared no better in Belgium, where, although Prost took pole again, and Arnoux P2, the latter went out on lap 7 with throttle cable failure, and Prost had an accident on lap 59.

Monaco Grand Prix, 23 May 1982

The new side-pods which appeared for Monaco never got a chance to prove their worth, as both cars went out: Arnoux spun off on lap 14, and Prost was classified 7th after an accident on his last lap. Once again, Arnoux had demonstrated how quick the cars were by taking pole.

US East Coast Grand Prix, Detroit, 6 June 1982

Detroit saw Prost on pole but unable to capitalise on it; although taking fastest lap, he was unclassified, Arnoux finishing 10th.

Zolder race statistics.

Arnoux leads the way at the start.

STARTING GRID		RESULTS - Monaco (251,712 km)				
Arnoux	Patrese	1. Patrese	Brabham-Ford	76	1h54'11.259"	
1'23.281"	1'23.791"				132.300 km/h	
Giacomelli	Prost	2. Pironi	Ferrari	75	Out of fuel	
1'23.939"	1'24.439"	3. De Cesaris	Alfa Romeo	75	Electrical	
Pironi	Rosberg	4. Mansell	Lotus-Ford	75	+ 1 lap	
1'24.585"	1'24.649"	5. De Angelis	Lotus-Ford	75	+ 1 lap	
De Cesaris	Daly	6. Daly	Williams-Ford	74	Accident	
1'24.928"	1'25.390"	7. Prost	Renault	73	Accident	
Alboreto	Watson	8. Henton	Tyrrell-Ford	72	+ 4 laps	
1'25.449"	1'25.583"	9. Surer	Arrows-Ford	70	+ 6 laps	
Mansell	Lauda	10. Alboreto	Tyrrell-Ford	69	Accident	
1'25.642"	1'25.838"					
Piquet	Winkelhock					
1'26.075"	1'26.260"	**FASTEST LAP**				
De Angelis	Cheever					
1'26.456"	1'26.463"	Patrese	Brabham-Ford		1'26.354"	
Henton	Laffite				138.073 km/h	
1'26.690"	1'27.007"					
Surer	Salazar	**RETIREMENTS**				
1'27.019"	1'27.022"					
		Rosberg	Williams-Ford	65	Front suspension	
		Lauda	McLaren-Ford	57	Engine	
		Piquet	Brabham-BMW	50	Gearbox	
		Watson	McLaren-Ford	36	Oil leak, battery	
		Winkelhock	ATS-Ford	31	Differential	
		Laffite	Ligier-Matra	30	Road-holding	
		Cheever	Ligier-Matra	28	Engine	
		Salazar	ATS-Ford	22	Extincteur	
		Arnoux	Renault	14	Spin	
		Giacomelli	Alfa Romeo	5	Transmission	

Monaco race statistics.

Refuelling.

STARTING GRID		RESULTS - Detroit (258,230 km)			
Prost	De Cesaris	1. Watson	McLaren-Ford	62	1h58'41.043"
1'48.537"	1'48.872"				130.547 km/h
Rosberg	Pironi	2. Cheever	Ligier-Matra	62	1h58'56.769"
1'49.264"	1'49.903"	3. Pironi	Ferrari	62	1h59'09.120"
Winkelhock	Giacomelli	4. Rosberg	Williams-Ford	62	1h59'53.019"
1'50.066"	1'50.252"	5. Daly	Williams-Ford	62	2:00'04.800"
Mansell	De Angelis	6. Laffite	Ligier-Matra	61	+ 1 lap
1'50.294"	1'50.443"	7. Mass	March-Ford	61	+ 1 lap
Cheever	Lauda	8. Surer	Arrows-Ford	61	+ 1 lap
1'50.520"	1'51.026"	9. Henton	Tyrrell-Ford	60	+ 2 laps
Guerrero	Daly	10. Arnoux	Renault	59	+ 3 laps
1'51.039"	1'51.227"	11. Serra	Fittipaldi-Ford	59	+ 3 laps
Laffite	Patrese				
1'51.270"	1'51.508"	**NOT CLASSIFIED**			
Arnoux	Alboreto				
1'51.514"	1'51.618"	Prost	Renault	54	+ 8 laps
Watson	Mass				
1'51.868"	1'52.271"	**FASTEST LAP**			
Surer	Henton				
1'52.316"	1'52.867"	Prost	Renault		1'50.438"
Boesel	Jarier				135.866 km/h
1'52.870"	1'52.988"				
Paletti	Baldi	**RETIREMENTS**			
1'54.084"	1'54.332"				
Salazar	Serra	Mansell	Lotus-Ford	44	Engine
1'55.633"	1'55.848"	Lauda	McLaren-Ford	40	Collision Rosberg
		Alboreto	Tyrrell-Ford	40	Accident
		Giacomelli	Alfa Romeo	30	Collision Watson
		De Angelis	Lotus-Ford	17	Gearbox
		Salazar	ATS-Ford	13	Accident
		Guerrero	Ensign-Ford	6	Collision Patrese
		Patrese	Brabham-Ford	6	Accident
		De Cesaris	Alfa Romeo	2	Transmission
		Jarier	Osella-Ford	2	Electrical
		Winkelhock	ATS-Ford	1	Accident
		Boesel	March-Ford	1	Collision Baldi
		Baldi	Arrows-Ford	0	Collision Boesel

Detroit race statistics.

STARTING GRID		RESULTS - Montréal (308,700 km)			
Pironi 1'27.509"	Arnoux 1'27.895"	1. Piquet	Brabham-BMW	70	1h46'39.577" 173.650 km/h
Prost 1'28.563"	Piquet 1'28.663"	2. Patrese	Brabham-Ford	70	1h46'53.376"
Giacomelli 1'28.740"	Watson 1'28.822"	3. Watson	McLaren-Ford	70	1h47'41.413"
Rosberg 1'28.874"	Patrese 1'28.999"	4. De Angelis	Lotus-Ford	69	+ 1 lap
De Cesaris 1'29.183"	De Angelis 1'29.228"	5. Surer	Arrows-Ford	69	+ 1 lap
Lauda 1'29.544"	Cheever 1'29.590"	6. De Cesaris	Alfa Romeo	68	Out of fuel
Daly 1'29.883"	Mansell 1'30.048"	7. Daly	Williams-Ford	68	Out of fuel
Alboreto 1'30.146"	Surer 1'30.518"	8. Baldi	Arrows-Ford	68	+ 2 laps
Baldi 1'30.599"	Jarier 1'30.717"	9. Pironi	Ferrari	67	+ 3 laps
Laffite 1'30.946"	Guerrero 1'31.235"	10. Cheever	Ligier-Matra	66	Out of fuel
Boesel 1'31.759"	Mass 1'31.861"	11. Mass	March-Ford	66	+ 4 laps
Paletti 1'31.901"	Salazar 1'32.203"				
Lees 1'32.205"	Henton 1'32.325"				

NOT CLASSIFIED

Henton	Tyrrell-Ford	59	+ 11 laps

FASTEST LAP

Pironi	Ferrari	1'28.323" 179.749 km/h

RETIREMENTS

Rosberg	Williams-Ford	52	Gearbox
Boesel	March-Ford	47	Engine
Alboreto	Tyrrell-Ford	41	Gearbox
Prost	Renault	30	Engine
Arnoux	Renault	28	Spin
Salazar	ATS-Ford	20	Transmission
Lauda	McLaren-Ford	17	Clutch
Laffite	Ligier-Matra	8	Road-holding
Guerrero	Ensign-Ford	2	Clutch
Giacomelli	Alfa Romeo	1	Collision Mansell
Mansell	Lotus-Ford	1	Collision Giacomelli
Jarier	Osella-Ford		Withdraw (2ª start)
Lees	Theodore-Ford		Withdraw (2ª start)
Paletti	Osella-Ford		Fatal accident

Montreal race statistics.

Canadian Grand Prix, Montreal, 13 June 1982

A week later in Canada, Arnoux started on P2 and Prost on P3, Pironi of Ferrari pipping them to pole in his new turbo car. In the race, Arnoux spun out on lap 28; Prost's engine failed on lap 30.

Dutch Grand Prix, Zandvoort, 3 July 1982

Returning to Europe for the second time, Arnoux grabbed pole from Prost. Here, a new waste-gate appeared after turbo failure had been caused in Canada by it being too small. Again, Prost's car suffered failure on lap 33, while Arnoux had an accident on lap 21.

British Grand Prix, Brands Hatch, 18 July 1982

The British GP proved a low-key affair for the Renaults after a

STARTING GRID		RESULTS - Zandvoort (306,144 km)			
Arnoux 1'14.233"	Prost 1'14.660"	1. Pironi	Ferrari	72	1h38'03.254" 187.3 km/h
Piquet 1'14.723"	Pironi 1'15.825"	2. Piquet	Brabham-BMW	72	1h38'24.903"
Lauda 1'15.832"	Tambay 1'16.154"	3. Rosberg	Williams-Ford	72	1h38'25.619"
Rosberg 1'16.260"	Giacomelli 1'16.513"	4. Lauda	McLaren-Ford	72	1h39'26.974"
De Cesaris 1'16.576"	Patrese 1'16.630"	5. Daly	Williams-Ford	71	+ 1 lap
Watson 1'16.700"	Daly 1'16.832"	6. Baldi	Arrows-Ford	71	+ 1 lap
Warwick 1'17.094"	Alboreto 1'17.237"	7. Alboreto	Tyrrell-Ford	71	+ 1 lap
De Angelis 1'17.620"	Baldi 1'18.020"	8. Tambay	Ferrari	71	+ 1 lap
Surer 1'18.296"	Winkelhock 1'18.352"	9. Watson	McLaren-Ford	71	+ 1 lap
Serra 1'18.438"	Henton 1'18.476"	10. Surer	Arrows-Ford	71	+ 1 lap
Laffite 1'18.478"	Boesel 1'18.658"	11. Giacomelli	Alfa Romeo	70	+ 2 laps
Jarier 1'18.953"	Mass 1'19.083"	12. Winkelhock	Toleman-Hart	70	+ 2 laps
Salazar 1'19.120"	Lammers 1'19.274"	13. Salazar	ATS-Ford	70	+ 2 laps
		14. Jarier	Osella-Ford	69	+ 3 laps
		15. Patrese	Brabham-BMW	69	+ 3 laps

FASTEST LAP

Warwick	Toleman-Hart	1'19.780" 191.867 km/h

RETIREMENTS

Mass	March-Ford	60	Engine
Lammers	Theodore-Ford	41	Engine
De Angelis	Lotus-Ford	40	Road-holding
De Cesaris	Alfa Romeo	35	Electrical
Prost	Renault	33	Engine
Arnoux	Renault	21	Accident suspension failure
Henton	Tyrrell-Ford	21	Accelerator cable
Boesel	March-Ford	21	Engine
Serra	Fittipaldi-Ford	18	Fuel pump
Warwick	Toleman-Hart	15	Engine, Oil leak
Laffite	Ligier-Matra	4	Road-holding

Zandvoort race statistics.

Oops … Arnoux has an accident!

STARTING GRID	
Rosberg 1'09.540"	Patrese 1'09.627"
Piquet 1'10.060"	Pironi 1'10.066"
Lauda 1'10.638"	Arnoux 1'10.641"
De Angelis 1'10.650"	Prost 1'10.728"
Alboreto 1'10.892"	Daly 1'10.980"
De Cesaris 1'11.347"	Watson 1'11.418"
Tambay 1'11.430"	Giacomelli 1'11.502"
Fabi 1'11.728"	Warwick 1'11.761"
Henton 1'12.080"	Jarier 1'12.436"
Guerrero 1'12.668"	Laffite 1'12.695"
Serra 1'13.096"	Surer 1'13.181"
Mansell 1'13.212"	Cheever 1'13.301"
Mass 1'13.622"	Baldi 1'13.721"

RESULTS - Brands Hatch (320,188 km)

1. Lauda	McLaren-Ford	76	1h35'33.812" 201.031 km/h	
2. Pironi	Ferrari	76	1h35'59.538"	
3. Tambay	Ferrari	76	1h36'12.248"	
4. De Angelis	Lotus-Ford	76	1h36'15.054"	
5. Daly	Williams-Ford	76	1h36'15.242"	
6. Prost	Renault	76	1h36'15.448"	
7. Giacomelli	Alfa Romeo	75	+ 1 lap	
8. Henton	Tyrrell-Ford	75	+ 1 lap	
9. Baldi	Arrows-Ford	74	Engine	
10. Mass	March-Ford	73	+ 3 laps	

NOT CLASSIFIED

Alboreto	Tyrrell-Ford	44	+ 32 laps

FASTEST LAP

Henton	Tyrrell-Ford	1'13.028" 207.389 km/h

RETIREMENTS

De Cesaris	Alfa Romeo	66	Electrical
Cheever	Ligier-Matra	60	Engine
Surer	Arrows-Ford	59	Gearbox
Rosberg	Williams-Ford	51	Fuel pressure
Laffite	Ligier-Matra	42	Gearbox
Warwick	Toleman-Hart	41	Seal transmission
Mansell	Lotus-Ford	30	Road-holding and exhausted
Piquet	Brabham-BMW	9	Fuel feed
Guerrero	Ensign-Ford	3	Engine
Jarier	Osella-Ford	2	Collision Serra
Serra	Fittipaldi-Ford	2	Collision Jarier
Watson	McLaren-Ford	2	Spin
Fabi	Toleman-Hart	0	Accident (start)
Arnoux	Renault	0	Accident (start) collision Patrese
Patrese	Brabham-BMW	0	Stall (start) Collision Arnoux

Brands Hatch race statistics.

A sunny day; the 1982 British GP.

huge accident at the start took out Arnoux. Prost could only manage 6th.

French Grand Prix, Le Castellet (Paul Ricard), 23 July 1982

New front suspension was to appear at the French GP, and must have worked as Arnoux took pole with Prost on P2. At the finish of the race, the positions were the same: Arnoux 1st, Prost 2nd. There was a difficult political incident at one point in the race when Arnoux was instructed to let Prost pass him, but he didn't comply with this.

François Guiter: "After the race, something funny happened, as Prost himself told me: on his way home he stopped to buy some fuel for his car and the pump attendant told him, 'You did well, Mr Arnoux, not to let that idiot Prost pass you!'"

Le Castellet (Paul Ricard).

STARTING GRID			
Arnoux		Prost	
1'34.406"		1'34.688"	
Pironi		Patrese	
1'35.790"		1'35.811"	
Tambay		Piquet	
1'35.905"		1'36.359"	
De Cesaris		Giacomelli	
1'37.573"		1'37.705"	
Lauda		Rosberg	
1'37.778"		1'37.780"	
Daly		Watson	
1'38.767"		1'38.944"	
De Angelis		Warwick	
1'39.118"		1'39.306"	
Alboreto		Laffite	
1'39.330"		1'39.605"	
Jarier		Winkelhock	
1'39.909"		1'39.917"	
Cheever		Surer	
1'40.187"		1'40.335"	
Fabi		Salazar	
1'40.421"		1'40.673"	
Henton		Lees	
1'40.852"		1'40.974"	
Baldi		Mass	
1'40.997"		1'41.579"	

RESULTS - Le Castellet (313,740 km)				
1. Arnoux	Renault	54	1h33'33.217"	
			201.2 km/h	
2. Prost	Renault	54	1h33'50.525"	
3. Pironi	Ferrari	54	1h34'15.345"	
4. Tambay	Ferrari	54	1h34'49.458"	
5. Rosberg	Williams-Ford	54	1h35'04.211"	
6. Alboreto	Tyrrell-Ford	54	1h35'05.556"	
7. Daly	Williams-Ford	53	+ 1 lap	
8. Lauda	McLaren-Ford	53	+ 1 lap	
9. Giacomelli	Alfa Romeo	53	+ 1 lap	
10. Henton	Tyrrell-Ford	53	+ 1 lap	
11. Winkelhock	ATS-Ford	52	+ 2 laps	
12. Lees	Lotus-Ford	52	+ 2 laps	
13. Surer	Arrows-Ford	52	+ 2 laps	
14. Laffite	Ligier-Matra	51	+ 3 laps	
15. Warwick	Toleman-Hart	50	+ 4 laps	
16. Cheever	Ligier-Matra	49	+ 5 laps	

FASTEST LAP			
Patrese	Brabham-BMW	1'40.075"	
		209.003 km/h	

RETIREMENTS			
De Cesaris	Alfa Romeo	25	Accident, puncture
Piquet	Brabham-BMW	23	Engine
De Angelis	Lotus-Ford	17	Fuel pressure
Watson	McLaren-Ford	13	Battery
Mass	March-Ford	10	Collision Baldi
Baldi	Arrows-Ford	10	Collision Mass
Patrese	Brabham-BMW	8	Engine
Salazar	ATS-Ford	2	Accident
Fabi	Toleman-Hart	0	Oil pump
Jarier	Osella-Ford	0	Transmission shaft

Le Castellet (Paul Ricard) race statistics.

Opposite: Renaults lead the way at Hockenheim.

German Grand Prix, Hockenheim, 8 August 1982

At Hockenheim chassis RE30-10 appeared. The new carbon fibre brake discs were also tried again briefly, but then removed. Prost started on P1 and Arnoux on P2. Arnoux finished 2nd, but Prost had injection failure on lap 14.

Austrian Grand Prix, Zeltweg, 15 August 1982

The following week in Austria, Renault was upstaged by Piquet and Patrese; Prost was on P3 and Arnoux on P5 on the grid. Both cars failed during the race with engine malfunction (turbo and injection) on the 15th and 48th laps respectively.

Swiss Grand Prix, Dijon-Prenois (France), 29 August 1982

At the Swiss Grand Prix, held at Dijon-Prenois, Prost took pole from Arnoux, going on to finish 2nd, with Arnoux trailing in last after injection problems.

STARTING GRID	
Prost	Arnoux
1'48.890"	1'49.256"
Piquet	Tambay
1'49.415"	1'49.570"
Alboreto	De Cesaris
1'52.625"	1'52.786"
Rosberg	Watson
1'52.892"	1'53.073"
Giacomelli	Cheever
1'53.887"	1'54.211"
De Angelis	Warwick
1'54.476"	1'54.594"
Laffite	Winkelhock
1'54.982"	1'55.223"
Henton	Mansell
1'55.474"	1'55.866"
Daly	Jarier
1'55.876"	1'56.250"
Guerrero	Salazar
1'56.489"	1'56.537"
Baldi	Boesel
1'56.680"	1'57.245"
Serra	Surer
1'57.337"	1'57.402"

RESULTS - Hockenheim (305,865 km)

1. Tambay	Ferrari	45	1h27'25.178"
			209.9 km/h
2. Arnoux	Renault	45	1h27'41.557"
3. Rosberg	Williams-Ford	44	+ 1 lap
4. Alboreto	Tyrrell-Ford	44	+ 1 lap
5. Giacomelli	Alfa Romeo	44	+ 1 lap
6. Surer	Arrows-Ford	44	+ 1 lap
7. Henton	Tyrrell-Ford	44	+ 1 lap
8. Guerrero	Ensign-Ford	44	+ 1 lap
9. Mansell	Lotus-Ford	43	+ 2 laps
10. Warwick	Toleman-Hart	43	+ 2 laps
11. Serra	Fittipaldi-Ford	43	+ 2 laps

FASTEST LAP

Piquet	Brabham-BMW	1'54.035"
		214.576 km/h

RETIREMENTS

Watson	McLaren-Ford	36	Front suspension ... accident
Laffite	Ligier-Matra	36	Road-holding
Daly	Williams-Ford	25	Engine
Boesel	March-Ford	22	Puncture
De Angelis	Lotus-Ford	21	Transmission
Piquet	Brabham-BMW	18	Collision Salazar
Salazar	ATS-Ford	17	Collision Piquet
Prost	Renault	14	Injection
Patrese	Brabham-BMW	13	Engine
De Cesaris	Alfa Romeo	9	Collision Watson/ Oil radiator broken
Cheever	Ligier-Matra	8	Road-holding
Baldi	Arrows-Ford	6	Ignition
Jarier	Osella-Ford	3	Steering
Winkelhock	ATS-Ford	3	Clutch/Gearbox

Hockenheim race statistics.

Italian Grand Prix, Monza, 12 September 1982

Renault's competition was considered to be on equal terms – or possibly even superior – when in qualifying the Renaults were down the grid. However, Arnoux won the race although Prost again had injection problems and went out on lap 27.

US Las Vegas Grand Prix, Caesar's Palace, 25 September 1982

For the final race of the season in Las Vegas, Prost again put his car on pole with Arnoux on P2. Prost was to finish 4th but Arnoux experienced engine failure, this time on lap 20.

Overall, this was a frustrating season race-wise. Generally, the problem lay in the failure of a small electric motor within the injection system, which combined electronic control with a Bosch-Kugelfischer mechanical pump designed to produce a considerable performance advantage. The power was obvious, as evidenced by the qualifying positions – 10 pole positions!

STARTING GRID

Piquet 1'27.612"	Patrese 1'27.971"
Prost 1'28.864"	Tambay 1'29.522"
Arnoux 1'30.261"	Rosberg 1'30.300"
De Angelis 1'31.626"	Alboreto 1'31.814"
Daly 1'32.062"	Lauda 1'32.131"
De Cesaris 1'32.308"	Mansell 1'32.881"
Giacomelli 1'32.950"	Laffite 1'32.957"
Warwick 1'33.208"	Guerrero 1'33.555"
Fabi 1'33.971"	Watson 1'34.164"
Henton 1'34.184"	Serra 1'34.187"
Surer 1'34.422"	Cheever 1'34.620"
Baldi 1'34.715"	Keegan 1'34.770"
Winkelhock 1'34.984"	Byrne 1'34.985"

RESULTS - Zeltweg (314,926 km)

1. De Angelis	Lotus-Ford	53	1h25'02.212" 222.2 km/h
2. Rosberg	Williams-Ford	53	1h25'02.262"
3. Laffite	Ligier-Matra	52	+ 1 lap
4. Tambay	Ferrari	52	+ 1 lap
5. Lauda	McLaren-Ford	52	+ 1 lap
6. Baldi	Arrows-Ford	52	+ 1 lap
7. Serra	Fittipaldi-Ford	50	+ 3 laps

FASTEST LAP

Piquet	Brabham-BMW	1'33.699" 228.297 km/h

RETIREMENTS

Prost	Renault	48	Injection
Watson	McLaren-Ford	44	Engine
Henton	Tyrrell-Ford	32	Engine/Valves
Piquet	Brabham-BMW	31	Engine/transmission shaft
Byrne	Theodore-Ford	28	Spin
Surer	Arrows-Ford	28	Fuel feed
Patrese	Brabham-BMW	27	Engine
Cheever	Ligier-Matra	22	Engine/Valves
Mansell	Lotus-Ford	17	Engine
Arnoux	Renault	15	Turbo
Winkelhock	ATS-Ford	14	Spin
Warwick	Toleman-Hart	7	Rear suspension
Fabi	Toleman-Hart	7	Transmission
Guerrero	Ensign-Ford	6	Transmission
Alboreto	Tyrrell-Ford	1	Spin
Keegan	March-Ford	1	Steering
De Cesaris	Alfa Romeo	0	Accident (start)
Daly	Williams-Ford	0	Collision De Cesaris
Giacomelli	Alfa Romeo	0	Collision De Cesaris

Zeltweg race statistics.

Gérard Larrousse with engine customer, Colin Chapman.

Twins that live at number 30.

STARTING GRID

Prost 1'01.380"	Arnoux 1'01.740"
Patrese 1'02.710"	Lauda 1'02.984"
De Cesaris 1'03.023"	Piquet 1'03.183"
Daly 1'03.291"	Rosberg 1'03.589"
Giacomelli 1'03.776"	(Tambay) (1'03.896")
Watson 1'03.995"	Alboreto 1'04.069"
Laffite 1'04.087"	Surer 1'04.928"
De Angelis 1'04.967"	Cheever 1'05.001"
Jarier 1'05.179"	Henton 1'05.391"
Guerrero 1'05.395"	Winkelhock 1'05.451"
Warwick 1'05.877"	Keegan 1'06.011"
Fabi 1'06.017"	Boesel 1'06.136"
Salazar 1'06.168"	Mansell 1'06.211"

RESULTS - Dijon-Prenois (304 km)

1. Rosberg	Williams-Ford	80	1h32'41.087" 196.8 km/h
2. Prost	Renault	80	1h32'45.529"
3. Lauda	McLaren-Ford	80	1h33'41.430"
4. Piquet	Brabham-BMW	79	+ 1 lap
5. Patrese	Brabham-BMW	79	+ 1 lap
6. De Angelis	Lotus-Ford	79	+ 1 lap
7. Alboreto	Tyrrell-Ford	79	+ 1 lap
8. Mansell	Lotus-Ford	79	+ 1 lap
9. Daly	Williams-Ford	79	+ 1 lap
10. De Cesaris	Alfa Romeo	78	+ 2 laps
11. Henton	Tyrrell-Ford	78	+ 2 laps
12. Giacomelli	Alfa Romeo	78	+ 2 laps
13. Watson	McLaren-Ford	77	+ 3 laps
14. Salazar	ATS-Ford	77	+ 3 laps
15. Surer	Arrows-Ford	76	+ 4 laps
16. Arnoux	Renault	75	Injection

FASTEST LAP

Prost	Renault	1'07.477" 202.735 km/h

RETIREMENTS

Cheever	Ligier-Matra	70	Jupe abimée
Winkelhock	ATS-Ford	55	Support engine
Jarier	Osella-Ford	44	Engine
Laffite	Ligier-Matra	33	Road-holding
Fabi	Toleman-Hart	31	Ignition
Boesel	March-Ford	31	Oil leak
Keegan	March-Ford	25	Spin
Warwick	Toleman-Hart	24	Engine
Guerrero	Ensign-Ford	4	Engine

Dijon-Prenois (France) race statistics.

STARTING GRID		RESULTS - Monza (301,600 km)			
Andretti 1'28.473"	Piquet 1'28.508"	1. Arnoux	Renault	52	1h22'25.734" 219.5 km/h
Tambay 1'28.830"	Patrese 1'29.898"	2. Tambay	Ferrari	52	1h22'39.798"
Prost 1'30.026"	Arnoux 1'30.097"	3. Andretti	Ferrari	52	1h23'14.186"
Rosberg 1'31.834"	Giacomelli 1'32.352"	4. Watson	McLaren-Ford	52	1h23'53.579"
De Cesaris 1'32.546"	Lauda 1'32.782"	5. Alboreto	Tyrrell-Ford	51	+ 1 lap
Alboreto 1'33.134"	Watson 1'33.185"	6. Cheever	Ligier-Matra	51	+ 1 lap
Daly 1'33.333"	Cheever 1'33.377"	7. Mansell	Lotus-Ford	51	+ 1 lap
Jarier 1'33.531"	Warwick 1'33.628"	8. Rosberg	Williams-Ford	50	+ 2 laps
De Angelis 1'33.629"	Guerrero 1'34.058"	9. Salazar	ATS-Ford	50	+ 2 laps
Surer 1'34.343"	Henton 1'34.379"	10. De Cesaris	Alfa Romeo	50	+ 2 laps
Laffite 1'34.379"	Fabi 1'34.780"	11. Serra	Fittipaldi-Ford	49	+ 3 laps
Mansell 1'34.964"	Baldi 1'34.977"	12. Baldi	Arrows-Ford	49	+ 3 laps
Salazar 1'34.991"	Serra 1'35.230"				

NOT CLASSIFIED

Guerrero	Ensign-Ford	40	+ 12 laps

FASTEST LAP

Arnoux	Renault	1'33.619" 223.031 km/h

RETIREMENTS

De Angelis	Lotus-Ford	34	Throttle cable
Giacomelli	Alfa Romeo	32	Road-holding
Surer	Arrows-Ford	28	Engine
Prost	Renault	27	Injection
Lauda	McLaren-Ford	22	Road-holding/brakes
Jarier	Osella-Ford	10	Accident/rear wheel
Piquet	Brabham-BMW	8	Clutch
Patrese	Brabham-BMW	7	Clutch
Laffite	Ligier-Matra	6	Gearbox
Fabi	Toleman-Hart	2	Engine
Daly	Williams-Ford	1	Rear suspension Collision Guerrero
Henton	Tyrrell-Ford	0	Spin/collision
Warwick	Toleman-Hart	0	Spin/collision Henton

Monza race statistics.

Réné Arnoux celebrates a win. (© DPPI/Ren.)

STARTING GRID		RESULTS - Las Vegas (273,750 km)			
Prost 1'16.356"	Arnoux 1'16.786"	1. Alboreto	Tyrrell-Ford	75	1h41'56.888"
Alboreto 1'17.646"	Cheever 1'17.683"	2. Watson	McLaren-Ford	75	1h42'24.180"
Patrese 1'17.772"	Rosberg 1'17.886"	3. Cheever	Ligier-Matra	75	1h42'53.338"
Andretti 1'17.921"	(Tambay) (1'17.958")	4. Prost	Renault	75	1h43'05.536"
Watson 1'17.986"	Warwick 1'18.012"	5. Rosberg	Williams-Ford	75	1h43'08.263"
Laffite 1'18.056"	Piquet 1'18.275"	6. Daly	Williams-Ford	74	+ 1 lap
Lauda 1'18.333"	Daly 1'18.418"	7. Surer	Arrows-Ford	74	+ 1 lap
(Guerrero) (1'18.496")	Giacomelli 1'18.622"	8. Henton	Tyrrell-Ford	74	+ 1 lap
Surer 1'18.734"	De Cesaris 1'18.761"	9. De Cesaris	Alfa Romeo	73	+ 2 laps
Henton 1'18.765"	De Angelis 1'19.302"	10. Giacomelli	Alfa Romeo	73	+ 2 laps
Mansell 1'19.439"	Winkelhock 1'19.767"	11. Baldi	Arrows-Ford	73	+ 2 laps
Baldi 1'20.271"	Boesel 1'20.766"	12. Keegan	March-Ford	73	+ 2 laps
Keegan 1'21.180"	Byrne 1'21.555"	13. Boesel	March-Ford	69	+ 6 laps

NOT CLASSIFIED

Winkelhock	ATS-Ford	62	+ 13 laps

FASTEST LAP

Alboreto	Tyrrell-Ford	1'19.639" 164.994 km/h

RETIREMENTS

Lauda	McLaren-Ford	53	Engine
Byrne	Theodore-Ford	39	Spin
Warwick	Toleman-Hart	32	Sparking plugs
De Angelis	Lotus-Ford	28	Engine
Andretti	Ferrari	26	Rear suspension
Piquet	Brabham-BMW	26	Sparking plugs
Arnoux	Renault	20	Engine
Patrese	Brabham-BMW	17	Clutch
Mansell	Lotus-Ford	8	Collision Baldi Suspension failure
Laffite	Ligier-Matra	5	Ignition
Guerrero	Ensign-Ford	0	Engine (start)

Left to right: Réné Arnoux, Michel Têtu, Gérard Larrousse, Daniel Champion (chief mechanic), Alain Prost, and Jean-Pierre Menrath (engine technician).

Caesar's Palace race statistics.

Now up to 650bhp. (© Bernard Assett)

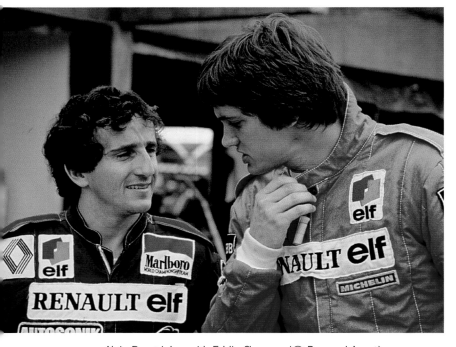

Alain Prost jokes with Eddie Cheever. (© Bernard Asset)

Fortunately, once this faulty part was modified it did become reliable through 1983. Renault also had a series of accidents and used four replacement chassis. In 1982, 32 starts were made (16 races x 2 cars), but they finished only 12 times; Prost won twice, as did Arnoux; Prost finished fourth in the championship. It was a case of what might have been!

1983: RE30C AND RE40

For 1983, the team wanted even more power and adequate reliability. Michel Têtu designed a new car – the RE40 – with a carbon-composite chassis, but Renault management decided that an interim RE30C would be used in the opening races. Power was now around 650bhp at 12,000rpm.

New rules: the governing body now required the cars to have a flat bottom within the confines of the wheelbase, with no ground-effect. Renault thought that everyone would be running interim cars, but, once again Brabham, for one, was ready with a car suited to the new regulations. The RE40 programme was accelerated. Jean-Pierre Boudy found ways to squeeze extra power from the ageing V6, modifying the turbo and developing a water-injection system for extra cooling that he had tested on his Renault 18 road car! It was to be a season which saw a lot of pit action with refuelling and tyre changes. Also some questionable fuel used by another team. François Guiter: "I know for certain that their use of that fuel cost us the championship."

> ## "New rules: the governing body now required the cars to have a flat bottom within the confines of the wheelbase, with no ground-effect."

Brazilian Grand Prix, Jacarepagua, 13 March 1983
Three interim RE30Cs set out for the first race at the Jacarepagua track. Prost started from P2, but new team-mate, Eddie Cheever, on P8 went out on lap 41. Prost finished 7th – not a good start.

US West Coast Grand Prix, Long Beach, 27 March 1983
Têtu's men had made up time, working hard to ready the new RE40 prototype for Long Beach. Poor grid positions, though, were not improved in the race and Cheever again went out, on lap 67 this time, with Prost trailing in 11th. Electrical problems were plaguing the new composite cars' early appearance; apparently they couldn't get a good earth!

STARTING GRID		RESULTS - Jacarepagua (316,953 km)			
Rosberg 1'34.526"	Prost 1'34.672"	1. Piquet	Brabham-BMW	63	1h48'27.731" 175.3 km/h
Tambay 1'34.758"	Piquet 1'35.114"	3. Lauda	McLaren-Ford	63	1h49'19.614"
Warwick 1'35.206"	Arnoux 1'35.547"	4. Laffite	Williams-Ford	63	1h49'41.682"
Patrese 1'35.958"	Cheever 1'36.051"	5. Tambay	Ferrari	63	1h49'45.848"
Lauda 1'36.054"	Baldi 1'36.126"	6. Surer	Arrows-Ford	63	1h49'45.938"
Alboreto 1'36.291"	Jarier 1'36.393"	7. Prost	Renault	62	+ 1 lap
De Angelis 1'36.454"	Guerrero 1'36.694"	8. Warwick	Toleman-Hart	62	+ 1 lap
Giacomelli 1'36.747"	Watson 1'36.977"	9. Serra	Arrows-Ford	62	+ 1 lap
Boesel 1'37.729"	Laffite 1'38.234"	10. Arnoux	Ferrari	62	+ 1 lap
Cecotto 1'38.378"	Surer 1'38.468"	11. Sullivan	Tyrrell-Ford	62	+ 1 lap
Sullivan 1'38.686"	Mansell 1'39.154"	12. Mansell	Lotus-Ford	61	+ 2 laps
Serra 1'39.965"	Fabi 1'40.309"	14. Cecotto	Theodore-Ford	60	+ 3 laps
Winkelhock 1'41.153"	Salazar 1'41.478"	15. Salazar	March-Ford	59	+ 4 laps
		16. Winkelhock	ATS-BMW	59	+ 4 laps

NOT CLASSIFIED

Guerrero	Theodore-Ford	53	+ 10 laps

DISQUALIFIED

(2) Rosberg*	Williams-Ford	63	1h48'48.362"
(13)De Angelis*	Lotus-Ford	60	+ 3 laps

FASTEST LAP

Piquet	Brabham-BMW		1'39.829" 181.426 km/h

RETIREMENTS

* Rosberg > disqualified for having been pushed after a pit-stop

* De Angelis > disqualified for having raced with a Ford engine after having been qualified with a Renault Turbo engine

Cheever	Renault	41	Turbo
Watson	McLaren-Ford	34	Engine
Boesel	March-Ford	25	Electrical
Baldi	Alfa Romeo	23	Collision Warwick
Jarier	Ligier-Ford	22	Rear suspension
Patrese	Brabham-BMW	19	Exhaust failure
Fabi	Osella-Ford	17	Engine
Giacomelli	Toleman-Hart	16	Spin
Alboreto	Tyrrell-Ford	7	Collision Baldi Oil radiator

Jacarepagua race statistics.

STARTING GRID		RESULTS - Long Beach (245,625 km)			
Tambay 1'26.117"	Arnoux 1'26.935"	1. Watson	McLaren-Ford	75	1h53'34.889" 129.720 km/h
Rosberg 1'27.145"	Laffite 1'27.818"	2. Lauda	McLaren-Ford	75	1h54'02.882"
De Angelis 1'27.982"	Warwick 1'28.130"	3. Arnoux	Ferrari	75	1h54'48.527"
Alboreto 1'28.425"	Prost 1'28.558"	4. Laffite	Williams-Ford	74	+ 1 lap
Sullivan 1'28.833"	Jarier 1'28.913"	5. Surer	Arrows-Ford	74	+ 1 lap
Patrese 1'28.958"	Jones 1'29.112"	6. Cecotto	Theodore-Ford	74	+ 1 lap
Mansell 1'29.167"	Giacomelli 1'29.266"	7. Boesel	March-Ford	73	+ 2 laps
Cheever 1'29.422"	Surer 1'29.521"	8. Sullivan	Tyrrell-Ford	73	+ 2 laps
Cecotto 1'29.559"	Guerrero 1'29.585"	9. Alboreto	Tyrrell-Ford	73	+ 2 laps
De Cesaris 1'29.603"	Piquet 1'30.034"	10. Patrese	Brabham-BMW	72	Distributeur
Baldi 1'30.070"	Watson 1'30.100"	11. Prost	Renault	72	+ 3 laps
Lauda 1'30.188"	Winkelhock 1'30.220"	12. Mansell	Lotus-Ford	72	+ 3 laps
Salazar 1'31.126"	Boesel 1'31.759"				

FASTEST LAP

Lauda	McLaren-Ford		1'28.330" 133.476 km/h

RETIREMENTS

Cheever	Renault	67	Gearbox
Jones	Arrows-Ford	58	Road-holding
Piquet	Brabham-BMW	51	Throttle
De Cesaris	Alfa Romeo	48	Gearbox
De Angelis	Lotus-Renault	29	Tyres
Guerrero	Theodore-Ford	27	Gearbox
Jarier	Ligier-Ford	26	Accident Rosberg
Giacomelli	Toleman-Hart	26	Flat battery
Baldi	Alfa Romeo	26	Accident
Tambay	Ferrari	25	Accident Rosberg
Rosberg	Williams-Ford	25	Collision Jarier
Salazar	March-Ford	25	Gearbox selector
Warwick	Toleman-Hart	11	Puncture / accident
Winkelhock	ATS-BMW	3	Accident

Long Beach race statistics.

French Grand Prix, Paul Ricard, 17 April 1983

Back to Europe for an early season French GP at Le Castellet on 17th April. This was much better: Prost was on pole and Cheever on P2. Prost went on to victory with Cheever 3rd on the podium.

San Marino Grand Prix, Imola, 1 May 1983

In the next race at Imola Cheever was to run carbon discs, but it was Prost who started from P4 and Cheever from P6, with Prost finishing 2nd in the race, Cheever having gone out on lap 2 due to turbo failure.

Monaco Grand Prix, 15 May 1983

For the Monaco GP Prost got the car on pole with Cheever on P3, but Prost was outpaced in the race and finished in third, whilst Cheever suffered electrical problems again and went out on lap 30. Interestingly, they both used an extended rear 'diffuser' that

Victory for Prost on home ground.

STARTING GRID		RESULTS - Le Castellet (313,740 km)			
Prost	Cheever	1. Prost	Renault	54	1h34'13.913"
1'36.672"	1'38.980"				199.866 km/h
Patrese	Arnoux	2. Piquet	Brabham-BMW	54	1h34'43.633"
1'39.104"	1'39.115"	3. Cheever	Renault	54	1h34'54.145"
De Angelis	Piquet	4. Tambay	Ferrari	54	1h35'20.793"
1'39.312"	1'39.601"	5. Rosberg	Williams-Ford	53	+ 1 lap
De Cesaris	Baldi	6. Laffite	Williams-Ford	53	+ 1 lap
1'39.611"	1'39.618"	7. Arnoux	Ferrari	53	+ 1 lap
Warwick	Winkelhock	8. Alboreto	Tyrrell-Ford	53	+ 1 lap
1'39.881"	1'40.233"	9. Jarier	Tyrrell-Ford	53	+ 1 lap
Tambay	Lauda	10. Surer	Arrows-Ford	53	+ 1 lap
1'40.393"	1'41.065"	11. Cecotto	Theodore-Ford	52	+ 2 laps
Giacomelli	Watson	12. De Cesaris	Alfa Romeo	50	+ 4 laps
1'41.775"	1'41.838"	13. Giacomelli	Toleman-Hart	49	Gearbox
Alboreto	Rosberg				
1'42.177"	1'42.450"	**FASTEST LAP**			
Cecotto	Mansell				
1'42.615"	1'42.650"	Prost	Renault		1'42.695"
Laffite	Jarier				203.671 km/h
1'42.678"	1'42.737"				
Surer	Guerrero	**RETIREMENTS**			
1'42.962"	1'43.367"				
Fabi	Sullivan	Boesel	March-Ford	47	Engine
1'43.411"	1'43.654"	Fabi	Osella-Ford	36	Engine
Boesel	Serra	Winkelhock	ATS-BMW	36	Exhaust
1'44.470"	1'44.778"	Lauda	McLaren-Ford	29	Rolling bearing
		Baldi	Alfa Romeo	28	Collision Winkelhock
		Serra	Arrows-Ford	26	Gearbox
		Guerrero	Theodore-Ford	23	Engine
		Sullivan	Tyrrell-Ford	21	Clutch
		De Angelis	Lotus-Renault	20	Electrical
		Patrese	Brabham-BMW	19	Engine/overheating
		Warwick	Toleman-Hart	14	Engine
		Mansell	Lotus-Ford	6	Foot pain
		Watson	McLaren-Ford	3	Throttle control

Paul Ricard race statistics.

Cheever in the pit lane. (© Bernard Asset)

Prost in the now very forward driving position typical of cars of that period.

STARTING GRID		RESULTS - Imola (302,400 km)			
Arnoux	Piquet	1. Tambay	Ferrari	60	1h37'52.460"
1'31.238"	1'31.964"				185.480 km/h
Tambay	Prost	2. Prost	Renault	60	1h38'41.241"
1'31.967"	1'32.138"	3. Arnoux	Ferrari	59	+ 1 lap
Patrese	Cheever	4. Rosberg	Williams-Ford	59	+ 1 lap
1'32.969"	1'33.450"	5. Watson	McLaren-Ford	59	+ 1 lap
Winkelhock	De Cesaris	6. Surer	Arrows-Ford	59	+ 1 lap
1'33.470"	1'33.528"	7. Laffite	Williams-Ford	59	+ 1 lap
De Angelis	Baldi	8. Serra	Arrows-Ford	58	+ 2 laps
1'34.332"	1'35.000"	9. Boesel	Ligier-Ford	58	+ 2 laps
Rosberg	Surer	10. Baldi	Alfa Romeo	57	Engine
1'35.086"	1'35.411"	11. Winkelhock	ATS-BMW	57	+ 3 laps
Alboreto	Warwick	12. Mansell	Lotus-Ford	56	Accident/Rear wing
1'35.525"	1'35.676"	13. Patrese	Brabham-BMW	54	Accident
Mansell	Laffite				
1'35.703"	1'35.707"	**FASTEST LAP**			
Giacomelli	Lauda				
1'35.969"	1'36.099"	Patrese	Brabham-BMW		1'34.437"
Jarier	Serra				192.128 km/h
1'36.116"	1'36.258"				
Guerrero	Sullivan	**RETIREMENTS**			
1'36.324"	1'36.359"				
Cecotto	Watson	De Cesaris	Alfa Romeo	46	Differential
1'36.638"	1'36.652"	De Angelis	Lotus-Renault	44	Road-holding
Boesel	Fabi	Piquet	Brabham-BMW	42	Engine
1'37.322"	1'37.711"	Jarier	Ligier-Ford	40	Radiator
		Sullivan	Tyrrell-Ford	37	Accident
		Warwick	Toleman-Hart	27	Accident
		Fabi	Osella-Ford	20	Accident
		Giacomelli	Toleman-Hart	21	Rear suspension
		Lauda	McLaren-Ford	11	Accident
		Cecotto	Theodore-Ford	11	Accident
		Alboreto	Tyrrell-Ford	10	Accident/Rear suspension
		Guerrero	Theodore-Ford	3	Collision Sullivan
		Cheever	Renault	2	Turbo

Imola race statistics.

STARTING GRID		Results - Monaco (251,712 km)			
Arnoux 1'25.182"	**Prost** 1'24.840"	1. Rosberg	Williams-Ford	76	1h56'38.121" 129.586 km/h
Tambay 1'26.298"	Cheever 1'26.279"	2. Piquet	Brabham-BMW	76	1h56'56.596"
Piquet 1'27.273"	Rosberg 1'26.307"	3. Prost	Renault	76	1h57'09.487"
Laffite 1'27.726"	De Cesaris 1'27.680"	4. Tambay	Ferrari	76	1h57'42.418"
Warwick 1'28.017"	Jarier 1'27.906"	5. Sullivan	Tyrrell-Ford	74	+ 2 laps
Surer 1'28.346"	Alboreto 1'28.256"	6. Baldi	Alfa Romeo	74	+ 2 laps
Mansell 1'28.721"	**Baldi** 1'28.639"	7. Serra	Arrows-Ford	74	+ 2 laps
Winkelhock 1'28.975"	Serra 1'28.784"	**FASTEST LAP**			
Boesel 1'29.222"	Patrese 1'29.200"	Piquet	Brabham-BMW		1'27.283" 136.603 km/h
Sullivan 1'29.530"	De Angelis 1'29.518"	**RETIREMENTS**			
		Patrese	Brabham-BMW	64	Electrical
		Laffite	Williams-Ford	54	Gearbox
		Warwick	Toleman-Hart	50	Collision Surer
		De Angelis	Lotus-Renault	50	Transmission shaft
		Surer	Arrows-Ford	49	Collision Warwick
		Jarier	Ligier-Ford	33	Suspension hydraulic pump
		Cheever	Renault	30	Electrical/Engine
		De Cesaris	Alfa Romeo	14	Gearbox
		Arnoux	Ferrari	6	Accident
		Boesel	March-Ford	3	Collision Winkelhock
		Winkelhock	ATS-BMW	3	Collision Boesel
		Alboreto	Tyrrell-Ford	0	Collision Mansell
		Mansell	Lotus-Ford	0	Collision Alboreto

Monaco race statistics.

went the full width of the car, terminating below the trailing edge of the rear wing. Renault claimed this was to reduce exhaust temperature and thus avoid overheating the tyres, but, as Bernard Dudot now says, "Making good use of the heat from the twin turbos on each side of the car allowed us to create a special exhaust system which, aided by the huge diffuser, gave more grip at the rear of the car." Other teams were not so sure and protested about it at Spa, saying that the system had a movable aerodynamic device (the exhaust gas!), but the FIA declared the system legal and everyone tried to replicate it in the races that followed Spa ...

Belgian Grand Prix, Spa, 22 May 1983
At Spa, Prost again put the RE40 on pole and went on to win the race, with Cheever finishing 3rd. Jean Sage had logistical problems to deal with, as the team was off again across the Atlantic to the Detroit GP on 5 June.

Prost in full flight.

STARTING GRID		RESULTS - Spa-Francorchamps (278,620 km)			
Prost 2'04.615"	Tambay 2'04.626"	1. Prost	Renault	40	1h27'11.502" 192.729 km/h
De Cesaris 2'04.840"	Piquet 2'05.628"	2. Tambay	Ferrari	40	1h27'34.684"
Arnoux 2'05.737"	Patrese 2'06.137"	3. Cheever	Renault	40	1h27'51.371"
Winkelhock 2'06.264"	Cheever 2'07.294"	4. Piquet	Brabham-BMW	40	1h27'53.797"
Rosberg 2'07.975"	Surer 2'08.587"	5. Rosberg	Williams-Ford	40	1h28'01.982"
Laffite 2'09.153"	Baldi 2'09.225"	6. Laffite	Williams-Ford	40	1h28'44.609"
De Angelis 2'09.310"	Guerrero 2'09.322"	7. Warwick	Toleman-Hart	40	1h29'10.041"
Lauda 2'09.475"	Giacomelli 2'09.706"	8. Giacomelli	Toleman-Hart	40	1h29'49.775"
Alboreto 2'09.739"	Boutsen 2'09.876"	9. De Angelis	Lotus-Renault	39	+ 1 lap
Mansell 2'09.924"	Watson 2'10.318"	10. Cecotto	Theodore-Ford	39	+ 1 lap
Jarier 2'11.354"	Warwick 2'11.474"	11. Surer	Arrows-Ford	39	+ 1 lap
Sullivan 2'11.683"	Fabi 2'11.734"	12. Sullivan	Tyrrell-Ford	39	+ 1 lap
Cecotto 2'11.860"	Boesel 2'12.310"	13. Boesel	Ligier-Ford	39	+ 1 lap
		14. Alboreto	Tyrrell-Ford	38	+ 2 laps
		FASTEST LAP			
		De Cesaris	Alfa Romeo		2'07.493" 196.218 km/h
		RETIREMENTS			
		Lauda	McLaren-Ford	33	Engine
		Mansell	Lotus-Ford	30	Gearbox
		De Cesaris	Alfa Romeo	25	Engine
		Guerrero	Theodore-Ford	23	Engine
		Arnoux	Ferrari	22	Engine
		Fabi	Osella-Ford	19	Rear suspension
		Winkelhock	ATS-BMW	18	Rear wheel off
		Watson	McLaren-Ford	8	Collision Jarier
		Jarier	Ligier-Ford	8	Collision Watson
		Boutsen	Arrows-Ford	4	Rear suspension
		Baldi	Alfa Romeo	3	Throttle
		Patrese	Brabham-BMW	0	Engine

Spa race statistics.

STARTING GRID · RESULTS

Spy in the sky.

STARTING GRID		RESULTS

Arnoux	Prost
1'28.729"	1'28.830"
Piquet	Tambay
1'28.887"	1'28.992"
Patrese	Cheever
1'29.549"	1'29.863"
Winkelhock	De Cesaris
1'30.966"	1'31.173"
Rosberg	Giacomelli
1'31.840"	1'31.586"
De Angelis	Warwick
1'31.822"	1'32.116"
Laffite	Surer
1'32.185"	1'32.540"
Boutsen	Jarier
1'32.576"	1'32.642"
Alboreto	Mansell
1'33.175"	1'33.588"
Lauda	Watson
1'33.671"	1'33.705"
Guerrero	Sullivan
1'33.721"	1'33.791"
Cecotto	Boesel
1'34.314"	1'34.486"
Fabi	Baldi
1'34.544"	1'34.755"

RESULTS

1. Arnoux	Ferrari	70	1h48'31.838"
			170.661 km/h
2. Cheever	Renault	70	1h49'13.867"
3. Tambay	Ferrari	70	1h49'24.448"
4. Rosberg	Wiliams-Ford	70	1h49'48.886"
5. Prost	Renault	69	+ 1 lap
6. Watson	Mclaren-Ford	69	+ 1 lap
7. Boutsen	Arrows-Ford	69	+ 1 lap
8. Alboreto	Tyrrell-Ford	68	+ 2 laps
9. Winkelhock	ATS-BMW	67	+ 3 laps
10. Baldi	Alfa Romeo	67	+ 3 laps

DISQUALIFIED (unconform weight)

(9) Sullivan	Tyrrell-Ford	68	+ 2 laps

FASTEST LAP

Tambay	Ferrari	1'30.851"
		174.747 km/h

RETIREMENTS

Patrese	Brabham-BMW	57	Gearbox
Warwick	Toleman-Hart	47	Turbo
Giacomelli	Toleman-Hart	43	Overheating
Mansell	Lotus-Ford	43	Road-holding
De Cesaris	Alfa Romeo	43	Engine
Laffite	Williams-Ford	38	Gearbox
Boesel	March-Ford	32	Rolling bearing
Guerrero	Theodore-Ford	27	Engine
Fabi	Osella-Alfa Romeo	27	Engine
Cecotto	Theodore-Ford	18	Differential
Piquet	Brabham-BMW	16	Throttle cable
Lauda	McLaren-Ford	11	Spun off
De Angelis	Lotus-Renault	2	Throttle cable
Jarier	Ligier-Ford	1	Gearbox
Surer	Arrows-Ford	1	Transmission

Montreal race statistics.

STARTING GRID	RESULTS - Detroit (241,380 km)

Arnoux	Piquet
1'44.734"	1'44.933"
Tambay	De Angelis
1'45.991"	1'46.258"
Surer	Alboreto
1'46.745"	1'47.013"
Cheever	De Cesaris
1'47.334"	1'47.453"
Warwick	Boutsen
1'47.534"	1'47.586"
Guerrero	Rosberg
1'47.701"	1'47.728"
Prost	Mansell
1'47.855"	1'48.395"
Patrese	Sullivan
1'48.537"	1'48.648"
Giacomelli	Lauda
1'48.785"	1'48.992"
Jarier	Laffite
1'48.994"	1'49.245"
Watson	Winkelhock
1'49.250"	1'49.466"
Boesel	Ghizani
1'49.540"	1'49.885"
Baldi	Cecotto
1'49.916"	1'51.709"

RESULTS - Detroit (241,380 km)

1. Alboreto	Tyrrell-Ford	60	1h50'53.669"
			129.852 km/h
2. Rosberg	Williams-Ford	60	1h51'01.371"
3. Watson	McLaren-Ford	60	1h51'02.952"
4. Piquet	Brabham-BMW	60	1h52'05.854"
5. Laffite	Williams-Ford	60	1h52'26.272"
6. Mansell	Lotus-Ford	59	+ 1 lap
7. Boutsen	Arrows-Ford	59	+ 1 lap
8. Prost	Renault	59	+ 1 lap
9. Giacomelli	Toleman-Hart	59	+ 1 lap
10. Boesel	March-Ford	58	+ 2 laps
11. Surer	Arrows-Ford	58	+ 2 laps
12. Baldi	Alfa Romeo	56	+ 4 laps

FASTEST LAP

Watson	McLaren-Ford	1'47.668"
		134.513 km/h

RETIREMENTS

Lauda	McLaren-Ford	49	Amortisseur
Guerrero	Theodore-Ford	38	Gearbox selector
Cecotto	Theodore-Ford	34	Gearbox selector
De Cesaris	Alfa Romeo	33	Turbo
Arnoux	Ferrari	31	Electrical
Sullivan	Tyrrell-Ford	30	Electrical
Jarier	Ligier-Ford	29	Wheel
Winkelhock	ATS-BMW	26	Accident
Warwick	Toleman-Hart	25	Engine/Water leak
Patrese	Brabham-BMW	24	Brakes
De Angelis	Lotus-Renault	5	Transmission
Cheever	Renault	4	Drive shaft
Ghinzani	Osella-Alfa Romeo	4	Overheating
Tambay	Ferrari	0	Stall (start)

Detroit race statistics.

Prost in Canada.

US East Coast Grand Prix, Detroit, 5 June 1983
From poor grid positions the pair struggled. Prost finished 8th, Cheever going out with a broken driveshaft on lap 4.

Canadian Grand Prix, Montreal, 12 June 1983
The Canadian GP was held the following week and Prost managed P2 on the grid to Arnoux, who was now in the Ferrari for 1983. In the race Cheever finished a credible second from a P6 grid slot, with Prost coming in 5th.

British Grand Prix, Silverstone, 16 July 1983
It was then back to Europe and this time to Silverstone. RE40/04 was to start from P3 on the grid for Prost, who won the race, whilst Cheever's 05 engine failed him on lap 3 (head gasket!). Prost's points were starting to pile up: could this be the year of that championship?

German Grand Prix, Hockenheim, 7 August 1983
Three weeks later, in Germany, Prost started from 5th and Cheever

STARTING GRID		RESULTS - Silverstone (316,173 km)			
Arnoux 1'09.462"	Tambay 1'10.104"	1 Prost	Renault	67	1h24'39.780" 224.001 km/h
Prost 1'10.170"	De Angelis 1'10.771"	2. Piquet	Brabham-BMW	67	1h24'58.941"
Patrese 1'10.881"	Piquet 1'10.933"	3. Tambay	Ferrari	67	1h25'06.026"
Cheever 1'11.055"	Winkelhock 1'11.687"	4. Mansell	Lotus-Renault	67	1h25'18.732"
De Cesaris 1'12.150"	Warwick 1'12.528"	5. Arnoux	Ferrari	67	1h25'38.654"
Baldi 1'12.860"	Giacomelli 1'13.422"	6. Lauda		66	+ 1 lap
Rosberg 1'13.755"	Johansson 1'13.962"	7. Baldi		66	+ 1 lap
Lauda 1'14.267"	Alboreto 1'14.651"	8. De Cesaris		66	+ 1 lap
Boutsen 1'14.964"	Mansell 1'15.133"	9. Watson		66	+ 1 lap
Surer 1'15.135"	Laffite 1'15.234"	10. Jarier		65	+ 2 laps
Guerrero 1'15.317"	Boesel 1'15.386"	11. Rosberg		65	+ 2 laps
Sullivan 1'15.449"	Watson 1'15.609"	12. Laffite		65	+ 2 laps
Jarier 1'15.767"	Ghinzani 1'16.544"	13. Alboreto		65	+ 2 laps
		14. Sullivan		65	+ 2 laps
		15. Boutsen		64	+ 3 laps
		16. Guerrero		64	+ 3 laps
		17. Surer		64	+ 3 laps

MEILLEUR TOUR EN COURSE		
Prost	Renault	1'14.212" 228.917 km/h

RETIREMENTS			
Winkelhock	ATS-BMW	49	Overheating
Boesel	March-Ford	48	Hydraulic suspension leak
Ghinzani	Osella-Alfa Romeo	46	Fuel pressure
Warwick	Toleman-Hart	27	Gearbox
Patrese	Brabham-BMW	9	Turbo
Johansson	Spirit-Honda	5	Fuel pump
Cheever	Renault	3	Engine Head gasket
Giacomelli	Toleman-Hart	3	Turbo
De Angelis	Lotus-Renault	1	Ignition

Silverstone race statistics.

STARTING GRID		RESULTS - Hockenheim (305,865 km)			
Tambay 1'49.328"	Arnoux 1'49.435"	1. Arnoux	Ferrari	45	1h27'10.319"
De Cesaris 1'50.845"	Piquet 1'51.082"	2. De Cesaris	Alfa Romeo	45	1h28'20.971"
Prost 1'51.228"	Cheever 1'51.540"	3. Patrese	Brabham-BMW	45	1h28'54.412"
Baldi 1'51.867"	Patrese 1'52.105"	4. Prost	Renault	45	1h29'11.069"
Warwick 1'54.199'	Giacomelli 1'54.648"	Lauda	McLaren-Ford	44	Disqualified
De Angelis 1'54.831"	Rosberg 1'55.289"	5. Watson	McLaren-Ford	44	+ 1 lap
Johansson 1'55.870"	Boutsen 1'56.015"	6. Laffite	Williams-Ford	44	+ 1 lap
Laffite 1'56.318"	Alboreto 1'56.398"	7. Surer	Arrows-Ford	44	+ 1 lap
Mansell 1'56.490"	Lauda 1'56.730"	8. Jarier	Ligier-Ford	44	+ 1 lap
Jarier 1'57.018"	Surer 1'57.072"	9. Boutsen	Arrows-Ford	44	+ 1 lap
Sullivan 1'57.426"	Cecotto 1'57.744"	10. Rosberg	Williams-Ford	44	+ 1 lap
Watson 1'57.776"	Guerrero 1'57.790"	11. Cecotto	Theodore-Ford	44	+ 1 lap
Boesel 1'58.413"	Ghinzani 1'58.473"	12. Sullivan	Tyrrell-Ford	43	+ 2 laps
		13. Piquet	Brabham-BMW	42	Fire Fuel pressure

FASTEST LAP		
Arnoux	Ferrari	1'53.938" 214.759 km/h

RETIREMENTS			
Cheever	Renault	38	Fuel pump
Ghinzani	Osella-Alfa Romeo	34	Engine
Boesel	March-Ford	27	Engine
Baldi	Alfa Romeo	24	Engine
Giacomelli	Toleman-Hart	19	Turbo
Warwick	Toleman-Hart	17	Engine
Johansson	Spirit-Honda	11	Engine
Tambay	Ferrari	11	Engine
De Angelis	Lotus-Renault	10	Overheating
Alboreto	Tyrrell-Ford	4	Fuel pump
Mansell	Lotus-Renault	1	Engine
Guerrero	Theodore-Ford	0	Engine

Hockenheim race statistics.

Cheever in for service.

Zeltweg race statistics

STARTING GRID

Piquet 1'27.612"	Patrese 1'27.971"
Prost 1'28.864"	Tambay 1'29.522"
Arnoux 1'30.261"	Rosberg 1'30.300"
De Angelis 1'31.626"	1'31.814"
Daly 1'32.062"	Lauda 1'32.131"
De Cesaris 1'32.308"	Mansell 1'32.881"
Giacomelli 1'32.950"	Laffite 1'32.957"
Warwick 1'33.208"	Guerrero 1'33.555"
Fabi 1'33.971"	Watson 1'34.164"
Henton 1'34.184"	Serra 1'34.187"
Surer 1'34.422"	Cheever 1'34.620"
Baldi 1'34.715"	Keegan 1'34.770"
Winkelhock 1'34.984"	Byrne 1'34.985"

RESULTS - Zeltweg (314,926 km)

1. Prost	Renault	53	1h24'32.745" 223.494 km/h
2. Arnoux	Ferrari	53	+ 6.835"
3. Piquet	Brabham-BMW	53	+ 27.659"
4. Cheever	Renault	53	+ 28.395"
5. Mansell	Lotus-Renault	52	+ 1 lap
6. Lauda	McLaren-Ford	50	+ 2 laps
7. Jarier	Ligier-Ford	50	+ 2 laps
8. Rosberg	Williams-Ford	50	+ 2 laps
9. Watson	McLaren-Ford	50	+ 2 laps
10. Fabi	Osella-Alfa Romeo	49	+ 3 laps
11. Ghinzani	Osella-Alfa Romeo	48	+ 4 laps
12. Johansson	Spirit-Honda	47	+ 5 laps
13. Boutsen	Arrows-Ford	47	+ 5 laps

FASTEST LAP

Prost	Renault	1'33.961" 227.660 km/h

RETIREMENTS

Winkelhock	ATS-BMW	34	Engine
De Cesaris	Alfa Romeo	31	Fuel pressure
Tambay	Ferrari	30	Ignition
Patrese	Brabham-BMW	30	Turbo
Guerrero	Theodore-Ford	26	Gearbox
Laffite	Williams-Ford	20	Road-holding
Baldi	Alfa Romeo	14	Engine
Alboreto	Tyrrell-Ford	9	Accident
Warwick	Toleman-Hart	3	Turbo
Giacomelli	Toleman-Hart	2	Collision
Sullivan	Tyrrell-Ford	1	Collision
Surer	Arrows-Ford	1	Collision
De Angelis	Lotus-Renault	1	Collision

Zeltweg race statistics.

Zandvoort race statistics

STARTING GRID

Piquet 1'15.630"	Tambay 1'16.370"
De Angelis 1'16.411"	Prost 1'16.611"
Mansell 1'16.711"	Patrese 1'16.940"
Warwick 1'17.198"	De Cesaris 1'17.233"
Winkelhock 1'17.306"	Arnoux 1'17.397"
Cheever 1'17.676"	Baldi 1'17.887"
Giacomelli 1'17.902"	Surer 1'17.696"
Watson 1'19.787"	Johansson 1'19.966"
Laffite 1'19.979"	Alboreto 1'20.149"
Lauda 1'20.169"	Guerrero 1'20.190"
Boutsen 1'20.245"	Jarier 1'20.247"
Rosberg 1'20.391"	Boesel 1'20.660"
Fabi 1'20.815"	Sullivan 1'20.842"

RESULTS - Zandvoort (306,144 km)

1. Arnoux	Ferrari	72	1h38'41.950" 186.105 km/h
2. Tambay	Ferrari	72	1h39'02.789"
3. Watson	McLaren-Ford	72	1h39'25.691"
4. Warwick	Toleman-Hart	72	1h39'58.789"
5. Baldi	Alfa Romeo	72	1h40'06.242"
6. Alboreto	Tyrrell-Ford	71	+ 1 lap
7. Johansson	Spirit-Ford	70	+ 2 laps
8. Surer	Arrows-Ford	70	+ 2 laps
9. Patrese	Brabham-BMW	70	+ 2 laps
10. Boesel	March-Ford	70	+ 2 laps
11. Fabi	Osella-Alfa Romeo	68	Engine
12. Guerrero	Theodore-Ford	68	+ 4 laps
13. Giacomelli	Toleman-Hart	68	+ 4 laps
14. Boutsen	Arrows-Ford	68	Engine

FASTEST LAP

Arnoux	Ferrari	1'19.863" 191.668 km/h

RETIREMENTS

Rosberg	Williams-Ford	53	Engine/ignition
Piquet	Brabham-BMW	41	Collision Prost
Prost	Renault	41	Accident
Cheever	Renault	39	Electrical/turbo
Laffite	Williams-Ford	37	Road-holding
Mansell	Lotus-Renault	26	Spin
Lauda	McLaren-TAG Porsche	25	Brakes
Sullivan	Tyrrell-Ford	20	Engine
De Angelis	Lotus-Renault	12	Fuel pressure
De Cesaris	Alfa Romeo	5	Engine
Jarier	Ligier-Ford	3	Hydraulic suspension
Winkelhock	ATS-BMW	50	Black flag (DQ).
(for having not respected the start procedure)			

Zandvoort race statistics.

6th. Prost finished 4th and Cheever went out yet again, this time with a fuel pump problem on lap 38. At this circuit Renault had gone back to the shorter rear diffuser where ultimate downforce was of secondary importance to low drag and top speed.

Austrian Grand Prix, Zeltweg, 14 August 1983

Just one week later in Austria, Prost was to win again from P3 on the grid, with Cheever a remarkable 4th from 21st on the grid! For Prost, the championship win now looked a distinct possibility.

Dutch Grand Prix, Zandvoort, 28 August 1983

The Dutch race at Zandvoort brought a reversal in fortunes; it was a disaster, as both cars failed.

Italian Grand Prix, Monza, 11 September 1983

Monza brought frustration as Prost had turbo failure on lap 26, though Cheever saved the day for Renault's championship hopes with the RE40, coming in 3rd. Interestingly, Boudy had introduced the single-nozzle 'super-cooling' process that was

used in qualifying, which cooled both sides of the intercooler matrix in an effort to come up with even more power.

European Grand Prix, Brands Hatch, 25 September 1983

A second UK race saw Brands Hatch hosting the European Grand Prix, in which Prost, although out-qualified by Cheever, was to finish in 2nd place with Cheever back in 10th.

South African Grand Prix, Kyalami, 15 October 1983

The last race spelt doom as Prost failed to finish – turbo failure again on lap 35. Cheever came home 6th, one lap down on the winner, Patrese, in the Brabham. Piquet (Brabham) took the title win and Prost the consolation prize of second, missing the title by just 2 points. There was more to this than met the eye, however, as Elf felt there was a question mark over the Brabham's fuel, and raised the matter with Renault management.

To the viewing public, however, it was once again a case of "what might have been," most of the technical failures this time

Monza race statistics.

STARTING GRID		RESULTS - Monza (301,600 km)			
Patrese	Tambay	1. Piquet	Brabham-BMW	52	1h23'10.880"
1'29.122"	1'29.650"				
Arnoux	Piquet	2. Arnoux	Ferrari	52	1h23'21.092"
1'29.901"	1'30.202"	3. Cheever	Renault	52	1h23'29.492"
Prost	De Cesaris	4. Tambay	Ferrari	52	1h23'29.903"
1'31.144"	1'31.272"	5. De Angelis	Lotus-Renault	52	1h24'04.560"
Cheever	De Angelis	6. Warwick	Toleman-Hart	52	1h24'24.228"
1'31.564"	1'31.628"	7. Giacomelli	Toleman-Hart	52	1h24'44.802"
Winkelhock	Baldi	8. Mansell	Lotus-Renault	52	1h24'46.915"
1'31.959"	1'32.407"	9. Jarier	Ligier-Ford	51	+ 1 lap
Mansell	Warwick	10. Surer	Arrows-Ford	51	+ 1 lap
1'32.423"	1'32.677"	11. Rosberg	Williams-Ford	51	+ 1 lap
Lauda	Giacomelli	12. Cecotto	Theodore-Ford	50	+ 2 laps
1'33.133"	1'33.384"	13. Guerrero	Theodore-Ford	50	+ 2 laps
Watson	Rosberg				
1'34.705"	1'35.291"				
Johansson	Boutsen	**FASTEST LAP**			
1'35.483"	1'35.624"				
Jarier	Surer	Piquet	Brabham-BMW		1'34.431"
1'36.220"	1'36.435"				221.114 km/h
Guerrero	Sullivan				
1'36.619"	1'36.644"	**RETIREMENTS**			
Ghinzani	Alboreto				
1'36.647"	1'36.788"	Fabi	Osella-Alfa Romeo	46	Oil circuit
Fabi	Cecotto	Sullivan	Tyrrell-Ford	44	Fuel pump
1'36.834"	1'37.105"	Johansson	Spirit-Honda	42	Engine
		Winkelhock	ATS-BMW	35	Exhaust failure
		Alboreto	Tyrrell-Ford	29	Clutch
		Prost	Renault	26	Turbo
		Lauda	McLaren-TAG Porsche	24	Electrical
		Watson	McLaren-TAG Porsche	13	Engine
		Ghinzani	Osella-Alfa Romeo	10	Gearbox
		Baldi	Alfa Romeo	5	Turbo
		Johansson	Spirit-Honda	4	Fuel feed
		Patrese	Brabham-BMW	3	Electrical/engine
		De Cesaris	Alfa Romeo	2	Spin

Prost, frustrated by turbo failure.

coming from the turbo. It looked like Renault's best-ever chance of the championship title had evaporated, despite 15 races, 30 starts, 3 poles, 3 wins and 9 podium places. But let's hear from François Guiter: "Our engineer, Jean-Claude Fayard, told me he was sure that the fuel Brabham was using, invented by a German chemist, was illegal. All we had to do was to put in a complaint and I asked Renault to do so, but they didn't want to; there was a bigger picture and the image of the Régie would be on show." So, not only did Renault lose the last race, but a furious Prost lost the championship by two points. He left Renault.

"It looked like Renault's best-ever chance of the championship title had evaporated, despite 15 races, 30 starts, 3 poles, 3 wins and 9 podium places."

François Guiter again: "Several months later, the boss of the Brabham stable at the time allowed himself the indulgence of admitting to me that their fuel was indeed 'suspect,' but he said

Brands Hatch race statistics

STARTING GRID		RESULTS - Brands Hatch (GB) (319,732 km)			
De Angelis 1'12.092"	Patrese 1'12.458"	1. Piquet	Brabham-BMW	76	1h36'45.865" 198.172 km/h
Mansell 1'12.623"	Piquet 1'12.724"	2. Prost	Renault	76	1h36'52.436"
Arnoux 1'13.113"	Tambay 1'13.157"	3. Mansell	Lotus-Renault	76	1h37'16.180"
Cheever 1'13.253"	Prost 1'13.342"	4. De Cesaris	Alfa Romeo	76	1h37'20.261"
Winkelhock 1'13.679"	Watson 1'13.783"	5. Warwick	Toleman-Hart	76	1h37'30.780"
Warwick 1'13.855"	Giacomelli 1'13.949"	6. Giacomelli	Toleman-Hart	76	1h37'38.055"
Lauda 1'13.972"	De Cesaris 1'14.403"	7. Patrese	Brabham-BMW	76	1h37'58.549"
Baldi 1'14.727"	Rosberg 1'14.917"	8. Winkelhock	ATS-BMW	75	+ 1 lap
Surer 1'15.436"	Boutsen 1'15.428"	9. Arnoux	Ferrari	75	+ 1 lap
Johansson 1'15.912"	Sullivan 1'16.640"	10. Cheever	Renault	75	+ 1 lap
Guerrero 1'16.769"	Jarier 1'16.880"	11. Boutsen	Arrows-Ford	75	+ 1 lap
Boesel 1'17.177"	Ghinzani 1'17.408"	12. Guerrero	Theodore-Ford	75	+ 1 lap
Palmer 1'17.432"	Alboreto 1'17.456"	13. Palmer	Williams-Ford	74	+ 2 laps
		14. Johansson	Spirit-Honda	74	+ 2 laps
		15. Boesel	Ligier-Ford	73	+ 3 laps

FASTEST LAP

Mansell	Lotus-Renault	1'14.342" 203.723 km/h

RETIREMENTS

Tambay	Ferrari	67	Spin
Alboreto	Tyrrell-Ford	65	Engine
Ghinzani	Osella-Alfa Romeo	63	Not classified
Surer	Arrows-Ford	51	Engine
Rosberg	Williams-Ford	43	Engine
Baldi	Alfa Romeo	39	Clutch
Watson	McLaren-TAG Porsche	36	Accident/wing
Sullivan	Tyrrell-Ford	27	Fire/oil circuit
Lauda	McLaren-TAG Porsche	26	Engine
De Angelis	Lotus-Renault	13	Engine
Jarier	Ligier-Ford	0	Transmission (start)

Brands Hatch race statistics.

Kyalami race statistics

STARTING GRID		RESULTS - Kyalami (316,008 km)			
Tambay 1'06.554"	Piquet 1'06.792"	1. Patrese	Brabham-BMW	77	1h33'25.708" 202.939 km/h
Patrese 1'07.001"	Arnoux 1'07.105"	2. De Cesaris	Alfa Romeo	77	1h33'35.027"
Prost 1'07.186"	Rosberg 1'07.256"	3. Piquet	Brabham-BMW	77	1h33'47.677"
Mansell 1'07.643"	Winkelhock 1'07.682"	4. Warwick	Toleman-Hart	76	+ 1 lap
De Cesaris 1'07.759"	Laffite 1'07.931"	5. Rosberg	Williams-Honda	76	+ 1 lap
De Angelis 1'07.937"	Lauda 1'07.974"	6. Cheever	Renault	76	+ 1 lap
Warwick 1'08.061"	Cheever 1'08.069"	7. Sullivan	Tyrrell-Ford	75	+ 2 laps
Watson 1'08.328"	Giacomelli 1'08.350"	8. Surer	Arrows-Ford	75	+ 2 laps
Baldi 1'08.628"	Alboreto 1'11.096"	9. Boutsen	Arrows-Ford	74	+ 3 laps
Sullivan 1'11.382"	Boutsen 1'11.658"	10. Jarier	Ligier-Ford	73	+ 4 laps
Jarier 1'12.017"	Surer 1'12.049"	11. Lauda	McLaren-Ford	71	Electrical
Boesel 1'12.745"	Acheson 1'13.352"	12. Acheson	March-Ford	71	Engine
Fabi 1'13.656"	Ghinzani 1'14.903"				

FASTEST LAP

Piquet	Brabham-BMW	1'09.948" 211.219 km/h

RETIREMENTS

Mansell	Lotus-Renault	68	Gearbox
Boesel	March-Ford	66	Engine
Alboreto	Tyrrell-Ford	60	Engine
Tambay	Ferrari	56	Turbo
Giacomelli	Toleman-Hart	56	Turbo/feu
Prost	Renault	35	Turbo
Fabi	Osella-Alfa Romeo	28	Engine
De Angelis	Lotus-Renault	20	Ignition
Watson	McLaren-TAG Porsche	18	Disqualified
Arnoux	Ferrari	9	Engine
Baldi	Alfa Romeo	5	Engine
Ghinzani	Osella-Alfa Romeo	1	Engine
Winkelhock	ATS-BMW	1	Engine
Laffite	Williams-Honda	1	Accident

Kyalami race statistics.

that it didn't give them such a great advantage. Not very much – only 40bhp!"

1984 – THE RE50 CARS

Prost, on leaving Renault, joined McLaren. Renault Sport had to find a new driver line-up, and signed Derek Warwick to join Patrick Tambay in a reconstructed Renault team to drive a new Têtu-designed model, the RE50. Dudot had not been happy with the KKK turbochargers in 1983, so decided to go for the larger American Garrett AiResearch model for 1984. There was also a change in manufacturing plants: Bernard Dudot's engine plant, now with 100 employees, completely took over the original premises at Viry-Châtillon, while Jean Sage moved with the chassis, gearbox and race teams to new premises at Evry.

Alloy was now used for the engine blocks in all cases, though the basic design had remained the same since the very start. But costs were high, compared with the previous iron blocks that never needed changing, as these had to be changed twice a year.

Refuelling during a race had been banned, and several teams tried cooling the fuel in order to get more into the tanks, which were now restricted to 220 litres. By now, the Renault turbo engine was giving 750bhp.

Brazilian Grand Prix, Jacarepagua, 25 March 1984

The unraced prototype 01 became a show car, and so it was RE50/02, 03 and 04 which were seen at the opening race in Brazil.

Warwick started on P3 and Tambay on P8. In the race, Tambay finished 8th and Warwick went out with suspension failure on lap 51.

South African Grand Prix, Kyalami, 7 April 1984

Kyalami: Warwick was to start from 9th place, and Tambay got near the front with 4th spot on the grid. However, it was Warwick who claimed 3rd place on the podium, whilst Tambay went out with ignition problems on lap 66.

Patrick Tambay and Derek Warwick.

STARTING GRID		RESULTS - Kyalami (307,800 km)			
Piquet 1'04.871"	Rosberg 1'05.058"	1. Lauda	McLaren-TAG Porsche	75	1h29'23.430" 206.599 km/h
Mansell 1'05.125"	Tambay 1'05.339"	2. Prost	McLaren-TAG Porsche	75	1h30'29.380"
Prost 1'05.254"	Fabi 1'05.923"	3. Warwick	Renault	74	+ 1 lap
De Angelis 1'05.953"	Lauda 1'06.043"	4. Patrese	Alfa Romeo	73	+ 2 laps
Warwick 1'06.056"	Alboreto 1'06.323"	5. De Cesaris	Ligier-Renault	73	+ 2 laps
Laffite 1'06.762"	Winkelhock 1'06.974"	6. Senna	Toleman-Hart	72	+ 3 laps
Senna 1'06.981"	De Cesaris 1'07.245"	7. De Angelis	Lotus-Renault	71	+ 4 laps
Arnoux 1'07.345"	Cheever 1'07.704"	8. Baldi	Spirit-Hart	71	+ 4 laps
	Hesnault 1'07.787"	9. Surer	Arrows-Ford	71	+ 4 laps
Patrese 1'08.298"	Baldi 1'09.923"	10. Hesnault	Ligier-Renault	71	+ 4 laps
Palmer 1'10.383"	Alliot 1'10.619"	11. Brundle*	Tyrrell-Ford	71	+ 4 laps
Surer 1'11.808"	Bellof 1'12.022"	12. Alboreto	Ferrari	70	Electronics
Brundle 1'12.233"	Boutsen 1'12.274"	13. Boutsen	Arrows-Ford	70	+ 5 laps

FASTEST LAP		
Tambay	Renault	1'08.877" 214.492 km/h

RETIREMENTS			
Tambay	Renault	66	Ignition
Laffite	Williams-Honda	60	Head gasket
Bellof	Tyrrell-Ford	60	Engine
Winkelhock	ATS-BMW	53	Battery/engine
Rosberg	Williams-Honda	51	Lost a wheel
Mansell	Lotus-Renault	51	Turbo
Arnoux	Ferrari	40	Injector pump drive
Piquet	Brabham-BMW	29	Turbo
Cecotto	Toleman-Hart	26	Puncture
Alliot	RAM-Hart	24	Water leak/engine
Palmer	RAM-Hart	22	Engine
Fabi	Brabham-BMW	18	Turbo
Cheever	Alfa Romeo	4	Radiator broken

Kyalami race statistics.

STARTING GRID		RESULTS - Jacarepagua (306,891 km)			
De Angelis 1'28.392"	Alboreto 1'28.898"	1. Prost	McLaren-TAG Porsche	61	1h42'34.492" 179.511 km/h
Warwick 1'29.025"	Prost 1'29.330"	2. Rosberg	Williams-Honda	61	1h43'15.006"
Mansell 1'29.364"	Lauda 1'29.854"	3. De Angelis	Lotus-Renault	61	1h43'33.620"
Piquet 1'30.149"	Tambay 1'30.554"	4. Cheever	Alfa Romeo	60	+ 1 lap
Rosberg 1'30.611"	Arnoux 1'30.695"	5. Brundle*	Tyrrell-Ford	60	+ 1 lap
Patrese 1'30.973"	Cheever 1'31.282"	6. Tambay	Renault	59	Out of fuel
Laffite 1'31.548"	De Cesaris 1'32.895"	7. Boutsen	Arrows-Ford	59	+ 2 laps
Fabi 1'33.277"	Senna 1'33.525"	8. Surer	Arrows-Ford	59	+ 2 laps
Cecotto 1'35.300"	Brundle 1'36.081"	9. Palmer	RAM-Hart	58	+ 3 laps
Hesnault 1'36.238"	Boutsen 1'36.312"				
Ghinzani 1'36.434"	Bellof 1'36.609"				
Baldi 1'36.816"	Surer 1'37.204"				
Alliot 1'37.709"	Palmer 1'37.919"				

FASTEST LAP		
Prost	McLaren-TAG Porsche	1'36.499" 187.686 km/h

RETIREMENTS			
Warwick	Renault	51	Front suspension
De Cesaris	Ligier-Renault	42	Gearbox
Patrese	Alfa Romeo	41	Gearbox
Lauda	McLaren-TAG Porsche	38	Electrical
Mansell	Lotus-Renault	35	Accident
Piquet	Brabham-BMW	32	Engine
Fabi	Brabham-BMW	32	Turbo
Arnoux	Ferrari	30	Battery
Ghinzani	Osella-Alfa Romeo	28	Gearbox
Hesnault	Ligier-Renault	25	Overheating
Alliot	RAM-Hart	24	Fixation battery
Cecotto	Toleman-Hart	18	Turbo pressure
Laffite	Williams-Honda	15	Electrical
Alboreto	Ferrari	14	Brakes
Baldi	Spirit-Hart	12	Fuel feed
Bellof	Tyrrell-Ford	11	Throttle cable
Senna	Toleman-Hart	8	Turbo pressure

Jacarepagua race statistics.

Patrick Tambay.

Tambay receives attention.

Belgian Grand Prix, Zolder, 29 April 1984
The long trek back to Europe saw Warwick starting on P4. He drove a good race to take 2nd place on the podium, with Tambay driving the new RE50/05 into 8th.

San Marino Grand Prix, Imola, 6 May 1984
At Imola, Warwick finished 4th from P4 on the grid, but Tambay was to go out in an accident with Cheever on the first lap.

French Grand Prix, Dijon, 20 May 1984
The French Grand Prix elicited a huge effort from the whole team – not that it hadn't been trying before, it was just that this season it was experiencing many failures. However, the past was forgotten for a short while as Tambay put the car on pole. Warwick was back in 7th, and, getting caught up in a collision on lap 53, it was his turn to go out this time. Tambay kept the flag flying by finishing 2nd, just a few seconds behind Lauda's charging McLaren.

STARTING GRID	
Alboreto 1'14.846"	**Arnoux** 1'15.398"
Rosberg 1'15.414"	**Warwick** 1'15.611"
De Angelis 1'15.979"	**Winkelhock** 1'16.130"
Patrese 1'16.431"	**Prost** 1'16.587"
Piquet 1'16.604"	**Mansell** 1'16.720"
Cheever 1'16.746"	**Tambay** 1'17.171"
De Cesaris 1'17.471"	**Lauda** 1'18.071"
Laffite 1'18.125"	**Cecotto** 1'18.321"
Boutsen 1'18.351"	**Fabi** 1'18.848"
Senna 1'18.876"	**Ghinzani** 1'19.734"
Bellof 1'19.811"	**Brundle** 1'20.123"
Hesnault 1'20.439"	**Surer** 1'20.615"
Baldi 1'20.644"	**Palmer** 1'20.793"

RESULTS - Zolder (298,340 km)

1. Alboreto	Ferrari	70	1h36'32.048" 185.430 km/h
2. Warwick	Renault	70	1h37'14.434"
3. Arnoux	Ferrari	70	1h37'41.851"
4. Rosberg	Williams-Honda	69	Out of fuel
5. De Angelis	Lotus-Renault	69	+ 1 lap
6. Bellof*	Tyrrell-Ford	69	+ 1 lap
7. Senna	Toleman-Hart	68	+ 2 laps
8. Tambay	Renault	68	+ 2 laps
9. Surer	Arrows-Ford	68	+ 2 laps
10. Piquet	Brabham-BMW	66	Engine
11. Palmer	RAM-Hart	64	+ 6 laps

FASTEST LAP

Arnoux	Ferrari	1'19.294" 193.497 km/h

RETIREMENTS

Baldi	Spirit-Hart	53	Suspension
Brundle	Tyrrell-Ford	51	Lost a wheel
Fabi	Brabham-BMW	42	Spin
De Cesaris	Ligier-Renault	42	Accident
Winkelhock	ATS-BMW	39	Exhaust
Lauda	Mclaren-TAG Porsche	35	Water pump
Cheever	Alfa Romeo	28	Engine
Laffite	Williams-Honda	15	Electrical
Hesnault	Ligier-Renault	15	Radiator
Boutsen	Arrows-BMW	15	Engine
Ghinzani	Osella-Alfa Romeo	14	Transmission
Mansell	Lotus-Renault	14	Clutch
Prost	McLaren-TAG Porsche	5	Injector pump drive
Patrese	Alfa Romeo	2	Ignition
Cecotto	Toleman-Hart	1	Clutch

Derek Warwick. (© TVA)

Zolder race statistics.

Têtu talks to Warwick (in car). (© TVA)

STARTING GRID — RESULTS - Dijon-Prenois (307,073 km)

STARTING GRID			
Tambay 1'02.200"	De Angelis 1'02.336"		
Piquet 1'02.806"	Rosberg 1'02.908"		
Prost 1'02.982"	Mansell 1'03.200"		
Warwick 1'03.540"	Winkelhock 1'03.865"		
Lauda 1'04.419"	Alboreto 1'04.459"		
Arnoux 1'04.917"	Laffite 1'05.410"		
Senna 1'05.744"	Boutsen 1'05.972"		
Patrese 1'06.172"	Cheever 1'06.281"		
Fabi 1'06.370"	Cecotto 1'08.189"		
Surer 1'08.457"	Bellof 1'08.608"		
Palmer 1'09.047"	Alliot 1'09.447"		
Brundle 1'09.554"	Baldi 1'09.629"		
Ghinzani 1'11.625"	De Cesaris 1'22.388"		

RESULTS - Dijon-Prenois (307,073 km)			
1. Lauda	McLaren-TAG Porsche	79	1h31'11.951" 202.023 km/h
2. Tambay	Renault	79	1h31'19.105"
3. Mansell	Lotus-Renault	79	1h31'35.920"
4. Arnoux	Ferrari	79	1h31'55.657"
5. De Angelis	Lotus-Renault	79	1h32'18.076"
6. Rosberg	Williams-Honda	78	+ 1 lap
7. Prost	McLaren-TAG Porsche	78	+ 1 lap
8. Laffite	Williams-Honda	78	+ 1 lap
9. Fabi	Brabham-BMW	78	+ 1 lap
10. De Cesaris	Ligier-Renault	77	+ 2 laps
11. Boutsen	Arrows-Ford	77	+ 2 laps
12. Brundle*	Tyrrell-Ford	76	+ 3 laps
13. Ghinzani	Osella-Alfa Romeo	74	+ 5 laps
14. Palmer	RAM-Hart	72	+ 7 laps

FASTEST LAP

Prost	McLaren-TAG Porsche	1'05.257" 214.432 km/h

RETIREMENTS

Baldi	Spirit-Hart	61	Engine
Warwick	Renault	53	Collision with Surer
Surer	Arrows-Ford	51	Collision Warwick
Cheever	Alfa Romeo	51	Engine
Senna	Toleman-Hart	35	Turbo
Alboreto	Ferrari	33	Engine
Cecotto	Toleman-Hart	22	Turbo
Patrese	Alfa Romeo	15	Engine
Piquet	Brabham-BMW	11	Turbo
Bellof	Tyrrell-Ford	11	Engine
Winkelhock	ATS-BMW	5	Clutch
Aliott	RAM-Hart	4	Electrical

Dijon race statistics.

STARTING GRID — RESULTS - Imola (302,400 km)

STARTING GRID	
Piquet 1'28.517"	**Prost** 1'28.628"
Rosberg 1'29.418"	Warwick 1'29.682"
Lauda 1'30.325"	Arnoux 1'30.411"
Winkelhock 1'30.723"	Cheever 1'30.843"
Fabi 1'30.950"	Patrese 1'31.163"
De Angelis 1'31.173"	De Cesaris 1'31.256"
Alboreto 1'31.282"	Tambay 1'31.663"
Laffite 1'32.600"	Surer 1'33.063"
Hesnault 1'33.186"	Mansell 1'34.477"
Cecotto 1'35.568"	Boutsen 1'36.018"
Bellof 1'36.059"	Brundle 1'36.531"
Alliot 1'36.733"	Baldi 1'36.916"
Palmer 1'37.262"	Gartner 1'38.948"

RESULTS - Imola (302,400 km)			
1. Prost	McLaren-TAG Porsche	60	1h36'53.679" 187.254 km/h
2. Arnoux	Ferrari	60	1h37'07.095"
3. De Angelis	Lotus-Renault	59	Out of fuel
4. Warwick	Renault	59	+ 1 lap
5. Bellof*	Tyrrell-Ford	59	+ 1 lap
6. Boutsen	Arrows-Ford	59	+ 1 lap
7. De Cesaris	Ligier-Renault	58	Out of fuel
8. Cheever	Alfa Romeo	58	Out of fuel
9. Baldi	Spirit-Hart	58	+ 2 laps
10. Palmer	RAM-Hart	57	+ 3 laps
11. Brundle*	Tyrrell-Ford	55	Fuel feed

FASTEST LAP

Piquet	Brabham-BMW	1'33.275" 194.275 km/h

RETIREMENTS

Alliot	RAM-Hart	53	Engine
Cecotto	Toleman-Hart	52	Engine
Piquet	Brabham-BMW	48	Turbo
Fabi	Brabham-BMW	48	Turbo
Gartner	Osella-Alfa Romeo	46	Engine
Surer	Arrows-BMW	40	Turbo
Winkelhock	ATS-BMW	31	Turbo
Alboreto	Ferrari	23	Exhaust
Lauda	Mclaren-TAG Porsche	15	Engine
Laffite	Williams-Honda	11	Engine
Patrese	Alfa Romeo	6	Electrical
Mansell	Lotus-Renault	2	Brakes/Spin
Rosberg	Williams-Honda	2	Electrical
Tambay	Renault	1	Collision Cheever
Hesnault	Ligier-Renault	0	Collision Laffite

Imola race statistics.

Together again, but only one would finish.

Derek Warwick with Gérard Larrousse.

STARTING GRID		RESULTS - Monaco (102,672 km)			
Prost	Mansell	1. Prost	McLaren-TAG Porsche	31	1h01'07.740"
1'22.661"	1'22.752"				100.775 km/h
Arnoux	Alboreto	2. Senna	Toleman-Hart	31	1h01'15.186"
1'22.935"	1'22.937"	3. Bellof*	Tyrrell-Ford	31	1h01'28.881"
Warwick	Tambay	4. Arnoux	Ferrari	31	1h01'36.817"
1'23.237"	1'23.414"	5. Rosberg	Williams-Honda	31	1h01'42.986"
De Cesaris	Lauda	6. De Angelis	Lotus-Renault	31	1h01'52.179"
1'23.578"	1'23.886"	7. Alboreto	Ferrari	30	+ 1 lap
Piquet	Rosberg	8. Ghinzani	Osella-Alfa Romeo	30	+ 1 lap
1'23.918"	1'24.151"	9. Laffite	Williams-Honda	30	+ 1 lap
De Angelis	Winkelhock				
1'24.426"	1'24.473"				
Senna	Patrese		FASTEST LAP		
1'25.009"	1'25.101"				
Fabi	Laffite	Senna	Toleman-Hart		1'54.334"
1'25.290"	1'25.719"				104.283 km/h
Hesnault	Cecotto				
1'25.815"	1'25.872"				
Ghinzani	Bellof		RETIREMENTS		
1'25.877"	1'26.117"				
		Patrese	Alfa Romeo	24	Steering
		Lauda	Mclaren-TAG Porsche	23	Spin
		Winkelhock	ATS-BMW	22	Spin
		Mansell	Lotus-Renault	15	Accident
		Piquet	Brabham-BMW	14	Ignition
		Hesnault	Ligier-Renault	12	Ignition
		Fabi	Brabham-BMW	9	Spin
		Cecotto	Toleman-Hart	1	Spin
		De Cesaris	Ligier-Renault	1	Accident
		Warwick	Renault	0	Accident
		Tambay	Renault	0	Collision Hesnault
		Hesnault	Ligier-Renault	0	Collision Tambay

Monaco race statistics.

Monaco Grand Prix, 3 June 1984
Monaco was best forgotten; both RE50/05 and 06 were written off in a first-corner accident.

Canadian Grand Prix, Montreal, 17 June 1984
It was a dismal Canadian Grand Prix for Renault. Warwick did start from P4 in the RE 50/07, but went out on lap 57, whilst Tambay didn't even make the start.

US East Coast Grand Prix, Detroit, 24 June 1984
Detroit was bright and sunny, but only 6 cars finished the race out of 26 starters. Warwick took fastest lap but then fell foul to gearbox failure; Tambay fared no better, with transmission failure on lap 33.

US Grand Prix, Dallas, 8 July 1984
A good grid position of P3 could not be translated into success

Montreal race statistics.

STARTING GRID		RESULTS - Montréal (308,700 km)			
Piquet	Prost	1. Piquet	Brabham-BMW	70	1h46'23.748"
1'25.442"	1'26.198"				174.085 km/h
De Angelis	Warwick	2. Lauda	Mclaren-TAG Porsche	70	1h46'26.360"
1'26.306"	1'26.420"	3. Prost	McLaren-TAG Porsche	70	1h47'51.780"
Arnoux	Alboreto	4. De Angelis	Lotus-Renault	69	+ 1 lap
1'26.549"	1'26.764"	5. Arnoux	Ferrari	68	+ 2 laps
Mansell	Lauda	6. Mansell	Lotus-Renault	68	+ 2 laps
1'27.246"	1'27.392"	7. Senna	Toleman-Hart	68	+ 2 laps
Senna	De Cesaris	8. Winkelhock	ATS-BMW	68	+ 2 laps
1'27.448"	1'27.922"	9. Cecotto	Toleman-Hart	68	+ 2 laps
Cheever	Winkelhock	10. Brundle*	Tyrrell-Ford	68	+ 2 laps
1'28.032"	1'28.909"	11. Alliot	RAM-Hart	65	+ 5 laps
Hesnault	Patrese	12. Cheever	Alfa Romeo	63	Out of fuel
1'29.187"	1'29.205"				
Rosberg	Fabi		FASTEST LAP		
1'29.284"	1'29.764"				
Laffite	Boutsen	Piquet	Brabham-BMW		1'28.763"
1'29.915"	1'30.073"				178.858 km/h
Ghinzani	Cecotto				
1'30.918"	1'31.459"		RETIREMENTS		
Brundle	Bellof				
1'31.785"	1'31.797"	Surer	Arrows-Ford	59	Engine
Surer	Rothengatter	Warwick	Renault	57	Chassis
1'32.756"	1'32.920"	Rothengatter	Spirit-Hart	56	Not classified
Thackwell	Alliot	Bellof	Tyrrell-Ford	52	Transmission shaft
1'33.750"	1'35.286"	De Cesaris	Ligier-Renault	40	Brakes
		Fabi	Brabham-BMW	39	Turbo
		Boutsen	Arrows-BMW	38	Engine
		Patrese	Alfa Romeo	37	Accident
		Rosberg	Williams-Honda	32	Fuel feed
		Laffite	Williams-Honda	31	Turbo
		Thackwell	RAM-Hart	29	Wastegate failure
		Ghinzani	Osella-Alfa Romeo	11	Gearbox
		Alboreto	Ferrari	10	Engine
		Hesnault	Ligier-renault	7	Turbo

STARTING GRID

Piquet	Prost
1'40.980"	1'41.640"
Mansell	Alboreto
1'42.172"	1'42.246"
De Angelis	Warwick
1'42.434"	1'42.637"
Senna	Cheever
1'42.651"	1'43.065"
Tambay	Lauda
1'43.289"	1'43.484"
Brundle	De Cesaris
1'43.754"	1'43.998"
Boutsen	Winkelhock
1'44.063"	1'44.228"
Arnoux	Bellof
1'44.748"	1'44.940"
Cecotto	Hesnault
1'45.231"	1'45.419"
Laffite	Alliot
1'46.225"	1'46.333"
Rosberg	Surer
1'46.495"	1'46.626"
Fabi	Palmer
1'47.335"	1'47.743"
Patrese	Ghinzani
1'47.974"	1'48.865"

RESULTS - Detroit (253,449 km)

1. Piquet	Brabham-BMW	63	1h55'41.842"
2. Brundle*	Tyrrell-Ford	63	1h55'42.670"
3. De Angelis	Lotus-Renault	63	1h56'14.480"
4. Fabi	Brabham-BMW	63	1h57'08.370"
5. Prost	McLaren-TAG Porsche	63	1h57'37.100"
6. Laffite	Williams-Honda	62	+ 1 lap

FASTEST LAP

Warwick	Renault	1'46.221" 136.346 km/h

RETIREMENTS

Alboreto	Ferrari	49	Engine
Rosberg	Williams-Honda	47	Exhaust/turbo
Warwick	Renault	40	Gearbox
Bellof*	Tyrrell-Ford	33	Accident
Tambay	Renault	33	Transmission
Alliot	RAM-Hart	33	Brakes/accident
Lauda	Mclaren-TAG Porsche	33	Electronics
Mansell	Lotus-Renault	27	Gearbox
Boutsen	Arrows-BMW	27	Engine
De Cesaris	Ligier-Renault	24	Overheating
Cecotto	Toleman-Hart	23	Clutch
Cheever	Alfa Romeo	21	Engine
Senna	Toleman-Hart	21	Accident
Patrese	Alfa Romeo	20	Spin, suspension failure
Hesnault	Ligier-Renault	3	Collision Ghinzani
Ghinzani	Osella-Alfa Romeo	3	Collision Hesnault
Arnoux	Ferrari	2	Accident
Palmer	RAM-Hart	2	Tyre/accident
Winkelhock	ATS-BMW	0	Accident
Surer	Arrows-Ford	0	Accident

STARTING GRID

Mansell	De Angelis
1'37.041"	1'37.635"
Warwick	Arnoux
1'37.708"	1'37.785"
Lauda	Senna
1'37.987"	1'38.256"
Prost	Rosberg
1'38.544"	1'38.767"
Alboreto	Tambay
1'38.793"	1'38.907"
Fabi	Piquet
1'38.960"	1'39.439"
Winkelhock	Cheever
1'39.860"	1'39.911"
Cecotto	De Cesaris
1'40.027"	1'40.095"
Bellof	Ghinzani
1'40.336"	1'41.176"
Hesnault	Boutsen
1'41.303"	1'41.318"
Patrese	Surer
1'41.328"	1'42.592"
Rothengatter	Alliot
1'43.084"	1'43.222"
Laffite	Palmer
1'43.304"	1'44.676"

RESULTS - Dallas (261,367 km)

1. Rosberg	Williams-Honda	67	2:01'22.617" 129.175 km/h
2. Arnoux	Ferrari	67	2:01'45.081"
3. De Angelis	Lotus-Renault	66	+ 1 lap
4. Laffite	Williams-Honda	65	+ 2 laps
5. Ghinzani	Osella-Alfa Romeo	65	+ 2 laps
6. Mansell	Lotus-Renault	64	Accident
7. Fabi	Brabham-BMW	64	+ 3 laps
8. Winkelhock	ATS-BMW	64	+ 3 laps

FASTEST LAP

Lauda	McLaren-TAG Porsche	1'45.353" 133.300 km/h

RETIREMENTS

Lauda	McLaren-TAG Porsche	60	Accident
Prost	McLaren-TAG Porsche	56	Accident
Boutsen	Arrows-BMW	55	Accident
Alboreto	Ferrari	54	Accident
Surer	Arrows-BMW	54	Accident
Senna	Toleman-Hart	47	Transmission shaft
Palmer	RAM-Hart	46	Electrical
Piquet	Brabham-BMW	45	Throttle cable
Tambay	Renault	25	Accident
Cecotto	Toleman-Hart	25	Accident
De Cesaris	Ligier-Renault	15	Accident
Rothengatter	Spirit-Hart	15	Fuel leak into the cockpit
Patrese	Alfa Romeo	12	Accident
Warwick	Renault	10	Spin
Bellof	Tyrrell-Ford	9	Accident
Cheever	Alfa Romeo	8	Accident
Hesnault	Ligier-Renault	0	Accident

Detroit race statistics.

Outside the Cotton Bowl, Dallas.

Dallas race statistics.

Warwick, Lauda, Senna. 2nd place: maybe there was hope ...

STARTING GRID		RESULTS - Brands Hatch (298,697 km)				
Piquet	Prost	1. Lauda	McLaren-TAG Porsche	71	1h29'28.532"	
1'10.869"	1'11.076"				200.206 km/h	
Lauda	De Angelis	2. Warwick	Renault	71	1h30'10.655"	
1'11.344"	1'11.573"	3. Senna	Toleman-Hart	71	1h30'31.860"	
Rosberg	Warwick	4. De Angelis	Lotus-Renault	70	+ 1 lap	
1'11.603"	1'11.703"	5. Alboreto	Ferrari	70	+ 1 lap	
Senna	Mansell	6. Arnoux	Ferrari	70	+ 1 lap	
1'11.890"	1'12.435"	7. Piquet	Brabham-BMW	70	+ 1 lap	
Alboreto	Tambay	8. Tambay	Renault	69	Turbo	
1'13.122"	1'13.138"	9. Ghinzani	Osella-Alfa Romeo	68	+ 3 laps	
Winkelhock	Boutsen	10. De Cesaris	Ligier-Renault	68	+ 3 laps	
1'13.374"	1'13.528"	11. Bellof*	Tyrrell-Ford	68	+ 3 laps	
Arnoux	Fabi	12. Surer	Arrows-BMW	67	+ 4 laps	
1'13.934"	1'14.040"	13. Patrese	Alfa Romeo	66	Gearbox	
Surer	Laffite					
1'14.336"	1'14.568"	**FASTEST LAP**				
Patrese	Cheever					
1'14.568"	1'14.609"	Lauda	McLaren-TAG Porsche		1'13.191"	
De Cesaris	Hesnault				206.927 km/h	
1'15.112"	1'15.837"					
Ghinzani	Rothengatter	**RETIREMENTS**				
1'16.466"	1'16.759"					
Palmer	Alliot	Rothengatter	Spirit-Hart	62	Not classified + 9 laps	
1'17.265"	1'17.517"	Hesnault	Ligier-Renault	43	Electrical	
Johansson	Bellof	Prost	McLaren-TAG Porsche	37	Gearbox	
1'17.777"	1'17.893"	Mansell	Lotus-Renault	24	Gearbox	
Gartner		Boutsen	Arrows-BMW	24	Electrical	
1'18.121"		Laffite	Williams-Honda	14	Water pump	
		Palmer	RAM-Hart	10	Steering/accident	
		Fabi	Brabham-BMW	9	Electrical	
		Winkelhock	ATS-BMW	8	Spin	
		Rosberg	Williams-Honda	1	Accident	
		Cheever	Alfa Romeo	1	Accident	
		Johansson	Tyrrell-Ford	1	Accident	
		Alliot	RAM-Hart	0	Accident	
		Gartner	Osella-Alfa Romeo	0	Accident	

Brands Hatch race statistics.

STARTING GRID		RESULTS - Hockenheim (299,068 km)				
Prost	De Angelis	1. Prost	McLaren-TAG Porsche	44	1h24'43.210"	
1'47.012"	1'47.065"				211.803 km/h	
Warwick	Tambay	2. Lauda	McLaren-TAG Porsche	44	1h24'46.359"	
1'48.382"	1'48.425"	3. Warwick	Renault	44	1h25'19.633"	
Piquet	Alboreto	4. Mansell	Lotus-Renault	44	1h25'34.873"	
1'48.584"	1'48.847"	5. Tambay	Renault	44	1h25'55.159"	
Lauda	Fabi	6. Arnoux	Ferrari	43	+ 1 lap	
1'48.912"	1'49.302"	7. De Cesaris	Ligier-Renault	43	+ 1 lap	
Senna	Arnoux	8. Hesnault	Ligier-Renault	43	+ 1 lap	
1'49.395"	1'49.857"	9. Johansson*	Tyrrell-Ford	42	+ 2 laps	
De Cesaris	Laffite	10. Rothengatter	Spirit-Hart	40	+ 4 laps	
1'50.117"	1'50.511"					
Winkelhock	Surer	**FASTEST LAP**				
1'50.686"	1'51.475"					
Boutsen	Mansell	Prost	McLaren-TAG Porsche		1'53.538"	
1'51.551"	1'51.715"				215.515 km/h	
Hesnault	Cheever					
1'51.872"	1'51.950"	**RETIREMENTS**				
Rosberg	Patrese					
1'52.003"	1'52.769"	Winkelhock	ATS-BMW	31	Turbo	
Ghinzani	Alliot				Gearbox	
1'54.546"	1'55.505"	Cheever	Alfa Romeo	29	Engine	
Gartner	Rothengatter	Fabi	Brabham-BMW	28	Pression turbo	
1'55.594"	1'56.112"	Piquet	Brabham-BMW	23	Gearbox	
Palmer	Johansson	Patrese	Alfa Romeo	16	Engine base	
1'56.797"	1'59.461"	Ghinzani	Osella-Alfa Romeo	14	Electrical	
		Gartner	Osella-Alfa Romeo	13	Turbo	
		Alboreto	Ferrari	13	Engine	
		Palmer	RAM-Hart	11	Turbo	
		Rosberg	Williams-Honda	10	Electrical	
		Laffite	Williams-Honda	10	Engine	
		Boutsen	Arrows-BMW	8	Oil pressure	
		De Angelis	Lotus-Renault	8	Turbo	
		Alliot	RAM-Hart	7	Overheating	
		Senna	Toleman-Hart	4	Accident (wing)	
		Surer	Arrows-BMW	1	Turbo	

Hockenheim race statistics.

for Warwick, as he was to go out with a spin on lap 10. And then Tambay had an accident on lap 25. A double whammy ...

British Grand Prix, Brands Hatch, 22 July 1984

An excellent result from 6th on the grid as Warwick grabbed 2nd place in the RE50/08. Tambay, who started 4 places back from Warwick, was to finish 8th.

German Grand Prix, Hockenheim, 5 August 1984

Things were looking in fine form – almost like the old days – when Warwick qualified in P3 on the second row of the grid, with Tambay alongside, just a fraction slower. Warwick held his position as he continued the good fortune from Brands Hatch and finished in 3rd on the podium, with Tambay just a little further back in 5th in RE50/09.

Austrian Grand Prix, Zeltweg, 19 August 1984

The Austrian GP at Zeltweg looked OK, with Warwick on P4 and

Oh dear! The Teapot remembered!

Zeltweg race statistics.

STARTING GRID	
Piquet 1'26.173"	Prost 1'26.203"
De Angelis 1'26.318"	Lauda 1'26.715"
Tambay 1'26.748"	Warwick 1'27.123"
Fabi 1'27.201"	Mansell 1'27.558"
Rosberg 1'28.760"	Senna 1'29.200"
Laffite 1'29.228"	Alboreto 1'29.694"
Patrese 1'30.736"	(Winkelhock) (1'30.853")
Arnoux 1'31.003"	Cheever 1'31.045"
Boutsen 1'31.189"	De Cesaris 1'31.588"
Surer 1'31.655"	Berger 1'31.904"
Hesnault 1'32.270"	Gartner 1'33.019"
Ghinzani 1'33.172"	Palmer 1'34.128"
Alliot 1'34.495"	Rothengatter 1'35.605"

RESULTS - Zeltweg (303,042 km)

1. Lauda	McLaren-TAG Porsche	51	1h21'13.851" 223.883 km/h	
2. Piquet	Brabham-BMW	51	1h21'36.376"	
3. Alboreto	Ferrari	51	1h22'01.849"	
4. Fabi	Brabham-BMW	51	1h22'09.163"	
5. Boutsen	Arrows-BMW	50	+ 1 lap	
6. Surer	Arrows-BMW	50	+ 1 lap	
7. Arnoux	Ferrari	50	+ 1 lap	
8. Hesnault	Ligier-Renault	49	+ 2 laps	
9. Palmer	RAM-Hart	49	+ 2 laps	
10. Patrese	Alfa Romeo	48	Out of fuel	
11. Alliot	RAM-Hart	48	+ 3 laps	
12. Berger	ATS-BMW	48	+ 3 laps	

FASTEST LAP

Lauda	McLaren-TAG Porsche	1'32.882" 230.305 km/h

RETIREMENTS

Tambay	Renault	42	Engine
Senna	Toleman-Hart	35	Oil pressure
Mansell	Lotus-Renault	32	Engine
Prost	McLaren-TAG Porsche	28	Spin
De Angelis	Lotus-Renault	28	Engine
Rothengatter	Spirit-Hart	23	Fuel feed
Cheever	Alfa Romeo	18	Engine
Warwick	Renault	17	Engine
De Cesaris	Ligier-Renault	15	Fuel pump
Rosberg	Williams-Honda	15	Road-holding
Laffite	Williams-Honda	12	Engine
Gartner	Osella-Alfa Romeo	6	Engine
Ghinzani	Osella-Alfa Romeo	4	Gearbox

Tambay on P5. But engine blow-ups dominated and, in the race, Warwick went out on lap 17 and Tambay on lap 43.

Dutch Grand Prix, Zandvoort, 26 August 1984
Things improved a little here when Tambay came in 6th, one lap down. Unfortunately, Warwick spun out on the oil left by Laffite's engine that blew up on lap 23.

Italian Grand Prix, Monza, 9 September 1984
Although Tambay had tested the new electronic ignition system over the equivalent of three Grand Prix distances at Paul Ricard ahead of Monza, the Italian GP turned out to be a complete washout with both cars retired: Tambay with a broken throttle cable and Warwick with failing oil pressure.

European Grand Prix, Nürburgring, 7 October 1984
Things looked up again at the Nürburgring. Tambay qualified in P3, but it proved to be a false dawn when he went out on lap 47 – the problem ... out of fuel! Warwick, starting from the 4th row, trailed in 11th, seven laps down, and, would you believe, he too was out of fuel!

Ducarouge, Dudot, Larrousse, Warr.

No luck for Warwick.

STARTING GRID		RESULTS - Monza (295,800 km)			
Piquet	Prost	1. Lauda	McLaren-TAG Porsche	51	1h20'29.065"
1'26.584"	1'26.671"				220.514 km/h
De Angelis	Lauda	2. Alboreto	Ferrari	51	1h20'53.314"
1'27.538"	1'28.533"	3. Patrese	Alfa Romeo	50	+ 1 lap
Fabi	Rosberg	4. Johansson	Toleman-Hart	49	+ 2 laps
1'28.587"	1'28.818"	5. Gartner	Osella-Alfa Romeo	49	+ 2 laps
Mansell	Tambay	6. Berger	ATS-BMW	49	+ 2 laps
1'28.969"	1'29.253"	7. Ghinzani	Osella-Alfa Romeo	49	Out of fuel
Patrese	Cheever	8. Rothengatter	Spirit-Hart	49	+ 2 laps
1'29.382"	1'29.797"				
Alboreto	Warwick	**FASTEST LAP**			
1'29.810"	1'30.113"				
Laffite	Arnoux	Lauda	McLaren-TAG Porsche		1'31.912"
1'30.578"	1'30.695"				227.173 km/h
Surer	De Cesaris				
1'31.108"	1'31.198"	**RETIREMENTS**			
Johansson	Hesnault				
1'31.203"	1'31.274"	Cheever	Alfa Romeo	46	Out of fuel
Boutsen	Berger	Boutsen	Arrows-BMW	45	Not classified + 6 lap
1'31.342"	1'31.549"	Tambay	Renault	43	Throttle cable
(Winkelhock)	Ghinzani	Fabi	Brabham-BMW	43	Engine
(1'32.866")	1'33.456"	Surer	Arrows-BMW	43	Engine
Alliot	Gartner	Warwick	Renault	31	Oil pressure
1'34.120"	1'34.472"	Palmer	RAM-Hart	20	Oil pressure
Rothengatter	Palmer	Piquet	Brabham-BMW	15	Engine/Water leak
1'34.719"	1'35.412"	De Angelis	Lotus-Renault	14	Gearbox
		Mansell	Lotus-Renault	13	Spin
		Laffite	Williams-Honda	10	Turbo
		Rosberg	Williams-Honda	8	Engine
		De Cesaris	Ligier-Renault	7	Engine
		Hesnault	Ligier-Renault	7	Spin
		Alliot	RAM-Hart	6	Electrical
		Arnoux	Ferrari	5	Gearbox
		Prost	McLaren-TAG Porsche	4	Engine

Monza race statistics.

STARTING GRID		RESULTS - Zandvoort (301,892 km)			
Prost	Piquet	1. Prost	McLaren-TAG Porsche	71	1h37'21.468"
1'13.567"	1'13.872"				
De Angelis	Warwick	2. Lauda	McLaren-TAG Porsche	71	1h37'31.751"
1'13.883"	1'14.405"	3. Mansell	Lotus-Renault	71	1h38'41.012"
Tambay	Lauda	4. De Angelis	Lotus-Renault	70	+ 1 lap
1'14.566"	1'14.866"	5. Fabi	Brabham-BMW	70	+ 1 lap
Rosberg	Laffite	6. Tambay	Renault	70	+ 1 lap
1'15.177"	1'15.231"	7. Hesnault	Ligier-Renault	69	+ 2 laps
Alboreto	Fabi	8. Johansson*	Tyrrell-Ford	69	+ 2 laps
1'15.264"	1'15.338"	9. Bellof*	Tyrrell-Ford	69	+ 2 laps
Boutsen	Mansell	10. Rosberg	Williams-Honda	68	Out of fuel
1'15.735"	1'15.811"	11. Palmer	RAM-Hart	67	+ 4 laps
Senna	De Cesaris	12. Alliot	RAM-Hart	67	+ 4 laps
1'15.960"	1'16.070"	13. Arnoux	Ferrari	66	Electrical
Arnoux	Winkelhock	14. Gartner	Osella-Alfa Romeo	66	+ 5 laps
1'16.121"	1'16.450"	15. Cheever	Alfa Romeo	65	Out of fuel
Cheever	Patrese				
1'16.991"	1'17.124"	**FASTEST LAP**			
Surer	Hesnault				
1'17.368"	1'17.905"	Arnoux	Ferrari		1'19.465"
Ghinzani	Palmer				192.628 km/h
1'19.454"	1'19.598"				
Gartner	Bellof	**RETIREMENTS**			
1'20.071"	1'20.092"				
Johansson	Alliot	Boutsen	Arrows-BMW	59	Collision Arnoux
1'20.236"	1'20.270"	Rothengatter	Spirit-Hart	53	Throttle cable
Rothengatter		Patrese	Alfa Romeo	51	Engine
1'21.063"		De Cesaris	Ligier-Renault	31	Engine
		Laffite	Williams-Honda	23	Engine
		Warwick	Renault	23	Spin on Laffite' oil
		Winkelhock	ATS-BMW	22	Spin
		Senna	Toleman-Hart	19	Engine
		Surer	Arrows-BMW	17	Rolling bearing
		Piquet	Brabham-BMW	10	Oil pressure
		Ghinzani	Osella-Alfa Romeo	8	Fuel pump
		Alboreto	Ferrari	7	Engine

Zandvoort race statistics.

The McLaren of Prost and Tambay. (© Bernard Asset)

STARTING GRID		RESULTS - Nürburgring (D) (304,314 km)			
Piquet 1'18.871"	Prost 1'18.875"	1. Prost	McLaren-TAG Porsche	67	1h35'13.284" 191.751 km/h
Tambay 1'19.499"	Rosberg 1'20.625"	2. Alboreto	Ferrari	67	1h35'37.195"
Alboreto 1'20.910"	Arnoux 1'21.180"	3. Piquet	Brabham-BMW	67	1h35'38.206"
Warwick 1'21.571"	Mansell 1'21.710"	4. Lauda	McLaren-TAG Porsche	67	1h35'56.370"
Patrese 1'21.937"	Fabi 1'22.206"	5. Arnoux	Ferrari	67	1h36'14.714"
Boutsen 1'22.248"	Senna 1'22.439"	6. Patrese	Alfa Romeo	66	+ 1 lap
Cheever 1'22.525"	Laffite 1'22.613"	7. De Cesaris	Ligier-Renault	65	+ 2 laps
Lauda 1'22.643"	Surer 1'22.708"	8. Baldi	Spirit-Hart	65	+ 2 laps
De Cesaris 1'23.034"	Berger 1'23.116"	9. Boutsen	Arrows-Ford	64	Out of fuel
Hesnault 1'23.322"	Ghinzani 1'24.699"	10. Hesnault	Ligier-Renault	64	+ 3 laps
Palmer 1'25.050"	Gartner 1'26.156"	11. Warwick	Renault	60	Out of fuel
De Angelis 1'26.161"	Baldi 1'28.137"				
Alliot 1'30.259"	Johansson 1'41.178"				

FASTEST LAP

Piquet	Brabham-BMW	1'23.146" 196.656 km/h

RETIREMENTS

Gartner	Osella-Alfa Romeo	60	Out of fuel
Fabi	Brabham-BMW	57	Gearbox
Mansell	Lotus-Renault	51	Engine
Tambay	Renault	47	Essence
Cheever	Alfa Romeo	37	Fuel pump
Alliot	RAM-Hart	37	Turbo
Palmer	RAM-Hart	35	Turbo
Laffite	Williams-Honda	27	Turbo
De Angelis	Lotus-Renault	25	Turbo
Johansson	Toleman-Hart	17	Overheating
Rosberg	Williams-Honda	0	Pile-up
Berger	ATS-BMW	0	Pile-up
Surer	Arrows-BMW	0	Pile-up
Ghinzani	Osella-Alfa Romeo	0	Pile-up
Senna	Toleman-Hart	0	Pile-up

Nürburgring race statistics.

STARTING GRID		RESULTS - Estoril (304,500 km)			
Piquet 1'21.703"	Prost 1'21.774"	1. Prost	McLaren-TAG Porsche	70	1h41'11.753" 180.540 km/h
Senna 1'21.936"	Rosberg 1'22.049"	2. Lauda	McLaren-TAG Porsche	70	1h41'25.178"
De Angelis 1'22.291"	Mansell 1'22.319"	3. Senna	Toleman-Hart	70	1h41'31.795"
Tambay 1'22.583"	Alboreto 1'22.686"	4. Alboreto	Ferrari	70	1h41'32.070"
Warwick 1'22.801"	Johansson 1'22.942"	5. De Angelis	Lotus-Renault	70	1h42'43.922"
Lauda 1'23.183"	Patrese 1'24.048"	6. Piquet	Brabham-BMW	69	+ 1 lap
Streiff 1'24.089"	Cheever 1'24.235"	7. Tambay	Renault	69	+ 1 lap
Laffite 1'24.437"	Surer 1'24.688"	8. Patrese	Alfa Romeo	69	+ 1 lap
Arnoux 1'24.848"	Boutsen 1'25.155"	9. Arnoux	Ferrari	69	+ 1 lap
Winkelhock 1'25.289"	De Cesaris 1'26.082"	10. Winkelhock	Brabham-BMW	69	+ 1 lap
Hesnault 1'26.701"	Ghinzani 1'26.840"	11. Johansson	Toleman-Hart	69	+ 1 lap
Berger 1'28.106"	Gartner 1'28.229"	12. De Cesaris	Ligier-Renault	69	+ 1 lap
Baldi 1'29.001"	Palmer 1'29.397"	13. Berger	ATS-BMW	68	+ 2 laps
Alliot 1'30.406"		14. Laffite	Williams-Honda	67	+ 3 laps
		15. Baldi	Spirit-Hart	66	+ 4 laps
		16. Gartner	Osella-Alfa Romeo	65	Out of fuel
		17. Cheever	Alfa Romeo	64	+ 6 laps

FASTEST LAP

Lauda	McLaren-TAG Porsche	1'22.996" 188.683 km/h

RETIREMENTS

Ghinzani	Osella-Alfa Romeo	60	Engine
Mansell	Lotus-Renault	52	Brakes' liquid leak Spin
Warwick	Renault	51	Gearbox
Streiff	Renault	48	Transmission shaft
Rosberg	Williams-Honda	39	Engine
Hesnault	Ligier-Renault	31	Electrical
Boutsen	Arrows-BMW	24	Transmission shaft
Palmer	RAM-Hart	19	Gearbox
Surer	Arrows-BMW	8	Electrical
Alliot	RAM-Hart	2	Engine

Estoril race statistics.

Portuguese Grand Prix, Estoril, 21 October 1984

The last race at Estoril saw Tambay start and finish in 7th place, but Warwick, who started from 9th, went out with gearbox trouble on lap 51.

The carbon-Kevlar race cars had been a little disappointing, not from a design point of view, but the reliability of components again. During the season the SEP-Renault carbon fibre brakes had continued testing, though they were not raced until Monza. Both Tambay and Warwick quite liked them in the race, so maybe this was a step forward.

In 1984, the pair started 31 times but were classified as finishers only 12 times. From 1978 to 1983, Renault Sport had been placed in sequence 12th, 6th, 4th, 3rd, 3rd and 2nd in the Constructors' Championship, so the drop to 5th in 1984 was the lowest since the first two years of development ...

1985 – RE60, RE60B: A SAD FINAL YEAR

Renault board members were having problems with the vast conglomerate, and had seen its main core business in the world commercial sector suffer huge trading losses, which had forced them to make many employees redundant. Putting employees out of work whilst spending huge sums on Formula 1 led to the board looking closely at this expenditure, especially in light of recent results. Sadly, the buck stopped at Gérard Larrousse: having so gamely taken control of Renault Sport in 1976, and been the mastermind behind nearly all its successes, he was moved aside and a new man, Gérard Toth, with little experience of motor sport, was put in charge of the team. After all he had done, Gérard Larrousse was naturally disillusioned and decided to leave. Michel Têtu, the man responsible for successful chassis design since 1979, also left before the season started. Both men moved to Ligier; the new RE60 design was complete but no cars had been built. One can only imagine the feeling in the team at that time. Sadly, the unwieldy management structure of the huge organisation – typical of many companies – also affected the Renault Régie, which was unable to respond quickly to changes.

Ready to go.

STARTING GRID		RESULTS - Jacarepagua (306,891 km)			
Alboreto	Rosberg	1. Prost	McLaren-TAG Porsche	61	1h41'26.115"
1'27.768"	1'27.864"				181.529 km/h
De Angelis	Senna	2. Alboreto	Ferrari	61	1h41'29.374"
1'28.081"	1'28.389"	3. De Angelis	Lotus-Renault	60	+ 1 lap
Mansell	Prost	4. Arnoux	Ferrari	59	+ 2 laps
1'28.848"	1'29.117"	5. Tambay	Renault	59	+ 2 laps
Arnoux	Piquet	6. Laffite	Ligier-Renault	59	+ 2 laps
1'29.612"	1'29.855"	7. Johansson	Tyrrell-Ford	58	+ 3 laps
Lauda	Warwick	8. Brundle	Tyrrell-Ford	58	+ 3 laps
1'29.984"	1'30.100"	9. Alliot	RAM-Hart	58	+ 3 laps
Tambay	Boutsen	10. Warwick	Renault	57	+ 4 laps
1'30.254"	1'30.953"	11. Boutsen	Arrows-BMW	57	+ 4 laps
De Cesaris	Patrese	12. Ghinzani	Osella-Alfa Romeo	57	+ 4 laps
1'31.411"	1'31.790"	13. Winkelhock	RAM-Hart	57	+ 4 laps
Laffite	Winkelhock				
1'32.021"	1'32.560"	**FASTEST LAP**			
Hesnault	Cheever				
1'32.904"	1'33.091"	Prost	McLaren-TAG Porsche		1'36.702"
Berger	Alliot				187.292 km/h
1'34.773"	1'35.726"				
Brundle	Ghinzani	**RETIREMENTS**			
1'36.152"	1'36.743"				
Johansson	Baldi	Berger	Arrows-BMW	51	Suspension
1'37.293"	1'41.330"	Senna	Lotus-Renault	48	Electrical
Martini		Cheever	Alfa Romeo	42	Engine
1'44.046"		Martini	Minardi-Ford	41	Engine
		Lauda	McLaren-TAG Porsche	27	Fuel feed
		De Cesaris	Ligier-Renault	26	Accident
		Patrese	Alfa Romeo	20	Puncture
		Rosberg	Williams-Honda	10	Turbo
		Hesnault		9	Accident
		Mansell	Williams-Honda	7	Exhaust/accident
		Baldi	Spirit-Hart	7	Turbo
		Piquet	Brabham-BMW	2	Transmission

Jacarepagua race statistics.

The Formula 1 team's budget was under review; frustration was rife, and the organisation went from bad to worse.

On the bright side, Bernard Dudot's incredible turbo engine team was now coaxing 810bhp out of the unit, and had completed a new EF15 V6 engine to complement the existing EF4s. Warwick and Tambay were retained, but the team was really only a shadow of its former self, and it was Lotus and Ligier which were to make good use of Dudot's power unit. Renault now supplied four teams: its own, Lotus, Ligier, and Tyrrell; ironically, it will be remembered that Tyrrell was a ferocious opponent of the turbo in previous years. On 21 April 1985, Ayrton Senna won his first race in the Lotus Renault.

> ## "Bernard Dudot's incredible turbo engine team was now coaxing 810bhp out of the unit, and had completed a new EF15 V6 engine to complement the existing EF4s."

Brazilian Grand Prix, Jacarepagua, 7 April 1985

Under the new management of Gérard Toth, three RE60 chassis were taken to the opening race in Brazil, where Warwick qualified on the 5th row and Tambay on the 7th. Warwick finished in 10th, with Tambay up the field in 5th place.

Portuguese Grand Prix, Estoril, 21 April 1985

Things were looking up back in Europe at the Portuguese GP as

Tambay. (© Bernard Asset)

Tambay, starting from the 6th row, climbed onto the podium in 3rd place, with Warwick just missing the points in 7th.

San Marino Grand Prix, Imola, 5 May 1985
The glimmer of hope from the old days continued, as, from the middle of the grid, both cars got to the finish with Tambay on the podium in 3rd, although Warwick struggled in on 10th spot only.

Monaco Grand Prix, 19 May 1985
In Monaco neither driver was happy with his grid position, with Warwick on row 5 and Tambay 2nd row from the back. However, it was Warwick who got to the finish in 5th place, Tambay having gone out after an accident with Berger on the first lap.

Canadian Grand Prix, Montreal, 16 June 1985
After the flight to Canada, Warwick qualified on the 3rd row with Tambay on the 5th. This time the roles were reversed, with Tambay managing to finish in 7th place and Warwick getting caught up in an accident, going out on lap 25.

US East Coast Grand Prix, Detroit, 23 June 1985
Warwick got his car on the third row, whilst Tambay was again back down the grid. The team was frustrated, though hopes were a little higher for Warwick's chances. But this US GP brought no better luck, as both cars failed to finish.

Renault-powered Ayrton Senna takes victory.

STARTING GRID		RESULTS - Estoril (291,450 km)			
Senna 1'21.007"	Prost 1'21.420"	1. Senna	Lotus-Renault	67	2:00'28.006" 145.160 km/h
Rosberg 1'21.904"	De Angelis 1'22.159"	2. Alboreto	Ferrari	67	2:01'30.984"
Alboreto 1'22.577"	Warwick 1'23.084"	3. Tambay	Renault	66	+ 1 lap
Lauda 1'23.288"	De Cesaris 1'23.302"	4. De Angelis	Lotus-Renault	66	+ 1 lap
Mansell 1'23.594"	Piquet 1'23.618"	5. Mansell	Williams-Honda	65	+ 2 laps
Johansson 1'23.652"	Tambay 1'24.111"	6. Bellof	Tyrrell-Ford	65	+ 2 laps
Patrese 1'24.230"	Cheever 1'24.563"	7. Warwick	Renault	65	+ 2 laps
Winkelhock 1'24.721"	Boutsen 1'24.747"	8. Johansson	Ferrari	62	+ 5 laps
Berger 1'24.842"	Laffite 1'24.943"	9. Ghinzani	Osella-Alfa Romeo	61	+ 6 laps
Hesnault 1'25.717"	Alliot 1'26.187"				
Bellof 1'27.284"	Brundle 1'27.602"		**FASTEST LAP**		
Palmer 1'28.166"	Baldi 1'28.473"	Senna	Lotus-Renault		1'44.121" 150.401 km/h
Martini 1'28.596"	Ghinzani 1'30.855"				

RETIREMENTS

Winkelhock	RAM-Hart	51	Not classified
Lauda	McLaren-TAG Porsche	50	Engine
Cheever	Alfa Romeo	37	Engine
Prost	McLaren-TAG Porsche	31	Accident
De Cesaris	Ligier-Renault	30	Road-holding
Boutsen	Arrows-BMW	29	Electrical
Piquet	Brabham-BMW	29	Road-holding
Brundle	Tyrrell-Ford	21	Gear selector
Baldi	Spirit-Hart	20	Accident
Rosberg	Williams-Honda	17	Accident
Laffite	Ligier-Renault	16	Road-holding
Berger	Arrows-BMW	13	Accident
Martini	Minardi-Ford	13	Accident
Patrese	Alfa Romeo	5	Accident
Alliot	RAM-Hart	4	Accident
Hesnault	Brabham-BMW	4	Electrical
Palmer	Zakspeed	3	Collision Rosberg

Estoril race statistics.

New engine. (© TVA)

Imola race statistics.

Patrick Tambay. (© Bernard Asset)

Monaco race statistics.

STARTING GRID

Senna	Rosberg
1'27.327"	1'27.354"
De Angelis	Alboreto
1'27.852"	1'27.871"
Boutsen	Prost
1'27.918"	1'28.099"
Mansell	Lauda
1'28.202"	1'28.399"
Piquet	Berger
1'28.489"	1'28.697"
Tambay	Cheever
1'29.102"	1'29.259"
De Cesaris	Warwick
1'29.406"	1'29.466"
Johansson	Laffite
1'29.806"	1'30.982"
(Palmer)	Patrese
(1'31.028")	1'31.108"
Martini	Hesnault
1'32.770"	1'33.142"
Alliot	Ghinzani
1'34.201"	1'34.209"
Winkelhock	Bellof
1'34.579"	1'35.653"
Brundle	Baldi
1'36.397"	1'36.922"

RESULTS - Imola (302,400 km)

1.	De Angelis	Lotus-Renault	60	1h34'35.955"
				191.180 km/h
2.	Boutsen	Arrows-BMW	59	+ 1 lap
3.	Tambay	Renault	59	+ 1 lap
4.	Lauda	McLaren-TAG Porsche	59	+ 1 lap
5.	Mansell	Williams-Honda	59	+ 1 lap
6.	Johansson	Ferrari	58	Out of fuel
7.	Senna	Lotus-Renault	57	Out of fuel
8.	Piquet	Brabham-BMW	57	Out of fuel
9.	Brundle	Tyrrell-Ford	56	+ 3 laps
10.	Warwick	Renault	56	+ 3 laps

FASTEST LAP

Alboreto	Ferrari	1'30.961"
		199.470 km/h

RETIREMENTS

Cheever	Alfa Romeo	51	Out of fuel
Ghinzani	Osella-Alfa Romeo	46	Gearbox
Alboreto	Ferrari	30	Electrical
Winkelhock	RAM-Hart	28	Engine
Alliot	RAM-Hart	24	Engine
Rosberg	Williams-Honda	24	Throttle control brakes
Laffite	Ligier-Renault	23	Turbo
Martini	Minardi-Motori Moderni	15	Turbo
De Cesaris	Ligier-Renault	12	Accident
Baldi	Spirit-Hart	10	Electrical
Hesnault	Brabham-BMW	6	Spin
Bellof	Tyrrell-Ford	6	Engine
Berger	Arrows-BMW	5	Electrical/engine
Patrese	Alfa Romeo	5	Engine
Palmer	Zakspeed	1	Engine

DISQUALIFIED (unconform weight)

(1)Prost	McLaren-TAG Porsche	60	1h33'57.188"

STARTING GRID

Senna	Mansell
1'20.450"	1'20.536"
Alboreto	Cheever
1'20.563"	1'20.729"
Prost	Boutsen
1'20.885"	1'21.302"
Rosberg	De Cesaris
1'21.320"	1'21.347"
De Angelis	Warwick
1'21.465"	1'21.531"
Berger	Patrese
1'21.665"	1'21.813"
Piquet	Lauda
1'21.817"	1'21.907"
Johansson	Laffite
1'22.635"	1'22.880"
Tambay	Brundle
1'22.912"	1'23.827"
Palmer	Fabi
1'23.840"	1'23.965"

RESULTS - Monaco (258,336 km)

1.	Prost	McLaren-TAG Porsche	78	1h51'58.034"
				138.435 km/h
2.	Alboreto	Ferrari	78	1h52'05.575"
3.	De Angelis	Lotus-Renault	78	1h52'25.205"
4.	De Cesaris	Ligier-Renault	77	+ 1 lap
5.	Warwick	Renault	77	+ 1 lap
6.	Laffite	Ligier-Renault	77	+ 1 lap
7.	Mansell	Williams-Honda	77	+ 1 lap
8.	Rosberg	Williams-Honda	76	+ 2 laps
9.	Boutsen	Arrows-BMW	76	+ 2 laps
10.	Brundle	Tyrrell-Ford	74	+ 4 laps
11.	Palmer	Zakspeed	74	+ 4 laps

FASTEST LAP

Alboreto	Ferrari	1'22.637"
		144.284 km/h

RETIREMENTS

Lauda	McLaren-TAG Porsche	17	Spin
Patrese	Alfa Romeo	16	Collision Piquet
Piquet	Brabham-BMW	16	Collision Patrese
Fabi	Toleman-Hart	16	Turbo
Senna	Toleman-Hart	13	Engine
Cheever	Alfa Romeo	10	Electrical
Johansson	Ferrari	1	Accident
Tambay	Renault	0	Collision Berger
Berger	Arrows-BMW	0	Collision Tambay

Warwick.

STARTING GRID		RESULTS - Detroit (253,449 km)			
Senna	Mansell	1. Rosberg	Williams-Honda	63	1h55'39.851"
1'42.051"	1'43.249"				131.458 km/h
Alboreto	Prost	2. Johansson	Ferrari	63	1h56'37.400"
1'43.748"	1'44.088"	3. Alboreto	Ferrari	63	1h56'43.021"
Rosberg	Warwick	4. Bellof	Tyrrell-Ford	63	1h56'46.076"
1'44.156"	1'44.163"	5. De Angelis	Lotus-Renault	63	1h57'06.817"
Cheever	De Angelis	6. Piquet	Brabham-BMW	62	+ 1 lap
1'44.231"	1'44.769"	7. Boutsen	Arrows-BMW	62	+ 1 lap
Johansson	Piquet	8. Surer	Brabham-BMW	62	+ 1 lap
1'44.921"	1'45.194"	9. Cheever	Alfa Romeo	61	+ 2 laps
Surer	Lauda	10. De Cesaris	Ligier-Renault	61	+ 2 laps
1'45.979"	1'46.266"	11. Berger	Arrows-BMW	60	+ 3 laps
Fabi	Patrese	12. Laffite	Ligier-Renault	58	+ 5 laps
1'46.546"	1'46.592"				
Tambay	Laffite	**FASTEST LAP**			
1'47.028"	1'47.267"				
De Cesaris	Brundle	Senna	Lotus-Renault		1'45.612"
1'47.393"	1'47.563"				137.132 km/h
Bellof	Winkelhock				
1'47.911"	1'47.926"	**RETIREMENTS**			
Boutsen	Ghinzani				
1'48.023"	1'48.546"	Senna	Lotus-Renault	51	Accident
Alliot	Berger	Brundle	Tyrrell-Ford	30	Collision Alliot
1'50.455"	2'05.307"	Alliot	RAM-Hart	27	Collision Brundle
Martini		Mansell	Williams-Honda	26	Accident
3'04.446"		Prost	McLaren-TAG Porsche	19	Brakes/accident
		Patrese	Alfa Romeo	19	Electrical
		Warwick	Renault	18	Transmission
		Tambay	Renault	15	Accident
		Martini	Minardi-Motori Moderni	11	Engine
		Lauda	McLaren-TAG Porsche	10	Brakes
		Fabi	Toleman-Hart	4	Clutch
		Winkelhock	RAM-Hart	3	Turbo
		Ghinzani	Osella-Alfa Romeo	0	Collision Boutsen

Detroit race statistics.

French Grand Prix, Paul Ricard, 7 July 1985

A major effort had to be made at the French GP, and new RE60Bs – chassis 06 and 07 – were on show. However, such was the pace of the competition that grid positions of 7th for Tambay and 8th for Warwick were all there was to show for it. Nevertheless, this time, the cars did last – why could they not do this more often? Both drivers finished, in 6th and 7th position respectively.

British Grand Prix, Silverstone, 21 July 1985

The next race was the British GP at Silverstone. Middle grid positions for both drivers produced a 5th place for Warwick, but Tambay went out after a spin on the first lap.

German Grand Prix, Nürburgring, 4 August 1985

Tambay lined up directly in front of Warwick, but on row 9. Tambay spun out on lap 19, while Warwick suffered ignition failure on lap 25.

Montreal race statistics.

STARTING GRID		RESULTS - Montréal (308,700 km)			
De Angelis	Senna	1. Alboreto	Ferrari	70	1h46'01.813"
1'24.567"	1'24.816"				174.686 km/h
Alboreto	Johansson	2. Johansson	Ferrari	70	1h46'03.770"
1'25.127"	1'25.170"	3. Prost	McLaren-TAG Porsche	70	1h46'06.154"
Prost	Warwick	4. Rosberg	Williams-Honda	70	1h46'29.634"
1'25.557"	1'25.622"	5. De Angelis	Lotus-Renault	70	1h46'45.162"
Boutsen	Rosberg	6. Mansell	Williams-Honda	70	1h47'19.691"
1'25.846"	1'26.097"	7. Tambay	Renault	69	+ 1 lap
Piquet	Tambay	8. Laffite	Ligier-Renault	69	+ 1 lap
1'26.301"	1'26.340"	9. Boutsen	Arrows-BMW	68	+ 2 laps
Cheever	Berger	10. Patrese	Alfa Romeo	68	+ 2 laps
1'26.354"	1'26.743"	11. Bellof	Tyrrell-Ford	68	+ 2 laps
Patrese	Winkelhock	12. Brundle	Tyrrell-Ford	68	+ 2 laps
1'26.995"	1'27.266"	13. Berger	Arrows-BMW	67	+ 3 laps
De Cesaris	Mansell	14. De Cesaris	Ligier-Renault	67	+ 3 laps
1'27.403"	1'27.728"	15. Surer	Brabham-BMW	67	+ 3 laps
Lauda	Fabi	16. Senna	Lotus-Renault	65	+ 5 laps
1'28.126"	1'28.625"	17. Cheever	Alfa Romeo	64	+ 6 laps
Laffite	Surer				
1'28.750"	1'29.473"	**FASTEST LAP**			
Alliot	Ghinzani				
1'29.501"	1'31.576"	Senna	Lotus-Renault		1'27.445"
Bellof	Brundle				181.554 km/h
1'31.733"	1'31.923"				
Martini		**RETIREMENTS**			
1'34.985"					
		Martini	Minardi-Motori Moderni	57	Accident
		Lauda	McLaren-TAG Porsche	37	Engine
		Ghinzani	Osella-Alfa Romeo	35	Engine
		Alliot	RAM-Hart	28	Accident
		Warwick	Renault	25	Accident
		Winkelhock	RAM-Hart	5	Accident
		Fabi	Toleman-Hart	3	Turbo
		Piquet	Brabham-BMW	0	Transmission

STARTING GRID		RESULTS - Le Castellet (307,930 km)			
Rosberg 1'32.462"	Senna 1'32.835"	1. Piquet	Brabham-BMW	53	1h31'46.266" 201.325 km/h
Alboreto 1'33.267"	Prost 1'33.335"	2. Rosberg	Williams-Honda	53	1h31'52.926"
Piquet 1'33.812"	Lauda 1'33.860"	3. Prost	McLaren-TAG Porsche	53	1h31'55.551"
De Angelis 1'34.022"	Berger 1'34.674"	4. Johansson	Ferrari	53	1h32'39.757"
Tambay 1'34.680"	Warwick 1'34.976"	5. De Angelis	Lotus-Renault	53	1h32'39.956"
Boutsen 1'35.488"	De Cesaris 1'35.571"	6. Tambay	Renault	53	1h33'01.433"
Surer 1'35.572"	Laffite 1'36.133"	7. Warwick	Renault	53	1h33'30.478"
Johansson 1'36.140"	Patrese 1'36.729"	8. Surer	Brabham-BMW	52	+ 1 lap
Cheever 1'36.931"	Fabi 1'37.142"	9. Boutsen	Arrows-BMW	52	+ 1 lap
Winkelhock 1'37.654"	Brundle 1'40.015"	10. Cheever	Alfa Romeo	52	+ 1 lap
Palmer 1'40.289"	Alliot 1'41.647"	11. Patrese	Alfa Romeo	52	+ 1 lap
Ghinzani 1'42.136"	Martini 1'44.350"	12. Winkelhock	RAM-Hart	50	+ 3 laps
Bellof 1'44.404"		13. Bellof	Tyrrell-Ford	50	+ 3 laps
		14. Fabi	Toleman-Hart	49	Fuel pressure
		15. Ghinzani	Osella-Alfa Romeo	49	+ 4 laps

FASTEST LAP		
Rosberg	Williams-Honda	1'39.914" 209.340 km/h

RETIREMENTS			
Brundle	Tyrrell-Renault	32	Gearbox
Lauda	McLaren-TAG Porsche	30	Gearbox
Senna	Lotus-Renault	26	Engine accident
Berger	Arrows-BMW	20	Collision Martini
Martini	Minardi-Motori Moderni	19	Collision Berger
Alliot	RAM-Hart	8	Fuel pressure
Palmer	Zakspeed	6	Engine
Alboreto	Ferrari	5	Turbo
De Cesaris	Ligier-Renault	4	Transmission
Laffite	Ligier-Renault	2	Turbo

Paul Ricard race statistics.

Austrian Grand Prix, Zeltweg, 18 August 1985

Austria – another disaster. Tambay was classified in 10th place but was 6 laps down on Prost; Senna once again claimed the podium after he drove his Renault-powered car to 2nd place. Our photo (right) clearly shows the engine failure on Warwick's car.

Dutch Grand Prix, Zandvoort, 25 August 1985

No luck here, either, as both cars went out with gearbox and transmission failures.

Italian Grand Prix, Monza, 8 September 1985

While other teams running with Renault engines were getting consistent finishes, the Renault team was struggling, and this time it was only Tambay who got home (in 7th). Monza failed to raise hopes when Warwick went out on lap 9, again with transmission failure.

Warwick giving it his all.

STARTING GRID		RESULTS - Silverstone (306,735 km)			
Rosberg 1'05.591"	Piquet 1'06.249"	1. Prost	McLaren-TAG Porsche	65	1h18'10.436" 235.354 km/h
Prost 1'06.308"	Senna 1'06.324"	2. Alboreto	Ferrari	64	+ 1 lap
Mansell 1'06.675"	Alboreto 1'06.793"	3. Laffite	Ligier-Renault	64	+ 1 lap
De Cesaris 1'07.448"	De Angelis 1'07.581"	4. Piquet	Brabham-BMW	64	+ 1 lap
Fabi 1'07.678"	Lauda 1'07.743"	5. Warwick	Renault	64	+ 1 lap
Johansson 1'07.887"	Warwick 1'08.238"	6. Surer	Brabham-BMW	63	+ 2 laps
Tambay 1'08.240"	Patrese 1'08.384"	7. Brundle	Tyrrell-Renault	63	+ 2 laps
Surer 1'08.587"	Laffite 1'08.656"	8. Berger	Arrows-BMW	63	+ 2 laps
Berger 1'08.672"	Winkelhock 1'09.114"	9. Patrese	Alfa Romeo	62	+ 3 laps
Boutsen 1'09.131"	Brundle 1'09.242"	10. Senna	Lotus-Renault	60	Electronics
Alliot 1'09.609"	Cheever 1'10.345"	11. Bellof	Tyrrell-Ford	59	+ 6 laps
Martini 1'13.645"	Palmer 1'13.713"				
Ghinzani 1'16.400"	Bellof 1'16.596"				

FASTEST LAP		
Prost	McLaren-TAG Porsche	1'09.886" 243.036 km/h

RETIREMENTS			
Lauda	McLaren-TAG Porsche	57	Electrical
Boutsen	Arrows-BMW	57	Accident
De Cesaris	Ligier-Renault	41	Clutch
Martini	Minardi-Motori Moderni	38	Transmission
De Angelis	Lotus-Renault	37	Not classified, 28 laps
Winkelhock	RAM-Hart	28	Turbo
Rosberg	Williams-Honda	21	Exhaust
Mansell	Willimas-Honda	17	Clutch
Cheever	Alfa Romeo	17	Turbo
Palmer	Zakspeed	6	Engine
Fabi	Toleman-Hart	4	Differential
Johansson	Ferrari	1	Accident
Tambay	Renault	1	Spin
Alliot	RAM-Hart	1	Pile-up
Ghinzani	Osella-Alfa Romeo	1	Pile-up

Silverstone race statistics.

STARTING GRID

Fabi 1'17.429"	Johansson 1'18.616"
Prost 1'18.725"	Rosberg 1'18.781"
Senna 1'18.792"	Piquet 1'18.802"
De Angelis 1'19.120"	Alboreto 1'19.194"
Patrese 1'19.338"	Mansell 1'19.475"
Surer 1'19.558"	Lauda 1'19.652"
Laffite 1'19.656"	De Cesaris 1'19.738"
Boutsen 1'19.781"	Tambay 1'19.917"
Berger 1'20.666"	Cheever 1'21.074"
Bellof 1'21.219"	Warwick 1'21.237"
Alliot 1'22.017"	Winkelhock 1'22.607"
Hesnault 1'23.161"	Palmer 1'24.217"
Rothengatter 1'26.478"	Brundle 1'27.621"
Martini 1'40.506"	

RESULTS - Nürburgring (304,314 km)

Pos	Driver	Car	Laps	Time/Gap
1.	Alboreto	Ferrari	67	1h35'31.337" 191.147 km/h
2.	Prost	McLaren-TAG Porsche	67	1h35'42.998"
3.	Laffite	Ligier-Renault	67	1h36'22.491"
4.	Boutsen	Arrows-BMW	67	1h36'26.616"
5.	Lauda	McLaren-TAG Porsche	67	1h36'45.309"
6.	Mansell	Williams-Honda	67	1h36'48.157"
7.	Berger	Arrows-BMW	66	+ 1 lap
8.	Bellof	Tyrrell-Renault	66	+ 1 lap
9.	Johansson	Ferrari	66	+ 1 lap
10.	Brundle	Tyrrell-Ford	63	+ 4 laps
11.	Martini	Minardi-Motori Mod.	62	Engine
12.	Rosberg	Williams-Honda	61	Brakes

FASTEST LAP

Lauda	McLaren-TAG Porsche	1'22.806" 197.464 km/h

RETIREMENTS

Driver	Car	Lap	Reason
Cheever	Alfa Romeo	45	Turbo
De Angelis	Lotus-Renault	40	Engine
Rothengatter	Osella-Alfa Romeo	32	Gearbox
Fabi	Toleman-Hart	29	Clutch
Senna	Lotus-Renault	27	Engine
Warwick	Renault	25	Ignition
Piquet	Brabham-BMW	23	Turbo
Tambay	Renault	19	Spin
Surer	Brabham-BMW	12	Engine
Winkelhock	RAM-Hart	8	Engine
Patrese	Alfa Romeo	8	Gearbox
Hesnault	Brabham-BMW	8	Clutch
Alliot	RAM-Hart	8	Oil pressure
Palmer	Zakspeed	7	Battery
De Cesaris	Ligier-Renault	0	Collision Laffite

Nürburgring race statistics.

A lot of hard work but nothing to show for it. (© Bernard Asset)

Another smoky end for Renault. (© Bernard Asset)

STARTING GRID

Prost 1'25.490"	Mansell 1'26.052"
Lauda 1'26.250"	Rosberg 1'26.333"
Piquet 1'26.404"	Fabi 1'26.664"
De Angelis 1'26.799"	Tambay 1'27.502"
Alboreto 1'27.516"	Patrese 1'27.851"
Surer 1'27.954"	Johansson 1'27.961"
Warwick 1'28.006"	Senna 1'28.123"
Laffite 1'28.249"	Boutsen 1'28.262"
Berger 1'28.566"	De Cesaris 1'28.666"
(Ghinzani) (1'28.894")	Cheever 1'29.031"
Alliot 1'29.827"	Bellof 1'30.514"
Acheson 1'35.072"	Rothengatter 1'35.329"
Palmer 1'35.787"	Martini 1'36.765"

RESULTS - Zeltweg (308,984 km)

Pos	Driver	Car	Laps	Time/Gap
1.	Prost	McLaren-TAG Porsche	52	1h20'12.583" 191.147 km/h
2.	Senna	Lotus-Renault	52	1h20'42.585"
3.	Alboreto	Ferrari	52	1h20'46.939"
4.	Johansson	Ferrari	52	1h20'51.656"
5.	De Angelis	Lotus-Renault	52	1h21'34.675"
6.	Surer	Brabham-BMW	51	+ 1 lap
7.	Bellof	Tyrrell-Renault	49	Out of fuel
8.	Boutsen	Arrows-BMW	49	+ 3 laps
9.	Rothengatter	Osella-Alfa R.	48	+ 4 laps
10.	Tambay	Renault	46	Engine

FASTEST LAP

Prost	McLaren-TAG Porsche	1'29.241" 239.701 km/h

RETIREMENTS

Driver	Car	Lap	Reason
Laffite	Ligier-Renault	43	Wheel
Martini	Minardi-Motori Moderni	40	Suspension
Lauda	McLaren-TAG Porsche	39	Engine
Berger	Arrows-BMW	32	Turbo
Fabi	Toleman-Hart	31	Electrical
Warwick	Renault	29	Engine
Acheson	RAM-Hart	28	Engine
Piquet	Brabham-BMW	26	Exhaust
Mansell	Williams-Honda	25	Engine
Patrese	Alfa Romeo	25	Engine
Palmer	Zakspeed	17	Engine
Alliot	RAM-Hart	16	Turbo
De Cesaris	Ligier-Renault	13	Accident
Cheever	Alfa Romeo	6	Turbo
Rosberg	Williams-Honda	4	Engine

Zeltweg race statistics.

STARTING GRID		RESULTS - Zandvoort (297,640 km)			
Piquet 1'11.074"	Rosberg 1'11.647"	1. Lauda	McLaren-TAG Porsche	70	1h32'29.263" 193.089 km/h
Prost 1'11.801"	Senna 1'11.837"	2. Prost	McLaren-TAG Porsche	70	1h32'29.495"
Fabi 1'12.310"	Tambay 1'12.486"	3. Senna	Lotus-Renault	70	1h33'17.754"
Mansell 1'12.614"	Boutsen 1'12.746"	4. Alboreto	Ferrari	70	1h33'18.100"
Surer 1'12.856"	Lauda 1'13.059"	5. De Angelis	Lotus-Renault	69	+ 1 lap
De Angelis 1'13.078"	Warwick 1'13.289"	6. Mansell	Williams-Honda	69	+ 1 lap
Laffite 1'13.435"	Berger 1'13.680"	7. Brundle	Tyrrell-Renault	69	+ 1 lap
Ghinzani 1'13.705"	Alboreto 1'13.725"	8. Piquet	Brabham-BMW	69	+ 1 lap
Johansson 1'13.768"	De Cesaris 1'13.797"	9. Berger	Arrows-BMW	68	+ 2 laps
Patrese 1'14.240"	Cheever 1'14.912"	10. Surer	Brabham-BMW	65	Exhaust
Brundle 1'14.920"	Bellof 1'15.236"				
Palmer 1'16.257"	Martini 1'17.919"	**FASTEST LAP**			
Alliot 1'18.525"	Rothengatter 1'19.410"	Prost	McLaren-TAG Porsche		1'16.538" 199.995 km/h

RETIREMENTS

Rothengatter	Osella-Alfa Romeo	46	Not classified, 14 laps
Boutsen	Arrows-BMW	44	Suspension
Alliot	RAM-Hart	42	Engine
Bellof	Tyrrell-Renault	39	Engine
Warwick	Renault	37	Gearbox
De Cesaris	Ligier-Renault	35	Turbo
Tambay	Renault	32	Transmission
Rosberg	Williams-Honda	20	Engine
Fabi	Toleman-Hart	18	Rolling bearing
Laffite	Ligier-Renault	17	Electrical
Palmer	Zakspeed	13	Oil pressure
Ghinzani	Toleman-Hart	12	Engine
Johansson	Ferrari	9	Engine
Martini	Minardi-Motori Moderni	1	Accident
Cheever	Alfa Romeo	1	Turbo
Patrese	Alfa Romeo	1	Turbo

Zandvoort race statistics.

Tambay waits ... (© Bernard Asset)

Belgian Grand Prix, Spa, 15 September 1985

Whilst it was a Renault engine that powered Senna to victory in the Belgian Grand Prix, the Renault team could only watch hopelessly as Warwick came in to finish in 6th place. This time, it was Tambay who went out on lap 24 with gearbox failure.

European Grand Prix, Brands Hatch, 6 October 1985

Brands Hatch, home to the European Grand Prix, saw Warwick qualify on row 4, but Tambay was way down the grid, eventually coming in last. Warwick went out with fuel problems on lap 4.

These were desperate times. By now, the Renault Sport team was in serious difficulty, and the new management was struggling to resolve the situation. Neither car appeared on the grid in South Africa.

Australian Grand Prix, Adelaide, 3 November 1985

The final race of 1985 – Renault's last as an F1 team in the turbo era – was the Australian GP on 3 November 1985. Neither car finished. It was the end.

STARTING GRID		RESULTS - Monza (295,800 km)			
Senna 1'25.084"	Rosberg 1'25.230"	1. Prost	McLaren-TAG Porsche	51	1h17'59.451" 257.595 km/h
Mansell 1'25.486"	Piquet 1'25.584"	2. Piquet	Brabham-BMW	51	1h18'51.086"
Prost 1'25.790"	De Angelis 1'26.044"	3. Senna	Lotus-Renault	51	1h18'59.841"
Alboreto 1'26.468"	Tambay 1'27.020"	4. Surer	Brabham-BMW	51	1h19'00.060"
Surer 1'27.153"	Johansson 1'27.473"	5. Johansson	Ferrari	50	Out of fuel
Berger 1'27.723"	Warwick 1'28.112"	6. De Angelis	Lotus-Renault	50	+ 1 lap
Patrese 1'28.340"	Boutsen 1'28.369"	7. Tambay	Renault	50	+ 1 lap
Fabi 1'28.386"	Lauda 1'28.472"	8. Brundle	Tyrrell-Renault	50	+ 1 lap
Cheever 1'28.629"	Brundle 1'28.793"	9. Boutsen	Arrows-BMW	50	+ 1 lap
Streiff 1'29.839"	Laffite 1'30.186"	10. Streiff	Ligier-Renault	49	+ 2 laps
Ghinzani 1'30.271"	Rothengatter 1'33.529"	11. Mansell	Williams-Honda	47	Engine
Martini 1'33.981"	Acheson 1'34.919"	12. Fabi	Toleman-Hart	47	+ 4 laps
Jones 1'34.943"	Alliot 1'36.221"	13. Alboreto	Ferrari	45	Out of fuel

FASTEST LAP

Mansell	Williams-Honda		1'28.283" 236.512 km/h

RETIREMENTS

Rosberg	Williams-Honda	44	Engine
Laffite	Ligier-Renault	40	Engine
Lauda	McLaren-TAG Porsche	33	Transmission
Patrese	Alfa Romeo	31	Exhaust
Rothengatter	Osella-Alfa Romeo	26	Engine
Alliot	RAM-Hart	19	Turbo
Berger	Arrows-BMW	13	Engine
Warwick	Renault	9	Transmission
Jones	Lola Haas-Hart	6	Fuel feed
Cheever	Alfa Romeo	3	Engine
Acheson	RAM-Hart	2	Clutch
Martini	Minardi-Motori Moderni	0	Fuel pump
Ghinzani	Toleman-Hart	0	Stall (start)

Monza race statistics.

Tambay leads Warwick, who just got in the points.

STARTING GRID		RESULTS - Brands Hatch (GB) (315,525 km)			
Senna 1'07.169"	Piquet 1'07.482"	1. Mansell	Williams-Honda	75	1h32'58.109" 202.430 km/h
Mansell 1'08.059"	Rosberg 1'08.197"	2. Senna	Lotus-Renault	75	1h33'19.505"
Streiff 1'09.080"	Prost 1'09.429"	3. Rosberg	Williams-Honda	75	1h33'56.642"
Surer 1'09.762"	Warwick 1'09.904"	4. Prost	McLaren-TAG Porsche	75	1h34'04.230"
De Angelis 1'10.041"	Laffite 1'10.081"	5. De Angelis	Lotus-Renault	74	+ 1 lap
Patrese 1'10.251"	Boutsen 1'10.323"	6. Boutsen	Arrows-BMW	73	+ 2 laps
Johansson 1'10.517"	Ghinzani 1'10.570"	7. Watson	McLaren-TAG Porsche	73	+ 2 laps
Alboreto 1'10.659"	Brundle 1'10.731"	8. Streiff	Ligier-Renault	73	+ 2 laps
Tambay 1'10.934"	Cheever 1'11.500"	9. Patrese	Alfa Romeo	73	+ 2 laps
Berger 1'11.608"	Fabi 1'12.090"	10. Berger	Arrows-BMW	73	+ 2 laps
Watson 1'12.496"	Jones 1'13.084"	11. Cheever	Alfa Romeo	73	+ 2 laps
Alliot 1'13.537"	Capelli 1'13.721"	12. Tambay	Renault	72	+ 3 laps
Danner 1'15.054"	Martini 1'15.127"				

FASTEST LAP

Laffite	Ligier-Renault	1'11.526" 211.744 km/h

RETIREMENTS

Surer	Brabham-BMW	62	Turbo
Johansson	Ferrari	59	Electrical
Laffite	Ligier-Renault	58	Engine
Danner	Zakspeed	50	Engine
Capelli	Tyrrell-Renault	44	Accident
Brundle	Tyrrell-Renault	40	Water pipe
Fabi	Toleman-Hart	33	Engine
Alliot	RAM-Hart	31	Engine
Ghinzani	Toleman-Hart	16	Engine
Jones	Lola Haas-Hart	13	Water radiator
Alboreto	Ferrari	13	Turbo
Piquet	Brabham-BMW	6	Accident
Warwick	Renault	4	Fuel feed
Martini	Minardi-Motori Moderni	3	Accident

Brands Hatch race statistics.

STARTING GRID		RESULTS - Spa-Francorchamps (298,420 km)			
Prost 1'55.306"	Senna 1'55.403"	1. Senna	Lotus-Renault	43	1h34'19.893" 189.811 km/h
Piquet 1'55.648"	Alboreto 1'56.021"	2. Mansell	Williams-Honda	43	1h34'48.315"
Johansson 1'56.585"	Boutsen 1'56.697"	3. Prost	McLaren-TAG Porsche	43	1h35'15.002"
Mansell 1'56.727"	Berger 1'56.770"	4. Rosberg	Williams-Honda	43	1h35'35.183"
De Angelis 1'57.322"	Rosberg 1'57.465"	5. Piquet	Brabham-BMW	42	+ 1 lap
Fabi 1'57.588"	Surer 1'57.729"	6. Warwick	Renault	42	+ 1 lap
Tambay 1'58.105"	Warwick 1'58.407"	7. Berger	Arrows-BMW	42	+ 1 lap
Patrese 1'58.414"	Ghinzani 1'58.706"	8. Surer	Brabham-BMW	42	+ 1 lap
Laffite 1'58.933"	Streiff 1'59.245"	9. Streiff	Ligier-Renault	42	+ 1 lap
Cheever 1'59.370"	Alliot 1'59.626"	10. Boutsen	Arrows-BMW	40	+ 3 laps
Brundle 2'00.950"	Danner 2'05.059"	11. Laffite	Ligier-Renault	38	Accident
Rothengatter 2'05.776"	Martini 2'06.007"	12. Martini	Minardi-Motori Mod.	38	+ 5 laps
		13. Brundle	Tyrrell-Renault	38	+ 5 laps

FASTEST LAP

Prost	McLaren-TAG Porsche	2'01.730" 205.241 km/h

RETIREMENTS

Rothengatter	Osella-Alfa Romeo	37	Not classified, 6 laps
Patrese	Alfa Romeo	31	Engine
Cheever	Alfa Romeo	26	Gearbox
Tambay	Renault	24	Gearbox
Fabi	Toleman-Hart	23	Accelerator control
De Angelis	Lotus-Renault	19	Turbo
Danner	Zakspeed	16	Gearbox
Alliot	RAM-Hart	10	Accident
Johansson	Ferrari	7	Engine Spun off
Ghinzani	Toleman-Hart	7	Accident
Alboreto	Ferrari	3	Clutch

Spa race statistics.

Derek gives it his best shot, but fuel problems let him down. (© Bernard Asset)

During the year, the electronic management box was moved to allow a lower engine cover; smaller radiators, a slimmer nose-cone, new uprights and wishbones had all been tried to achieve a smaller package passing through the air, but to no avail. Engines and gearboxes had continued to fail. Both drivers started 15 of the 16 Grands Prix, but the cars were no longer the serious competitors that they once had been.

Régie management had lost interest in a house Formula 1 team, so it was therefore no surprise when Renault announced that it was pulling out of the F1 World Championship at the end of the season. The drivers had done their best, but it looked like they were just making up the numbers in the final Grand Prix. They put on a brave face, but were bitterly disappointed. It was also a shock to France's national pride and, for sure, the Grand Prix world

The last team photo.

STARTING GRID	
Senna	Mansell
1'19.843"	1'20.537"
Rosberg	Prost
1'21.887"	1'21.889"
Alboreto	Surer
1'22.337"	1'22.561"
Berger	Tambay
1'22.592"	1'22.683"
Piquet	De Angelis
1'22.718"	1'23.077"
Boutsen	Warwick
1'23.196"	1'23.426"
Cheever	Patrese
1'23.597"	1'23.758"
Johansson	Lauda
1'23.902"	1'23.941"
Brundle	Streiff
1'24.241"	1'24.286"
Jones	Laffite
1'24.369"	1'24.830"
Ghinzani	Capelli
1'25.021"	1'27.120"
Martini	Fabi
1'27.196"	1'28.110"
Rothengatter	
1'30.319"	

RESULTS - Adelaïde (309,960 km)

1. Rosberg	Williams-Honda	82	2:00'40.473"
			154.032 km/h
2. Laffite	Ligier-Renault	82	2:01'26.603"
3. Streif	Ligier-Renault	82	2:02'09.009"
4. Capelli		81	+ 1 lap
5. Johansson		81	+ 1 lap
6. Berger		81	+ 1 lap
7. Rothengatter		78	+ 4 laps
8. Martini		78	+ 4 laps

FASTEST LAP

Rosberg	Williams-Honda	1'23.758"
		162.758 km/h

RETIREMENTS

Senna	Toleman-Hart	63	Engine
Alboreto	Ferrari	62	Gear selector
Lauda	McLaren-TAG Porsche	58	Accident
Warwick	Renault	57	Transmission
Brundle	Tyrrell-Renault	49	Not classified, 33 laps
Surer	Brabham-BMW	43	Engine
Patrese	Alfa Romeo	43	Exhaust
Fabi	Toleman-Hart	41	Engine
Boutsen	Arrows-BMW	38	Oil leak
Ghinzani	Toleman-Hart	29	Clutch
Prost	McLaren-TAG Porsche	27	Engine
Tambay	Renault	21	Transmission
Jones	Lola Haas-Hart	21	Electrical
De Angelis	Lotus-Renault	19	Disqualified
Piquet	Brabham-BMW	15	Court-circuit
Cheever	Alfa Romeo	6	Engine
Mansell	Williams-Honda	2	Transmission

Adelaide race statistics.

needed industrial giants like Renault. Fortunately, Bernard Dudot's efforts were still paying dividends with engines being supplied to other teams. That department was now producing even more engines to be used by Lotus, Ligier, and Tyrrell in 1986, which it continued to do until the end of the turbo era.

Bernard Dudot: "We saw 1200bhp on several occasions in qualifying, but I know that more was claimed by others. Also, we sometimes saw flashes of much higher figures in the later years."

Incredible is not too strong a word to describe the basic V6 design created by François Castaing for the 2-litre sports cars in 1972/73 that had been modified to create the 1500 Grand Prix engine, and then gone on to become one of the greatest and most powerful Grand Prix engines of all time. Renault had made a brave and determined effort with its own team; company and top management commitment in 1976 – and the efforts of

"Renault had brought use of the turbocharger to the Grand Prix world. The fact that others were able to exploit it further is a tribute to the far-sighted vision of the men involved."

the technical engineers, designers, team managers and team personnel to try to make it work – were of the highest order.

Renault had brought use of the turbocharger to the Grand Prix world. The fact that others were able to exploit it further is a tribute to the far-sighted vision of the men involved, who, as this story tells, were dedicated to a dream. That it so nearly brought them the World Championship is to be commended, but, in Grand Prix racing, so near can also be so far ...

Part 5

THE LAST WORD

Gérard Larrousse: "I remember Michel Têtu with a couple of Renault 5 bodies and a big powerful hack-saw, cutting up the chassis to create the shell for the first R5 Turbo."

When Jean Terramorsi first put forward the idea of using a turbocharger to increase performance, he was thinking primarily of the development of road cars. Bernard Dudot had done it in 1972 with a primitive but very effective installation in the A110. As far as road cars were concerned, that's where the idea stopped for a number of years as the racing engines were created, but Terramorsi and his colleague, Henri Lherm, had not lost sight of the marketing potential and began to consider the Renault R5 as the basis for a new car.

Renault's successful R5 was the mainstay of the company's private car sales in the early 1970s, and, up at Alpine in Dieppe, a hotter version was being tried out, eventually to be known as the R5 Alpine and sold in the UK as the R5 Gordini, because copyright of the name Alpine belonged to Sunbeam. Mauro Bianchi had also built a car for his wife – a very hot R5 Alpine – during the time that he was helping to develop the A310.

By early 1975, various feasibility discussions had already occurred, and, following Terramorsi's thinking, Marc Deschamps, stylist at Renault's design centre at Rueil, came up with a sketch, dated 7 May 1976, that was remarkably similar to the final car which appeared some years later. A small team was put together, joined a couple of months later by Michel Têtu, a man we have met before in the Turbo F1 story. In January of 1976, Gérard Larrousse had taken on the role of head of Renault's competition department, now known as Renault Sport, and had brought Têtu along to develop the idea of a rear-engined super car and turn the chassis into a serious prospect utilising the already recognised capabilities and experience he acquired at Charles Deutsche, Ligier, and Auto Delta Alfa Romeo.

Usually, a manufacturer creates a production model and then makes the racing and sporting versions afterward, but, on this occasion, the idea was to create a competition car first, specifically intended to compete in the World Rally Championship. The project had been given the name 822, and, following earlier discussions, Renault management had come up with a specification for a vehicle which was to be "a powerful,

manoeuvrable car, with excellent road-holding. It must not exceed a weight of 810kg," – the weight limit for 2-litre cars in the World Rally Championship at the time. From the marketing point of view, Renault wanted a road car that would be able to achieve competition success with only a limited amount of modification. Plus, the production car was required to attain speeds that were usually associated with pure sports cars, around 200kmh at the time, and should have a serious visual 'wow' factor.

The gearbox was to be 5-speed; the engine should develop power to the order of 150-160bhp, and performance must be easily extendable for competition. Even four-wheel drive was briefly considered, but rejected after an evaluation of cost, which was perceived as too high from the point of view of producing for sale the 400 cars required for competition homologation at the time. Unfortunately, that conservative judgement, unlike the decision to go into F1, meant that the 5 Turbo missed the opportunity to replace the Alpine berlinette in everyone's hearts. However, the idea of creating a super car capable of taking on the likes of Peugeot, Lancia, Ford, etc, in rallying was conceived, though it would not be until spring of 1977 that the development was given the go-ahead.

> **"Even four-wheel drive was briefly considered, but rejected after an evaluation of cost, which was perceived as too high from the point of view of producing for sale the 400 cars required for competition homologation at the time."**

Several engines were considered (even 3-litre, originally), including a 2-litre and the 1400cc which, applying the equivalence formula of 1.4 for turbo engines demanded by competition rules, corresponded to a 2-litre format. It was decided to go turbo and it was the R5 Alpine engine that was chosen; a solid, compact unit which could withstand severe stress, plus it had an advantageous cylinder head design. Its main asset, though, was its capacity, which made it ideal for a turbo to be added without modification to stroke or bore, along the lines of the Dudot/Terramorsi criteria. This 1397cc capacity engine, after application of that ratio of 1.4, in effect became a 1955cc unit, perfect for the under 2-litre category. And with the gearbox and drive train from the V6 Alpine PRV engine, it was a strong combination.

With these ideas in mind, the creation of a prototype was instigated and, in the spring of 1977, an R5 shell was delivered to Dieppe. Work was begun, but, due to preparations for Le Mans, the workforce that could be devoted to the new project was limited, though it did, in due course, create the first, now well-known 'black prototype.' Just as in the early Alpine days, the work was carried out in a cramped workshop with no windows, which meant that the mechanics had to down tools on many occasions to go outside for fresh air because of the fumes coming from the welding process!

Work on the engine had begun in a different plant but in parallel with the chassis, and the knowledge gained from work on the F1 turbo was applied to the new little engine. The first engine was built and tested on a dyno, then installed in the car. Initially, a tubular framework was made to carry the engine and transmission units, and add strength to the now dismantled original R5 bodyshell. Rear suspension from the A310 was installed, while the front end came from the R5 Alpine Group 2

The first prototype 822 on test at Lédenon, 23 November 1978.

rally car. By July 1977, the basics were completed, with just the many teething problems to attend to that were typical of setting up a new turbocharged, fuel-injected engine, and details like the gear linkage, steering, pedals, etc, awaiting refinement to produce a usable car.

> **"This 1397cc capacity engine, after application of that ratio of 1.4, in effect became a 1955cc unit, perfect for the under 2-litre category. And with the gearbox and drive train from the V6 Alpine PRV engine, it was a strong combination."**

Following the death of Terramorsi the year previously, in August 1976, his colleague-at-arms, Henri Lherm, took up the torch to push the project forward, as the styling side had lost some of its direction. In October 1977, it was decided to give the job of creating final body style, based on the original Marc Deschamps ideas, to Bertone in Turin. Marcello Gandini was immediately impressed and began to build a superb plaster mock-up, beautifully finished and looking like a real car rather than a prototype racer.

Larrousse was ready to pounce! The car was placed in a room near to the area where the new Renault 9 was being presented to Bernard Hanon. As Hanon moved to leave after the R9 presentation, he was sidetracked to look at the new R5 Turbo styled by Bertone. He was amazed and totally convinced: the project could officially progress to the next stage.

Société Heuliez was commissioned in April 1978 to do a study for the production of the car, though the remit to produce the various plastic body parts went to the ex-Alpine workforce at the soon-to-be-renamed BEREX plant in Dieppe. Richard Bouleau, together with Yves Legal and Alain Serpaggi, was already preparing a customer road-car version, and had secretly fitted an engine into a Lancia Stratos which underwent extensive testing carried out by Alain Serpaggi. Final assembly of the first production R5 Turbos would be done at Heuliez in Cerisay.

It was on the evening of 9 March 1978, not far from Dieppe, that the prototype was driven for the first time by Gérard Larrousse and Michel Têtu. Michel Têtu: "I was delighted when Gérard asked me to take the car out for the tests – it was quite an honour." A secluded road had been chosen, and Larrousse took François Castaing with him for the first run in the car for 10 laps of the secret route. Têtu then took Patrick Landon with him and drove for 11 laps. Of course, there were things which required improvement, but the only problem requiring the mechanics' attention over this first 260km test was an electrical short circuit under the dashboard!

A second test was held on 14 March at the Renault testing ground at Lardy, where the reaction from the senior management present resulted in the go-ahead for continuation of the study. In the summer of 1978, the second prototype, 822/01 – which had a rear section bodyshell rather than the fabricated tubular construction of the original – was created. To conform to the weight requirement of rally regulations, it was decided to manufacture the doors and tailgate in aluminium. 822/01 was painted a beautiful metallic red and presented to the press at the Ermonville Pavilion on 4 October 1978.

A third car, 822/02, was built and painted in blue, and was shown at the Salon de Bruxelles in 1979. Chassis 822/03 was built at the same time. This would be developed for Group 4 and competed in the 1979 Giro d'Italia. By 1979, the Turbo was producing impressive performance figures.

The rest, as they say, is history and this concluding chapter tells how Renault's turbocharging philosophy was not only to take over in F1, but also to influence rallying and customer road cars, too.

Maxi Turbo, Tour de Corse, May 1985.

"... the first production series of 1678 Renault 5 Turbos, along with the special versions that followed, has achieved cult status, and turbo technology has been taken up by most of the major motor manufacturers."

It is fascinating to reflect, at the end of our story, that the idea of turbocharging a small-engined car was first tried out by a young engineer with a bright idea in the kitchen at Alpine in Dieppe. Such is the interest in turbocharging now that the first production series of 1678 Renault 5 Turbos, along with the special versions that followed, has achieved cult status, and turbo technology has been taken up by most of the major motor manufacturers.

Our story concludes with a pictorial look at the first Renault Sport road car to use a turbo.

Maxi engine on test at Le Luc, 1985.

Engine layout on the first prototype.

R5 turbo-engine prototype, Montlhéry, September 1979.

The first car presented to the press, October 1978.

R5 production at Viry-Châtillon, November 1979.

HISTOIRE & COLLECTION

It would be understandable to imagine that old cars from the 1970s and 1980s are of little concern to today's digitised world, but, in fact, the interest in what many regard as a classic era is enormous. Renault – which has a huge customer base and, as we have learnt, an incredible pedigree – decided in 2002 to create a living, moving, vibrant collection of cars from throughout the company's history, which is called the Service Histoire & Collection.

The idea of saving and collecting the cars originated in the mid-1980s, and, in the early 1990s, the likes of Jean Sage, Gilbert Hatry, Jean Robert, Patrick Landon, and several others all thought it might be a good plan, or the cars would, in time, be lost to museums as static exhibits. Initially, despite a lack of formal structure, several of these men began to collect what they considered to be the most important vehicles. Various clubs and associations throughout France, and departments within Renault, financed by the commercial networks within the company, began to acquire cars, also.

(© RS)

"... in 2003, the entire department – now including some 600 cars – was moved to a new home at the Renault Flins plant just outside Paris, close to the A13 Rouen motorway: the 12,000m² (129,167ft²) first floor of a former parts storage building, which was opened up to house the collection."

Early in the new millennium Renault management decided it was time to bring the cars together in one place. Christian Schmaltz, from within the Renault organisation, was appointed the new director of Histoire & Collection in 2002, and initially assembled the cars in Billancourt. Then, in 2003, the entire department – now including some 600 cars – was moved to a new home at the Renault Flins plant just outside Paris, close to the A13 Rouen motorway: the 12,000m² (129,167ft²) first floor of a former parts storage building, which was opened up to

Some of the F1-powered Renaults in the 650-strong collection. (© RS)

The workshops: cars await checks. (© RS)

Mechanics' corner: keeping history alive. (© RS)

'Etoile Filante' waits to go out to a display. (© RS)

house the collection. In addition to this, as the collection was to be a living entity, a workshop was required to tend to the needs of the vehicles, some of which were in poor repair. A new 2000m² (21,528ft²) workshop was built nearby, and incorporated hydraulic ramps, a pit, a painting chamber, a number of machine tools, and a considerable spare parts storage area of some 500m² (5381ft²). Today, nine highly qualified technicians work on the premises; their passion and knowledge mean that the words 'impossible' and 'can't' do not form part of their vocabulary, and they can recreate on-site any old and unavailable part in almost any material, including creative restorations in leather and wooden frameworks, where required for the very old cars. These fine engineers, led by Jean-Louis Le-Tohic, can do anything that is required to keep yesterday's cars alive today.

"The workshops were officially opened by Louis Schweitzer, President Director General of Renault, on 24 April 2003 in the presence of a large audience which included Jean Rédélé, whose company had created the Alpines in the collection."

1982 RE30. (© RS)

R8 Gordinis ready to go on track. (© H&C)

The workshops were officially opened by Louis Schweitzer, President Director General of Renault, on 24 April 2003 in the presence of a large audience which included Jean Rédélé, whose company had created the Alpines in the collection.

Many of the turbo cars featured in this book (save those that, sadly, are no longer in one piece) can be seen running full flight on the track, bringing the glorious sounds of the past to the ears of today's enthusiasts. It's not only the cars, either – the drivers of the time can often be seen in the cockpit, including many of the famous names mentioned in previous chapters. There some 55 Formula 1 machines to choose from in a collection that now stands at 650 cars, depicting every era from the very beginning: record-breaking cars like the 'Etoile Filante;' rally cars from every period; Alpine A106, 108, 110, 310, GTA, Renault Turbos of every description: sports cars, road-cars, and some fabulous concept cars.

Histoire & Collection cars are kept extremely busy attending between 150 and 250 events a year.

Finally, at the end of our story, it gives me much pleasure to say that, if you have enjoyed this story, you should go and see these amazing cars – because you can!

The RS01: first turbo F1 car running in 2007. (© H&C)

R5 Turbo Maxi. (© H&C)

The Le Mans-winning A442B. (© H&C)

The RS01 at Donington Park, England. (© RS)

R5 Turbo. (© H&C)

THE END

MORE FROM VELOCE PUBLISHING:

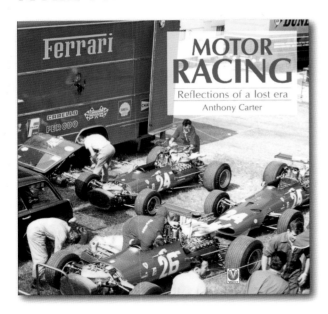

MOTOR RACING – REFLECTIONS OF A LOST ERA
Anthony Carter

• Hardback • 250mm x 250mm • 208 pages • 300 black and white photographs • £39.99*
• ISBN 978-1-904788-10-2 • UPC 6-36847-00310-4

A defining era in motorsport documented in words and intimate photographs, both black and white and colour, from the mid-1950s through the 1960s, when motor racing was still accessible to all, and the 1970s when overt sponsorship and television changed the sport for ever.

AUTODROME
S S Collins & Gavin D Ireland

• Hardback • 250mm x 250mm • 176 pages • 160 colour photographs
• £35.99* • ISBN 978-1-904788-31-7 • UPC 6-36847-00331-9

Windswept and abandoned, the derelict buildings and crumbling tarmac are all that remain of once grand motor racing circuits. From the great speed bowls of Monza and Brooklands to the parkland of Crystal Palace; all are photographed as they are now, but remembered in their prime.

1½-LITRE GRAND PRIX RACING 1961-63
Mark Whitelock

• Hardback • 25x25cm • £39.99* • 336 pages • 200+ illustrations • ISBN: 978-1-84584-016-7
• UPC: 6-36847-04016-1

This is the story of a Grand Prix formula that no British constructor wanted but which they came to almost totally dominate. It saw the career of Stirling Moss come to a premature end, and in his absence the rise to prominence of a new breed of British driver in Jim Clark, Graham Hill and John Surtees.

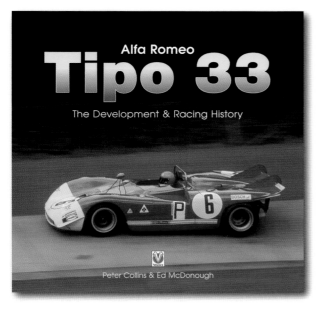
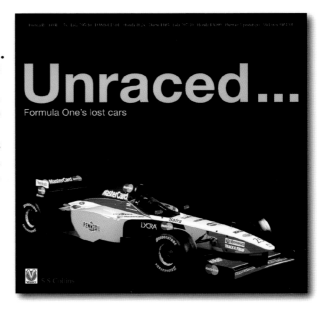

INDEX